AF736485

Human Rights Research Series

Volume 104

Series Editors

Andrea Broderick, Maastricht University, Maastricht, The Netherlands

Antenor Hallo de Wolf, University of Groningen, Groningen, The Netherlands

Nicola Jägers, Tilburg University, Tilburg, The Netherlands

Jasper Krommendijk, Radboud University, Nijmegen, The Netherlands

Alberto Quintavalla, Erasmus University, Rotterdam, The Netherlands

Noor Swart, University of Groningen, Groningen, The Netherlands

The *Human Rights Research Series* offers leading scholarship on the evolving landscape of international human rights norms and their practical implementation. This collection explores the complex interplay between global standards and national legal frameworks, examining how human rights principles are interpreted, applied, and enforced across diverse contexts. Authored by members of the Netherlands Network for Human Rights Research, each volume in this series provides an in-depth analysis of critical issues at the intersection of law, policy, and human rights advocacy. The series encompasses a wide range of methodological approaches, from rigorous doctrinal analysis to innovative empirical studies, reflecting the multidisciplinary nature of human rights research. This series serves as an essential resource for academics, policymakers, legal practitioners, and human rights defenders seeking to deepen their understanding of contemporary human rights challenges. By bridging theoretical insights with practical applications, these books contribute to ongoing debates about the role of human rights in shaping just and equitable societies. The Human Rights Research Series aims to foster dialogue, inspire innovative approaches, and ultimately advance the protection and promotion of human rights at both the national and international levels.

The NNHRR Series was previously published by Intersentia, and continued from 2025 by T.M.C. Asser Press/Springer.

Roman Girma Teshome

The Human Cost of Development

Situating Development-Induced Displacement in International Human Rights Law

ASSER PRESS

Springer

Roman Girma Teshome
School of Law
Utrecht University
Utrecht, The Netherlands

Human Rights Research Series
ISBN 978-94-6265-750-2 ISBN 978-94-6265-751-9 (eBook)
https://doi.org/10.1007/978-94-6265-751-9

Published by T.M.C.ASSER PRESS, The Hague, The Netherlands www.asserpress.nl
Produced and distributed for T.M.C. ASSER PRESS by Springer-Verlag Berlin Heidelberg

© T.M.C. ASSER PRESS and the authors 2026

No part of this work may be reproduced, stored in a retrieval system, or transmitted in any form or by any means, electronic, mechanical, photocopying, microfilming, recording or otherwise, without written permission from the Publisher, with the exception of any material supplied specifically for the purpose of being entered and executed on a computer system, for exclusive use by the purchaser of the work.
The use of general descriptive names, registered names, trademarks, service marks, etc. in this publication does not imply, even in the absence of a specific statement, that such names are exempt from the relevant protective laws and regulations and therefore free for general use.

This T.M.C. ASSER PRESS imprint is published by the registered company Springer-Verlag GmbH, DE, part of Springer Nature.
The registered company address is: Heidelberger Platz 3, 14197 Berlin, Germany

If disposing of this product, please recycle the paper.

Acknowledgements

This book is based on the Ph.D. research I conducted at the University of Amsterdam, and it would not have been possible without the support and assistance of many people.

First of all, I am deeply grateful to my supervisors, Yvonne Donders and Maarten den Heijer, for their continuous guidance, support, and mentorship throughout this process. This research would not have been completed without your critical feedback and thoughtful comments. Your positive attitude and encouragement kept me going during times when writing a Ph.D. inevitably became overwhelming. I appreciate you tremendously.

I also want to extend my heartfelt gratitude to the members of the doctoral committee: Ingo Venzke, Marjoleine Zieck, Rosanne van Alebeek, Karin Arts, and Margot Salomon. Thank you for taking the time from your busy schedules to read and evaluate my work.

I would like to express my appreciation to the faculty members and staff of the International and European Law Department and the Amsterdam Center for International Law. Attending and organizing seminars, engaging in teaching activities, and interacting with you all not only enriched my research but also made the four years I spent there more enjoyable.

I am especially grateful to my fellow Ph.D. candidates; it is comforting and therapeutic to vent with people who are going through the same experience. It has been a pleasure knowing and working with you. I would particularly like to thank my two paranymphs, Debadatta Bose and Lara Talsma; thank you for graciously agreeing to assist me during one of the most crucial stages of my Ph.D., among many other moments.

This work also benefited from my research stay at American University, Washington College of Law. Thank you for welcoming me.

Last but not least, my deepest gratitude goes to my family and friends for their unwavering support in all my academic endeavours and beyond.

Contents

Abbreviations

ACHR	American Convention on Human Rights
ADB	Asian Development Bank
AU	African Union
CEDAW	Convention on the Elimination of All Forms of Discrimination Against Women
CESCR	Committee on Economic, Social and Cultural Rights
COHRE	Sudan Human Rights Organisation & Centre on Housing Rights and Evictions
CRPD	Convention on the Rights of Persons with Disabilities
DID	Development-induced displacement
ECHR	European Convention on Human Rights
ECOSOC	United Nations Economic and Social Council
ESC	Economic, social and cultural
GNP	Gross national product
HRBA	Human rights-based approach
HRBAD	Human rights-based approach to development
HRC	Human Rights Committee
IADB	Inter-American Development Bank
IBRD	International Bank for Reconstruction and Development
ICCPR	International Covenant on Civil and Political Rights
ICESCR	International Covenant on Economic, Social and Cultural Rights
ICJ	International Court of Justice
ICOLD	International Commission on Large Dams
IDA	International Development Association
IDP	Internally displaced person
IEG	The Independent Evaluation Group
IFI	International financial institution
IHL	International humanitarian law
ILC	International Law Commission
ILO	International Labour Organization
IMF	International Monetary Fund

IRR	Impoverishment risks and reconstruction
KSDP	Kuraz Sugar Development Project
OAS	Organization of American States
OHCHR	Office of High Commissioner on Human Rights
PCIJ	Permanent Court of International Justice
SDG	Sustainable development goal
SERAC	Social and Economic Rights Action Centre
UDHR	Universal Declaration of Human Rights
UN	United Nations
UNDRIP	United Nations Declaration on the Rights of Indigenous Peoples
UNHCR	United Nations High Commissioner for Refugees
WGIP	Working Group on Indigenous Peoples

Part I
A Conceptual Background

Chapter 1
Introduction: Framing the Problem and Approach

Contents

Abstract This chapter frames the problem, research questions, and methodology that underpin the book. Development-induced displacement (DID) is a form of internal displacement in which individuals are involuntarily removed from their homes or residences to make room for development projects. DID, which can be caused by a range of small and large-scale development projects, is one of the leading causes of internal displacement affecting millions of people each year. While these development projects carry a significant economic potential, the involuntary displacement they cause comes with a plethora of risks and consequences that often result in chronic impoverishment. These adverse consequences further interfere with and potentially violate a range of human rights, such as the right to housing, the right to property, the right to work, and the right to education. Moreover, DID and its adverse consequences often hit the hardest vulnerable and marginalized groups potentially perpetuating existing vulnerabilities and inequalities. Against this background, the current work seeks to situate DID and its adverse consequences in international human rights law. Using the human rights-based approach as a theoretical framework, it seeks to (re)frame the adverse consequences of DID as human rights issues and explore rights-based solutions to address these issues.

Keywords Development-induced displacement · Indigenous peoples · Violation approach · Human rights-based approach · Impoverishment risk · Vulnerability

© T.M.C. ASSER PRESS and the authors 2026

R. G. Teshome, *The Human Cost of Development*, Human Rights Research Series 104,
https://doi.org/10.1007/978-94-6265-751-9_1

1.1 The Indigenous Peoples of the Lower Omo Valley

The lower Omo valley, a remote area extending along the banks of the Omo River in Southern Ethiopia, is home to several distinct groups of indigenous peoples.[1] These communities are largely pastoralists and small-scale farmers who heavily rely on the Omo River for their livelihoods.[2] Not only do they use the river as their main source of water but they also rely on the seasonal flooding caused by the river to cultivate their lands.[3] Their identity, culture, and way of life are deeply connected to their ancestral lands and the river itself.[4] Overall, the economic, social, and cultural well-being of these communities is intrinsically tied to the Omo River and the surrounding land.[5] As with many indigenous peoples, these communities do not hold formal legal titles to the land they have traditionally occupied.[6] Nor have they seen the need to seek such recognition. They believe that their ancestral land, which they have occupied for generations, belongs to them.

In 2006, the Ethiopian government commenced the construction of the Gilgel Gibe III Dam project on the Omo River[7]—a decision that monumentally changed the lives of thousands of indigenous peoples inhabiting the lower Omo valley. The project was aimed at generating electricity and providing irrigation for the Kuraz Sugar Development Project (KSDP), a large-scale government-owned plantation downstream of the river.[8] The KSDP, which was launched in 2011, is a large-scale sugarcane cultivation project that involves several factories and plantations.[9] The

[1] The Oakland Institute 2019, p. 6 (studies show there are more than eight different groups of indigenous peoples that inhabit the lower Omo valley); see also Beirne 2014, p. 216.

[2] The Oakland Institute 2019, p. 3.

[3] Ibid., pp. 6 and 7; see also Beirne 2014, p. 216 (These indigenous peoples practice "flood-retreat agriculture" where they use the land naturally irrigated by the flood to grow crops and graze their cattle).

[4] The Oakland Institute 2019, pp. 6 and 7 (the cultural lives of these indigenous peoples are also connected to their economic life and, hence, to their land and the Omo River).

[5] The Oakland Institute 2019, p. 3.

[6] Human Rights Watch 2012, p. 68; see also Schapper and Urban 2021, p. O71.

[7] The Oakland Institute 2019, p. 8. The Gilgel Gibe III dam has been one of the most controversial projects due to the social and environmental costs it imposes, which was the main reason why the World Bank, the African Development Bank, and the European Investment Bank originally refused to finance the project. It was eventually constructed with a loan obtained from the financial institutions of China and funding from the local banks (see The Economist, 'Ethiopia opens Africa's tallest and most controversial dam' (The Economist, 21 December 2016), available at https://www.economist.com/middle-east-and-africa/2016/12/21/ethiopia-opens-africas-tallest-and-most-controversial-dam, accessed 28 June 2025; see also Sean Avery, 'Fears over Ethiopian dam's costly impact on environment, people' (The Conversation, 12 September 2017), available at https://theconversation.com/fears-over-ethiopian-dams-costly-impact-on-environment-people-80757, accessed 28 June 2025; see also The Oakland Institute 2019, pp. 8 and 9.

[8] The Oakland Institute 2019, p. 7.

[9] Beirne 2014, p. 218; The Oakland Institute 2019, p. 7.

construction of the dam was completed in 2015 and it started generating electricity in the same year.[10]

These two projects have directly and indirectly caused the involuntary displacement of a significant number of the indigenous peoples of the lower Omo valley.[11] Thousands were involuntarily removed from their lands and relocated in multiple resettlement sites as their lands were taken for the projects.[12] Others were forced to leave their homes and residences due to the unbearable conditions caused by the projects. The dam, in particular, halted or significantly decreased the seasonal flooding,[13] which the indigenous peoples used to cultivate their lands. This disruption, combined with other environmental impacts caused by the projects, forced many to flee their homes.[14]

This is development-induced displacement (DID)—a phenomenon where individuals or groups are involuntarily moved from their homes or residences to make room for development projects. Displacement, in this context, occurs when the implementation of development projects involves the acquisition of land and the involuntary relocation of its inhabitants or results in deteriorating living conditions that compel individuals to abandon their homes.

The displacement prompted by the Gilgel Gibe III Dam and the KSDP projects has imposed a range of economic, social, and cultural consequences and risks on the affected indigenous communities.[15] A large number of individuals have lost their lands, sources of income, and access to common resources.[16] As a result, many have been exposed to heightened levels of food insecurity.[17] The displacement has also disrupted the traditional way of life and cultural practices of these indigenous communities.[18] Studies have shown that the people displaced by these projects were not offered adequate safeguards and remedies to restore—let alone enhance—their

---

[10] The Oakland Institute 2019, p. 9.

[11] Schapper and Urban 2021, p. O71. The data on the number of people displaced by these projects is not conclusive (see Beirne 2014, p. 222).

[12] Human Rights Watch 2012, pp. 33 and 51–53; see also Schapper and Urban 2021, p. O71; see also Zikargie and Cochrane 2022, pp. 1 and 2. The initial environmental and social impact assessment conducted on the Gilgel Gibe III dam project, for instance, predicted that around 2627 people would be displaced by the project (see Beirne 2014, p. 220; see also Human Rights Watch 2012, 33). This does not fully represent the total number of people displaced by these projects. Moreover, some of the involutory relocations caused by the KSDP had been disguised as voluntary villagization (see Beirne 2014, pp. 222 and 223; see also Human Rights Watch 2012, p. 32). "[V]illagization involves moving people who live in dispersed settlements into large, government designed villages." (see Stevenson and Buffavand 2018, p. 111).

[13] The Oakland Institute 2019, pp. 9 and 10; see also Solomon 2019. As a large proportion of the flow of the river is used to fill the dam reservoir, the seasonal flooding has been halted (Beirne 2014, p. 219).

[14] The Oakland Institute 2019, p. 13; see also Schapper and Urban 2021, p. O71.

[15] Schapper and Urban 2021, p. O72.

[16] The Oakland Institute 2019, pp. 11 and 12; see also Schapper and Urban 2021, p. O72.

[17] The Oakland Institute 2019, pp. 11 and 18; see also Human Rights Watch 2012, p. 56; see also Stevenson and Buffavand 2018, p. 110.

[18] The Oakland Institute 2019, pp. 13 and 14.

livelihoods.[19] The state failed to provide adequate replacement land, sustainable employment opportunities, and sufficient public services at the resettlement sites.[20] In addition, reports show that government authorities and security forces used violence, harassment, and intimidation in the course of relocation.[21] Now, several years later, the indigenous peoples of the Omo valley still grapple with the economic and social adversities caused by the displacement and the other adverse consequences of those projects.[22]

This story of the indigenous peoples of the lower Omo valley captures the dilemma associated with DID, which the name itself indicates. On the one hand, "development" has a positive connotation as it represents the social and economic advancement of a given society. On the other hand, displacement entails the involuntary removal of people(s) from their homes or residences, which comes with a plethora of socio-economic risks. The economic potential of the two projects, i.e. the Gilgel Gibe III Dam and the KSDP, is undeniable. The electricity generated from the dam not only contributed towards meeting the increasing energy needs of Ethiopia but also those of the neighbouring countries.[23] The plantation has created thousands of jobs and generated significant revenue.[24] However, for those uprooted from their homes and residences, these projects posed substantial threats to their socio-economic and cultural subsistence.

This is compounded by the fact that the costs of development, DID in this context, are frequently borne by an underprivileged portion of society who are often neither the participants nor the beneficiaries of the development project for which they are paying the price.[25] Studies evince that the indigenous peoples of the Omo valley were not sufficiently consulted and did not meaningfully participate in the decision-making process regarding the projects or the displacement that followed.[26] The resettlement plan proposed by the government failed to take into account their cultural practices and way of life on which their very identity as indigenous peoples depend.[27] Moreover, the people displaced by these projects did not meaningfully benefit from the

---

[19] Ibid., p. 11.

[20] Ibid., pp. 11–13; see also Human Rights Watch 2012, p. 2; see also Beirne 2014, pp. 230–232; see also Schapper and Urban 2021, pp. O71 and O72.

[21] Human Rights Watch 2012, pp. 1–2 and 45–51.

[22] The Oakland Institute 2019, p. 11.

[23] Beirne 2014, p. 218; see also Human Rights Watch 2012, p. 1; see also Schapper and Urban 2021, p. O64. At the time the dam was completed, the electricity generated from the dam was estimated to provide around 40 percent of Ethiopia's electricity demand (Solomon 2019). In addition, Ethiopia has been selling the electricity generated from the dam to neighbouring states, namely Sudan, Djibouti, and Kenya (see Schapper and Urban 2021, p. O64).

[24] Human Rights Watch 2012, p. 31 (it was estimated that the project could create more than 150,000 jobs); see also Kamski 2016, pp. 568, 569.

[25] Robinson 2003, p. 10; see also Mathur 1995, p. 21.

[26] Human Rights Watch 2012, pp. 2, 37–38 and 72; Beirne 2014, p. 230; see also Schapper and Urban 2021, p. O73.

[27] The Oakland Institute 2019, pp. 13 and 18 (for instance, there were complaints that the government had been pressuring them to abandon cattle breeding); see also Human Rights Watch 2012, p. 58.

proceeds of the projects. The indigenous peoples of the Omo valley did not get the electricity generated from the dam; the irrigation system did not cultivate their lands; and the sustainable jobs created by the projects mainly went to "outsiders".[28] "Development" rather led to the impoverishment and marginalization of these groups. These issues raise various human rights and social justice concerns. This is the problem that the current work seeks to address.

1.2 Background and Context

DID is one of the main causes of internal displacement affecting millions of people every year. With the proliferation of large scale development projects, it has emerged as one of the most prevalent forms of internal displacement in terms of magnitude and geographical scope.[29] This is particularly evident in developing and highly populated countries in Asia, Africa, and South America.[30] The number of people affected by DID in developing countries, in particular, has increased since the 1960s and 1970s,[31] which coincides with the time formerly colonized African states obtained their independence.[32] Newly independent states resorted to large-scale projects to meet their development needs and translate their political independence into economic independence.[33] Studies have also depicted a continuous increase in the number of people displaced by DID in the last few decades. For instance, in the 1980s and 1990s around 10 million people were displaced every year as a result of development projects while in the first decade of the 21st century this number has increased to approximately 15 million per year.[34]

Displacement can be caused by a range of public and private development projects undertaken by states and private companies, respectively. Some of the main causes of DID include the construction of dams, transportation and infrastructure projects, and the extraction of natural resources.[35] While these development projects ostensibly have significant economic potential, the socio-economic and cultural cost they

[28] The Oakland Institute 2019, p. 14 (it was reported that most of the decent-paying jobs were given to migrant workers who came from the other parts of the country).

[29] Terminski 2015, pp. 32 and 33.

[30] Ibid., p. 15; see also Stanley 2004, p. 4; see also McDowell 2014, p. 333 (China and India are particularly prominent in this regard, which also correlates with their economic capacity to undertake large-scale development projects. In China, for instance, 70 million people were displaced between 1950 and 2008 due to development projects alone).

[31] Rahmato 2003, p. 1.

[32] Terminski 2015, pp. 35 and 36 (African countries particularly embarked on the construction of large-scale dam projects to meet their energy needs).

[33] Adeola 2017, p. 92.

[34] Terminski 2015, p. 56; see also Cernea 2009, pp. xxv–xxx; see also McDowell 2014, p. 333. It has to be noted that due to insufficient statistics on the exact number of people displaced by DID, most studies on the subject show only the approximate number.

[35] Stanley 2004, pp. 6–11; see also Terminski 2015, pp. 37–42.

impose, which is usually borne by the underprivileged portion of society, cannot be overlooked. The involuntary displacement often caused by these projects particularly imposes a range of consequences and risks on those displaced, extending from inherent socio-economic problems that come with forcible displacement to grave human rights violations.[36] As Robinson asserted, "for millions of people around the world—development has cost them their homes, their livelihoods, their health, and even their very lives."[37] The "Impoverishment Risks and Reconstruction (IRR) Model", a theoretical framework developed by Michael Cernea to identify the adverse consequences of DID and to inform policy responses,[38] outlined eight interrelated risks of displacement based on empirical evidence, namely: landlessness, joblessness, homelessness, marginalization, food insecurity, increased morbidity and mortality, loss of access to common property, and social disintegration.[39] These consequences collectively contribute to the impoverishment of displaced persons that often follows DID.[40] Overall, studies have evinced that people who have been involuntarily displaced from their homes or residences bear the "long-term risks of becoming poorer than before displacement".[41]

DID and its adverse consequences often hit vulnerable and marginalized groups the hardest.[42] Those that are economically and socially marginalized are often disproportionately affected by displacement prompted by development projects.[43] Among these marginalized groups are indigenous peoples, who, as various studies show, are disproportionately represented in the number of people displaced by DID. For instance, a study conducted on development projects undertaken in India from 1951 to 1991 showed that of the total number of people displaced by these projects, 40% were indigenous peoples, even if they only made up 8% of the general population.[44] Moreover, certain groups, such as indigenous peoples, women, children, and disabled persons, face special challenges in the course of displacement due to their specific socio-economic status and historical and ongoing marginalization.[45] Physical displacement imposes severe consequences on indigenous peoples given their deep cultural, spiritual, and economic ties to their ancestral land.[46] Women face

[36] Being forcibly displaced from one's home and residence is inherently disruptive and taxing. However, in some cases, displacement leads to long-term socio-economic problems and chronic impoverishment.

[37] Robinson 2003, p. 1.

[38] Cernea 1997, pp. 1569, 1570 and 1571.

[39] Cernea 1999; see also Cernea 1995, pp. 245, 251 and 252; see also Cernea 2000, pp. 19 and 20; see also Nayak 2013, pp. 397, 398 and 404).

[40] Cernea 1995, pp. 251 and 252.

[41] Cernea 1996, p. 304; see also Robinson 2003, p. 11.

[42] Robinson 2003, p. 10.

[43] Ibid., p. 10; see also Stanley 2004, p. 14.

[44] Rew et al. 2000, pp. 104 and 105; see also Stanley 2004, p. 14.

[45] Thukral 1996, p. 1500.

[46] Stanley 2004, p. 14.

distinct socio-economic challenges in displacement settings due to existing gender-based social and legal discrimination, especially in relation to property ownership and land rights.[47] Studies also show that displacement exposes women to gender-based violence and abuse.[48] The severity of the adverse consequences of DID also correlates with the level of dependency of those displaced on land. Apart from indigenous peoples, farmers and pastoralists also rely on land and other natural resources for their livelihoods. Consequently, displacement or land acquisition significantly affects these groups particularly when they are not provided with replacement land of equal or better quality. Overall, DID imposes varying levels of risks and impacts on displaced persons. This has the effect of potentially perpetuating existing vulnerabilities and marginalization. As this book aims to establish, these factors, i.e. the varying consequences of DID vis-à-vis the socio-economic standing and vulnerability of different groups, should be taken into account in the determination of the human rights safeguards that need to be provided for people affected by DID and the corresponding obligations of states.

Furthermore, the process and outcome of DID interfere with and potentially violate a range of human rights. The socio-economic impoverishment that DID often results in has a particularly adverse impact on the protection of economic, social, and cultural rights, such as the right to an adequate standard of living, the right to work, the right to health, and cultural rights.[49] The effects of DID, however, are not limited to this group of rights. Civil and political rights, such as freedom of movement and choice of residence, freedom of religion, and the right to life, are also among the rights potentially infringed by displacement.[50] The *Endorois case* decided by the African Commission on Human and Peoples' Rights is a good example to demonstrate the wide-ranging impacts of DID on the protection of human rights.[51] The case concerns the involuntary removal of the indigenous people of Endorois from their ancestral land for development purposes.[52] The African Commission, in this case, found violations of several human rights including the right to freedom of religion, the right to property, the right to development, peoples' right to freely dispose of their natural resources, and cultural rights.[53] The Commission attributed most of these violations to the lack of meaningful participation of the people concerned in the process of development or displacement and the provision of adequate compensation and other safeguards.[54] While this case involves indigenous peoples, being forcibly uprooted

---

[47] UN CESCR 1997, para 10; see also Thukral 1996, pp. 1500 and 1501.

[48] UN CESCR 1997, para 10; see also Nayak 2013, p. 402.

[49] Terminski 2015, p. 473; see also van der Ploeg and Vanclay 2017, p. 35.

[50] Barutciski 2006, pp. 75 and 76.

[51] *Centre for Minority Rights Development (Kenya) and Minority Rights Group International on behalf of Endorois Welfare Council v Kenya*, 276/2003, African Commission on Human and Peoples' Rights, 4 February 2010 ('*Endorois case*'), para 3; see also Juma 2013, p. 214.

[52] *Endorois case* (n 51) paras 1–2; see also Juma 2013, p. 214 (the land of the Endorois community was taken for the development of a game reserve).

[53] *Endorois case* (n 51) para 298.

[54] Ibid., paras 173, 234–238, 249–251, 268, and 297–298; see also Juma 2013, pp. 222 and 223–224.

from one's home or residence inherently interferes with human rights irrespective of the identity or characteristics of the people affected. It is important to note that some of these interferences can be justified based on the permissible limitations under international human rights law. Limitations allow states to restrict rights in order to protect a higher individual or public interest.[55] Hence, it is imperative to examine to what extent DID and its adverse consequences can be justified within the framework of permissible limitations on human rights.

In addition, the disproportionate impact of DID on vulnerable or protected groups as well as differential treatment in the course of DID, if any, might constitute discrimination. Non-discrimination, which is a cross-cutting obligation and principle in international human rights law, obliges states to guarantee the rights recognized in human rights treaties without any discrimination based on any of the protected grounds, such as race, gender, religion, and political opinion.[56] Hence, discrimination, whether direct or indirect, constitutes a human rights violation in conjunction with the corresponding substantive right.

As this book also aims to establish, the adverse economic, social, and cultural consequences of DID as well as the human rights interferences it constitutes are largely attributable to the lack or inadequacy of the procedural and substantive safeguards put in place by states. Hence, most of these consequences can be mitigated, if not avoided, by the provision of adequate safeguards at all phases of displacement—from the inception of the development project to the implementation of the resettlement. This work argues that the integration of human rights norms and principles in the process of development in general and of DID in particular can aid the determination and provision of adequate safeguards. This can lead to a better outcome in terms of protecting the rights and interests of displaced persons in the course of DID. Hence, it is important to examine what these human rights norms are and how they can apply in the context of DID.

There is currently no binding and comprehensive international law framework specifically addressing displacement prompted by development projects. However, the people affected by DID can benefit from the general human rights protections available in international human rights law. Moreover, certain human rights, such as the rights to housing, property, protection against interference with one's home, and choice of residence, are thematically more pertinent in the context of DID.[57] These rights offer normative standards that can inform the process of DID and protect the rights of the people affected thereby. Thus, it is important to explore the normative contents of these rights and how they apply in the context of displacement prompted by development projects.

In addition, there are some specialized human rights regimes that deal with specific subject matters relevant to DID or offer normative protections to specific

[55] See, for instance, UN General Assembly, International Covenant on Economic, Social and Cultural Rights, 16 December 1966, 993 United Nations Treaty Series 3 ('ICESCR'), Article 4.

[56] Ibid., Article 2(2); see also UN General Assembly, International Covenant on Civil and Political Rights, 16 December 1966, 999 United Nations Treaty Series 171 ('ICCPR'), Article 2(1).

[57] Barutciski 2006.

groups affected by DID. Accordingly, the frameworks on the rights of internally displaced persons, the rights of indigenous peoples, and the right to development offer normative standards applicable in the context of DID. The frameworks on internally displaced persons, i.e. the UN Guiding Principles on Internal Displacement and the African Union Convention for the Protection and Assistance of Internally Displaced Persons in Africa,[58] are particularly relevant in the context of internal displacement. These frameworks recognize the right to be protected against arbitrary displacement[59]—displacement that is not justified or undertaken in accordance with the relevant international law norms.[60] In addition, they envisage normative standards applicable before, during, and after displacement.[61] While these norms can inform the process of DID, they only marginally address a form of internal displacement caused by development projects.[62] As DID is pre-planned, foreseeable, and instigated and/or supported by states, it is distinct from internal displacement caused by emergency situations, such as conflict and natural disaster.[63] Thus, whether or not the frameworks on internal displacement sufficiently appreciate these factors needs to be examined. Similarly, the frameworks on the rights of indigenous peoples protect the rights of indigenous peoples to the land they traditionally occupy and the surrounding environment.[64] These frameworks particularly enshrine norms that protect indigenous peoples from being forcibly removed from their ancestral land,[65] which will come into effect when DID affects these groups. The right to development also enunciates important norms on the process and outcome of development,[66] which are pertinent in the context of DID. The scope of these frameworks, however,

[58] UN Commission on Human Rights, Guiding Principles on Internal Displacement, 11 February 1998, E/CN.4/1998/53/Add.2; see also African Union, African Union Convention for the Protection and Assistance of Internally Displaced Persons in Africa, 23 October 2009 ('Kampala Convention').

[59] The Guiding Principles on Internal Displacement (n 58) Principle 6(1); see also Kampala Convention (n 58) Article 3(1)(a).

[60] Deng and Adeola 2021, p. 66.

[61] The Guiding Principles on Internal Displacement (n 58); see also Kampala Convention (n 58).

[62] Juma 2013, p. 211. As will be discussed in Chap. 6, the Guiding Principles and the Kampala Convention only contain one or two provisions that specifically address a form of internal displacement caused by development projects, which is planned and, hence, avoidable (see the Guiding Principles on Internal Displacement (n 58) Principles 6(2)(c) and 7(3); see also Kampala Convention (n 58) Article 10).

[63] Robinson 2003, p. 54; see also Muggah 2003, pp. 15 and 16.

[64] UN General Assembly, United Nations Declaration on the Rights of Indigenous Peoples: resolution/adopted by the General Assembly, 2 October 2007, A/RES/61/295 ('UNDRIP'); see also International Labour Organization (ILO), Indigenous and Tribal Peoples Convention, C169, 27 June 1989 ('ILO Convention No. 169'); see also Organization of American States, American Declaration on the Rights of Indigenous Peoples, 15 June 2016, AG/RES. 2888 (XLVI-O/16).

[65] UNDRIP (n 64) Article 10; see also ILO Convention No. 169 (n 64) Article 16.

[66] UN General Assembly, Declaration on the Right to Development: resolution/adopted by the General Assembly, 4 December 1986, A/RES/41/128; see also Organization of African Unity (OAU), African Charter on Human and Peoples' Rights, 27 June 1981, CAB/LEG/67/3 rev. 5, 21 I.L.M. 58 (1982), Article 22.

is limited to the specific groups or subject matters they address. They do not specifically or comprehensively deal with the legal and practical issues associated with this form of displacement. Hence, it is legitimate to question the adequacy of these frameworks in addressing the peculiar features of DID and its adverse consequences.

The normative standards that are applicable in the context of involuntary displacement and resettlement caused by development projects can also be derived from several policy frameworks adopted by international financial institutions. These institutions, such as the World Bank, the African Development Bank, the Inter-American Development Bank, and the Asian Development Bank, are important actors in the DID discourse as they finance development projects that, in many cases, cause displacement. These financial institutions have operational policies on involuntary resettlement that enunciate standards of protection that need to be provided at all phases of displacement in order to restore the livelihoods of those affected.[67] While these policy frameworks do not form part of the international human rights law regime, they can inform the procedural and substantive safeguards that need to be put in place in the course of DID. Hence, it is important to explore the standards of protection envisaged in these policy frameworks and their role in protecting the rights of those affected by DID.

Against this background, the current work seeks to situate DID and its adverse consequences in international human rights law. Using a human rights-based approach (HRBA) as a theoretical framework, it seeks to (re)frame the consequences of DID as human rights issues and explore international human rights law responses to these issues. The HRBA is a theoretical framework advanced to redefine and address various socio-economic and political problems using international human rights law as a guiding normative framework.[68] This approach was initially developed and is predominantly employed in the context of development. It rests on the assumption that integrating human rights norms and principles in the process of development—both as instrumental tools and end goals—is essential to achieve socially just development outcomes.[69] Hence, the HRBA purports that human rights norms and principles should not only guide the process of development but also that the outcome of development should advance the realization of rights.[70] Moreover, the HRBA seeks to address structural inequalities and injustices that impede this broader

[67] World Bank, Operational Manual OP 4.12—Involuntary Resettlement, December 2001; see also The World Bank, Environmental and Social Framework (ESF), 2017, available at https://documents1.worldbank.org/curated/en/383011492423734099/pdf/The-World-Bank-Environmental-and-Social-Framework.pdf, accessed 28 June 2025; see also the African Development Bank Involuntary Resettlement Policy, November 2003; see also Asian Development Bank Involuntary Resettlement Policy, August 1995; see also Inter-American Development Bank, Operational Policy on Involuntary Resettlement, OP-710, October 1998.

[68] Boesen and Sano 2010, p. 45.

[69] As will be elucidated further in Chap. 4, this also forms an integral component of the right to development (see Chap. 8, Sect. 8.3).

[70] Office of the United Nations High Commissioner for Human Rights (OHCHR), Frequently asked questions on a human rights-based approach to development cooperation, 1 January 2006, HR/PUB/06/8, p. 15; see also Boesen and Sano 2010, pp. 50 and 51.

objective of development and, hence, the process of development should particularly take into account the needs and rights of vulnerable and marginalized groups.[71] Using this approach, this book aims to elucidate how international human rights law can be integrated in the process of DID. Accordingly, it seeks to identify and analyse the human rights frameworks and norms applicable in the context of displacement, the rights of people affected thereby, and the corresponding obligations of states.

1.3 Research Questions

Generally, the objectives of this book are twofold: (1) to map out existing international human rights law norms that apply to DID and (2) to assess the adequacy of these norms in addressing the adverse consequences and salient features of DID. To these ends, the book identifies the relevant frameworks and norms applicable to this form of displacement, examines their application in the context of DID, and critically engages with their gaps and limitations, if any.

Hence, the central question that this book seeks to address is:

How and to what extent do existing international human rights instruments protect the rights of people(s) affected by DID?

Under this general framework, the book will raise and systematically address the following three interrelated questions. First, it assesses to what extent the economic, social, and cultural consequences of DID interfere with and potentially violate human rights. Drawing on pertinent socio-legal research and case studies, the book identifies the adverse consequences of DID, examines how these adverse consequences interfere with human rights, and identifies the factors contributing to these interferences. It then explores how some of these interferences can be justified based on the relevant limitation clauses in international human rights law. It also highlights instances where these interferences cannot be justified and therefore constitute human rights violations. In doing so, the book seeks to (re)frame the adverse consequences of DID as human rights issues.

Second, the book examines the rights-based procedural and substantive safeguards states need to provide at different phases of displacement in order to protect the rights of people affected by DID. To this end, it identifies and maps out the general and specialized human rights frameworks and norms applicable to DID and contextually analyses their application in the course of displacement. In other words, the book explores the rights of individuals or groups affected by this form of displacement and the corresponding obligations of states. Thus, it draws on the pertinent human rights treaties, soft-law documents, interpretations of human rights bodies, and policy documents to identify the safeguards that need to be provided in the course of DID.

Third, the book explores the extent to which existing human rights frameworks adequately address the adverse consequences of DID and its distinctive features.

---

[71] Boesen and Sano 2010, p. 51; see also OHCHR (2006) (n 70) p. 16; see also Gready 2008, p. 736; see also Braniff and Hainsworth 2015, p. 42.

Using a critical approach, it assesses whether and to what extent the human rights frameworks and norms covered in this work adequately and effectively address the legal and practical issues arising from DID. In doing so, the book identifies the gaps and limitations of the current international human rights law regime in sufficiently protecting the rights and interests of the people(s) affected by DID.

1.4 Scope and Methodology

This book is based on legal research that falls within the ambit of international human rights law. Thus, a significant portion of this work is dedicated to the analysis of international human rights norms and practices relevant to the issues under consideration. As mentioned before, the book uses the human rights-based approach, which is "a conceptual framework for the process of human development that is normatively based on international human rights standards and operationally directed to promoting and protecting human rights",[72] to situate DID in international human rights law. Using this approach, it (re)frames DID and its consequences as human rights issues and explores how and to what extent international human rights law addresses these issues. Under this general framework, the book will be guided by the following methodological choices to answer the research questions stated above.

The book employs both doctrinal and normative research methods. Using the doctrinal method, it examines "what the law is". It identifies the applicable law based on normative principles recognized in different human rights instruments and reinforced in the case law as well as the authoritative interpretations of human rights monitoring bodies. Accordingly, a range of international and regional human rights treaties and soft-law instruments directly or indirectly relevant to the issue of DID will be systematically examined. Indeed, a comprehensive analysis of all relevant norms from all international and regional human rights systems would be neither feasible nor desirable in this work. Thus, necessary choices are made based on the subject matter and contextual significance of the norms.

The applicable human rights frameworks and norms are identified using two approaches. First, the book uses, what Audrey Chapman calls, a "violation approach"[73] to identify the pertinent norms using inductive reasoning. Chapman proposed this approach as a monitoring mechanism to evaluate the compliance of states with the norms enunciated under the International Covenant on Economic, Social and Cultural Rights (ICESCR), as opposed to the "progressive realization" approach.[74] The violation approach involves identifying human rights violations and the factors contributing to those violations "in order to end and rectify" violations and advance the realization of these rights in general.[75] The violation approach, according

[72] OHCHR 2006 (n 70), p. 15.

[73] Chapman 1996, pp. 23–66.

[74] Ibid., p. 24.

[75] Ibid., pp. 36 and 37.

to Chapman, helps to "[translate] the abstract legal norms, in which various human rights covenants are framed, into operational standards."[76] This work uses the violation approach to identify the general human rights norms applicable to DID and the safeguards that need to be put in place at all phases of displacement. This is predicated on the assumption that the safeguards that need to be provided in the course of DID should be aimed at preventing the violation of human rights. Hence, it is important to understand how DID can potentially violate human rights in order to identify these safeguards. Accordingly, the book identifies the rights that are most affected by DID by looking at the literature, case law, and relevant documents produced by human rights monitoring bodies. It then explores the normative contents of these rights and the state obligations they entail as well as how they are implicated in the context of DID. In doing so, it identifies the human rights protections and safeguards that need to be provided in the course of DID by contextually analysing these general norms.

The analysis in this part of the book, part II, draws on the frameworks adopted in the UN human rights system. This methodological choice is based on the fact that the substantive contents of the general human rights norms selected for this work are mostly similar across various human rights systems. Nevertheless, references will be made to the regional human rights systems intermittently to give a general overview of the recognition or sources of the rights under consideration and to clarify certain concepts or norms as the need arises. While the case law and interpretative documents of one human rights monitoring body might not be formally used to interpret the human rights frameworks of another system, they play a crucial role in the development of human rights norms across different systems. This is also evident from the practices of several human rights monitoring bodies in different systems that refer to and draw inspiration from each other frequently.[77] Hence, this book also draws on the norms and interpretations of the regional human rights systems to aid the analysis of the norms and clarify certain concepts under the UN system. The regional norms and case law are selected based on their thematic relevance to the norms or issues being discussed.

Second, the book employs a "thematic approach" to identify relevant frameworks and norms pertinent to DID. Accordingly, specialized human rights frameworks or regimes that deal with specific groups or subject matters relevant to DID, i.e. instruments on the rights of internally displaced persons, the rights of indigenous peoples, and the right to development, will be analysed. Even though the right to development can be considered a specific human right, the author has opted to include it in the part that deals with specialized human rights regimes for two reasons. First, the right to

---

[76] Ibid., pp. 24 and 37.

[77] See, for instance, *Endorois case* (n 51) paras 187–190 (in this case, the African commission referred to some of the judgments of the European Court of Human Rights, such as the *case of Doğan and others v Turkey*, and the Inter-American Court of Human Rights including the case of *The Mayagna (Sumo) Awas Tingni v Nicaragua*); see also *Chiara Sacchi et al. v Argentina*, communication No. 104/2019, decision on admissibility, Committee on the Rights of the Child, 22 September 2021, CRC/C/88/D/104/2019, paras 4.3, 10.5, 10.7, 10.12 (in this case, the Committee referred to interpretations of the European Court of Human Rights and the Inter-American Court of Human Rights).

development is developed separately and incorporated in separate instruments in the UN human rights system, i.e. the Declaration on the Right to Development[78] and the Draft Convention on the Right to Development (which is currently under review).[79] Second, the right to development encompasses various rights and different normative aspects as this book will elaborate on later. These norms can inform the process and outcome of DID. Based on this understanding, the book explores the normative content of the specialized instruments mentioned above and their application in the context of DID. Furthermore, pertinent policy frameworks that enunciate standards of protection applicable in the context of involuntary displacement and resettlement caused by development projects will be explored. Particularly, the book engages with the resettlement policies of international financial institutions and explores their role in protecting the rights of people displaced by DID. In these parts of the book, part III and part IV, jurisdictions or institutions that have relevant frameworks on the subject under consideration will be covered. Moreover, flexible and contextual methodological choices will be made depending on the topic and the research needs, which will be made explicit in the relevant parts.

It is important to note that international financial institutions arguably do not have explicit mandates to promote human rights, and their policy frameworks do not form part of the international human rights law regime. However, they play an important norm-setting role as they have policy frameworks and standards with which states seeking to obtain funding from these institutions need to comply. This is particularly relevant in the context of DID as these institutions finance development projects that potentially cause displacement. In addition, they have relatively comprehensive policy frameworks on involuntary displacement and resettlement prompted by development projects. These policy frameworks set out the standards states need to follow and the safeguards they need to provide in the course of displacement. These policies can inform the discourse on DID in general and the safeguards needed to prevent or mitigate its adverse consequences in particular. Hence, it is important to explore the substantive contents of these policy frameworks and their role in protecting the rights of people affected by DID, which this book seeks to do. The book makes the necessary correlation between these policy standards and the relevant human rights norms in order to fit this part into its overall scope. Thus, the book examines the role, if any, of these institutions in advancing human rights, the contents of their policy standards on DID, the extent to which these policy standards align with relevant human rights norms, and the role of these policies in protecting the right of displaced persons. It also engages with the limitations of these policy frameworks.

The book further employs a normative research method to explore "what the law ought to be". It assesses the adequacy of existing human rights frameworks in addressing the adverse consequences of DID and its distinctive features. Drawing on relevant literature and case studies, the book identifies these adverse consequences as well as the legal and practical issues raised in the course of DID. Then, it assesses

---

[78] The Declaration on the right to development (n 66).

[79] Human Rights Council, Working Group on the Right to Development, Revised Draft Convention on the Right to Development, 6 April 2022, A/HRC/WG.2/23/2.

to what extent the human rights instruments and norms identified in the book address these consequences and issues. The "adequacy" of the human rights norms will be tested against the practical need. Thus, in doing so, the book highlights the gaps and limitations of international human rights law vis-à-vis DID and the protection of the rights of the people affected thereby and proposes normative solutions.

The book employs case studies derived from secondary sources to demonstrate the adverse consequences of DID and the human rights interferences it involves. These case studies are selected based on their contextual relevance—their relevance in demonstrating the specific issue under consideration. The selection of case studies is not intended to be geographically representative or to cover the various causes of DID as this is not necessary for the purposes for which the case studies are used in this book. In addition, the case studies primarily illustrate negative experiences in which DID has led to various socio-economic and human rights consequences. While there is a risk of confirmation bias in this approach, the selection is justified for two main reasons. First, the case studies are intended to exemplify the human rights issues raised in this book rather than to prove a hypothesis per se. In other words, this work will not draw statistical conclusions based on the case studies cited. The case studies will mainly be used to demonstrate the adverse consequences of DID and the human rights interferences it involves. Accordingly, the case studies mostly represent negative experiences of DID by design. Hence, the case studies will only be used in a way that aligns with the objectives of the book in general or of the particular section in which they are mentioned in particular. Second, studies show that, in most cases, DID results in adverse socio-economic outcomes and often exposes the people affected to the risk of impoverishment.[80] Displacement prompted by development seldom leads to positive outcomes where the livelihoods of those displaced are restored or improved. Hence, the existing literature and case studies on DID also predominantly deal with the adverse consequences of DID. Thus, the choice of case studies in this research also reflects that. Nonetheless, the book also mentions positive displacement and resettlement experiences where it is needed.

As mentioned before, DID can be caused by public and private projects undertaken by states and private companies, respectively. The applicable human rights frameworks and norms might also differ based on the actors involved. International human rights law, as it stands today, is predominantly state-centric and does not have a direct horizontal effect. The obligation to realize human rights primarily rests with states, and, in principle, private actors do not have direct human rights obligations under international human rights treaties. Instead, states have a duty to protect rights holders from infringement of their rights by third parties, which is the indirect horizontal effect of human rights treaties. Nevertheless, the emerging business and human rights regime, crystalized by the UN Guiding Principles on Business and Human Rights and the draft treaty, imposes the responsibility to respect human rights on businesses.[81] Against this backdrop, the thematic scope of this research is

---

[80] See, for instance, Cernea 1996, p. 304.

[81] OHCHR, Guiding Principles on Business and Human Rights: Implementing the United Nations "Protect, Respect and Remedy" Framework, HR/PUB/11/04, 2011, para 11; see also Human Rights

limited to public projects. In other words, the book focuses on displacement caused by projects undertaken by states. It does not engage with displacement prompted by the operations of private companies and the corresponding human rights norms, particularly the corporate responsibility to respect human rights. Thus, the book identifies and examines human rights norms applicable in the case of displacement directly instigated by states.

1.5 Structure

The book is structured into five parts consisting of ten chapters. Part I offers a conceptual background and it involves two chapters including this introductory chapter, which formulates the research problem and approach. Chapter 2 provides a conceptual framework by setting out the definition, causes, and consequences of DID. In doing so, the chapter seeks to lay the foundation for the doctrinal and normative analysis provided in the subsequent chapters.

Part II explores the normative protections available for people affected by DID in general human rights frameworks by using the violation approach elucidated above. Accordingly, it examines how DID can interfere with and potentially violate human rights as well as what factors contribute to those violations. Three rights are selected for in-depth analysis in this part: the right to housing, the right to property, and the right to work, which will be covered in Chaps. 3, 4 and 5, respectively. Thus, these chapters explore the normative contents of these rights, the state obligations they entail, and their implication in the course of DID.

Part III, consisting of three chapters, focuses on specialized human rights regimes that deal with subject matters relevant to DID or the specific groups of people affected thereby. Consequently, the instruments on the rights of internally displaced persons, the rights of indigenous peoples, and the right to development will be systematically analysed in Chaps. 6, 7 and 8, respectively. The chapters identify the normative standards incorporated in these frameworks and assess their application in the course of DID.

Part IV looks beyond international human rights law and in Chap. 9 examines the involuntary resettlement policies adopted by international financial institutions, specifically, the World Bank, the African Development Bank, the Inter-American Development Bank, and the Asian Development Bank. The chapter explores the safeguards enshrined in these policy frameworks and their role in protecting the rights of people affected by DID.

Part V presents the main findings of the study in Chap. 10. This concluding chapter takes a broader perspective examining how international human rights law can guide and inform the overall process of DID as well as the safeguards that should be implemented throughout. Building on the doctrinal analysis developed in

---

Council, the Third Revised Draft of the Binding Treaty on Business and Human Rights, January 2022, A/HRC/49/65/Add.1.

the preceding chapters, it proposes a framework for a human rights-based approach to DID—outlining how displacement can be planned and carried out in a manner that respects and promotes human rights. The chapter also identifies key gaps and limitations within the existing international human rights framework as it relates to DID and proposes recommendations to address these shortcomings.

References

Adeola R (2017) The Legal Protection of Development-Induced Displaced Persons in Africa. (2017) 10(1) African Journal of Legal Studies 91–104.

Barutciski M (2006) International Law and Development-induced Displacement. In: de Wet C (ed) Development-induced displacement: Problems, Policies and People. Berghahn, New York, NY.

Beirne J (2014) Gilgel Gibe III: Dam-Induced Displacement in Ethiopia and Kenya. SEM 2014, available at http://labos.ulg.ac.be/hugo/wp-content/uploads/sites/38/2017/11/The-State-of-Environmental-Migration-2014-215-234.pdf, accessed 28 June 2025.

Boesen J K, Sano H-O (2010) The Implications and Value-Added of a Human Rights-Based Approach. In: Andreassen B V, Marks S P (eds) Development as a Human Right: Legal, Political and Economic Dimensions, 2nd edn. Intersentia.

Braniff M, Hainsworth P (2015) A Human Rights Based Approach to Development. In: McCann G, McCloskey S (eds) From the Local to the Global: Key Issues in Development Studies, 3rd edn. Pluto Press, London.

Cernea M M (1995) Understanding and Preventing Impoverishment from Displacement: Reflections on the State of Knowledge. (1995) 8(3) Journal of Refugee Studies.

Cernea M M (1996) Bridging the Research Divide: Studying Development Oustees. In: Allen T (ed) In Search of Cool Ground: War, Flight and Homecoming in Northeast Africa. United Nations Research Institute for Social Development, Africa World Press/ James Currey, London.

Cernea M M (1997) The Risks and Reconstruction Model for Resettling Displaced Populations. 25(10) World Development.

Cernea M M (1999) Why Economic Analysis is Essential to Resettlement: A Sociologist's View. In: Cernea M (ed) The Economics of Involuntary Resettlement: Questions and Challenges. World Bank, Washington DC.

Cernea M M (2009) Preface: An original contribution to country-wide displacement analysis. In: Pankhurst A, Piguet F (eds) Moving People in Ethiopia: Development, Displacement and The State. James Currey, Woodbridge, Suffolk/Rochester, NY.

Cernea M M (2000) Risks, Safeguards, and Reconstruction: a Model for Population Displacement and Resettlement. In: Cernea M M, McDowell C (eds) Risks and Reconstruction: Experiences of Resettlers and Refugees. The World Bank, Washington DC.

Chapman A R (1996) A "Violations Approach" for Monitoring the International Covenant on Economic, Social and Cultural Rights. (1996) 18(1) Human Rights Quarterly 23–66.

Deng F M, Adeola R (2021) The Normative Influence of the UN Guiding Principles on the Kampala Convention in the Protection of Internally Displaced Persons in Africa. (2021) 65(S1) Journal of African Law 59–72.

Gready P (2008) Rights-based approaches to development: what is the value-added? (2008) 18(6) Development in Practice 735–747.

Human Rights Watch (2012) "What Will Happen if Hunger Comes?": Abuses against the Indigenous Peoples of Ethiopia's Lower Omo Valley. Human Rights Watch, June 2012.

Juma L (2013) Protection of development-induced internally displaced persons under the African Charter: the case of the Endorois community of Northern Kenya. (2013), 46(2) The Comparative and International Law Journal of Southern Africa 211–233.

Kamski B (2016) The Kuraz Sugar Development Project (KSDP) in Ethiopia: between 'sweet visions' and mounting challenges. (2016) 10(3) Journal of Eastern African Studies 568–580.
Mathur H M (1995) The Resettlement of People Displaced by Development Projects: Issues and Approaches. In: Mathur H M, Cernea M (eds) Development, Displacement and Resettlement: Focus on Asian Experience, 1st edn. New Delhi: Vikas Publishing House.
McDowell C (2014) Development Created Population Displacement. In: Fiddian-Qasmiyeh E, Loescher G, Long K, Sigona N (eds) The Oxford Handbook of Refugee and Forced Migration Studies. Oxford University Press, Oxford.
Muggah R (2003) A Tale of Two Solitudes: Comparing Conflict and Development induced Internal Displacement and Involuntary Resettlement. (2003) 41(5) International Migration 5–31.
Nayak A K (2013) Development, Displacement and Justice in India: Study of Hirakud Dam. (2013) 43(3) Social Change 397–419.
Rahmato D (2003) Resettlement in Ethiopia: The Tragedy of Population Relocation in the 1980s. Forum for Social Studies, Addis Ababa, June 2003.
Rew A, Fisher E, Pande B (2000) Addressing Policy Constraints and Improving Outcomes in Development-Induced Resettlement Projects. Refugee Studies Centre, Oxford.
Robinson C W (2003) Risks and Rights: The Causes, Consequences, and Challenges of Development-Induced Displacement. The Brookings Institution-SAIS Project on Internal Displacement, An Occasional Paper May 2003.
Schapper A, Urban F (2021) Large dams, norms and Indigenous Peoples. 39(S1) Development Policy Review O61–O80.
Solomon S (2019) Forced Displacement Causes Controversy in Ethiopia's Omo Valley. VOA News, 19 July 2019, available at https://www.voanews.com/a/africa_forced-displacement-causes-controversy-ethiopias-omo-valley/6172224.html, accessed 28 June 2025.
Stanley J (2004) Development-induced Displacement and Resettlement. Forced Migration Online.
Stevenson E G J, Buffavand L (2018) "Do Our Bodies Know Their Ways?" Villagization, Food Insecurity, and Ill-Being in Ethiopia's Lower Omo Valley. (2018) 61(1) African Studies Review 109–133.
Terminski B (2015) Development-Induced Displacement and Resettlement: Causes, Consequences, and Socio-Legal Context. Ibidem-Verlag, Stuttgart.
The Oakland Institute (2019) "How They Tricked Us": Living with the Gibe III Dam and Sugarcane Plantations in Southwest Ethiopia. The Oakland Institute.
Thukral E G (1996) Development, Displacement and Rehabilitation: Locating Gender. (1996) 31(24) Economic and Political Weekly 1500–1503.
UN Committee on Economic, Social and Cultural Rights (UN CESCR) (1997) General Comment No. 7: The right to adequate housing (Art.11.1): forced evictions, 20 May 1997, E/1998/22.
Van der Ploeg L, Vanclay F (2017) A Human Rights-based Approach to Project Induced Displacement and Resettlement. (2017) 35(1) Impact Assessment and Project Appraisal 34–52.
Zikargie Y A, Cochrane L (2022) Modernist Land Development-Induced Villagisation: Deconstructing Socio-Economic Rights of Pastoralists in South Omo, Ethiopia. (2022) Forum for Development Studies 1–24.

Chapter 2
Development-Induced Displacement: Concept, Causes, and Consequences

Contents

Abstract Development-induced displacement (DID) concerns the forcible removal of individuals from their homes or residences to make way for development projects. Similar to other forms of internal displacement, DID is characterized by two key elements: its involuntary nature and the fact that it occurs within the national borders of the state. However, DID differs in that it is pre-planned, foreseeable, and initiated or supported by the state. As this work will argue, these distinct characteristics should be taken into account in the determination of the human rights safeguards that need to be provided in the course of DID and, in turn, heighten the obligations of states. This chapter provides a conceptual foundation for the book by formulating the definition, causes, and consequences of DID.

Keywords Forced migration · Internal displacement · Refugee · Development-induced displacement · Impoverishment · Vulnerability

© T.M.C. ASSER PRESS and the authors 2026

R. G. Teshome, *The Human Cost of Development*, Human Rights Research Series 104, https://doi.org/10.1007/978-94-6265-751-9_2

2.1 Introduction

Forced migration pertains to the involuntary movement of people within or outside their country of origin prompted by a host of foreseeable or unforeseeable external factors. Forced migrants include both those who have crossed international borders—refugees, or asylum seekers pending their status,—and those who are internally relocated—internally displaced persons (IDPs). IDPs constitute almost two-thirds of the number of forced migrants in the world, the majority of whom reside in developing countries.[1] One of the main causes of internal displacement is the implementation of development projects. As depicted in the preceding chapter, development-induced displacement (DID), a phenomenon where people are forced to leave their homes or residences to make room for development projects, has emerged as one of the leading causes of internal displacement affecting millions of people every year.[2]

This chapter seeks to clarify the concept of DID and highlight the legal and practical issues related to the subject in order to lay the foundation for the normative analysis provided in subsequent chapters and define the overall scope of the book. It aims to set the scene for the human rights issues this book raises by elucidating the concept, causes, and adverse consequences of DID.

To this end, the chapter is divided into five main sections. Section 2.2 clarifies the concept of DID by providing a definition and identifying its distinctive features in relation to other forms of forced migration. Section 2.3 explores some of the principal causes of DID, specifically dam construction, urban (re)development and transportation, and the extraction of natural resources. Section 2.4 then examines the economic, social, and cultural consequences that DID imposes on displaced persons using examples of case studies. Section 2.5 engages with vulnerability in the context of DID, i.e. how the consequences of DID can perpetuate existing vulnerabilities and inequalities or even create new ones. Finally, Sect. 2.6 introduces ways in which the consequences of DID can be avoided or, at least, mitigated by drawing on positive displacement and resettlement experiences.

---

[1] According to the United Nations High Commissioner for Refugees (UNHCR) report, there are around 123.2 million forced migrants in the world as of the end of 2024, among which 73.5 million are internally displaced persons. (see UNHCR, Global Trends: Forced Displacement in 2024, https://www.unhcr.org/global-trends, accessed 5 July 2025, 2).

[2] Studies have depicted that, for instance, in the first decade of the 21st century, approximately 15 million people had been displaced every year to make room for development projects (Terminski 2015, pp. 32 and 56; see also McDowell 2014, p. 333).

2.2 Development-Induced Displacement: A Conceptual Background

2.2.1 *The Definition of Development-Induced Displacement*

As DID falls under the category of internal displacement, it is important to start from the concept of internal displacement in international law. Internal displacement indicates the involuntary movement of people within the borders of the state. The definition provided under the relevant UN framework on internal displacement, i.e. the Guiding Principles on Internal Displacement,[3] describes who qualify as IDPs rather than the phenomenon itself.[4] This is similar to the approach followed by the international instruments on refugees as will be discussed subsequently. The elements that constitute internal displacement, however, can be deduced from this definition of IDPs. The definition reads:

> ... internally displaced persons are persons or groups of persons who have been forced or obliged to flee or to leave their homes or places of habitual residence, in particular as a result of or in order to avoid the effects of armed conflict, situations of generalized violence, violations of human rights or natural or human-made disasters, and who have not crossed an internationally recognized state border.[5]

The definition provided under the African Union Convention for the Protection and Assistance of Internally Displaced Persons in Africa (Kampala Convention),[6] which is the first and the only legally binding instrument on the rights of IDPs, is a verbatim copy of the above definition.[7] The Kampala Convention, however, also defines the

---

[3] UN Commission on Human Rights, Guiding Principles on Internal Displacement, 11 February 1998, E/CN.4/1998/53/Add.2. The Guiding Principles were drafted by an ad-hoc expert group established under the auspices of the then UN Human Rights Commission. The Guiding Principles contain a set of non-binding standards, albeit they have significant normative weight. These standards will be further discussed in detail in Chap. 6.

[4] Guiding Principles on Internal Displacement (n 3) scope and purpose, para 2.

[5] Ibid. The first working definition at the UN level was adopted by the UN Secretary-General in 1992, according to which "[IDPs] are persons or groups who have been forced to flee their homes suddenly or unexpectedly in large numbers, as the result of armed conflict, internal strife, systematic violation of human rights or natural or man-made disaster, and who are within the territory of their own country." (UN Commission on Human Rights, Analytical report of the Secretary-General on Internally Displaced Persons, 14 February 1992, UN Doc. E/CN.4/1992/23, para 17). However, although the two main elements of the definition of IDPs were incorporated into this definition, the additional elements it included have been criticized for making it too restrictive. For instance, the term "suddenly and unexpectedly" leaves out a situation where displacement is pre-planned and undertaken over a long period. Moreover, the phrase "forced to flee" does not properly represent IDPs who are involuntarily removed from their homes or residence (see Mooney 2005, pp. 10 and 11). These concerns are addressed by the definition adopted in the Guiding Principles.

[6] African Union, African Union Convention for the Protection and Assistance of Internally Displaced Persons in Africa, 23 October 2009 ('Kampala Convention').

[7] Ibid., Article 1(k). This does not come as a surprise as the Convention heavily draws on the Guiding Principles.

phenomenon of internal displacement as "the involuntary or forced movement, evacuation or relocation of persons or groups of persons within internationally recognized state borders".[8] The two key elements of these definitions are the involuntary nature of the displacement and the fact that the migration, in this case, takes place within the national borders of the state.[9] This excludes persons who voluntarily move for economic or other reasons[10] and those who have crossed an international border.

Internal displacement can be caused by a number of foreseeable and unforeseeable factors, which include conflict, violence, human rights violations, and natural or human-made disasters.[11] As the term "in particular" in the definition quoted above indicates, the list of causes of displacement enumerated in the provision is illustrative rather than exhaustive.[12] Other causes of internal displacement can rightly fall under this definition provided that they result in the involuntary movement of people within the national borders of the state.[13] This—coupled with the subsequent principles of the framework that refer to displacements caused by development projects—also attests that people displaced by development projects are covered by the above definition of IDPs, even though development is not explicitly mentioned in the list. For instance, Principle 6 of the Guiding Principles, prohibiting arbitrary displacement, includes "large-scale development projects, which are not justified by compelling and overriding public interests" as one of the cases of arbitrary displacement.[14] As the substantive content of the Guiding Principles will be discussed in detail in Chap. 6, this brief remark suffices to indicate that persons displaced by DID are also included in the definition of IDPs.

Similar to the other forms of internal displacement, the two major elements of DID are the involuntary nature of the displacement and the fact that the people affected thereby do not cross international borders. The cause of the displacement, in this case, is the implementation of development projects. Thus, DID is a phenomenon where people are forced to leave their homes or habitual residences to make room for development projects. In other words, people are uprooted from their homes or residences when their land or place of residence is needed for development purposes. The prerogative of the state to displace people for development purposes is rooted in the "eminent domain" doctrine, which refers to the power of the state to acquire

---

8 Ibid., Article 1(l).

9 Internal Displacement Monitoring Centre, 'Who are Internally Displaced People?', available at http://www.internal-displacement.org/internal-displacement, accessed 19 July 2025; see also Kälin 2014, p. 2; see also Cohen 2006, p. 92; see also Kälin 2008, p. 3.

10 Muggah 2003, p. 7. However, as it will be clarified later on, the distinction between voluntary and involuntary displacement is not always clear.

11 Guiding Principles on Internal Displacement (n 3) scope and purpose, para 2; see also Kampala Convention (n 6) Article 1(k).

12 Cohen 2006, p. 93; see also Kälin 2014, p. 4.

13 Scholten 2016, p. 2; see also Kälin 2008, p. 2.

14 Guiding Principles on Internal Displacement (n 3) Principle 6; see also Robinson 2003, p. 3. (Principle 6 of the Guideline explicitly prohibits arbitrary displacement and non-exhaustively lists situations that amount to arbitrary displacement, the substantive content of which will be discussed in Chap. 6).

private property for public purposes.[15] This doctrine asserts that control over land and other resources is one of the inherent powers of a state, thus affording it a mandate to utilize such resources for the public good, even if they are owned or possessed by individuals or private entities.[16] Accordingly, a state can remove individuals from their homes or residences for development purposes provided that the relevant legal requirements are fulfilled.[17]

DID is often followed by resettlement, which refers to a planned "relocation of displaced population to new sites".[18] Resettlement involves a process in which people who are physically displaced from their homes or residences are relocated to a new place coupled with the measures taken to re-establish them socially and economically.[19] Accordingly, the notion of resettlement contains two main elements: "a movement of population; and an element of planning and control."[20] In DID literature and policy documents, (involuntary) resettlement and displacement are sometimes used interchangeably.[21] Displacement and resettlement, however, denote distinct, albeit interdependent, concepts. Displacement necessarily precedes resettlement, while in some cases, it occurs without any planned resettlement. This research looks into forced displacement induced by the implementation of development projects, irrespective of whether or not it is followed by formal resettlement. Thus, throughout this work, the term "development-induced displacement" will be used to denote this form of forced migration, while resettlement will be used in its strict sense to refer to the pre-planned relocation of displaced persons to a new site.

Development as a cause of displacement signifies the undertaking of a wide range of small and large scale projects aimed at, *inter alia*, economic development, conservation of nature, urbanization, and provision of public services.[22] These development projects can be private or public projects, undertaken by private companies and

---

15 Muggah 2003, p. 8; see also Meidinger 2008, p. 2.

16 Ramanathan 1996, p. 1488.

17 While the specific requirements and processes in which this doctrine is applied depend on domestic laws, there are two requirements that are commonly accepted, i.e. acquisition of private property should be justified by public purpose and the owner of the property must be duly compensated (see Meidinger 2008, p. 2; see also Ramanathan 1996, p. 1488). These requirements will be discussed in the subsequent chapters based on the relevant human rights frameworks.

18 Mathur 1995, p. 15; see also Muggah 2003, p. 10.

19 Terminski 2015, pp. 33 and 34.

20 Chambers 1969, p. 11.

21 For instance, the pertinent policies of international financial institutions employ the term "involuntary resettlement" to refer to the situation where people(s) are displaced and relocated to make room for development projects they finance (see World Bank, Operational Manual OP 4.12—Involuntary Resettlement, December 2001; see also the African Development Bank Involuntary Resettlement Policy, November 2003; see also Asian Development Bank Involuntary Resettlement Policy, August 1995; see also Inter-American Development Bank, Operational Policy on Involuntary Resettlement, OP-710, October 1998). It is important to note that this term makes sense in the context of the policy frameworks of these institutions as their main purpose is to provide policy guidance to the process of resettlement.

22 Scholten 2016, p. 4.

states respectively, which also determines the type of state obligations in international human rights law.[23] As established in the preceding chapter, the scope of this book is limited to the latter.

2.2.2 Differentiating Development-Induced Displacement

Forced migration, or forced displacement as it is referred to in some literature, denotes the involuntary movement of people either within or across state borders.[24] The distinction between voluntary and involuntary migration, however, can be ambiguous.[25] For instance, involuntary migration caused by the loss of livelihood due to external factors, such as drought, is often conflated with economic migration in which individuals move in search of a better life. The former qualifies as forced migration, although it may involve an element of choice in a strict sense, since the movement is prompted by an external factor and the people concerned have little or no choice.[26] Thus, as can be inferred from both the definitions of IDPs above and refugee status discussed below, two essential elements define forced migration: the presence of an external factor beyond the migrant's control and the absence of meaningful choice. As of the end of 2024, approximately 123.2 million people in the world have found themselves in this situation, which includes refugees, IDPs, and asylum seekers.[27] It is imperative to differentiate these groups of forced migrants or the different types of forced migration as the norms of international law applicable to each category and the corresponding state obligations can be distinct. Accordingly,

[23] International human rights law provides different sets of obligations depending on which actors are involved. States are obligated to respect rights, which refers to refraining from directly infringing rights. States also have an obligation to protect right-holders from infringements of their rights by third parties, i.e. individuals or corporations. (UN CESCR 2017, paras 10–22). Hence, with regard to public projects, states have an obligation to respect, while they have a duty to protect when it comes to projects undertaken by private companies.

[24] Muggah 2003, p. 7. The field or the subject of forced migration was initially conceptualized in the context of refugees (see Bakewell 2011, p. 14). Expanding the forced migration studies to include IDPs has received resistance from some scholars who argued that the scope of the field should only be limited to those who had to flee their countries for (fear of) persecution—refugees and asylum seekers; including IDPs in this field or merging refugee studies in the broader field of forced migration would potentially dilute the international system put in place to protect the former (Bakewell 2011, p. 15; see also Hathaway 2007, pp. 350 and 365–366). This argument has been rejected by others who contended that the field or subject should be broad to include all those who move against their choice whether or not they cross an international border (see Bakewell 2011, p. 15; see also Cohen 2007, pp. 370–376; see also DeWind 2007, pp. 381–385). This view is widely accepted now and this work also uses the term "forced migration" based on this broader understanding.

[25] Bakewell 2011, p. 18.

[26] Hugo and Bun 1990, p. 20; see also Muggah 2003, p. 10; see also Bakewell 2011, p. 20.

[27] UNHCR global trends (n 1) p. 2 (this number has shown a significant increase every year, nearly doubling over the last decade).

the following sections seek to elucidate the difference between DID and the other forms of forced migration as well as the people affected thereby.

2.2.2.1 Refugees and Internally Displaced Persons[28]

As the people displaced by DID fall under the category of IDPs, this section generally addresses the difference between IDPs and refugees. Refugees constitute persons who have fled their country of origin due to war or fear of persecution and are seeking protection in another country.[29] The 1951 Refugee Convention defines the term "refugee" as:

> …any person who…. owing to well-founded fear of being persecuted for reasons of race, religion, nationality, membership of a particular social group or political opinion, is outside the country of his nationality and is unable or, owing to such fear, is unwilling to avail himself of the protection of that country; or who, not having a nationality and being outside the country of his former habitual residence as a result of such events, is unable or, owing to such fear, is unwilling to return to it.[30]

This definition contains three cumulative elements. First, the person must be "outside of the country of [their] nationality" or cross an international border to be granted a refugee status,[31] which is also the main distinguishing factor between refugees and IDPs. Second, there must be a "well-founded fear of persecution", which involves both subjective and objective elements, due to one or more of the grounds listed in the

---

[28] As the instruments on refugee status and internal displacement define the persons who have such status rather than the phenomenon, this section has also opted to define and compare the two categories of forced migrants instead of the types of migrations.

[29] Refugees are one of the prominent groups of forced migrants. According to the UNHCR's 2024 report, there are close to 37 million refugees and 8.4 million asylum seekers around the world (see UNHCR global trends (n 1) p. 2).

[30] UN General Assembly, Convention Relating to the Status of Refugees, 28 July 1951, 189 United Nations Treaty Series 137, Article 1A(2).

[31] Ibid.

provision.[32] The grounds of persecution enumerated in the Convention, "race, religion, nationality, membership of a particular social group or political opinion",[33] are exhaustive and the reason of persecution a person is fleeing from must fall under one of those grounds in order to obtain refugee status.[34] The African and Inter-American regional frameworks on refugee status have expanded the definition of refugees by adding more grounds of persecution, namely "external aggression, occupation, foreign domination or events seriously disturbing public order",[35] the rationale of which can be traced back to the colonial history of these continents. The third element of the definition pertains to the lack of protection from the country of nationality, which is attributable to the fear of persecution. Thus, a person seeking refugee status must be "unable or unwilling" to obtain protection from their country of nationality due to such fear.[36]

In light of the definition of IDPs provided in the preceding section, it is not difficult to identify the main difference between refugees and IDPs. While both groups of migrants are forced to move due to external factors, the movement of IDPs, as opposed to refugees, is confined within the national borders of the state.[37] Thus, the main distinguishing element is whether or not the migrants concerned have crossed an international border. Apart from this major distinction, the other constituent elements of the refugee definition are not necessarily applicable in the case of IDPs or, in other words, those elements are not essential prerequisites for an individual to be considered an IDP. For instance, the element of "fear of persecution" is not a necessary condition in the context of internal displacement,[38] although IDPs may also experience such fear or persecution in certain cases. IDPs are forced to leave their homes or residences due to the occurrence of some foreseen or unforeseen

[32] Ibid. According to the UNHCR, "well-founded fear" contains both objective and subjective criteria, which means it should be assessed based on the objective situation in the country of origin and personal circumstances and family background as well as the perception of the person seeking refugee status. Hence, "Asylum-seekers are not required to prove their fear "beyond reasonable doubt", or that it would be "more probable than not" that the feared harm will materialize. The adjudicator should consider the applicants' fear well-founded, if there is a reasonable possibility that they would face some form of harm if they were to return to their country of origin or habitual residence." (see UNHCR 2011, p. 6). While the Convention does not explicitly define what the term "persecution" constitutes, according to the UNHCR, it can be inferred from Article 33 of the Convention—the provision on the principle of non-refoulement—that "a threat to life or physical freedom constitutes persecution, as would other serious violations of human rights." (see UNHCR 2011, pp. 6 and 7; see also Refugee Convention (n 30) Article 33(1)). However, not every infringement of human rights constitutes a persecution; it needs to have a certain level of gravity to meet the threshold.

[33] Refugee Convention (n 30) Article 1A(2).

[34] Goodwin-Gill 2014, p. 39.

[35] Organization of African Unity (OAU), Convention Governing the Specific Aspects of Refugee Problems in Africa, 10 September 1969, 1001 U.N.T.S. 45 ('OAU Convention'), Article 1(2); see also Cartagena Declaration on Refugees, Adopted by Colloquium on the International Protection of Refugees in Central America, Mexico and Panama, 22 November 1984, para III(3).

[36] UNHCR 2011, pp. 6 and 7.

[37] Loescher 2016, pp. 325 and 326.

[38] Bakewell 2011, p. 17.

events, such as conflict or natural disaster, or are forced to relocate in order to make room for development projects.[39] Moreover, the definition of refugee status contains an element of discrimination as the fear of persecution necessitating the individual's flight relates to membership in specific groups enumerated in the provision quoted above, i.e. "race, religion, nationality, membership of a particular social group", or to holding a particular political opinion.[40] While the conflict, human rights violations, and even the development project that caused displacement in the case of IDPs may target those group identities or political opinions, they are not necessary requirements to be considered as such. Internal displacement can occur with or without such discrimination or differential treatment.

Some commentators attribute a narrower definition to IDPs contending that this category of forced migrants should only include those who would qualify as refugees if they were to cross international borders.[41] Nevertheless, internal displacement denotes a broader concept covering numerous causes of migration that are excluded from the definition of refugee status. IDPs comprise both those who might be regarded as refugees if they cross international borders and those who are displaced by factors that do not fall under the definition of refugees, such as development projects and natural disasters.[42] Thus, as Robinson rightly noted, "[IDPs]...are not simply "internal refugees", differing from their international counterparts by fluke of geography."[43]

Furthermore, refugees are granted a special legal status in international law due to their inability to get protection from their state of nationality, which necessitates a "substitute protection" from the international community.[44] On the other hand, IDPs are, in principle, still in a position to get protection from their national state and the international and regional frameworks on IDPs do not confer upon them a special legal status as such.[45] IDPs remain under the jurisdiction of their state of nationality even in cases where their displacement is caused by that very state.[46] Hence, they are still subjected to the same domestic laws and entitled to similar rights granted to individuals within the territory of the state or to citizens under human rights and humanitarian laws.[47] This does not, however, rule out the special legal and humanitarian assistance displaced persons should be provided with due to their particular vulnerability.[48]

IDPs are entitled to rights similar to those granted to individuals in the territory of the state in general and to citizens in particular. In principle, the fact of displacement

39 Guiding Principles on Internal Displacement (n 3) scope and purpose, para 2.

40 Refugee Convention (n 30) Article 1A(2).

41 Scholten 2016, p. 2.

42 Cohen 2006, p. 93; see also Bakewell 2011, p. 17.

43 Robinson 2003, p. 8.

44 Kälin 2014, pp. 165 and 166.

45 Ibid., p. 164; see also Kälin 2008, pp. 4 and 5.

46 Kälin 2014, p. 166; see also Cohen 2006, p. 88.

47 Kälin 2008, pp. 4 and 5.

48 Kälin 2014, p. 167; see also UNHCR 2013, p. 19.

alone does not deprive IDPs from enjoying similar rights as other citizens—provided that they are citizens.[49] Whereas, as foreigners, there are certain rights refugees are not granted, such as the right to vote and some welfare rights.[50] In other words, IDPs should enjoy higher protections as normally granted to citizens, rather than the specific protections available to refugees due to their status as such.[51] As the former representative of the UN Secretary-General on the human rights of IDPs, Walter Kälin, rightly contended:

> To qualify IDPs as a kind of 'refugees' risks ultimately lowering the level of their rights: while refugees as foreigners regularly do not enjoy all the rights available to the citizens of a country, it is important to insist that IDPs do not lose any rights because they are displaced, even if in reality they may be discriminated against and treated as second class citizens.[52]

Hence, another main differences between refugees and IDPs is the type of rights they are entitled to, which relates to the nature of their legal status.

Despite these differences, however, both refugees and IDPs are exposed to the particular disadvantages and vulnerabilities that come with being forcibly uprooted from one's home or residence, the extent of which depend more on the circumstances of the case and the safeguards put in place rather than the cause of displacement. As will be described in the following sections, IDPs including people displaced by development projects face various economic, social, and cultural challenges. Most of these challenges are also shared by refugees who had to leave their homes and livelihoods for fear of persecution.[53] Nevertheless, in both cases, most of these calamities can be mitigated, save for the unfavourable consequences inherent to displacement, if adequate protection is provided by the state of nationality or the receiving state, respectively.

2.2.2.2 Development-Induced Displacement and Other Types of Internal Displacement

As mentioned before, internal displacement is the largest category of forced migration in terms of the number of people it affects.[54] Various causes of internal displacement contribute to this number including those specifically listed under the Guiding Principles, i.e. "armed conflict, situations of generalized violence, violations of human rights or natural or human-made disasters", and others that are not specifically mentioned therein.[55] Armed conflicts, which include both international and internal

[49] Kälin 2014, p. 166.

[50] Ibid.

[51] Barutciski 2006, p. 73.

[52] Kälin 2014, p. 166; it has to be noted here that while human rights are, generally, guaranteed to "everyone" including foreigners, there are certain rights that are only limited to citizens.

[53] Turton 2006, pp. 15 and 16; see also Cernea 1996a, p. 17.

[54] Kälin 2014, p. 165; see also UNHCR global trends (n 1) p. 2.

[55] Guiding Principles on Internal Displacement (n 3) Principle 2.

armed conflicts as defined under international humanitarian law,[56] are among the primary causes of internal displacement.[57] In addition, the Guiding Principles list generalized violence or sporadic conflicts that do not meet the threshold of armed conflict as causes of internal displacement.[58] Internal displacement can also be caused by human rights violations, especially those that specifically target protected groups, such as ethnic and religious minorities, forcing them to flee their homes and habitual residences.[59] Another major cause of internal displacement is natural or human-made disasters.[60] As mentioned before, the list of causes of internal displacement under the Guiding Principles is left open-ended. Thus, apart from the causes specifically enumerated therein, other causes of displacement, such as development, are also covered by the definition of IDPs.

The implementation of development projects is one of the principal causes of internal displacement. While the two main elements of the definition of IDPs, i.e. the involuntary nature of the displacement and the fact that those displaced do not cross international borders, are applicable to all causes or types of internal displacement, DID has certain distinctive characteristics. In particular, three key factors differentiate DID from the other two primary types of internal displacement: conflict-induced displacement and disaster-induced displacement. These distinguishing factors relate to the foreseeability of the displacement, the duration of the displacement, and the extent of state involvement. DID, regardless of whether or not it is followed by resettlement and rehabilitation measures, is foreseeable and pre-planned.[61] Moreover, in most cases, displacement caused by development projects results in the permanent relocation of the people(s) affected depriving them of the option to return to their homes or residences. In public projects, where the state is the principal actor, displacement is directly caused by state action. In other words, the state initiates the displacement and is directly involved in all stages of the process. Even in private projects, displacement often takes place with the approval and/or support of the state. These factors have a direct implication on the type and scope of state obligations under international human rights law as this book seeks to establish in the subsequent chapters.

On the other hand, internal displacement caused by other factors, particularly natural disasters and conflict, is usually unforeseeable, temporary, and the direct involvement of the state is often minimal, if not non-existent. Natural disasters, such as flooding, earthquake, and storms, are the principal causes of internal displacement in terms of the number of people they affect every year.[62] Most of these incidents,

---

[56] International armed conflicts are hostilities that involve two or more states fighting against each other while non-international armed conflict refers to hostilities between a state and non-state armed groups or between such groups themselves (see ICRC 2008, p. 1).

[57] IDMC 2021; see also UNHCR 2013, p. 20.

[58] UNHCR 2013, p. 20.

[59] Ibid., p. 21.

[60] IDMC 2021, p. 15.

[61] Robinson 2003, p. 54; see also Muggah 2003, pp. 15 and 16.

[62] The Internal Displacement Monitoring Centre (IDMC) data shows that in 2017 alone 18.8 million people have been internally displaced due to natural disasters (Internal Displacement Monitoring

however, are unforeseeable and the resulting displacement only lasts for a limited period or they often involve "short-term evacuations" in which cases the displaced persons may have the option to return to their residences.[63] Nevertheless, some natural disasters, such as tsunamis, may result in long term destruction, which makes it impossible for the displaced people to return to their homes. In such cases, natural disasters may cause long-term or permanent displacement.[64]

Similarly, conflict-induced displacement is also mostly unanticipated and temporary, although it can sometimes be long-term.[65] In light of this, the pertinent international instruments on internal displacement, namely the Guiding Principles, the Kampala Convention, and the Pinheiro Principles (the UN Economic and Social Council's Principles on Housing and Property Restitution for Refugees and Displaced Persons), specifically require states to facilitate the voluntary return of displaced persons to their homes or habitual residences when the situation that necessitated their flight ends.[66] With regard to state involvement, the likelihood of a state's action directly causing disaster-induced displacement is minimal, although not entirely impossible. It is, however, important to note that state inaction—specifically, the failure to implement adequate adaptation and mitigation measures to address the global climate crisis—can be the root cause of certain natural disasters. In conflict-induced displacement, the state might be involved in the armed conflict that caused the displacement, thus, taking part in actions that force people to flee, such as the destruction of houses.[67] In other cases, the conflict can be between non-state actors and the direct involvement of the state in the cause of displacement can be minimal. Thus, in the case of conflict-induced displacement, the state involvement varies depending on the nature of the conflict and the actors involved.

These distinguishing features of various causes of internal displacement are not without any effect, rather they (should) play an important role in determining the rights of displaced persons and the corresponding obligations of states concerning the protection and assistance of displaced persons.[68] As this book seeks to demonstrate in the subsequent chapters, due to these distinct features, DID calls for heightened obligations of states. In other words, the level of protection and assistance the state

---

Centre (IDMC), Global Report on Internal Displacement 2018, available at http://www.internal-displacement.org/global-report/grid2018/, accessed 19 July 2025).

63 Terminski 2015, p. 58; see also Kälin 2014, p. 165; see also IDMC 2021, p. 15.

64 Terminski 2015, p. 31; see also Kälin 2014, p. 165.

65 Robinson 2003, p. 54; see also Kälin 2014, p. 165; see also Muggah 2003, p. 15.

66 Guiding Principles on Internal Displacement (n 3) Principle 28; see also UN Economic and Social Council, Principles on Housing and Property Restitution for Refugees and Displaced Persons, 28 June 2005, E/CN.4/Sub.2/2005/17. (This instrument, commonly called the Pinheiro Principles, is adopted by the UN Economic and Social Council and it guarantees refugees and IDPs displaced due to armed conflicts a right to regain the possession of their houses and property after the conflict is over).

67 Lischer 2007, p. 144 (For instance, in the Darfur conflict where the government forces and rebel groups were fighting, around two million people were displaced following the destruction of their village by government soldiers).

68 Robinson 2003, p. 54.

has to provide in other unanticipated cases of displacement arguably would not be sufficient to fulfil state obligations under international human rights law when it comes to DID.

2.3 Causes of Development-Induced Displacement

DID can be caused by a range of development projects. This section briefly outlines some of the primary causes of DID, namely, dam construction, urban (re)development and transportation projects, and the extraction of natural resources, which are selected based on their scale—in terms of the number of people they affect and their prevalence across borders. It is important to note, however, that the causes of DID are not limited to these three categories of development projects. Numerous other large and small scale development projects are also responsible for the displacement of a large number of people worldwide including government-owned plantations and the development of national parks and reserves, among others.[69]

2.3.1 Construction of Dams

The construction of hydroelectric and irrigation dams is one of the most prominent causes of displacement in terms of the number of people it affects and the geographical area it covers.[70] Studies show that the construction of dams accounts for approximately 40% of displacements caused by development projects each year.[71] According to the World Commission on Dams'[72] comprehensive report, as of the year 2000, approximately between 40 and 80 millions of people have been displaced by large dam projects worldwide.[73] Reports also reveal that this number has shown a significant increase in the last two decades.[74] The fastest developing and highly populated countries, such as China and India, take the lion's share in the number of

69 Terminski 2015, pp. 37–41.

70 Stanley 2004, p. 6.

71 Ibid., p. 7; see also World Commission on Dams 2000, p. 103. Moreover, among the projects financed by the World Bank that involve displacement, construction of dams constitute 63 percent of the displacement (see the Report of the World Commission on Dams (n 71) 104; see also Stanley 2004, p. 7); see also Terminski 2015, pp. 40 and 86.

72 The World Commission on Dams is a global expert forum that existed from 1998 to 2000. The Commission worked to identify the economic potential as well as the socio-economic impacts of large dam projects. It sought to explore ways in which large dams can be built to prevent or mitigate their adverse impacts (see Schulz and Adams 2019, pp. 1 and 2).

73 World Commission on Dams 2000, pp. 16–17 and 104 (it is important to note that these numbers are estimates and displacement caused by development projects are often underreported mainly by states).

74 IDMC 2017, p. 2.

people displaced by large dam projects.[75] For instance, the Three Gorges dam project in China alone displaced an estimated number of 1.2 million people.[76] The construction of the Sardar Sarovar Dam in India has been responsible for the displacement of over 200,000 people.[77]

The construction of large dams has notably increased since the 1950s,[78] which coincides with the independence of formerly colonized states.[79] Newly independent and developing countries embarked on the construction of large-scale dam projects in pursuit of economic development and to meet their growing energy needs,[80] 90% of which were constructed in the last quarter of the twentieth century.[81] The construction of large-scale dams "...[has] become symbols of economic development in many countries of Africa, Asia, and Latin America."[82] This is also one of the reasons why the number of people affected by DID has significantly increased since then. According to the data from the International Commission on Large Dams (ICOLD),[83] the number of large dams in the world was 5000 in 1950 while forty years later, in the late 1990s, this number had increased to over 45,000.[84] Consequently, the number of people displaced due to large dam projects during this period ranges from 30 to 80 million people.[85] Overall, the construction of dams, particularly large-scale dams, is one of the main causes of involuntary displacement.

---

[75] World Commission on Dams 2000, p. 104 (between 1950 and 1990, the construction of dams had led to the displacement of around 10.2 million people. Similarly, between 16 and 38 million people had been displaced by large dams in India within the same period); see also Terminski 2015, p. 88.

[76] Stanley 2004, p. 6.

[77] Himanshu 1999.

[78] Stanley 2004, p. 6. Technically speaking, large dams refers to dams higher than 15 meters (see International Rivers: people, water, life, Questions and Answers About Large Dams, available at https://www.irn.org/files/basics/qanda.html, accessed 26 July 2025).

[79] For instance, out of more than 4000 dams India currently has, more than 3000 of them were built after 1947, which is when the country obtained its independence (see Debasree 2015, p. 448).

[80] Adeola 2017, pp. 245 and 246; see also Terminski 2015, p. 36.

[81] Gizachew 2017, p. 115.

[82] Terminski 2015, p. 50.

[83] The International Commission on Large Dams is an international organization that has over 100 member states. It studies the design, construction, and impacts of large dams and "[sets] standards and guidelines to ensure that dams are built and operated safely, efficiently, economically, and are environmentally sustainable and socially equitable." (International Commission on Large Dams, Organization and Mission, available at https://www.icold-cigb.org/GB/icold/organization__mission.asp, accessed 26 July 2025).

[84] Stanley 2004, p. 6; see also Terminski 2015, p. 86.

[85] Stanley 2004, p. 7; This is one of the reasons researchers on DID usually employ case studies on dam projects.

2.3.2 Urban (Re)development and Transportation

Urban (re)development encompasses a wide range of public projects undertaken in urban areas, including city renewal initiatives, industrial and commercial developments, the construction of schools, hospitals, transportation systems, and other communication infrastructure.[86] These projects are among the principal causes of displacement accounting for approximately 60% of DID every year.[87] Compared to large-scale dam projects, the number of people ousted by individual urban development undertakings is relatively smaller.[88] Due to the frequency of these types of projects, however, the overall number of people they displace is significantly larger.[89] Moreover, while the amount of land acquired for individual urban development projects is usually smaller compared to other large-scale development projects, "the ratio of people displaced per unit of expropriated land is usually higher as a result of high urban population densities."[90]

With the proliferation of urbanization around the world, the number of urban development projects and the resulting displacement have been particularly intensifying in recent decades.[91] For instance, the data on urbanization suggests that the percentage of people that live in large cities with 4 million or more residents is expected to reach "24.5 percent globally and 28.2 percent in developing countries" in 2025, while it was only 15.8% in 1980.[92] It is further estimated that by 2050, 68% of the world population will be living in urban areas in a significant increase from the current number—55%.[93] This increase in urbanization will consequently lead to an increase in public projects in urban areas, which will, in turn, lead to a potential increase in DID.

---

[86] Stanley 2004, p. 8.

[87] Terminski 2015, p. 38; see also Stanley 2004, p. 8. With regard to projects funded by the World Bank, the figure is quite different from the data on dams mentioned above; only 22.6 percent of DID has resulted from urban development projects financed by the World Bank (see Stanley 2004, p. 8).

[88] Terminski 2015, p. 38; see also Stanley 2004, p. 10.

[89] Stanley 2004, p. 10; Terminski 2015, p. 38.

[90] Stanley 2004, p. 8. For instance, The Mumbai Urban Transport Project in India has caused the displacement of around 100,000 people; water supply project in Nairobi relocated 10,000 people, to mention a few (see Terminski 2015, p. 38).

[91] Stanley 2004, p. 8.

[92] Ibid.

[93] United Nations Department of Economic and Social Affairs, 68% of the world population projected to live in urban areas by 2050, says UN, News, available at https://www.un.org/uk/desa/68-world-population-projected-live-urban-areas-2050-says-un, accessed 19 July 2025; see also The World Bank, Urban Development, last updated 20 April 2020, available at https://www.worldbank.org/en/topic/urbandevelopment/overview#1, accessed 19 July 2025.

2.3.3 Extraction of Natural Resources

Another category of development projects that frequently causes displacement is the extraction of natural resources, particularly minerals and oil.[94] Compared to the two previously mentioned categories, mining and oil extraction projects tend to displace a relatively smaller number of people.[95] In some cases, displacement occurs as an indirect consequence of development projects.[96] Those projects may cause environmental and ecological disruptions that, in turn, lead to the involuntary displacement of the inhabitants.[97] This indirect displacement is not commonly followed by a planned resettlement.[98] Rather, people are forced to abandon their homes and flee due to the unbearable living conditions caused by natural resource extraction projects.[99] In addition, extraction of natural resources is also often associated with the concerns of ethnic tensions, self-determination, and struggle for resources.[100] The implementation of these projects, therefore, can sometimes instigate or aggravate internal conflicts, which may subsequently cause displacement.[101] Hence, in these cases, DID, conflict-induced displacement, and environmentally-induced displacement can be overlapping,[102] which is one of the reasons why the data and literature on displacement caused by these projects is not as clear and extensive as the previous two causes.[103]

Moreover, displacement prompted by the extraction of natural resources disproportionately affects indigenous peoples as approximately "over 60 percent of the world's natural resources are located on indigenous lands."[104] This factor is particularly important in the DID discourse since indigenous peoples are granted special

---

[94] Terminski 2015, p. 39; see also Stanley 2004, p. 11.

[95] Stanley 2004, p. 11. However, even if the extraction of natural resources displaces a smaller number of people compared to other large-scale projects, such as dams and urban development, the fact that it still affects a significant number of people should not be overlooked. For instance, a gold mining project in Tarkwa region of Ghana has displaced approximately 20,000 to 30,000 people (see Terminski 2015, p. 39). Studies have also shown that in India, 2.5 million people had been displaced due to mining projects from 1950–1990 (see Terminski 2012, p. 2).

[96] Stanley 2004, p. 11.

[97] Ibid.; see also Terminski 2015, p. 40.

[98] Stanley 2004, p. 11.

[99] Ibid.

[100] Terminski 2015, p. 40.

[101] Ibid.

[102] The Ogoni case in Nigeria is a good example to demonstrate this overlap. As can be seen from the facts of the case, the oil extraction projects by private companies contaminated the environment, which made the lives of the Ogoni community members difficult. Moreover, the government of Nigeria responded to the protests challenging the environmental degradation caused by oil companies with violent measures, including the destruction of houses and execution of the community leaders. This has displaced a number of Ogoni people from their homes. (see *Social and Economic Rights Action Center (SERAC) and Center for Economic and Social Rights (CESR) / Nigeria*, 155/96, African Commission on Human and People's Rights, paras 2–8.)

[103] Stanley 2004, p. 9.

[104] Terminski 2015, p. 39.

rights to their land in international human rights law,[105] which also places limits on the state's power of expropriation,[106] as will be discussed in Chap. 7.

2.4 Consequences of Development-Induced Displacement

Being forcibly displaced from one's home or residence comes with a plethora of social, economic, and cultural consequences and risks. In his seminal work, the Impoverishment Risk and Reconstruction Model,[107] Michael Cernea identified eight interdependent risks associated with displacement, namely: landlessness, joblessness, homelessness, marginalization, increased morbidity, food insecurity, loss of access to common property, and social disintegration.[108] These consequences collectively contribute to the impoverishment of displaced persons that often follows DID.[109] As Cernea concluded, "being forcibly ousted from one's land and habitat by a dam, reservoir or highway is not only immediately disruptive and painful, it is also fraught with serious long term risks of becoming poorer than before displacement, more vulnerable economically, and disintegrated socially."[110] This section elucidates some of the main consequences of DID under three categories: economic, social, and cultural.

2.4.1 Economic Consequences

Forced displacement imposes several adverse economic consequences on displaced persons. Studies have evinced that people affected by DID bear the "risk of becoming poorer than before displacement".[111] This risk of impoverishment is the result of various interdependent consequences of DID that affect the livelihoods and sources

---

[105] UN General Assembly, United Nations Declaration on the Rights of Indigenous Peoples: resolution/adopted by the General Assembly, 2 October 2007, A/RES/61/295 ('UNDRIP'), Article 10; see also International Labour Organization (ILO), Indigenous and Tribal Peoples Convention, C169, 27 June 1989 ('ILO Convention No. 169'), Articles 13–19.

[106] States cannot forcibly remove indigenous peoples from their lands without their "free, prior and informed consent" (see UNDRIP (n 105) Article 10; see also ILO Convention No. 169 (n 105) Article 16).

[107] The impoverishment risk and reconstruction (IRR) model is a theoretical model developed by Michael Cernea in order to identify the adverse consequences of involuntary displacement prompted by development and formulate policy responses to address those consequences. As the name itself indicates, the IRR model identifies the impoverishment risks that DID involves and the reconstruction measures that need to be undertaken to avert these risks. (see Cernea and McDowell 2000, p. 5).

[108] Cernea 1995, pp. 251 and 252; see also Cernea 2000, pp. 19 and 20.

[109] Cernea 1995, pp. 251 and 252.

[110] Cernea 1996a, p. 304.

[111] Ibid.; see also Robinson 2003, p. 11.

of income of displaced persons including, *inter alia*, loss of land or decrease in landholding, loss of housing, and loss of jobs or decrease in income.[112]

Expropriation of land, which displaced people derive their livelihoods from through farming, pastoralism, and commercial undertakings, is the principal cause of the risk of economic impoverishment that displaced persons face. "This is the principal form of de-capitalization and pauperization of displaced people, through loss of both physical and [human-made] capital."[113] The acquisition of land that DID involves often leads to landlessness or decrease in landholdings, particularly when adequate in-kind or monetary compensation is not provided.[114] In some cases, even if compensation is provided and displaced persons are resettled, those short-term measures might not be sufficient to restore the landholdings they had before displacement.[115] This will, in turn, have a ripple effect as it affects production capacity, particularly those of farmers and pastoralists, and ultimately leads to food insecurity.[116] For instance, a study conducted on a coal mining project in Singrauli, India showed that the percentage of landless individuals among those displaced by the project increased significantly—from 20% to 72%—after relocation.[117] Similarly, the average landholding of people displaced by Kiambere Hydroelectric dam project in Kenya decreased from 13 to 6 hectares, which in turn significantly diminished their crop and livestock production and their family income by 82%.[118] Another study conducted on four development projects in Ethiopia found that the average landholding of the people displaced by these projects decreased from 1.2 to 0.68 hectares after relocation, which significantly reduced their incomes as they are mostly farmers.[119] In some cases, displaced persons are provided with replacement land of lesser quality in terms of agricultural productivity and/or location, which also significantly affects their economic well-being. This was, for instance, the case in the Merowe Dam Project in Sudan where studies showed that the lands provided to people displaced by the project were of poor quality.[120] These cases demonstrate that the loss of land, decrease in landholding, and poorer quality of land that DID results in impose significant economic costs on displaced persons particularly on those whose livelihoods depend on land.

The other consequence of DID that adversely affects the economic and social wellbeing of the people affected is loss of housing or subjection to poorer housing conditions after displacement. The process of DID often involves eviction, which, in some cases, constitutes "forced eviction"—a forcible removal from one's home

[112] Nayak 2013, pp. 398 and 404.

[113] Cernea 1995, p. 251.

[114] Cernea 2000, p. 23.

[115] Van der Ploeg and Vanclay 2017, p. 45.

[116] Cernea 2000, pp. 23 and 24.

[117] Ibid., p. 23.

[118] Ibid., pp. 23 and 24.

[119] Gebreyesus and Tadesse 2019, pp. 133 and 142.

[120] Ahmed 2019, pp. 148 and 149. The construction of the dam has displaced approximately 50,000 persons (Ahmed 2019, p. 131).

or residence without adequate legal protection.[121] This might result in temporary or permanent loss of housing depending on the resettlement options and remedies provided.[122] People displaced by development projects are often provided with "temporary shelters" until they are able to set up permanent housing, which can be financially challenging for most of them.[123] These temporary arrangements turn into long-term or permanent housing for a large number of displaced persons.[124] For instance, a study conducted on Kukadi-Krishna irrigation project in India showed that 59% of the people displaced by the project were living in temporary facilities for 10-15 years after displacement.[125] Similarly, a case study conducted on several development projects in the city of Ahmedabad, India found that a number of households displaced by these projects continued to live in temporary housing facilities for seven years.[126] In some cases, even if the displaced people are able to reconstruct houses, they are subjected to poorer housing conditions due to the inadequacy of safeguards provided by the state, such as inadequate compensation.[127] In other cases, the replacement housing provided by the state may fail to meet the standards of "adequate housing" as formulated in relevant human rights frameworks discussed in the next chapter. Thus, the risk of homelessness or diminished housing conditions contributes to the economic impoverishment as well as to the social challenges displaced persons face coupled with the loss of land and income sources associated with DID.

Apart from the loss of housing and land, physical displacement also results in "loss or significant reduction of access to [common] resources", such as water sources, grazing land, and forests, which the people affected depend upon to make or sustain a living.[128] Moreover, despite their socio-economic importance, these resources are not usually taken into account in the determination of compensation, if any, and the resettlement process.[129]

Another consequence of displacement that the risk of impoverishment is attributable to is loss or decrease of income sources. For people whose livelihoods depend on land, such as farmers and pastoralists, this might be the immediate

---

[121] According to the definition adopted by the Committee on Economic, Social and Cultural Rights (CESCR), forced eviction is "the permanent or temporary removal against their will of individuals, families and/or communities from the homes and/or land which they occupy, without the provision of, and access to, appropriate forms of legal or other protection." (UN CESCR 1997, para 3).

[122] Cernea 2000, p. 25.

[123] Ibid.

[124] Ibid., pp. 25 and 26.

[125] Ibid., p. 26.

[126] Patel et al. 2015, p. 235.

[127] Cernea 2000, p. 25.

[128] Terminski 2015, pp. 44 and 45; empirical studies suggest that these resources can be the source of a significant portion of household incomes. For instance, a study conducted on semi-arid regions of India states that "between 91 and 100 percent of firewood, between 66 and 89 percent of domestic fuel, and between 69 and 80 percent of poor households' grazing needs are supplied by land held under common property regime." (see Cernea 2000, p. 29).

[129] Cernea 1995, p. 252; see also Cernea 2000, p. 29.

consequence of the land acquisition discussed above. People who do not directly derive their income from the land they are displaced from can also have a hard time regaining the income they used to earn before displacement.[130] For instance, the study conducted on the DID cases in the city of Ahmedabad, India, revealed that 14% of workers displaced by the development projects covered by the study remained unemployed for a long time due to the remote location of the resettlement sites and other socio-economic difficulties created by the displacement.[131] Thus, the loss or decrease of income that DID causes can continue for a long period after displacement,[132] resulting in chronic impoverishment. In some cases, unemployment may not be an immediate result of displacement particularly when displaced persons are provided with project-related jobs.[133] Nonetheless, these jobs are typically short-term and with the completion of the project, those individuals are often left unemployed.[134] This pattern has been particularly shown by case studies undertaken on dam projects, the construction of which often creates numerous employment opportunities temporarily providing displaced persons with jobs.[135]

In addition, displacement disrupts trade links, established customer bases, and local economic associations,[136] which contributes to the overall economic impoverishment of the displaced population.

These consequences of DID put a severe strain on the income-earning capacity of the people affected potentially leading to impoverishment, if left unmitigated. Studies have also shown that this economic impoverishment will have ripple effects causing food insecurity and an increase in morbidity and mortality rates, among others.[137] Moreover, the economic consequences that DID results in can persist over a long time leading to the chronic impoverishment and marginalization of those affected.[138] Overall, DID exerts an immense impact on the economic wellbeing of the people affected by displacement particularly when adequate safeguards are not provided.

2.4.2 Social Consequences

In addition to economic hardships, displaced persons also face a range of social consequences related to, *inter alia*, access to education and healthcare services, as

[130] A study undertaken in Thailand confirmed the fact that people who have been resettled following DID were earning less than the income they had before displacement for reasons directly attributable to the displacement (see Dunning 1979, pp. 15–25).

[131] Patel et al. 2015, p. 242.

[132] Cernea 1995, p. 251.

[133] Cernea 2000, p. 24.

[134] Ibid., pp. 24 and 25.

[135] Ibid.

[136] Robinson 2003, p. 12.

[137] Cernea 2000, pp. 27 and 28.

[138] McDowell 2014, p. 338; see also Cernea 2000, pp. 27–29.

well as the disruption of community life. To start with, the economic consequences of DID described above directly affect the social wellbeing of displaced persons as they diminish their ability to afford and access pertinent public services. Displacement not only temporarily interrupts schooling but also can potentially have a long-term effect on access to education in cases where adequate educational facilities are not provided in the new resettlement sites or children are forced to join the labour market as the result of economic impoverishment.[139] For instance, a study conducted on development projects undertaken in the city of Ahmedabad, India, found that the displacement caused by these projects not only temporary interrupted schooling but also a number of students dropped out of school due to the socio-economic difficulties instigated by the displacement.[140] Displacement also adversely affects the physical and physiological health of those displaced.[141] This is mainly attributable to food insecurity that follows from the economic impoverishment and the lack or inadequacy of public services, such as clean water supply and healthcare facilities, at the places where displaced people are resettled.[142] For instance, a study conducted on the Hirakud dam project in India flagged that the site where the people displaced by the project were resettled lacked basic public amenities, such as healthcare facilities and schools.[143] Moreover, the psychological stress and mental health issues that being forcibly displaced from one's home or residence causes cannot be overlooked.

In communal societies, people often rely on informal social structures to get essential services, such as child-care, and to deal with emergency situations.[144] Displacement can potentially disrupt these social arrangements, which not only affects various social needs but also has an adverse impact on the economic self-sufficiency of the community.[145] In addition, displacement disrupts well-established "social support systems" where the most vulnerable portions of the society, such as the elderly and disabled people, are protected.[146] These social structures are particularly imperative in communities or countries where social security or social welfare and other safeguards that protect these vulnerable and marginalized groups are not sufficiently provided. Furthermore, these informal social structures are not usually taken into account in displacement and resettlement policies and practices.[147] For instance, a study conducted in several development projects in India found that displaced persons were resettled in different sites without taking into account their established social

139 Cernea 2000, p. 31.

140 Patel et al. 2015, p. 246.

141 Cernea 2000, pp. 27 and 28.

142 Cernea 1995, p. 252.

143 Nayak 2013, p. 413; see also Patel et al. 2015, pp. 246–248 (this study also found that the resettlement sites lack basic public services, which contributed to various health problems displaced persons were facing).

144 Parasuraman 1996, p. 1530.

145 Cernea 2000, p. 30.

146 Partridge 1989, p. 375.

147 Cernea 2000, p. 30.

units and networks.[148] Hence, displacement causes "an expensive yet unquantified loss of social capital".[149]

2.4.3 Cultural Consequences

Another adverse impact of DID pertains to the cultural life of the people(s) affected. Displacement potentially disrupts the cultural practices and way of life of those displaced from their homes or residences. In this context, culture represents a broader concept that includes both the spiritual and material traits with which a certain group identifies. In the *Endorois case*—a case related to the forcible removal of indigenous people from their ancestral land for development purposes—the African Commission on Human and Peoples' Rights defined culture as:

> [a] complex whole which includes a spiritual and physical association with one's ancestral land, knowledge, belief, art, law, morals, customs, and any other capabilities and habits acquired by humankind as a member of society - the sum total of the material and spiritual activities and products of a given social group that distinguish it from other similar groups….cultural identity [encompasses] a group's religion, language, and other defining characteristics.[150]

In some situations, the cultural practices and way of life of displaced people are closely tied to their homes, land, or place of residence, in which case they are inevitably disrupted by relocation from those sites. This is particularly the case for indigenous peoples whose way of life is closely intertwined with their ancestral land.[151] For instance, in the *Endorois case* where the indigenous communities concerned claimed the violation of cultural rights due to denial of access to their land, the Commission noted that indigenous peoples culture and way of life are intrinsically linked to their traditional land.[152] Hence, dispossession of land and displacement interfered with their cultural practices and continuation of that way of life.[153] Overall, DID imposes a plethora of adverse economic, social, and cultural consequences on displaced persons. The impacts of DID, however, are not limited to the people that are displaced by the project concerned but also extend to the host communities that inhabit the areas where the former are resettled.[154] As Cernea found in his study, "the inflows of displacees increase pressure on resources and scarce social

---

[148] Patel et al. 2015, p. 249.

[149] Cernea 1995, p. 252.

[150] *Centre for Minority Rights Development (Kenya) and Minority Rights Group International on behalf of Endorois Welfare Council v. Kenya,* 276/2003, African Commission on Human and Peoples' Rights, 4 February 2010 ('Endorois case'), para 241.

[151] Charters 2018, p. 396.

[152] *Endorois case* (n 150) para 244.

[153] Ibid., paras 244 and 251.

[154] Stanley 2004, p. 2; see also Cernea 2000, p. 32.

services, as well as competition for employment."[155] Moreover, host communities may also be subjected to inflation or an increase in the cost of living, health risks, and environmental degradation due to the sudden increase of population.[156] The resettlement of displaced populations to a new place inhabited by groups of people culturally or socially distinct from the former may also create cultural and social tensions.[157] Since the focus of this research is on the rights of persons displaced by DID and the correlative obligations of states, it does not extend to the challenges faced by host communities. Thus, this brief remark suffices to note that the impacts of DID also extend to the economic, social, and cultural well-being of the host communities and resettlement programs need to take into account this aspect as well.

2.5 Vulnerability in the Context of Development-Induced Displacement

The consequences of DID described above are not felt on the same level by all groups of people affected. Certain segments of the population are more vulnerable due to their specific economic and social status as well as their historical and ongoing marginalization.[158] Thus, the consequences of DID have the potential to perpetuate existing vulnerabilities or disadvantages and even create new ones. To begin with, studies have evinced that DID disproportionately affects "the poorest and most marginalized population"[159] who are not often the beneficiaries of the development projects of which they are bearing the cost. For instance, a study conducted on development projects undertaken in India from 1951 to 1991 showed that of the total number of people displaced by these projects, 40% of were indigenous peoples, even if they only made up 8% of the general population.[160] Another study conducted in India also found that religious and tribal minorities were disproportionately represented among the people displaced by the projects covered by the study.[161] Moreover, financially underprivileged people feel the costs of DID more severely than people with adequate financial means to re-establish themselves and cope with the changing circumstances.[162] Not only does DID usually target already marginalized people but also "those who enjoy the benefits of development [that caused displacement]

[155] Cernea 2000, p. 32.

[156] Ibid.

[157] Ibid.

[158] Ibid., p. 31; see also Stanley 2004, p. 14. The concept of marginalization, as used in this book, refers to the social, economic, and political standing of a group in a given society. Vulnerability is the result of that; marginalization makes a group susceptible to special challenges, human rights violations, and abuses. This work will employ both terms based on this understanding.

[159] Robinson 2003, p. 10.

[160] Rew et al. 2000, pp. 104 and 105; see also Debasree 2015, p. 448; see also Stanley 2004, p. 14.

[161] Patel et al. 2015, p. 248.

[162] Mathur 1995, p. 20.

may not be those who bear the risks."[163] This raises concerns of social justice and equity[164]—values upon which the human rights norms discussed in this book are founded.

Development processes that are not based on equitable standards often exacerbate already existing inequalities and vulnerabilities, not only because the burden of paying the costs could fall on the shoulders of those who are already marginalized but also because certain groups of people might face specific challenges due to their socio-economic status and other factors.[165] Similarly, DID poses varying levels of risk to different groups of people based on their special status or vulnerability. The consequences of DID often hit the hardest vulnerable and marginalized groups such as indigenous peoples, women, and children.[166] As mentioned above, indigenous peoples are often disproportionately affected by displacement prompted by development projects. Furthermore, physical displacement has severe consequences on these peoples since they have special ties to their land and environment.[167] This is also the main reason why indigenous peoples are accorded special rights to their ancestral land and states have a heightened obligation when the displacement in question affects the people identified as such.[168]

Similar to the other forms of forced migration, internal displacement, including DID, also imposes a more severe impact on women. Women are particularly vulnerable in the context of DID due to the existing social and legal discriminations with regard to property ownership and land rights,[169] which will, in turn, lead to discriminatory practices in the determination of compensation and resettlement.[170] Despite the international recognition of women's equal rights to land ownership and utilization,[171] and the significant progress made in the last few decades in this regard, there

---

[163] Ibid., p. 21; see also Cernea 2000, p. 12.

[164] Cernea 2000, p. 12.

[165] Thukral 1996, p. 1500.

[166] Stanley 2004, p. 14; see also UN CESCR 1997, para 7.

[167] Stanley 2004, p. 14.

[168] The ILO Convention No. 169 and the Declaration on the Rights of Indigenous Peoples recognize the right of ownership and possession of indigenous people to the land they 'traditionally occupy'. More importantly, Article 16 of the Convention and Article 10 of the Declaration specifically prohibit the removal of these people from their land save for exceptional circumstances where they have given "free, prior and informed consent" (see ILO Convention No. 169 (n 105) Articles 14 and 16; see also UNDRIP (n 105) Article 10).

[169] UN CESCR 1997, para 10; see also Thukral 1996, p. 1500.

[170] Nayak 2013, p. 403.

[171] UN General Assembly, Convention on the Elimination of All Forms of Discrimination Against Women, 18 December 1979, 1249 United Nations Treaty Series 13, Articles 14 and 15; see also UN CEDAW Committee 2016; see also UN CESCR 2005, para 28.

remains a gender gap and discrimination when it comes to land rights.[172] This differential treatment will directly reflect in the compensation and other remedies provided following displacement as their determination is usually based on ownership.[173]

Some studies have portrayed that in rural areas, disruption of access to common resources, which usually follows displacement, is more detrimental to women since they often use these resources as a source of income.[174] Similarly, women who live in urban areas are also disproportionately affected in comparison to men as their income sources can be dependent on small local businesses and established customer bases.[175] This is further compounded by resettlement and compensation standards that often discriminate against women.[176] For instance, a study undertaken on the Orissa region of India pointed out that the age to claim compensation for land acquisition for unmarried women was set at 30 years while it was only 18 years for their male counterparts.[177]

Moreover, displacement also increases the vulnerability of women to gender-based violence and abuse,[178] unless the necessary preventive measures are taken. Particularly when displaced persons are relocated to temporary shelters, like camps, or even left without any replacement shelter as often happens, women face an increased risk of violence.[179] Some studies have also documented an increase in domestic violence in the immediate years following involuntary resettlement.[180] Overall, women are one of the most vulnerable groups in the context of forced migration in general and DID in particular.

Another group that is particularly vulnerable in displacement settings is children. Displacement particularly affects the education of children when school is interrupted,[181] or adequate access to school is not guaranteed in the resettlement sites. For instance, a study conducted in development projects undertaken in Ahmedabad mentioned before revealed that 18% of children displaced by these projects dropped out of school due to the remote locations of the resettlement sites and lack of sufficient access to public transport, among others.[182] Moreover, the overall impoverishment

---

[172] Thukral 1996, 1500; According to the report of the Food Agricultural Organization of the United Nations (FAO), women constitute less than 15 percent of landholders, which is defined as a person who makes important decisions concerning the utilization of the land, in the world. Moreover, the report also depicted that women's ownership of land is significantly smaller than men's, and women landowners are less likely to have formal legal documents to that effect (see Food Agricultural Organization of the United Nations (FAO), The gender gap in land rights, available at https://www.fao.org/documents/card/en/c/I8796EN/, accessed 19 July 2025).

[173] Thukral 1996, p. 1501.

[174] Stanley 2004, p. 15.

[175] Ibid.

[176] Cernea 2000, p. 31; see also Stanley 2004, p. 15.

[177] Cernea 2000, p. 31.

[178] UN CESCR 1997, para 10; see also Nayak 2013, p. 402.

[179] Freccero 2015, pp. 55–58; see also UNHCR 2003.

[180] Colson 2008, pp. 31 and 32.

[181] Cernea 2000, p. 31; see also Stanley 2004, p. 15.

[182] Patel et al. 2015, p. 246.

of the household, which, as described before, is a common consequence of DID, adversely affects children's education and well-being in general.[183] As a result, they are, in some cases, forced to join the labour market earlier than they should in order to support themselves and their families.[184]

Generally, DID has varying levels of risks and impacts on displaced people(s) depending on their economic, social, and cultural status as well as their historical and ongoing vulnerability and marginalization. Displacement potentially intensifies existing inequalities and vulnerabilities or even creates new ones due to the economic marginalization it causes. In addition to the categories of vulnerable groups mentioned above, the consequences of DID also hit hard elders and disabled people, among others. Hence, the normative analyses in the subsequent chapters will adopt a vulnerability lens in order to understand and explore the specific normative responses to the differential degrees of risks that DID poses to marginalized groups.

2.6 Preventing or Mitigating the Adverse Consequences of Displacement

While displacement is inherently disruptive, most of the adverse consequences of DID are mainly attributable to the legality and legitimacy of the decision-making, the process of displacement and resettlement, and the adequacy of the procedural and substantive safeguards provided along the way, rather than the mere the fact of displacement. In other words, the measures undertaken at all phases of displacement—starting from the planning of the development project concerned to the implementation of the resettlement—and the safeguards put in place by the state determine the level of economic, social, and cultural costs displaced persons pay.[185] The adverse consequences of displacement discussed above can be prevented or at least mitigated if adequate resettlement and rehabilitation options are provided and the necessary safeguards are put in place.

This can be seen from the fact that although the displacement of people for development reasons is a situation that occurs worldwide, it does not arise as a significant social and economic problem in all countries.[186] Some commentators argue that democratic countries where public participation and human rights protections are guaranteed are in a relatively better position to deal with a situation of involuntary displacement prompted by development.[187] In these countries, if displacement is inevitable, it is arguably implemented with the meaningful participation of those affected in the decision-making and followed by adequate resettlement standards.[188]

---

[183] Stanley 2004, p. 15.

[184] Cernea 2000, p. 31.

[185] Stanley 2004, p. 11.

[186] Terminski 2015, p. 34.

[187] Ibid.

[188] Ibid.

On the other hand, in authoritarian systems or in countries where democratic practice is in its infancy, it is more likely that the displacement process will be arbitrary as there may be lack of proper safeguards and institutions to protect the rights of people affected by displacement.[189] This does not conclusively imply that positive resettlement experiences can only be achieved in a specific system or form of government. It rather shows that it is possible to prevent or mitigate the adverse consequences of DID.

Hence, most of the unfavourable social, economic, and cultural consequences of DID described above are attributable to the lack or inadequacy of the safeguards put in place by states. In fact, although it seldom occurs, in some instances, DID and resettlement have actually improved the income and living conditions of displaced persons.[190] For instance, a case study conducted on the Arena Hydroelectric Project in Costa Rica, which resulted in the displacement of a number of people, found that the socio-economic conditions of those displaced by the project improved due to the research-oriented planning of the resettlement, the extensive participation of the people affected in the process, and the continued assistance provided after resettlement to re-establish their livelihoods.[191] Similarly, the economic wellbeing of the people displaced by the Yacreta Hydroelectric project in Argentina improved after displacement since they were provided with economic choices that suited their needs.[192] Another positive displacement and resettlement experience was recorded in the Shuikou and Yantan hydroelectric dam projects in China.[193] Studies have depicted that the people relocated by these projects were left in a better economic condition after displacement as they were given an opportunity to participate in the decision-making process and the state had undertaken various initiatives to restore their livelihoods including creating employment opportunities.[194] Hence, while most cases of involuntary displacement and resettlement have worsened the social, economic, and cultural wellbeing of the people affected, these few cases illustrate that it is, in fact, possible that with proper safeguards the livelihoods of displaced people can improve after displacement.[195]

As Cernea rightly puts it, "[i]f involuntary displacements are, to a certain extent, inevitable, they must be carried out in a way that will protect the livelihoods of the displaced people. If this is not done, then some people will share in the gains, while others will share only in the pains, of development."[196] Hence, "[r]edressing the inequities caused by displacement and enabling affected people to share in the benefits of growth are not just possible but imperative, on both economic and moral

---

[189] Ibid.

[190] Randell 2016, p. 386; see also Stanley 2004, p. 11.

[191] Partridge 1993.

[192] Mejia 2000, pp. 149–160.

[193] Cernea 1996b, pp. 19–27; see also Randell 2016, p. 386.

[194] Randell 2016, p. 386; see also Cernea 1996b, pp. 19–27.

[195] Randell 2016, p. 386.

[196] Cernea 2000, pp. 12 and 13.

grounds."[197] As this work seeks to establish in the subsequent chapters, states not only have a moral responsibility but also international legal obligations to prevent or mitigate the adverse consequences of DID.

Overall, while displacement has some inherent risks, most of the negative impacts of DID can be mitigated, if not avoided, with proper safeguards at all phases of displacement. The subsequent chapters of this book will elucidate what these "proper safeguards" constitute based on the relevant human rights and policy frameworks.

2.7 Conclusion

DID is a form of internal displacement that represents the involuntary displacement and, possibly, resettlement of individuals and groups for development purposes. People are forcibly removed and relocated from their homes and/or lands to make room for development projects. It is distinct from refugee status as the migration in the case of DID takes place within the borders of the state and from other forms of internal displacement as the displacement, in this case, is prompted and pre-planned by the state and is permanent. These distinctions are important for determining the applicable legal framework as well as the type and scope of state obligations under international law, as will be examined in the subsequent chapters.

DID can be caused by a range of small and large-scale development projects including, *inter alia*, the construction of dams, the extraction of natural resources, infrastructure, urban (re)development, and transportation. Despite the ostensible economic potential and social benefit of these development projects, the displacement they cause comes with a range of economic, social, and cultural consequences. DID often causes landlessness or a decrease in landholding, loss of housing, loss of employment or income, disruption of access to public services, disruption of social and communal arrangements, and disruption of cultural life, which in turn severely affect the livelihoods of displaced persons. Moreover, these adverse consequences often have long-term impacts that can potentially lead to the chronic impoverishment of those affected. In addition, DID disproportionately affects marginalized and vulnerable groups who are not often equal participants in and beneficiaries of development. Those who are socially and economically marginalized often face special challenges and have a hard time coping with the changes that come with displacement. Hence, DID has the potential to perpetuate existing vulnerabilities and even create new ones.

As depicted in this chapter, most of the adverse consequences of DID are attributable to the inadequacy of the safeguards provided by the state, or lack thereof, in different stages of displacement and resettlement. The few case studies of positive resettlement experiences mentioned above also attest that it is, in fact, possible to prevent or at least mitigate most of the adverse consequences of DID with the provision of adequate short-term and long-term safeguards or remedies at all phases

[197] Cernea 2000, p. 13.

of displacement. Based on this conceptual introduction, the following chapters will explore to what extent and how these consequences of DID interfere with human rights and elaborate on the safeguards that need to be put in place to prevent or justify those interferences based on the relevant human rights norms.

References

Adeola R (2017) The Responsibility of Businesses to Prevent Development-induced Displacement in Africa. (2017) 17(1) African Human Rights Journal 245–265.

Ahmed I A I (2019) The Merowe Dam in Northern Sudan: A Case of Population Displacement and Impoverishment. In: Schmidt J D, Kimathi L, Owiso M O (eds) Refugees and Forced Migration in the Horn and Eastern Africa: Trends, Challenges and Opportunities. Springer.

Bakewell O (2011) Conceptualising Displacement and Migration: Processes, Conditions, and Categories. In: Koser K, Martin S (eds) The Migration-Displacement Nexus: Patterns, Processes, and Policies. Berghahn Books, New York.

Barutciski M (2006) International Law and Development-induced Displacement. In: de Wet C (ed) Development-induced displacement: Problems, Policies and People. Berghahn, New York.

Cernea M M (1995) Understanding and Preventing Impoverishment from Displacement: Reflections on the State of Knowledge. (1995) 8(3) Journal of Refugee studies 245–264.

Cernea M M (1996a) Bridging the Research Divide: Studying Development Oustees. In: Allen T (ed) In Search of Cool Ground: War, Flight and Homecoming in Northeast Africa. United Nations Research Institute for Social Development/Africa World Press/James Currey, London.

Cernea M M (1996b) Understanding and Preventing Impoverishment from Displacement. In: McDowell C (ed) Understanding Impoverishment: the Consequences of Development-induced Displacement. Berghahn Books.

Cernea M M (2000) Risks, safeguards, and reconstruction: a model for population displacement and resettlement. In: Cernea M M, McDowell C (eds) Risks and Reconstruction: Experiences of Resettlers and Refugees. The World Bank, Washington DC.

Cernea M M, McDowell C (2000) Introduction: Reconstructing resettlers' and refugees' livelihoods. In: Cernea M M, McDowell C (eds) Risks and Reconstruction: Experiences of Refugees and Resettlers. The World Bank, Washington DC.

Chambers R (1969) Settlement schemes in Tropical Africa: A Study of Organizations and Development. Routledge/Kegan Paul.

Charters C (2018) Part IV Rights to Land and Territory, Natural Resources, and Environment, Ch.14 Indigenous Peoples' Rights to Lands, Territories, and Resources in the UNDRIP: Articles 10, 25, 26, and 27. In: Hohmann J, Weller M (eds) The UN Declaration on the Rights of Indigenous Peoples: A Commentary. Oxford University Press, Oxford.

Cohen R (2006) Developing an International System for Internally Displaced Persons. (2006) 7(2) International Studies Perspectives 87–101.

Cohen R (2007) Response to Hathaway. (2007) 20(3) Journal of Refugee Studies 370–376.

Colson E (1971) The Social Consequences of Resettlement: The Impact of the Kariba Resettlement upon the Gwembe Tonga. Manchester University Press.

Colson E (2008) Gendering Those Uprooted by 'Development'. In: Indra D (ed) Engendering Forced Migration: Theory and Practice. Berghahn Books, New York.

Debasree D (2015) Development-induced displacement: impact on Adivasi women of Odisha. (2015) 50(3) Community Development Journal 448–462.

DeWind J (2007) Response to Hathaway. (2007) 20(3) Journal of Refugee Studies 381–385.

Dunning M H (1979) Government managed land settlement and resettlement in Thailand. In: Gosling L A P (ed) Population resettlement in the Mekong River Basin: Papers of the Third Carolina Geographical Symposium. University of North Carolina Press, Chapel Hill.

Freccero J (2015) Sheltering Displaced Persons from Sexual and Gender-based Violence. (2015) 50 Forced Migration Review 55–58.

Gebreyesus A, Tadesse S (2019) Livelihood Impacts of Development-Induced Displacements: an Investigation into Post-Project Livelihoods of PAPs. (2019) 35(1/2) Eastern Africa Social Science Research Review 123–151.

Gizachew A (2017) Causes of Big Development Projects: Development-induced Displacement and its Socio-economic Impacts on Displaced People in Tekeze Dam. (2017) 9(9) International Journal of Sociology and Anthropology 114–130.

Goodwin-Gill G S (2014) The International Law of Refugee Protection. In: Fiddian-Qasmiyeh E, Loescher G, Long K, Sigona N (eds) The Oxford Handbook of Refugee and Forced Migration Studies. Oxford University Press, Oxford.

Hathaway J C (2007) Forced Migration Studies: Could We Agree Just to 'Date'? (2007) 20(3) Journal of Refugee Studies 349–365.

Himanshu T (1999) Displacement and Development: Construction of the Sardar Dam (Cultural Survival, September 1999) available https://www.culturalsurvival.org/publications/cultural-survival-quarterly/displacement-and-development-construction-sardar-dam, accessed 19 July 2025.

Hugo G, Bun C K (1990) Conceptualizing and Defining Refugee and Forced Migrations in Asia. (1990) 18(1) Asian Journal of Social Science 19–42.

Internal Displacement Monitoring Centre (IDMC) (2017) Dams and Internal Displacement: an Introduction (IDMC, 11 April 2017) available at https://www.internal-displacement.org/publications/case-study-series-dam-displacement, accessed 19 July 2025.

Internal Displacement Monitoring Centre (IDMC) (2021) Internal displacement in a changing climate, 2021, available at https://www.internal-displacement.org/global-report/grid2021/#part1, accessed 19 July 2025.

International Committee of the Red Cross (ICRC) (2008) How is the Term "Armed Conflict" Defined in International Humanitarian Law? ICRC Opinion Paper, March 2008, available at https://www.icrc.org/en/article/armed-conflict-international-humanitarian-law, accessed 27 July 2025.

Kälin W (2008) Guiding Principles on Internal Displacement: Annotations, 2nd edn. Studies in Transnational Legal Policy No. 38, The American Society of International Law, Washington DC.

Kälin W (2014) Internal Displacement. In: Fiddian-Qasmiyeh E, Loescher G, Long K, Sigona N (eds) The Oxford Handbook of Refugee and Forced Migration Studies. Oxford University Press, Oxford.

Lischer S K (2007) Causes and Consequences of Conflict-Induced Displacement. (2007) 9(2) Civil Wars 142–155.

Loescher G (2016) Refugees and Internally Displaced Persons. In: Cogan J K, Hurd I, Johnstone I (eds) The Oxford Handbook of International Organizations. Oxford University Press, Oxford.

Mathur H M (1995) The Resettlement of People Displaced by Development Projects: Issues and Approaches. In: Mathur H M, Cernea M (eds) Development, Displacement and Resettlement: Focus on Asian Experience, 1st edn. Vikas Publishing House, New Delhi.

McDowell C (2014) Development Created Population Displacement. In: Fiddian-Qasmiyeh E, Loescher G, Long K, Sigona N (eds) The Oxford Handbook of Refugee and Forced Migration Studies. Oxford University Press, Oxford.

Meidinger E E (2008) The "Public Uses" of Eminent Domain: History and Policy. (2008) 11(1) Journal of Environmental Law 1–66.

Mejia M C (2000) Economic Recovery After Involuntary Resettlement: the Case of Brickmakers Displaced by the Yacyereta Hydroelectric Project. In: Cernea M M, McDowell C (eds) Risks and Reconstruction: Experiences of Resettlers and Refugees. The World Bank, Washington DC.

Mooney E (2005) The Concept of Internal Displacement and the Case for Internally Displaced Persons as a Category of Concern (2005) 24(3) Refugee Survey Quarterly 9–26.

Muggah R (2003) A Tale of Two Solitudes: Comparing Conflict and Development induced Internal Displacement and Involuntary Resettlement. (2003) 41(5) International Migration 5–31.

Nayak A K (2013) Development, Displacement and Justice in India: Study of Hirakud Dam. (2013) 43(3) Social Change 397–419.
Parasuraman S (1996) Development Projects, Displacement and Outcomes for Displaced: Two Case Studies. (1996) 31(24) Economic and Political Weekly 1529–1532.
Partridge W L (1989) Involuntary Resettlement in Development Projects. (1989) 2(3) Journal of Refugee Studies 373–384.
Partridge W L (1993) Successful Involuntary Resettlement: Lessons from the Costa Rican Arenal Hydroelectric Plant. In: Cernea M M, Guggenheim S E (eds) Anthropological Approaches to Resettlement: Policy, Practice and Theory. Routledge.
Patel S, Sliuzas R, Mathur N (2015) The risk of impoverishment in urban development-induced displacement and resettlement in Ahmedabad. (2015) 27(1) Environment & Urbanization 231–256.
Ramanathan U (1996) Displacement and the Law. (1996) 31(24) Economic and Political Weekly 1486–1491.
Randell H (2016) The short-term impacts of development-induced displacement on wealth and subjective well-being in the Brazilian Amazon. (2016) 87 World Development 385–400.
Rew A, Fisher E, Pande B (2000) Addressing Policy Constraints and Improving Outcomes in Development-Induced Resettlement Projects. Refugee Studies Centre, Oxford.
Robinson C W (2003) Risks and Rights: The Causes, Consequences, and Challenges of Development-Induced Displacement. The Brookings Institution-SAIS Project on Internal Displacement, An Occasional Paper.
Scholten A (2016) International Human Rights Law Aspects of Forced Migrations, Evictions and Displacement: Current Issues and Challenges, available at https://www.ssoar.info/ssoar/handle/document/47750, accessed 19 July 2025.
Schulz C, Adams W A (2019) Debating dams: The World Commission on Dams 20 years on. (2019) 6(5) WIREs Water 1–19.
Stanley J (2004) Development-induced Displacement and Resettlement. (2004) Forced Migration Online.
Terminski B (2012) Mining-Induced Displacement and Resettlement: Social Problem and Human Rights Issue. (2012) Universite de Geneve, Faculté de Droit, 2012.
Terminski B (2015) Development-Induced Displacement and Resettlement: Causes, Consequences, and Socio-Legal Context. Ibidem-Verlag, Stuttgart.
Thukral E G (1996) Development, Displacement and Rehabilitation: Locating Gender. (1996) 31(24) Economic and Political Weekly 1500–1503.
Turton D (2006) Who is a Forced Migrant? In: de Wet C (ed) Development-induced Displacement: Problems, Policies and People. Berghahn Books.
UN Committee on Economic, Social and Cultural Rights (UN CESCR) (1997) General Comment No. 7: The right to adequate housing (Art.11.1): forced evictions, 20 May 1997, E/1998/22.
UN Committee on Economic, Social and Cultural Rights (UN CESCR) (2005) General Comment No. 16: The Equal Right of Men and Women to the Enjoyment of All Economic, Social and Cultural Rights (Art. 3 of the Covenant), 11 August 2005, E/C.12/2005/4.
UN Committee on Economic, Social and Cultural Rights (UN CESCR) (2017) General Comment No. 24 (2017) on State obligations under the International Covenant on Economic, Social and Cultural Rights in the Context of Business Activities, 10 August 2017, E/C.12/GC/24.
UN Committee on the Elimination of Discrimination against Women (CEDAW Committee) (2016) General Comment No. 34 on the rights of rural women, 4 March 2016, CEDAW/C/GC/34.
United Nations High Commissioner for Refugees (UNHCR) (2003) Sexual and Gender-Based Violence against Refugees, Returnees and Internally Displaced Persons: Guidelines for Prevention and Response, UNHCR, May 20003.
United Nations High Commissioner for Refugees (UNHCR) (2011) Who is a Refugee? UNHCR Protection Training Manual for European Border and Entry Officials, 2011, available at https://www.unhcr.org/4d944c319.html, accessed 19 July 2025.

United Nations High Commissioner for Refugees (UNHCR) (2013) Internal Displacement: Responsibility and Action (UNHCR Handbook for Parliamentarians, No. 20, 2013).

Van der Ploeg L, Vanclay F (2017) A human Rights-based Approach to Project Induced Displacement and Resettlement. (2017) 35(1) Impact Assessment and Project Appraisal 34–52.

World Commission on Dams (2000) Dams and Development: a New Framework for Decision-Making, the Report of the World Commission on Dams. Earthscan Publication.

Part II
The Interference with Human Rights in the Course of Development-Induced Displacement

Chapter 3
The Right to Housing

Contents

Abstract The right to housing is among the rights most commonly affected by development-induced displacement (DID). As DID entails the involuntary removal of individuals from their homes and residences, it inherently impacts the enjoyment of this right. This chapter, therefore, examines the sources and normative content of the right to housing as well as how the process and outcome of DID can interfere with this right. International human rights law, however, allows states to impose legitimate limitations on the enjoyment of rights, including the right to housing, under exceptional circumstances in order to protect overriding individual or public interests. Economic development or the provision of public services that trigger displacement in the context of DID could be considered a justified public interest provided that all conditions for lawful limitation are met. Accordingly, the chapter also explores the extent to which interferences with the right to housing can be justified under relevant limitation clauses. In doing so, it outlines the human rights safeguards that must be in place during eviction or displacement to prevent violations.

Keywords Right to housing · Adequate Housing · Security of tenure · Forced eviction · Homelessness · Non-discrimination · Progressive realization

© T.M.C. ASSER PRESS and the authors 2026

R. G. Teshome, *The Human Cost of Development*, Human Rights Research Series 104,
https://doi.org/10.1007/978-94-6265-751-9_3

3.1 Introduction

The adverse economic, social, and cultural consequences of development-induced displacement (DID), discussed in the preceding chapters, interfere with and potentially violate a wide range of human rights. The right to housing, which guarantees access to adequate housing and protects individuals from forced eviction and other forms of undue interference, is among the rights most commonly and directly affected. DID evidently interferes with the right to housing as it often involves the eviction of individuals or groups from their homes or residences and, in many instances, leads to homelessness and poorer housing conditions. The right to housing could also be violated when the process of displacement involves direct or indirect discrimination against protected groups. As this chapter establishes, these unfavourable outcomes result from the lack or inadequacy of procedural and substantive safeguards put in place during displacement and, hence, can be prevented or at least mitigated.

This chapter marks the beginning of the normative analysis in this book by elucidating the interference and potential violation of the right to housing in the course of displacement. However, as most human rights, the right to housing is not absolute and can be subjected to limitations when there is an overriding public interest that outweighs its protection. In these cases, in addition to the existence of a legitimate ground that justifies the interference, the restriction has to comply with the conditions and safeguards provided under the relevant human rights frameworks. The interference constitutes a violation if these conditions are not met or if the state fails to implement the necessary safeguards. As this work argues, the human rights standards on the right to adequate housing and limitation of the right can and should inform the implementation of DID. Thus, the chapter also examines to what extent the interferences to the right to housing can be justified based on the relevant limitation clauses and the rights-based safeguards that states need to put in place in the course of eviction or displacement to prevent violation.

The chapter is divided into five substantive sections. Section 3.2 explores the recognition of the right to housing in international human rights law with reference to relevant treaties, case law, and other sources. Sections 3.3 and 3.4 examine the normative content of the right and the corresponding state obligations, respectively. The norms on the limitation of economic, social, cultural rights (hereinafter "ESC rights" or "socio-economic rights") in general and the right to housing in particular will be addressed in Sect. 3.5. Subsequently, Sect. 3.6 assesses how the process and outcomes of DID can interfere with this right, and outlines the human rights safeguards that states must implement during displacement to prevent violations.

3.2 The Recognition of the Right to Housing

The right to housing is explicitly recognised in a number of general human rights instruments, specifically, Article 25(1) of the Universal Declaration on Human Rights (UDHR)[1] and Article 11(1) of the International Covenant on Economic, Social, and Cultural Rights (ICESCR).[2] Moreover, several specialized human rights instruments, including the Convention on the Elimination of All Forms of Discrimination Against Women (CEDAW) and the Convention on the Rights of the Child (CRC), also guarantee the right to housing for the specific groups they seek to protect.[3] Article 11(1) of the ICESCR stipulates the right to housing as a component of the right to an adequate standard of living along with adequate food and clothing.[4] The provision reads, "[t]he States Parties to the present Covenant recognize the right of everyone to an adequate standard of living for himself and his family, including adequate food, clothing and housing, and to the continuous improvement of living conditions."[5] This provision reiterates Article 25(1) of the UDHR,[6] save for the fact that it does not include the right to health, which is recognized in a separate provision.[7] Overall, at the universal level, the right to housing is recognized in various human rights frameworks and further elaborated through the authoritative interpretations of their respective monitoring bodies and case law.

On the contrary, this right has not been expressly included in most regional human rights instruments. The African Charter on Human and Peoples' Rights, which includes all categories of rights in the same instrument,[8] does not contain a provision on the right to housing. Nevertheless, the African Commission on Human and Peoples' Rights has read this right into the Charter asserting that the right to housing is implicitly recognized in the Charter as an important element of some of the rights explicitly included therein.[9] In its seminal judgment, *SERAC v. Nigeria*,

[1] UN General Assembly, Universal Declaration of Human Rights, 10 December 1948, 217 A (III) ('UDHR'), Article 25(1).

[2] UN General Assembly, International Covenant on Economic, Social and Cultural Rights, 16 December 1966, 993 United Nations Treaty Series 3 ('ICESCR'), Article 11(1).

[3] UN General Assembly, Convention on the Elimination of All Forms of Discrimination Against Women, 18 December 1979, 1249 United Nations Treaty Series 13 ('CEDAW'), Article 14(2); see also UN General Assembly, Convention on the Rights of the Child, 20 November 1989, 1577 United Nations Treaty Series 3, Article 27(3); see also UN General Assembly, International Convention on the Elimination of All Forms of Racial Discrimination, 21 December 1965, 660 United Nations Treaty Series 195, Article 5(e) (iii); see also UN General Assembly, International Convention on the Protection of the Rights of All Migrant Workers and Members of their Families, 18 December 1990, A/RES/45/158, Article 43(1)(d).

[4] ICESCR (n 2), Article 11(1).

[5] Ibid.

[6] UDHR (n 1), Article 25(1).

[7] ICESCR (n 2), Article 12.

[8] Organization of African Unity (OAU), African Charter on Human and Peoples' Rights, 27 June 1981, CAB/LEG/67/3 rev. 5, 21 I.L.M. 58 (1982) ('African Charter').

[9] *Social and Economic Rights Action Center (SERAC) and Center for Economic and Social Rights (CESR) v. Nigeria*, Communication No. 155/96, 27 October 2001, African Commission on Human

the Commission proclaimed that interference with the right to housing affects the protection of the rights to health, property, and family life, which are enshrined under Articles 16, 14, and 18 of the Charter, respectively.[10] Thus, the cumulative effect of these provisions "reads into the [African] Charter a right to shelter or housing".[11] The normative content of the right and state obligations it entails are subsequently elaborated under the principles and guidelines on the implementation of ESC rights adopted by the Commission.[12] In contrast to the Charter, the Protocol to the African Charter on Human and Peoples' Rights on the Rights of Women in Africa expressly stipulates the right to adequate housing under Article 16.[13]

Similarly, neither the American Convention on Human Rights (ACHR)[14] nor the Additional Protocol to the American Convention on Human Rights in the Area of Economic, Social and Cultural Rights (San Salvador Protocol)[15] expressly recognize the right to housing. While "adequate housing for all sectors of the population" is mentioned in the Protocol of Buenos Aires—Protocol of Amendment to the Charter of the Organization of American States (OAS)—as one of the main goals member states need to pursue in order to achieve "economic and social development",[16] none of the binding human rights instruments incorporates this right. However, Article 26 of the American Convention, a general provision on progressive development and socio-economic rights, requires state parties to take measures in order to progressively realize ESC rights implied in the standards envisaged under the Charter of OAS and the Protocol of Buenos Aires.[17] Since the latter explicitly sets out the provision of adequate housing as one of the main goals member states should pursue, there is a compelling argument that the cumulative reading of Article 26 of the Convention and Article 31 of the Protocol of Buenos Aires results in the recognition of a separate

---

and Peoples' Rights, para 60; see also African Commission on Human and Peoples' Rights 2011, paras 77 and 78.

[10] *SERAC v. Nigeria* (n 9) para 60; see also African Commission on Human and Peoples' Rights 2011, para 77; see also African Charter (n 8) Articles 14, 16, and 18(1).

[11] *SERAC v. Nigeria* (n 9) para 60; see also African Commission on Human and Peoples' Rights 2011, para 77.

[12] African Commission on Human and Peoples' Rights 2011, paras 77–79. The Commission, however, is a quasi-judicial body whose recommendations and interpretative documents are not binding, which puts into question the normative weight of its decisions and documents. Nonetheless, as the Commission is established by the Charter itself with the mandate of interpreting the same, its interpretations are authoritative (African Charter (n 8) Article 45).

[13] African Union, Protocol to the African Charter on Human and Peoples' Rights on the Rights of Women in Africa, 11 July 2003, Article 16.

[14] Organization of American States (OAS), American Convention on Human Rights, 22 November 1969, 36 OAS Treaty Series ('American Convention on Human Rights').

[15] Organization of American States (OAS), Additional Protocol to the American Convention on Human Rights in the Area of Economic, Social and Cultural Rights, 17 November 1988, 69 OAS Treaty Series ('Protocol of San Salvador').

[16] Organization of American States (OAS), Protocol of Amendment to the Charter of the Organization of American States, 27 February 1967, 1-A OAS Treaty Series, Article 31(k).

[17] American Convention on Human Rights (n 14) Article 26.

right to adequate housing.[18] Apart from this, the protection against interference with one's home and the right to property explicitly recognized under Articles 11 and 21 of the ACHR,[19] respectively, can also be used to guarantee housing rights to the extent their normative scope allows.

The right to housing is also not explicitly provided under the European Convention on Human Rights (ECHR), which does not come as a surprise since the Convention does not include ESC rights as such save for the right to education.[20] Some of the rights recognized therein, however, can be interpreted in a way that protects certain socio-economic rights.[21] The European Court on Human Rights (ECtHR) has relied on some of the civil and political rights enshrined in the Convention, principally Article 8—"the right to respect for [one's] private and family life,...home and...correspondence"[22]—in several cases involving claims related to the right to housing.[23] Furthermore, while the initial version of the European Social Charter (ESC), a human rights framework in the Council of Europe that specifically guarantees socio-economic rights,[24] did not contain a general right to housing,[25] the revised version of the Charter has introduced a separate and general right to adequate housing under Article 31.[26] This is further affirmed and elaborated by the decisions of the

[18] Thiele 2003, pp. 470 and 471.

[19] American Convention on Human Rights (n 14) Article 11(2) and (3) and 21.

[20] Council of Europe, Protocol 1 to the European Convention for the Protection of Human Rights and Fundamental Freedoms, 20 March 1952, 9 ETS, Article 2.

[21] Ssenyonjo 2011, p. 972.

[22] Council of Europe, European Convention for the Protection of Human Rights and Fundamental Freedoms, as amended by Protocols Nos. 11 and 14, 4 November 1950, 5 ETS, Article 8.

[23] *Moldovan and Others v. Romania*, Application No. 41138/98; 64320/01, Judgment, European Court of Human Rights, 12 July 2005, paras 103–109 (In this case involving discrimination and ill-treatment of Roma people, the Court found the violation of Article 8 of the Convention due to the destruction of Roma houses by police officers, which forced the people affected to live in unfavourable housing conditions coupled with the failure of the state to provide adequate remedies. The Court further noted that Article 8 also entails "positive obligations inherent in an effective respect for private or family life and the home." (see *Moldovan and Others v. Romania*, n 23, para 93). The idea that these positive obligations of states may involve providing adequate housing assistance for a person in need, a disabled person in the case, is also mirrored in the case of *Marzari v. Italy*, although the application was found to be inadmissible for being manifestly ill-founded (see *Marzari v. Italy*, Application No. 36448/97, decision on admissibility, European Court of Human Rights, 4 May 1999, para 1; see also Kucs et al. 2008, p. 109); see also *Connors v. the United Kingdom*, Application No. 66746/01, Judgment, European Court of Human Rights, 27 May 2004.

[24] Council of Europe, European Social Charter (Revised), 3 May 1996, 163 ETS ('European Social Charter (revised)'); see the original version Council of Europe, European Social Charter, 18 October 1961, 35 ETS ('European Social Charter (1961)').

[25] The Charter rather mentioned this right in relation to specific groups that are accorded special protection therein, i.e. migrant workers and families (European Social Charter (n 24) Article 19(4) and Article 16; see also Leckie 1995, p. 109). The Additional Protocol to the Charter further provides the rights of the elderly to have access to adequate housing that suits their needs and puts a correlative duty on state parties to provide the same (see Council of Europe, Additional Protocol to the European Social Charter, 5 May 1988, 128 ETS, Article 4(2)).

[26] European Social Charter (revised) (n 24) Article 31.

European Committee of Social Rights,[27] a body entrusted with the task of monitoring states' compliance with the Charter.[28]

Overall, the right to housing is explicitly or impliedly recognized in a number of international and regional human rights instruments. Furthermore, it is also inextricably linked to other ESC rights as well as to civil and political rights, which also coincides with the principle of interdependence and indivisibility of rights.[29] Hence, even if the right to housing is not expressly recognized in some instruments, claims pertaining to this right can be raised under other rights including the right to property and the right to respect for family life and home, among others.

3.3 Normative Content of the Right to Housing

The Committee on Economic, Social and Cultural Rights (CESCR) has clarified the substantive content of the right to housing in General Comments No. 4 and No. 7 as well as through its case law.[30] According to the Committee, the right to housing should not be construed narrowly as "...merely having a roof over one's head or views shelter exclusively as a commodity."[31] Instead, "it should be seen as the right to live somewhere in security, peace and dignity."[32] As the wording of Article 11(1) indicates and as further elaborated by the Committee, housing must be "adequate", which involves various conditions that need to be taken into account cumulatively.[33] While adequacy, to some extent, is a subjective standard that is determined based on specific socio-economic, cultural, and environmental circumstances, it also involves

---

[27] *European Federation of National Organisations working with the Homeless (FEANTSA) v. Slovenia*, Complaint No. 53/2008, decision on the merits, European Committee of Social Rights, 8 September 2009; see also *European Federation of National Organisations Working with the Homeless (FEANTSA) v. France*, Complaint No. 39/2006, decision on the merits, European Committee of Social Rights, 5 December 2007; see also *European Federation of National Organisations working with the Homeless (FEANTSA) v. the Netherlands*, Complaint No. 86/2012, decision on the merits, European Committee of Social Rights, 2 July 2014 (in this case, the Committee dealt with the right to shelter, since the case involves undocumented migrants).

[28] European Social Charter (1961) (n 24) Articles 24 and 25; see also European Social Charter (revised) (n 24), part IV, Article C; see also European Committee of Social Rights, available at https://www.coe.int/en/web/european-social-charter/european-committee-of-social-rights, accessed 28 June 2025.

[29] UN General Assembly, Vienna Declaration and Programme of Action, 12 July 1993, A/CONF.157/23, para 5; see also *I.D.G v. Spain*, Communication No. 2/2014, adoption of views, Committee on Economic, Social and Cultural Rights, 13 October 2015, E/C.12/55/D/2/2014, para 11.1.

[30] UN CESCR 1991; see also UN CESCR 1997.

[31] UN CESCR 1991, para 7.

[32] Ibid.; see also African Commission Principles and Guidelines (n 9) para 78.

[33] ICESCR (n 2), Article 11; see also UN CESCR 1991, paras 7 and 8.

certain objective elements that are applicable in all cases.[34] Accordingly, the right to adequate housing encompasses the following main substantive elements.

The first element pertains to "legal security of tenure", which entails legal protection against interferences or threats, such as forced eviction and harassment, that undermine the enjoyment of the right to housing.[35] Tenure can take different forms ranging from ownership to informal settlement and legal security should be guaranteed irrespective of the type of tenure under consideration.[36] The protection against forced eviction is one of the principal elements of the right to housing, which is further elaborated by the Committee in a separate document, General Comment No. 7.[37] As the Committee has stressed, forced eviction constitutes a prima facie violation of the right to housing unless it is justified in the "most exceptional circumstances".[38] In the case of *I.D.G v. Spain*, the first case decided by the Committee on the merits, the Committee asserted that eviction is only justified in limited circumstances and must be undertaken in accordance with the relevant human rights norms.[39] The Committee further noted that states should put in place certain procedural safeguards in the process of eviction including consultation with those affected and "adequate and reasonable notice", which the state failed to comply with in this particular case.[40] This brief remark here suffices to note that protection against forced eviction is one of the substantive contents of the right to housing. What this specifically entails and the norms associated with it will be further examined in the subsequent sections in the context of DID.

Another element of adequacy is the availability of and access to essential public services, such as healthcare facilities, drinking water, energy, sanitation, and other infrastructures.[41] Adequate housing needs to contain these essential services and facilities.[42] This does not, however, imply that states are expected to provide all these facilities immediately. As will be discussed in the following section, state obligations required by ESC rights are qualified by the principles of resource availability and progressive realization, save for minimum core obligations.

Adequacy also involves the element of affordability—the costs of housing must be affordable vis-à-vis the income levels in a particular state.[43] As the Committee puts it, "costs associated with housing should be at such a level that the attainment and

---

34 UN CESCR 1991, para 8.

35 UN CESCR 1991, para 8(a); see also African Commission on Human and Peoples' Rights 2011, para 79(g).

36 UN CESCR 1991, para 8(a).

37 UN CESCR 1997.

38 UN CESCR 1991, para 18; see also UN CESCR 1997, para 11; see also African Commission on Human and Peoples' Rights 2011, para 79.

39 *I.D.G v. Spain* (n 29) para 11.

40 Ibid., paras 11.2 and 13.3-5.

41 UN CESCR 1991, para 8(b); see also African Commission on Human and Peoples' Rights 2011, para 78.

42 UN CESCR 1991, para 8(b).

43 Ibid., para 8(c).

satisfaction of other basic needs are not threatened or compromised."[44] This requires states to take appropriate legal and policy measures in order to ensure that housing is affordable, which also includes regulation of housing provided by private entities.[45] In addition, states have an obligation to provide subsidies for those who cannot afford housing,[46] the extent of this is again contingent on the economic capacity of the state concerned.

Another element of adequacy is habitability, which pertains to the suitability of the housing in providing adequate physical protection and a healthy living environment for the inhabitants.[47] In this regard, the "Health Principles of Housing" adopted by the World Health Organization provide guidance as it is also recommended by the Committee.[48] This framework dictates that housing should involve necessary amenities that protect physical and mental health.[49] To this end, it prescribes standards on, *inter alia*, safe water supply, sanitation, drainage, hygiene, waste management, indoor pollution, and housing environment, and the steps states and other stakeholders should take to meet these standards.[50] Thus, adequate housing should shield the inhabitants from health hazards as much as possible.

The next element of adequacy, accessibility, requires that housing needs to be accessible particularly to vulnerable groups, such as physically disabled persons, children, and the elderly.[51] These groups should be provided with "full and sustainable access to adequate housing resources" that cater to their specific needs.[52]

A further element of adequacy is the location of the housing, which should be convenient in terms of access to employment opportunities and essential public services mentioned before.[53] Moreover, housing sites should not be in the vicinity of sources of pollution that put the health of the occupants in danger.[54]

In addition, adequacy also includes the element of cultural acceptability, i.e. adequate housing should respect the cultural identity, practice, and way of life of the people concerned.[55] The policies and the process of housing construction as well as the general pursuit of modernization in the housing sector should not disregard the

---

[44] Ibid., para 8(c); see also African Commission on Human and Peoples' Rights 2011, para 79(i).

[45] Saul et al. 2014, p. 930.

[46] UN CESCR 1991, para 8(c).

[47] Ibid., para 8(d); see also African Commission on Human and Peoples' Rights 2011, para 79(j).

[48] UN CESCR 1991, para 8(d).

[49] World Health Organization (WHO), Health principles of housing (Geneva: World Health Organization, 1989) available at https://apps.who.int/iris/handle/10665/39847, accessed 28 June 2025 ('WHO Principles').

[50] Ibid.

[51] UN CESCR 1991, para 8(e).

[52] Ibid.

[53] UN CESCR 1991, para 8(f); see also African Commission on Human and Peoples' Rights 2011, para 79(k).

[54] UN CESCR 1991, para 8(f).

[55] Ibid., para 8(g).

cultural identity and diversity of the people involved.[56] This is particularly relevant in relation to indigenous peoples whose distinct cultural identities should be taken into account in housing projects and the provision of other public services.[57]

Overall, the right to housing contains several elements and standards that need to be considered collectively to determine the adequacy of the housing. The potential violation of this right in the process of DID, which will be examined in the subsequent sections, should also be assessed in light of these specific elements and the corresponding obligations of states described below.

3.4 State Obligations Related to the Right to Housing

3.4.1 The General Nature of State Obligations

Article 2(1) of ICESCR obliges states to take necessary measures to progressively realize the rights recognized in the Covenant, including the substantive elements of the right to adequate housing outlined above.[58] The provision reads:

> Each State Party to the present Covenant undertakes to take steps, individually and through international assistance and co-operation, especially economic and technical, to the maximum of its available resources, with a view to achieving progressively the full realization of the rights recognized in the present Covenant by all appropriate means, including particularly the adoption of legislative measures.[59]

Four main principles or elements of state obligations, which include both obligations of conduct and of result,[60] can be deduced from this provision: the obligation to take steps, the principle of progressive realization, the utilization of maximum of available resources, and international cooperation.[61]

---

[56] Ibid.; see also UN Committee on Economic, Social and Cultural Rights (CESCR), Concluding Observations of the Committee on Economic, Social and Cultural Rights: Greece, 7 June 2004, E/C.12/1/Add.97, para 44; see also African Commission on Human and Peoples' Rights 2011, para 79(l).

[57] African Commission on Human and Peoples' Rights 2011, para 79(o).

[58] ICESCR (n 2) Article 2. This provision is formulated differently than its counterpart under the International Covenant on Civil and Political Rights (ICCPR) (see UN General Assembly, International Covenant on Civil and Political Rights, 16 December 1966, 999 United Nations Treaty Series 171, Article 2(1)). While the former requires states to undertake positive measures in order to progressively realize the rights stipulated under the Covenant, the latter—Article 2 of the ICCPR—obliges states to "respect and ensure" the rights enunciated therein (see ICESCR (n 2) Article 2(1); see also ICCPR (n 58) Article 2(1)). While this distinction is partly attributable to the very nature of these categories of rights, the traditional or outdated categorization of human rights based on the nature of state obligations they entail cannot be maintained as both sets of rights have largely similar features and are highly interdependent (see Van Hoof 1984, p. 103).

[59] ICESCR (n 2) Article 2(1).

[60] UN CESCR 1990, para 1.

[61] Ibid.; see also Ssenyonjo 2011, pp. 974 and 975.

The first element, the obligation to take steps, obliges states to undertake "deliberate, concrete and targeted" measures in order to progressively realize the rights recognized in the Covenant.[62] While the state obligations socio-economic rights require are qualified by the principle of progressive realization, as will be discussed below, this obligation of conduct has immediate effect.[63] Accordingly, states need to start taking measures immediately, or as the Committee puts it "within a reasonably short time", after the Covenant is entered into force for the state concerned.[64] States are particularly expected to take legislative measures, among other appropriate measures, which are "highly desirable and in some cases may even be indispensable."[65] The undertaking of legislative measures alone does not, however, relieve states of their obligation to take steps.[66] Other appropriate measures should also be taken, which states are at liberty to determine based on the nature of the right in question and the circumstances of the case, although the Committee has the final say on the "appropriateness" of the measure.[67] In the case of *I.D.G v. Spain*, the Committee emphasized that the obligation to take steps particularly includes ensuring that "effective judicial remedies" are available and readily accessible as the protection of human rights in general is contingent on such access.[68] This interpretation holds particular significance given that the right to effective remedies is not explicitly mentioned in the Covenant. The state's failure to ensure this access to remedies was what prompted the violation in this particular case.[69]

In the context of the right to housing, states need to take legislative measures that ensure security of tenure and stipulate the specific conditions and standards of eviction.[70] Moreover, the Committee urges states to adopt "a national housing strategy" that sets specific goals for the improvement of shelter conditions within a definite time frame and the resources and actions required to reach those goals.[71] Moreover, this strategy should be adopted with sufficient and genuine consultation with those affected.[72] Apart from the measures specifically enumerated by the Committee, states

---

[62] UN CESCR 1990, para 2; see also African Commission Principles and Guidelines (n 9) para 2.

[63] UN CESCR 1990, para 2.

[64] Ibid.; see also *I.D.G v. Spain* (n 29) para 11.3; see also UN Commission on Human Rights, Note verbale dated 5 December 1986 from the Permanent Mission of the Netherlands to the United Nations Office at Geneva addressed to the Centre for Human Rights, 8 January 1987, E/CN.4/1987/17 ('Limburg Principles'), para 16; see also African Commission Principles and Guidelines (n 9) para 18.

[65] UN CESCR 1990, para 3; see also Alston and Quinn 1987, p. 167.

[66] UN CESCR 1990, para 4.

[67] Ibid; see also Ssenyonjo 2011, p. 976.

[68] *I.D.G v. Spain* (n 29) para 11.3.

[69] Ibid., paras 14 and 15.

[70] UN CESCR 1991, paras 8(a) and 17; see also UN CESCR 1997, para 9; see also African Commission on Human and Peoples' Rights 2011, para 79(a).

[71] UN CESCR 1991.

[72] UN CESCR 1991, para 12; see also African Commission on Human and Peoples' Rights 2011, para 79(d-f).

are generally required to take other pertinent steps in order to progressively realize the right to adequate housing.

Another main element of the nature of state obligations ESC rights entail is the availability of resources; as the provision quoted above indicates, states are expected to take steps "to the maximum of [their] available resources."[73] On the one hand, this notion leaves a certain latitude for states in light of their economic capacity and the resource constraint they may encounter.[74] On the other hand, it requires states to use "the maximum" of the resources available at their disposal, which includes actively seeking international assistance to procure resources.[75] One of the principal issues associated with this notion of "availability of resources" concerns the allocation of resources or budget.[76] While states enjoy a certain level of discretion in this regard, allocation of resources should give due consideration to the obligations envisaged under the Covenant, particularly to the minimum core obligations,[77] which will be discussed below. Moreover, states need to give priority to the special needs and rights of disadvantaged and marginalized groups in budget allocation. The Committee has also affirmed this in relation to the right to housing where it urged states to give priority to people living in unfavourable housing conditions.[78]

The principle of "progressive realization", which is an obligation of result, entails that the measures taken by states should be aimed at progressively realizing the rights recognized in the Covenant.[79] This is predicated on the pragmatic consideration that requiring the full realization of ESC rights immediately or within a short period of time might not be feasible.[80] Thus, states are obliged to make reasonable and sufficient progress or "to move as expeditiously and effectively as possible", in the Committee's words, towards the full realization of these rights.[81] As an

[73] ICESCR (n 2) Article 2(1); see also UN CESCR 1990, paras 10 and 11.

[74] UN CESCR 1990, paras 10 and 11.

[75] Ibid., paras 10 and 13; see also Limburg Principles (n 64) para 26.

[76] Ssenyonjo 2011, p. 980.

[77] Alston and Quinn 1987, p. 177; see also Limburg Principles (n 64) para 28. In evaluating states' adherence to this principle—utilization of the maximum of resources available at their disposal—the Committee usually refers to the percentage of budget reserved for the provision of essential public services that the realization of rights recognized in the Covenant is contingent upon, such as education and health facilities, compared to other sectors, for instance, military expenditure (see Ssenyonjo 2011, p. 980). The Committee has particularly condemned a misallocation of resources in its concluding observations to states reports (for instance, see UN Committee on Economic, Social and Cultural Rights (CESCR), Concluding observations of the UN Committee on Economic, Social and Cultural Rights: Senegal, 24 September 2001, E/C.12/1/Add.62, para 23; see also UN Committee on Economic, Social and Cultural Rights (CESCR), Consideration of reports submitted by States parties under arts 16 and 17 of the Covenant, Concluding observations of the Committee on Economic, Social and Cultural Rights: Democratic Republic of the Congo, 16 December 2009, E/C.12/COD/CO/4, para 16).

[78] UN CESCR 1991, para 11.

[79] UN CESCR 1990, para 9.

[80] Ibid.

[81] Ibid.; see also African Commission Principles and Guidelines (n 9) para 13. Progress in the realization of rights is evaluated by looking into the positive changes happening over time. With

extension of the obligation of progressive realization, in principle, intentional retrogressive measures—those that reduce the level of realization already achieved—are proscribed.[82] These measures are only justified in exceptional circumstances by taking into account "the totality of the rights provided for in the Covenant and in the context of the full use of the maximum available resources".[83] Retrogressive measures can be justified in cases of, for instance, economic recession, natural disaster, or other comparable circumstances that put a severe strain on available resources.[84] Accordingly, retrogressive measures are not compatible with the Covenant save for exceptional cases where they are taken to advance other rights and the state is facing resource constraints.

Notwithstanding the principle of progressive realization, socio-economic rights also entail immediate obligations that states are obliged to fulfil right away. One of these obligations, as mentioned before, is the obligation to take steps, which requires states to act within a reasonably short period of time.[85] Negative obligations that only require states to abstain from directly infringing these rights generally also have immediate effect. With regard to the right to housing, for instance, the Committee recognised that there are some measures that states are expected to take immediately despite their level of economic development.[86] According to the Committee, "many of the measures required to promote the right to housing would only require the abstention by the government from certain practices and a commitment to facilitating "self-help" by affected groups."[87] Hence, as long as these measures are not beyond the resource capacity of the state, including resources acquired through international cooperation, the state is required to take action without delay.[88]

The other obligation that has immediate effect is the obligation of non-discrimination.[89] States have a duty to ensure that the rights guaranteed under the Covenant are applied "without discrimination of any kind as to race, colour, sex, language, religion, political or other opinion, national or social origin, property, birth or other status."[90] This obligation has immediate effect and is not subject to the principle of progressive realization as it mainly requires making policy decisions

regard to this, the Committee urges states to set specific benchmarks or indicators against which their compliance and progress is evaluated, taking into account the circumstances and needs of their respective countries (UN CESCR 1981, paras 6 and 7).

[82] UN CESCR 1990, para 9; see also African Commission on Human and Peoples' Rights 2011, para 20.

[83] UN CESCR 1990, para 9; see also African Commission on Human and Peoples' Rights 2011, para 20.

[84] Muller 2009, pp. 586 and 587.

[85] UN CESCR 1990, para 2; see also African Commission on Human and Peoples' Rights 2011, para 18.

[86] UN CESCR 1991, para 10.

[87] Ibid.

[88] Ibid.

[89] UN CESCR 2009, para 7; see also UN CESCR 1990, para 1.

[90] ICESCR (n 2) Article 2(2); see also UN CESCR 2009, para 7; see also African Commission on Human and Peoples' Rights 2011, para 19.

that are in line with international human rights standards rather than undertaking resource-intensive measures.[91] This is also affirmed by the Committee with regard to the right to housing.[92]

Another set of immediate obligations under ESC rights relates to minimum core obligations.[93] These obligations correspond to the minimum core contents of each right, which, in several instances, have been identified by the Committee through its authoritative interpretations. These core contents refer to "essential prerequisites for leading an adequate and dignified life".[94] The disregard of these core contents undermines the essence of the right in question and deprives the Covenant of its "raison d'être".[95] Thus, the state obligations relating to these minimum core contents have immediate effect and the leeway left to states by the principle of progressive realization does not apply. Hence, non-compliance with the minimum core contents of rights amounts to a prima facie violation.[96] This does not, however, imply that the economic struggles of states and the resource constraints they may encounter in fulfilling these minimum core obligations will not be taken into account.[97] What is required from states is that they must make the utmost effort to utilize all resources available at their disposal by giving priority to these core obligations.[98] This entails a heightened standard and burden of proof; a state that has failed to comply with these minimum core obligations has to prove that compliance is "practically impossible" in the circumstances of the case.[99] With regard to the right to housing, the minimum core obligations of states include ensuring access to basic shelter at the very least, providing legal security of tenure, and refraining from carrying out forced eviction or providing protection against that.[100]

---

[91] Reidel et al. 2014, p. 14; see also UN CESCR 1990, para 1; see also UN CESCR 2009, para 7; see also African Commission on Human and Peoples' Rights 2011, para 19.

[92] UN CESCR 1991, para 9.

[93] UN CESCR 1990, para 10.

[94] Reidel et al. 2014, p. 14.

[95] UN CESCR 1990, para 10; see also African Commission on Human and Peoples' Rights 2011, para 17.

[96] International Commission of Jurists (ICJ), Maastricht Guidelines on Violations of Economic, Social and Cultural Rights, 26 January 1997, available at http://hrlibrary.umn.edu/instree/Maastrichtguidelines_.html, accessed 28 June 2025 ('Maastricht Guidelines'), para 9.

[97] UN CESCR 1990, para 10.

[98] Ibid; see also Reidel et al. 2014, p. 14; see also African Commission on Human and Peoples' Rights 2011, para 17.

[99] Reidel et al. 2014, p. 14.

[100] UN CESCR 1990, para 10; see also African Commission on Human and Peoples' Rights 2011, para 79(a-c); see also *Mohamed Ben Djazia and Naouel Bellili v. Spain*, Communication No. 5/2015, adoption of views, UN Committee on Economic, Social and Cultural Rights (CESCR), 21 July 2017, E/C.12/61/D/5/2015, para 15.2 (The CESCR often specifies the core contents of rights in the respective general comments. But the core contents of the right to housing are not explicitly stated under General Comment No. 4. They can, however, be deduced from the case of *Mohamed Ben Djazia and Naouel Bellili v. Spain* in which the Committee denounced homelessness caused by a state action).

The final element of state obligation under Article 2(1), duty to cooperate, requires states to "seek [and/or] provide international assistance and cooperation".[101] On the one hand, states should seek financial and other assistance from the international community to maximize their resources and improve the realization of socio-economic rights.[102] On the other hand, states that are in a position to do so are expected to provide assistance to other states.[103] The duty to cooperate will be further discussed in the next part of this book in relation to the right to development.

In addition, the tripartite typology of general human rights obligations, i.e. respect, protect and fulfil, is also applicable to ESC rights in general,[104] and the right to housing in particular. The obligation to respect, which has immediate application, obliges states to refrain from taking actions that directly or indirectly interfere with the enjoyment of rights recognized under human rights instruments.[105] When it comes to the right to housing, the duty to respect will be ostensibly infringed if the state destroys housing through its agents or denies access thereto[106] and undertakes forced eviction unless those measures fall under the justified limitation of the right. The duty to respect, nonetheless, should not be construed as mere abstinence. States are also required to put in place adequate legislative and institutional frameworks in order to ensure non-interference as well as provide effective remedies when interference occurs.[107] This is also clearly reiterated by the Committee in the case of *I.D.G. v. Spain* where it emphasized the state's obligation to provide effective procedural guarantees and remedies in order to protect the right to housing.[108]

The duty to protect requires states to take the necessary measures in order to protect rights holders from infringements of their rights by third parties.[109] This "indirect horizontal effect" of human rights treaties obliges states to regulate the actions of non-state actors,[110] including the commercial activities and overall operations of private

---

[101] Ssenyonjo 2011, p. 983; see also ICESCR (n 2) Article 2(1); UN CESCR 1990, para 13.

[102] UN CESCR 1990, para 13.

[103] Ibid., paras 13 and 14.

[104] Maastricht Guidelines (n 96) para 6 (these guidelines were adopted by a group of experts at the initiation of the International Commission of Jurists in order to further clarify Limburg Principles); moreover, each of these types of obligations contains elements of both obligations of conduct and result, against which the compliance of a state is evaluated (see Maastricht Guidelines (n 96) para 7).

[105] Maastricht Guidelines (n 96) para 6; see also Reidel et al. 2014, p. 18; see also African Commission on Human and Peoples' Rights 2011, para 5; see also *SERAC v. Nigeria* (n 9) para 45.

[106] For instance, see *SERAC v. Nigeria* (n 9) paras 61 and 62 (the state, in this case, destroyed the houses of Ogoni people and obstructed their effort to rebuild their houses, which violated the duty to respect).

[107] UN CESCR 1990, para 5.

[108] *I.D.G. v. Spain* (n 29) paras 11.3 and 11.4; see also African Commission on Human and Peoples' Rights 2011, para 6.

[109] Maastricht Guidelines (n 96) para 6; see also Reidel et al. 2014, p. 19; see also *SERAC v. Nigeria* (n 9) para 46; see also African Commission on Human and Peoples' Rights 2011, para 7.

[110] Lane 2018, p. 26.

entities.[111] Similarly, in relation to the right to housing, states are required to provide necessary safeguards to ensure that this right is not violated by private actors, such as "landlords, property developers, and landowners", and to put in place effective remedies if violation occurs.[112] The Committee also affirmed this in the case of *Mohamed Ben Djazia and Naouel Bellili v. Spain* where it stressed states' obligation to protect rights holders from direct or indirect interference by private actors.[113] The Committee further noted that even if eviction as a result of the expiration of a rental contract or inability to pay rent, which was the factual issue in this case, constitutes a dispute between private parties, the state still bears the obligation to ensure that the eviction procedure and implementation are in line with the rights enunciated under the Covenant, particularly the right to housing.[114]

The third aspect of this tripartite typology, the duty to fulfil, includes "obligations to facilitate, provide, and promote".[115] This positive obligation requires states to facilitate access to goods and services indispensable for the enjoyment of rights by taking adequate legal and administrative measures and to provide those goods and services when necessary to the extent their resource capacity allows.[116] In the context of the right to housing, for instance, the duty to fulfil includes offering subsidies for those who are unable to afford housing and providing essential public services.[117] Overall, the realization of the right to housing requires a range of negative and positive obligations.

3.4.2 *Non-discrimination*

Non-discrimination is a cross-cutting human rights obligation and principle.[118] States are obliged to guarantee all rights recognized in human rights treaties without discrimination based on any of the protected grounds, such as race, gender, language, and

[111] African Commission on Human and Peoples' Rights 2011, para 7. The case of *SERAC v. Nigeria* can be a good example here, since the state failed to properly regulate the Oil companies concerned and, rather, facilitated their operation and the exploitation of Ogoni resources without giving due regard to their rights. Hence, the Nigerian government, in this case, failed to comply with its duty to protect the rights stipulated under the Charter for it provided a 'green light' to the private entities involved (*SERAC v. Nigeria* (n 9) paras 55 and 58).

[112] *SERAC v. Nigeria* (n 9) para 61.

[113] *Mohamed Ben Djazia and Naouel Bellili v. Spain* (n 100) para 14.2.

[114] Ibid., para 14.1 (the Committee used this justification to reject Spain's argument that since the given dispute is between two individuals, it does not raise issues under the Covenant (see para 14.2)).

[115] Reidel et al. 2014, p. 19.

[116] Tadeg 2010, p. 51; see also Maastricht Guidelines (n 96) para 6; see also Reidel et al. 2014, 19 and 20; see also African Commission on Human and Peoples' Rights 2011, paras 10 and 11.

[117] UN CESCR 1991, para 8(c) and (d).

[118] UN CESCR 2009, para 7.

religion.[119] This is stipulated under Article 2(2) of the ICESCR, which provides, "[t]he States Parties to the present Covenant undertake to guarantee that the rights enunciated in the present Covenant will be exercised without discrimination of any kind as to race, colour, sex, language, religion, political or other opinion, national or social origin, property, birth or other status."[120] Discrimination constitutes differential treatment based on one or more of the grounds listed under the provision or other status that has "the purpose or effect of nullifying or impairing the equal enjoyment or exercise of [rights]".[121] As the term "other status" under the provision indicates, the list of protected grounds is not exhaustive.[122] Other socio-economic or political statuses that marginalize certain groups could also be considered prohibited grounds of discrimination.[123]

Indeed, not all differential treatments amount to discrimination. Differential treatment can be justified, in some cases, if "...the justification for differentiation is reasonable and objective."[124] For instance, differential treatment can be acceptable when it falls under "temporary special measures" aimed at rectifying past injustices by providing special treatment for historically disadvantaged groups.[125] A differential treatment that is not justified based on these standards leads to a violation of the obligation of non-discrimination in conjunction with the right to which the differential treatment is directed.

Discrimination can be formal (de jure) and substantive (de facto) depending on where the discrimination emanated from, i.e. the law or policy of the state or the practice, respectively.[126] Formal (de jure) discrimination occurs when domestic laws and policies involve discrimination or unjustified differential treatment.[127] In the context of DID, laws or policies that involve distinctions, for instance, in property ownership, housing, and eligibility for compensation based on any of the protected grounds are discriminatory save for cases where they are reasonably justified.[128] Substantive discrimination, on the other hand, denotes prejudice and differential

---

[119] ICESCR (n 2) Article 2(1); see also ICCPR (n 58) Article 2(1); see also African Charter (n 8) Article 2; see also European Convention on Human Rights (n 22) Article 14; see also American Convention on Human Rights (n 14) Article 1(1).

[120] ICESCR (n 2) Article 2(1).

[121] Maastricht Guidelines (n 96) para 11; see also UN CESCR 2009, para 7.

[122] ICESCR (n 2) Article 2(2); see also UN CESCR 2009, para 27.

[123] The other protected statuses that are prohibited grounds of discrimination include disability, health status, age, family and marital status, nationality, economic and social status, place of residence, sexual orientation and gender identity. (see UN CESCR 2009, paras 27–35; see also Reidel et al. 2014, p. 17; see also Limburg Principles (n 64) para 36).

[124] UN CESCR 2009, para 13.

[125] Reidel et al. 2014, p. 17; see also UN CESCR 2009, paras 9 and 13; see also Saul et al. 2014, 178 and 179.

[126] UN CESCR 2009, para 8.

[127] Ibid., para 8(a).

[128] For instance, women face discrimination in land ownership in several jurisdictions particularly in the past (see UN CESCR 1997, para 10; see also Thukral 1996, p. 1500).

treatment manifested in practice.[129] For instance, if certain groups are excluded from participating in the consultation process for DID or unjustifiably provided with lesser remedies, this can amount to substantive (de facto) discrimination even if the law is not discriminatory. The duty of non-discrimination obliges states to take measures in order to address both formal and substantive discrimination.[130]

Discrimination can also be direct or indirect depending on how it is manifested. "Direct discrimination occurs when an individual is treated less favourably than another person in a similar situation for a reason related to a prohibited ground".[131] In other words, laws, policies, and practices that involve unjustified differential treatment constitute direct discrimination. On the other hand, "[i]ndirect discrimination refers to laws, policies or practices which appear neutral at face value, but have a disproportionate impact" on certain groups.[132] Hence, not only the purpose or content but also the effect of laws, policies, and practices need to be taken into account to determine the existence of discrimination.

3.5 Limitations on the Right to Adequate Housing

Most human rights including ESC rights in general and the right to housing in particular are not absolute. They can be subjected to limitations in order to uphold a greater individual or public interest in accordance with the relevant human rights norms.[133] Unlike the rights stipulated under the ICCPR, specific limitation clauses are not included within the provisions recognizing rights under the ICESCR,[134] save for the right to form trade unions guaranteed under Article 8.[135] Instead, the latter has a general limitation clause under Article 4 of the Covenant, which applies to all rights enshrined therein.[136] The provision provides:

> The States Parties to the present Covenant recognize that, in the enjoyment of those rights provided by the State in conformity with the present Covenant, the State may subject such rights only to such limitations as are determined by law only in so far as this may be compatible with the nature of these rights and solely for the purpose of promoting the general welfare in a democratic society.[137]

---

[129] UN CESCR 2009, para 8.

[130] Ibid., paras 8 and 9.

[131] Ibid., para 10.

[132] Ibid.

[133] Saul et al. 2014, p. 247.

[134] Ibid., p. 240.

[135] Alston and Quinn 1987, p. 192; see also ICESCR (n 2) Article 8 (this provision includes a specific limitation clause and the legitimate aims for restriction listed therein, i.e. "national security or public order or for the protection of the rights and freedoms of others", resemble those of the ICCPR).

[136] ICESCR (n 2) Article 4.

[137] Ibid.

This provision, while allowing states to impose necessary limitations on the rights recognized under the Covenant, restricts both the grounds and the manner in which limitations can be legitimately applied.[138] Similarly, this general limitation clause is also applicable to the right to housing.

A justified limitation needs to comply with the three conditions enunciated under Article 4. The first condition is that a limitation on the enjoyment of these rights can only be imposed if it is prescribed by law.[139] The law in this context can take different forms depending on the legal system—common law or statute.[140] Nevertheless, the law, which the limitation emanates from, should be "a law of general application which is consistent with the Covenant and is in force at the time the limitation is applied."[141] Moreover, the law must be clear, accessible and foreseeable[142] in order to enable rights holders to regulate their conduct accordingly.[143] It must not also be "arbitrary or unreasonable or discriminatory."[144] In the context of DID, for instance, the law providing for limitation of rights for development reasons should not involve discrimination in the planning and undertaking of displacement or eviction.

The second condition requires the limitation to be "compatible with the nature of [the rights envisaged under the Covenant]."[145] This should be construed in light of the specific nature of each right under consideration. The limitation should not be incompatible with the very objective and essence of the right.[146] Consequently, limitations should not affect the minimum core contents of ESC rights,[147] which are also non-derogable.[148] A limitation on the right to be free from hunger, for instance, cannot be imposed without compromising the very nature of the right.[149] Similarly, with regard to the right to housing, a limitation that has the effect of rendering the individuals concerned homeless is clearly against the very nature of the right and the

---

[138] Alston and Quinn 1987, p. 193.

[139] ICESCR (n 2) Article 4.

[140] Alston and Quinn 1987, p. 200; see also Saul et al. 2014, p. 248.

[141] Limburg Principles (n 64) para 48.

[142] Alston and Quinn 1987, p. 200; see also Limburg Principles (n 64) para 50; see also UN Commission on Human Rights, The Siracusa Principles on the Limitation and Derogation Provisions in the International Covenant on Civil and Political Rights, 28 September 1984, E/CN.4/1985/4, paras 15–18 (Even if the Siracusa Principles regulate limitation of civil and political rights, several of the principles enunciated therein can be applied to limitations imposed on ESC rights by analogy).

[143] Saul et al. 2014, p. 248; see also Giacca 2014, p. 81.

[144] Limburg Principles (n 64) para 49; see also Giacca 2014, p. 81.

[145] ICESCR (n 2) Article 4.

[146] Limburg Principles (n 64) para 56; see also Saul et al. 2014, p. 257.

[147] Saul et al. 2014, pp. 257 and 258; see also Giacca 2014, pp. 81 and 82.

[148] African Commission Principles and Guidelines (n 9) para 17; apart from the limitation of rights, international human rights law also allows restrictions through derogation, which allows states to temporarily depart from their human rights obligations during the time of emergency, such as armed conflicts, natural disasters, and public emergency (see UN HRC 2001). However, there are some rights and obligations that cannot be derogated from and minimum core obligations fall under that.

[149] Alston and Quinn 1987, p. 201.

minimum core obligation it entails.[150] This is also reiterated by the Committee in relation to forced eviction,[151] as will be discussed below. Hence, the human rights interferences that DID involves cannot be justified as legitimate limitations if they encroach upon the minimum core contents including access to basic shelter.

Finally, the third condition envisaged under Article 4 of the Covenant pertains to the legitimate aim that the limitation in question aims to advance. Limitations on ESC rights can only be imposed "solely for the purpose of promoting the general welfare in a democratic society."[152] The first element of this condition, "promoting the general welfare", should be interpreted narrowly as its main objective is to restrict the discretion left to states in this regard.[153] General welfare, according to the Limburg Principles, refers to "the well-being of the people as a whole".[154] Nevertheless, what general welfare specifically constitutes is not clear from the drafting documents of the Covenant and it has not been subsequently clarified by the Committee.[155] Resort to the grounds of limitation enunciated under the ICCPR, such as public order, morality and the rights of others,[156] is not insightful either since these grounds of limitations were "explicitly rejected during the drafting process".[157] Thus, the argument of some commentators that these grounds of limitation can be drawn from the ICCPR and used to expand the permissible grounds of limitation under the ICESCR[158] goes against the original intent of the clause and the nature of ESC rights. The main reason why the legitimate aims under the ICCPR were not included under Article 4 of the ICESCR relates to the very nature of economic, social, and cultural rights.[159] As some delegates stressed, there is hardly any public order or morality ground that justifies limitations on, for instance, the rights to health, housing, and food.[160] The other grounds of limitation, such as national security, can only be legitimately used

---

[150] UN CESCR 1997, para 17; see also *Mohamed Ben Djazia and Naouel Bellili v. Spain* (n 100) para 15.2.

[151] Saul et al. 2014, p. 257; see also UN CESCR 1997, para 17.

[152] ICESCR (n 2) Article 4; This is quite different from the approach adopted by the European Social Charter, which allows limitation on diverse grounds of limitation, i.e. "the protection of the rights and freedoms of others or for the protection of public interest, national security, public health, or morals" (see European Social Charter (revised) (n 25) part V, Article G).

[153] Alston and Quinn 1987, p. 202.

[154] Limburg Principles (n 64) para 52.

[155] Saul et al. 2014, p. 250.

[156] See, for instance, ICCPR (n 58), Articles 18 and 19.

[157] Muller 2009, pp. 570–573; see also Saul 2016, pp. 555 and 556 (see, for instance, the Record of the 234th meeting of the UN Commission on Human Rights, 2 July 1951, E/CN.4/SR.234 and Record of the 235th meeting of the UN Commission on Human Rights, 2 July 1951, E/CN.4/SR.235).

[158] Saul et al. 2014, p. 250; see also Giacca 2014, pp. 77–80.

[159] Muller 2009, p. 571.

[160] Saul 2016, p. 555 (the Record of the 234th meeting, n); see also Muller 2009, p. 571; see also Alston and Quinn 1987, p. 202.

to limit these rights "in so far as they are genuinely synonymous with "the general welfare"[161] based on the strict understanding of the term described below.

A closer look at Article 8 of the ICESCR, which is the only provision in the Covenant that includes a specific limitation clause,[162] also arguably supports this position. According to this provision, the right to form and join trade unions can be restricted "in the interests of national security or public order or for the protection of the rights and freedoms of others".[163] The associative nature of this right resembles those of the rights stipulated under the ICCPR and the drafters, in this case, opted to use similar grounds of limitation.[164] The distinction between the legitimate aims of limitation envisaged under Article 4 and Article 8 of the ICESCR indicate that the permissible grounds of limitation coincide with the nature of the right(s) concerned. Thus, in the absence of interpretative guidance from the Committee, general welfare needs to be interpreted more strictly,[165] taking into account the general objectives of the Covenant and the substantive content of the rights it incorporates. Hence, the public interest that the limitation in question aims to advance should correspond to the "economic and social wellbeing" of the public.[166] General welfare should be assessed on a case-by-case basis taking into account the particular needs of different segments of the population.

As development projects that cause displacement often aim to advance economic development and, in some cases, the provision of public services, it is important to question whether these purposes can serve as legitimate grounds for limiting ESC rights. While the limitation of rights for economic reasons can be justified in some instances, the generic term "economic development" is too open-ended and ambiguous to warrant legitimate limitations.[167] What economic development constitutes, moreover, is controversial as the diversity of theories on the subject also suggests, which will be discussed in Chap. 8 in relation to the right to development. Thus, the economic interest the limitation seeks to advance should be clearly and narrowly defined and conform to the condition of the general welfare. Development projects aimed at promoting the socio-economic wellbeing or advancing the socio-economic rights of the general public can be used as legitimate grounds of limitation provided that the other conditions of limitation are fulfilled.

The reference to a democratic society under Article 4 should not be interpreted as requiring states to subscribe to a certain political ideology or form of government

---

161 Alston and Quinn 1987, p. 202; see also Muller 2009, p. 573.

162 ICESCR (n 2) Article 8.

163 Ibid., Article 8(1)(a).

164 Muller 2009, p. 572.

165 It is, however, important to note that although the interpretation of "general welfare" is theoretically debatable, in practice, the determination of a legitimate aim in human rights cases is fairly straightforward. Human rights monitoring bodies rarely engage with the existence of a legitimate aim extensively. The assessment of limitations is often based on the necessity and proportionality test.

166 Muller 2009, p. 573; see also Giacca 2014, p. 77.

167 Alston and Quinn 1987, p. 203; see also Muller 2009, p. 574.

per se.[168] Pursuant to the Siracusa Principles, "while there is no single model of a democratic society, a society which recognizes and respects the human rights set forth in the United Nations Charter and the [UDHR] may be viewed as meeting this definition."[169] This was also stressed by the delegate from Uruguay, among others, during the drafting process of the Covenant.[170] Thus, the state imposing a limitation, which bears the burden of proof, is required to demonstrate that the limitation does not hinder the functioning of a democratic society.[171]

In more concrete terms, the reference to a democratic society entails the requirements of "necessity and proportionality".[172] While Article 4 does not explicitly mention these conditions, the CESCR has read the conditions of necessity and proportionality into the provision in the cases of *Lorne Joseph Walters v. Belgium and Rosario Gómez-Limón Pardo v. Spain*, among others.[173] The interpretation of these conditions can be further informed by the norms of other human rights treaties, including the ICCPR, and by the relevant interpretations of human rights judicial and quasi-judicial bodies.[174] The requirement of necessity envisages that limitation should only be imposed as a last resort, or presuppose "the existence of a pressing social need" as the ECtHR puts it.[175] The principle of proportionality demands that the limitation must be relevant and proportionate to the legitimate aim it seeks to

---

168 Alston and Quinn 1987, p. 203.

169 Siracusa Principles (n 142) para 21; see also Alston and Quinn 1987, p. 203; Resort to the jurisprudence of the ECtHR on the principle of "necessary in a democratic society", which is one of the conditions of limitation of rights under the Convention, can provide guidance here. The Court emphasized that "a democratic society" in this context refers to the existence of certain principles or values that are indispensable for the protection of the rights recognised under the Convention (see, for instance, *Handyside v United Kingdom*, Application No 5493/72, A/24, [1976] ECHR 5, (1976) 1 EHRR 737, (1979) 1 EHRR 737, IHRL 14 (ECHR 1976), Merits, European Court of Human Rights, 7 December 1976, para 49).

170 Alston and Quinn 1987, p. 203.

171 Limburg Principles (n 64) para 54; see also Siracusa Principles (n 142) para 20.

172 Saul et al. 2014, p. 254.

173 *Lorne Joseph Walters v. Belgium*, communication No. 61/2018, adoption of views, Committee on Economic, Social and Cultural Rights, 12 October 2021, E/C.12/70/D/61/2018, paras 9.2. and 9.3; see also *Rosario Gómez-Limón Pardo v. Spain*, communication No. 52/2018, adoption of views, Committee on Economic, Social and Cultural Rights, 5 March 2020, E/C.12/67/D/52/2018, para 9.4.

174 It is important to note that Article 4 of the ICESCR is one of the most undeveloped norms of the Covenant. The Committee has not extensively dealt with what these conditions of limitations entail and how they can be applied in its General Comments. It only recently started referring to Article 4 in individual communications. The Human Rights Committee, on the other hand, has a more developed jurisprudence and interpretation on limitations of the rights provided under the ICCPR, which to a certain extent can be employed to aid the interpretation of the limitation clause under the ICESCR. This analogical interpretation can only be employed to the extent it is compatible with the object and purpose of the Covenant and the natures of the rights enunciated therein.

175 European Court of Human Rights, Guide on Article 8 of the European Convention on Human Rights: Right to respect for private and family life, home and correspondence (Council of Europe, December 2018) para 19; see also *Dudgeon v United Kingdom*, Application No. 7525/76, European Court of Human Rights, 22 October 1981, paras 51–53.

achieve; it must be the least intrusive measure available in the circumstances of the case.[176] In other words, this principle requires states to strike a fair balance between the competing interests of promoting the general welfare, on the one hand, and protecting the ESC rights of all persons, on the other hand.[177] Overall, the interferences with the right to housing that DID results in including forced eviction and the other consequences of DID, which will be discussed in the subsequent sections, need to be necessary to achieve the socio-economic aim in question, be the least restrictive alternatives available, and proportionate to the aim pursued.

3.6 Interference with the Right to Housing in the Course of Development-Induced Displacement

In light of the normative elements of the right to housing elucidated above, the forcible displacement of individuals from their homes or residences for development or other reasons directly interferes with the enjoyment of the right to housing. Indeed, not all these interferences amount to a violation. Displacement and the resulting interference with the enjoyment of the right to housing can be justified in exceptional circumstances. The human rights frameworks that enunciate this right also leave room for states to impose necessary limitations. This section will elaborate on the ways DID can interfere with the enjoyment of and potentially violate the right to housing as well as how violation can be avoided or the interferences can be justified. The section will also explore the factors that contribute to such interferences. Generally, DID can (potentially) constitute a violation of the right to housing when it involves forced eviction, when it leads to homelessness or deterioration of housing conditions, and when it involves direct or indirect discrimination.

3.6.1 Forced Eviction

DID often entails the eviction of displaced persons from their homes or residences. Whether that falls under the definition of forced eviction and constitutes a violation of the right to housing depends on the circumstances of the case and the legal safeguards put in place by states. Forced eviction, according to the definition adopted by the CESCR, constitutes "…the permanent or temporary removal against their will of individuals, families and/or communities from the homes and/or land which they occupy, without the provision of, and access to, appropriate forms of legal or other

[176] *Rosario Gómez-Limón Pardo v. Spain* (n 173) para 9.4; see also et al. 2014, p. 256; see also *Dudgeon v United Kingdom* (n 175) paras 51–53; see also Giacca 2014, p. 82.

[177] African Commission on Human and Peoples' Rights 2011, para 1(g); see also *Rosario Gómez-Limón Pardo v. Spain* (n 173) para 9.4.

protection."[178] Thus, the two elements that make up this definition are the involuntary nature of the removal from one's home or residence and the lack or inadequacy of legal and other safeguards.[179] Forced eviction constitutes a prima facie violation of the right to housing.[180]

Protection against forced eviction, one of the normative elements of the right to housing and entails an immediate obligation of states,[181] applies irrespective of the type of tenure in question, which may range from ownership to informal settlement.[182] In other words, this entitlement is not necessarily contingent upon a property right.[183] The Committee has also reiterated this in the case of *Mohamed Ben Djazia and Naouel Bellili v. Spain* where it dealt with the question of whether or not eviction from rental housing constituted a violation of the right to housing.[184] According to the Committee, "[security of tenure] also applies to persons living in rental accommodation. Whether public or private, such persons should enjoy the right to housing even when the lease expires."[185] The same goes for informal settlers who do not have formal title of ownership or possession of the house concerned. As the Committee indicated in the case of *Maribel Viviana López Albán v. Spain*, eviction of persons without a legal title to the house they occupy or illegal occupants should also comply with human rights standards discussed below.[186] The Committee in this case stressed that "the State party will be committing a violation of the right to adequate housing if it stipulates that a person who is occupying a property without legal title must be evicted immediately irrespective of the circumstances in which the eviction order would be carried out."[187]

Apart from the socio-economic impacts it imposes on the people affected,[188] "forced eviction [also constitutes] gross violation of human rights."[189] In addition to the right to housing, it may also result in the violation of a range of other rights, such as the right to life, freedom from cruel, inhuman, and degrading treatment, the right to private and family life, the right to security of a person, freedom of

---

[178] UN CESCR 1997, para 3; see also African Commission on Human and Peoples' Rights 2011, para 1(a).

[179] UN CESCR 1997, para 3; see also African Commission on Human and Peoples' Rights 2011, para 1(a).

[180] UN CESCR 1991, para 18; see also UN CESCR 1997, para 1.

[181] OHCHR 2014, p. 21.

[182] UN CESCR 1991, para 8(a); see also OHCHR 2014, p. 5.

[183] OHCHR 2014, p. 5.

[184] *Mohamed Ben Djazia and Naouel Bellili v. Spain* (n 100) paras 12.7 and 13.2.

[185] Ibid., para 13.2.

[186] *Maribel Viviana López Albán v. Spain*, communication No. 37/2018, adoption of views, Committee under the Optional Protocol to the International Covenant on Economic, Social and Cultural Rights, 11 October 2019, E/C.12/66/D/37/2018, para 11.7.

[187] Ibid.

[188] The economic, social, and cultural consequences of DID discussed in the previous chapter are also applicable to forced eviction to a large extent.

[189] OHCHR 2014, p. 5; see also UN Commission on Human Rights, Forced evictions, Resolution 1993/77, 10 March 1993, E/CN.4/RES/1993/77 ('Resolution on Forced Eviction') para 1.

movement and choice of residence, the right to work, the right to education, and the right to property, among others.[190] These violations are mainly attributable to the way eviction is decided, planned, and undertaken as well as its outcomes.[191] Forced eviction often involves the destruction of property, violence, and use of force, which may even result in human casualties.[192] Furthermore, forced eviction may also be discriminatory and target disadvantaged groups thereby intensifying already existing vulnerabilities and inequalities or even creating new ones.[193] As the Special Rapporteur on adequate housing put it, "forced evictions intensify inequality, social conflict, segregation and "ghettoization", and invariably affect the poorest, most socially and economically vulnerable and marginalized sectors of society, especially women, children, minorities and indigenous peoples."[194]

Consequently, forced eviction is prohibited under international human rights law, which can be deduced from the normative contents of the right to housing, as discussed above, as well as the right to protection against interference with one's home recognized under Article 17 of the ICCPR.[195] The latter proscribes "arbitrary and unlawful interference" with one's "privacy, family, home or correspondence" by private or public authorities and imposes a corresponding obligation on states to guarantee such protection through legal and other means.[196] Unlawful interference in this context refers to a situation where the interference to those protected spaces takes place without the existence of legal authority to that effect.[197] In other words, any interference with privacy, family, home, and correspondence must be explicitly provided by law.[198] Nevertheless, this does not imply that all grounds of interference are legitimate under the Covenant. As signified by the term "arbitrary interference" and the prohibition thereof, any interference provided by law must comply with the general objectives of the Covenant and the rights recognized therein.[199] Moreover, the notion of arbitrariness also requires that the interference should be reasonable under the specific circumstances of the case.[200] The Human Rights Committee

---

190 OHCHR 2014, p. 6; see also UN CESCR 1997, para 4; see also The Special Rapporteur on Adequate Housing 2007.

191 OHCHR 2014, p. 6.

192 Langford and du Plessis 2006, p. 6; for instance, in forced eviction carried out in Harare Zimbabwe in 2004, eleven people had lost their lives due to violent police responses. Moreover, eviction orders are often met with public protest and resistance, which increases the casualties depending on how law enforcement officials handle the situation (see Langford and Plessis 2006, pp. 6 and 7); see also Thiele 2003, p. 464.

193 OHCHR 2014, p. 6.

194 The Special Rapporteur on Adequate Housing 2007, para 7.

195 ICCPR (n 58) Article 17; see also *Mohamed Ben Djazia and Naouel Bellili v. Spain* (n 100) para 13.3.

196 ICCPR (n 58) Article 17; see also UN HRC 1988, para 1.

197 UN HRC 1988, para 3.

198 Ibid.

199 Ibid., para 4.

200 Ibid.

(HRC)[201] has further clarified this in its concluding observations on Kenya stressing that "the state party should develop transparent policies and procedures for dealing with evictions and ensure that evictions from settlements do not occur unless those affected have been consulted and appropriate resettlement arrangements have been made."[202] Hence, forced eviction, as defined under General Comment No. 7, falls under unlawful and arbitrary interference with one's home and family, unless it is justified based on these human rights standards.

The prohibition of forced eviction does not extend to evictions carried out on the basis of pre-existing law and in accordance with human rights norms,[203] as the definition itself suggests. In other words, in exceptional circumstances, eviction can be justified—even if it is involuntary—provided that adequate procedural and substantive safeguards are put in place.[204] In these instances, the manner in which eviction is planned and executed should aim to mitigate its adverse socio-economic consequences, if not leave those affected better off economically and socially.[205] This imposes on states not only the obligation to justify the necessity of the eviction but also to put in place necessary safeguards at all phases of eviction in order to protect the rights or socio-economic interests of the people affected thereby.[206]

In order to understand what these safeguards are, it is important to resort to the General Comments on the right to housing and protection of home adopted by the CESCR and the HRC, respectively,[207] the UN Commission on Human Rights Resolution on forced eviction,[208] and the Special Rapporteur's Principles and Guidelines on Development-based Eviction and Displacement,[209] which is particularly important for DID, among other soft law and interpretative documents. Drawing on these documents, the following sections explore how eviction in the context of DID can be justified based on the pertinent human rights norms and the safeguards that need to be provided at all phases of eviction or displacement.

---

201 The HRC is entrusted to monitor the implementation of the ICCPR. Since the protection from "arbitrary or unlawful interference with [one's] privacy, family, home or correspondence" stipulated under Article 17 of the ICCPR also includes the prohibition of arbitrary eviction, the HRC is also involved in issues related to forced eviction, in addition to the CESCR.

202 UN Human Rights Committee (HRC), Concluding Observations of the Human Rights Committee: Kenya, 29 April 2005, CCPR/CO/83/KEN, para 22.

203 OHCHR fact sheet (n 181) 5; see also *Mohamed Ben Djazia and Naouel Bellili v. Spain* (n 100) para 15.1; see also African Commission Principles and Guidelines (n 9) para 79(s).

204 UN CESCR 1997, paras 13–15.

205 OHCHR 2014, p. 19.

206 UN CESCR 1997, paras 13–15.

207 UN CESCR 1997; UN CESCR 1991; see also UNHRC 1988.

208 Resolution on Forced Eviction, n 189. UN Commission on Human Rights was a predecessor of the UN Human Rights Council established in 1946 and mandated with the task of promoting and protecting human rights globally (see information about the Commission and its work at https://www.ohchr.org/en/hr-bodies/chr/commission-on-human-rights, accessed 28 June 2025).

209 The Special Rapporteur on Adequate Housing 2007.

3.6.1.1 Justifying Eviction

As eviction constitutes an interference with the right to housing, it needs to comply with the conditions of limitation enunciated under Article 4 of the ICESCR and the authoritative interpretations described above.[210] The first condition is that the eviction needs to be provided by law.[211] The purpose of the law providing for the eviction and the corresponding obligations expected from states are twofold. First, the law needs to guarantee security of tenure and protect rights holders against forced eviction including by providing remedies or sanctions.[212] Second, the legislation should clearly specify the circumstances under which eviction can be justified and the standards that need to be followed or the safeguards that need to be put in place in the course of eviction.[213] Moreover, the law needs to be specific, accessible, and foreseeable as well as align with the pertinent human rights norms and principles as discussed before.[214]

The second condition is that the eviction needs be necessary to promote the "general welfare" of the public.[215] The general welfare aim pertains to the socio-economic wellbeing of the population, which corresponds to the rights provided under the ICESCR, and should particularly take into account the needs and rights of vulnerable groups.[216] In the context of evictions induced by development projects, not only the eviction but also the development project itself has to be justified by the general welfare requirement. This principle also correlates with the "public interest" requirement of the Guiding Principles on Internal Displacement,[217] which will be covered in Chap. 6.

The third condition demands that the eviction needs to be undertaken in accordance with the "general principles of reasonableness and proportionality".[218] These twin conditions entail that states should exhaust all other feasible alternatives and eviction should only be undertaken as a last resort.[219] Thus, priority should be accorded to preventive measures that minimize eviction and displacement. To this end, "eviction-impact assessment", which is aimed at exploring other alternatives and mapping out strategies for mitigating the negative consequences of eviction, should be carried

---

210 ICESCR (n 2) Article 4.

211 Ibid.

212 UN CESCR 1991, paras 8(a) and para 17.

213 UN CESCR 1997, para 9; see also The Special Rapporteur on Adequate Housing 2007, para 21.

214 Siracusa Principles (n 142) paras 16 and 17; see also Alston and Quinn 1987, p. 200; see also UNHRC 1988, para 3.

215 The Special Rapporteur on Adequate Housing 2007, para 21.

216 Ibid.

217 UN Commission on Human Rights, Guiding Principles on Internal Displacement, 11 February 1998, E/CN.4/1998/53/Add.2, Principle 6(2)(c).

218 UN CESCR 1997, para 9; see also The Special Rapporteur on Adequate Housing 2007, para 21; see also *Mohamed Ben Djazia and Naouel Bellili v. Spain* (n 100) para 13.4.

219 The Special Rapporteur on Adequate Housing 2007, para 38.

out prior to the approval of the development project that involves eviction.[220] This coincides with the duty of due diligence, which requires states to take necessary measures in order to identify, prevent, and address human rights risks of, for instance, their development endeavours.[221] The duty of due diligence consists of two elements, namely the duty to prevent harm or human rights violations and the duty to respond or remedy the harm if it occurred.[222] The obligation to conduct human rights impact assessment is part of the first element, i.e. prevention. States need to conduct a human rights impact assessment to identify and prevent the potential impacts of the project concerned.[223] This assessment should particularly take into consideration the heightened impacts of forced eviction on certain vulnerable groups, such as women, indigenous peoples, and children.[224] In addition, states need to undertake a balancing exercise taking into account the general welfare objectives, on the one hand, and the adverse impacts of the eviction, on the other hand. The eviction can only be justified if it is proportionate—the general welfare benefits outweigh the impacts of the eviction.

Hence, eviction in general and eviction induced by development projects in particular needs to be justified based on the conditions discussed above, i.e. legality, advancement of the general welfare, and reasonableness and proportionality. Moreover, the eviction process as a whole should be guided by international human rights norms and standards.[225] In other words, a rights-based approach should be applied in both the planning and implementation of evictions. The obligations of states, however, do not end there. States are also required to put in place necessary safeguards before, during, and after eviction and provide adequate remedies along the way in order to protect the rights of people affected and prevent or mitigate the negative consequences of eviction. These safeguards are particularly relevant in the context of evictions carried out to make room for development projects since the state has a direct role and control, especially in the case of public projects.

3.6.1.2 Safeguards Before, During, and After Eviction

States need to put in place a range of procedural and substantive safeguards at all stages of eviction or displacement as established by the case law and authoritative interpretations of the relevant human rights bodies. One of the safeguards

---

220 Ibid., para 30–32.

221 Monnheimer 2021, p. 69; see also Shelton and Gould 2013, pp. 578 and 579.

222 Monnheimer 2021 116.

223 The Special Rapporteur on Adequate Housing 2007, paras 30–32; see also Walker 2014, p. 395.

224 It is important to note that different norms are applicable when it comes to evictions that affect indigenous peoples due to the special ties they have to their ancestral land and the special land rights they are entitled to as the result (UN General Assembly, United Nations Declaration on the Rights of Indigenous Peoples: Resolution adopted by the General Assembly, 2 October 2007, A/RES/61/295 ('UNDRIP'), Article 10; see also International Labour Organization (ILO), Indigenous and Tribal Peoples Convention, C169, 27 June 1989, Articles 13–16). This will be further discussed in the next chapter.

225 OHCHR 2014, p. 5; see also The Special Rapporteur on Adequate Housing 2007, para 21.

that need to be provided prior to the eviction, particularly in the case of eviction induced by development projects, is adequate and meaningful consultation with the people(s) potentially affected by the eviction and their representatives.[226] To this end, all relevant information about the development project planned to be undertaken, the process of eviction, and the details of the planned consultation should be disseminated in due time to all persons and groups concerned.[227] The consultation should be meaningful in the sense that affected individuals are given a genuine opportunity to challenge the eviction, propose alternative solutions, and ensure that their rights are protected during its implementation if eviction is unavoidable.[228] This requires the state to facilitate access to legal and technical information on the matter to the people concerned.[229] The consultation should not be limited to the eviction decision. Rather, the people affected should also have a say on the remedies and resettlement options provided.[230] Moreover, the consultation should be inclusive, participatory, and open to those potentially affected, particularly to vulnerable and marginalized groups.[231] In situations where agreement cannot be reached, the eviction decision should be made by an independent judicial or other constitutional organs rather than the executive.[232] Overall, provision of or access to adequate information and meaningful consultation with the participation of all people(s) potentially affected by the eviction is one of the procedural safeguards states need to provide.

The other procedural safeguard that should be put in place prior to eviction is reasonable notice of the eviction procedure.[233] The eviction notice should contain detailed information including the justification for the eviction and the time and manner of its execution.[234] The notice should be given in due time in order to enable the individuals affected to make the necessary arrangements with their property and legally challenge the decision if they choose to do so.[235] Furthermore, as the Committee noted in the case of *I.D.G. v. Spain*, the means by which the notice is communicated should be one that gives sufficient opportunity for the person concerned to access the information, which the state failed to comply with in this

---

[226] The Special Rapporteur on Adequate Housing 2007, para 37; see also *Maribel Viviana López Albán v. Spain* (n 186) para 8.3; see also *Mohamed Ben Djazia and Naouel Bellili v. Spain* (n 100) para 13.4; see also *I.D.G. v. Spain* (n 29) para 11.2; see also African Commission on Human and Peoples' Rights 2011, para 79(v); see also Resolution on Forced Eviction (n 189) para 3.

[227] The Special Rapporteur on Adequate Housing 2007, para 37.

[228] Ibid.; see also *Maribel Viviana López Albán v. Spain* (n 186) para 8.3.

[229] The Special Rapporteur on Adequate Housing 2007, para 37; see also African Commission on Human and Peoples' Rights 2011, para 79(w).

[230] The Special Rapporteur on Adequate Housing 2007, para 37.

[231] Ibid., para 38 and 39; see also African Commission on Human and Peoples' Rights 2011, para 79(w).

[232] The Special Rapporteur on Adequate Housing 2007, para 38.

[233] *I.D.G. v. Spain* (n 29) para 11.2.

[234] The Special Rapporteur on Adequate Housing 2007, para 40.

[235] Ibid., para 40 and 41; see also African Commission on Human and Peoples' Rights 2011, para 79(w).

case.[236] Accordingly, all available methods should be exhausted in order to serve the notice in person and public posting of the notice should only be used as a last resort.[237] The individuals potentially affected by eviction should also be guaranteed "access to an effective and appropriate judicial remedy".[238]

In addition, a range of procedural and substantive safeguards should be provided during the execution of eviction. To start with, eviction should be carried out in the presence of government officials with formal authorization, especially when it affects a large number of households.[239] Furthermore, independent observers including civil society organizations and the media should be given access to eviction sites in order to ensure accountability and transparency.[240] As mentioned before, some of the human rights violations evictions may result in are attributable to the way eviction is undertaken.[241] In order to avoid that, the manner in which eviction is carried out must respect "the dignity and human rights to life and security of those affected".[242] Again, special attention should be given to vulnerable groups in the process of eviction. For instance, the state should protect women from gender-based violence and discrimination.[243]

In the course of eviction, states should refrain from the use of force as much as possible and any "legal use of force" must adhere to the norms on the use of force by government officials in international law.[244] The relevant norms are adopted by the General Assembly Resolution[245] and other relevant UN organs.[246] These norms are also endorsed by the Special Rapporteur on adequate housing.[247] As these frameworks indicate, state agents or law enforcement officials should, as much as

---

[236] *I.D.G. v. Spain* (n 29) paras 12.2 and 14.

[237] Ibid., para 12.3.

[238] Ibid., para 11.4.

[239] The Special Rapporteur on Adequate Housing 2007, para 45; see also African Commission on Human and Peoples' Rights 2011, para 79(w).

[240] The Special Rapporteur on Adequate Housing 2007, para 46; see also African Commission on Human and Peoples' Rights 2011, para 79(w).

[241] Langford and Plessis 2006, pp. 6 and 7.

[242] The Special Rapporteur on Adequate Housing 2007, para 47; see also African Commission on Human and Peoples' Rights 2011, para 79(t).

[243] The Special Rapporteur on Adequate Housing 2007, para 47.

[244] Ibid., para 48; see also African Commission on Human and Peoples' Rights 2011, para 79(bb); These rules are particularly derived from two instruments adopted by the UN organs, namely the 1979 Code of Conduct for Law Enforcement Officials, adopted by the General Assembly (see UN General Assembly, Code of Conduct for Law Enforcement Officials, Resolution 34/169, 17 December 1979 ('Resolution on Code of Conduct')) and the 1990 Basic Principles on the Use of Force and Firearms by Law Enforcement Officials (see Basic Principles on the Use of Force and Firearms by Law Enforcement Officials, Adopted by the Eighth United Nations Congress on the Prevention of Crime and the Treatment of Offenders, Havana, Cuba, 27 August to 7 September 1990 ('Basic principles on the use of force')).

[245] Resolution on Code of Conduct (n 244).

[246] Basic Principles on the Use of Force (n 244).

[247] The Special Rapporteur on Adequate Housing 2007, para 48.

possible, employ non-violent means, such as negotiation and mediation.[248] They can only resort to the use of force when it is "strictly necessary and to the extent required for the performance of their duty".[249] This encompasses the principle of necessity, which dictates that the use of force can only be justified when it is absolutely imperative to achieve the legitimate aim pursued, and the principle of proportionality, which imposes a limit on the level of force that can be used vis-à-vis the objective and the circumstances of the case.[250] Moreover, important precautionary measures, including those related to the means and methods of force, should be undertaken to minimize the risks associated with use of force.[251] Overall, these rules on the use of force should also be used in the context of forced eviction to regulate the conduct of the state or its authorities.

Moreover, the time and date the eviction is carried out should not be arbitrary or too disruptive. This means that evictions should not be undertaken during the holidays, around election time, school exam times, and at night times.[252] The people affected should also be given the option to demolish their properties themselves and, in any case, have an opportunity to salvage their belongings and building materials.[253]

States should also provide various short-term and long-term remedies or substantive safeguards in the course of eviction in order to protect the rights of those affected. Remedies for evictions induced by development projects should include adequate compensation, replacement housing and/or land, or resettlement, which must be provided within the shortest possible time following the eviction unless such immediacy is not possible due to force majeure.[254] Monetary compensation should be provided for the properties lost, loss or decrease of income, legal and other costs incurred, and loss of potential opportunities, such as employment or education, as well as any physical or moral damage incurred.[255] The amount of compensation is determined on a case-by-case basis taking into account all these factors and other

[248] Basic Principles on the Use of Force (n 244) para 4.

[249] Resolution on Code of Conduct (n 244), Article 3; see also Basic Principles on Use of Force (n 244) para 4; see also Geneva Academy 2016, p. 6.

[250] Resolution on Code of Conduct (n 244), Article 3; see also Geneva Academy 2016, pp. 6–9.

[251] Basic Principles on Use of Force (n 244) principle 3; see also Geneva Academy 2016, pp. 9 and 10.

[252] The Special Rapporteur on Adequate Housing 2007, para 49; see also African Commission on Human and Peoples' Rights 2011, para 79(dd).

[253] The Special Rapporteur on Adequate Housing 2007, para 51; see also African Commission on Human and Peoples' Rights 2011, para 79(ee).

[254] Resolution on Forced Eviction (n 189) para 4; see also The Special Rapporteur on Adequate Housing 2007, para 52; see also CESCR Concluding Observation on Greece (n 56) para 42; see also *Maribel Viviana López Albán v. Spain* (n 186) para 9.1.

[255] The Special Rapporteur on Adequate Housing 2007, para 60; the amount of compensation should take into consideration both the losses sustained as the result of eviction and the costs incurred in the process (e.g. legal costs, relocation costs). Particularly when the housing they are evicted from is not only used as a living space but also as a source of income, the calculation of the compensation must also take into account the loss related to that. (see The Special Rapporteur on Adequate Housing 2007, para 63).

particular circumstances of the case. As mentioned before, the entitlement to protection against forced eviction is not contingent on property rights and it applies irrespective of the type of tenure in question.[256] Similarly, in the case of eviction, the provision of compensation should not be limited only to those who have legal or formal ownership or possession right to the property from which they are evicted.[257] Informal dwellers are also entitled to compensation for the loss they sustained due to eviction.[258]

It is imperative to note that monetary compensation should not be used in lieu of real property replacements—housing and land—as much as possible.[259] According to the Special Rapporteur on adequate housing, "where land has been taken, the evicted should be compensated with land commensurate in quality, size and value, or better."[260] Moreover, the alternative housing provided by the state should comply with the criteria of adequacy of housing elucidated in the previous section.[261] States should also ensure that evicted people have access to minimum essential conditions, i.e. food, clean water, basic housing, education facilities, health services, and access to common resources that they depended upon prior to eviction.[262] Thus, temporary shelters provided until permanent relocation is arranged should also adhere to adequate housing standards to the extent possible and access to minimum essential services should be granted.[263] As the Committee stressed in the case of *Maribel Viviana López Albán v. Spain*, "States must endeavour to ensure that the temporary accommodation protects the human dignity of the persons evicted, meets all safety and security requirements and does not become a permanent solution, but is a step towards obtaining adequate housing."[264] Hence, basic shelter that does not fully comply with the standards of adequacy should not be used as a permanent or long-term option.

As established in the preceding chapter, displacement, or eviction in this context, caused by development projects has a permanent nature, which means that in most cases the evicted or displaced persons do not have the option to return to their homes or residences. If such an option is feasible, however, displaced persons should be given a choice to return and states should facilitate the restitution of their properties.[265] Thus, restitution and return should be prioritized. If this is not doable and

---

[256] General Comment No. 4 (n 30) para 8(a).

[257] The Special Rapporteur on Adequate Housing 2007, para 61.

[258] Ibid.

[259] Ibid., para 60.

[260] Ibid; see also African Commission on Human and Peoples' Rights 2011, para 79(gg).

[261] *Maribel Viviana López Albán v. Spain* (n 186) para 9.3; see also The Special Rapporteur on Adequate Housing 2007, para 55.

[262] The Special Rapporteur on Adequate Housing 2007, paras 52 and 54; see also *Maribel Viviana López Albán v. Spain* (n 186) para 9.3; see also African Commission on Human and Peoples' Rights 2011, para 79(ff).

[263] *Maribel Viviana López Albán v. Spain* (n 186) para 9.4.

[264] Ibid.

[265] Resolution on forced eviction (n 189) para 4; see also The Special Rapporteur on Adequate Housing 2007, para 64.

permanent relocation or resettlement is necessary, replacement of real properties is the next best option.[266] The planning and implementation of the resettlement plan should employ a human rights-based approach or give the utmost effect to the rights of displaced persons.[267] For instance, the site selected for relocation should not be adjacent to sources of pollution or other threats to the health of the inhabitants.[268] Moreover, resettlement should be undertaken taking into account the living conditions of both the resettled and host communities. Resettlement should not have the effect of worsening their socio-economic condition, if not enhancing it.[269]

The obligations of states, however, do not culminate upon the completion of the resettlement plan. States are also required to follow up on the conditions of resettled people and provide long-term assistance depending on the circumstances.[270] As established in the previous chapter, DID—or eviction caused by development projects in this context—has long-term consequences on displaced persons, which are not usually prevented or mitigated solely by the provision of short-term remedies, such as compensation. This calls for long-term remedies and rehabilitation measures that are aimed at restoring or, preferably, improving the lives of displaced persons and protecting their rights.

3.6.2 Homelessness and Inadequate Housing

One of the adverse consequences of DID, as discussed in the preceding chapter, is homelessness or deterioration of housing conditions after displacement. People displaced for development reasons are usually subjected to temporary or permanent loss of housing and poorer conditions of housing compared to their situation before displacement.[271] These outcomes of DID constitute a violation of the right to housing, although the latter can be justified in exceptional circumstances.

Measures that lead to homelessness and inadequate housing also amount to retrogressive measures, which constitute a prima facie violation of the right in question. A retrogressive measure refers to any undertaking by a state "that reduces the extent to which [rights] are guaranteed".[272] In the context of the right to housing, for instance, if the laws, policies, and administrative measures adopted by the state result in homelessness or poorer housing conditions compared to the level previously achieved, they amount to retrogressive measures. Such measures, if they are deliberate, constitute a

[266] The Special Rapporteur on Adequate Housing 2007, para 68.

[267] Ibid., paras 56(a) and 58.

[268] Ibid., para 56(g).

[269] Ibid., para 56(d).

[270] Ibid., paras 68 and 69.

[271] See the examples of case studies in Chap. 2, Sect. 2.4.

[272] Maastricht Guidelines (n 96) para 14(e).

violation of the right to housing save for exceptional cases where they can be justified.[273] As described above, retrogressive measures can only be justified if the state is able to prove that it has utilized all the resources available at its disposal to avert the situation and the measure is taken in the interest of protecting the totality of rights recognized under the Covenant.[274]

Moreover, even if the development project that necessitated the displacement, or even the displacement itself, is justified, the right to housing can still be violated if the outcome is unfavourable, i.e. leading to homelessness or inadequate housing. As the Committee contended in the case of *Mohamed Ben Djazia and Naouel Bellili v. Spain*, "the persons concerned must not remain in or be exposed to a situation constituting a violation",[275] which is the case in these specific situations of DID. The Committee specifically stressed that "eviction should not render individuals homeless."[276] Accordingly, "[w]here those affected do not have the means to acquire alternative housing, States parties must take all appropriate measures to ensure, where possible, that adequate alternative housing, resettlement or access to productive land, as the case may be, is available."[277] While the amount of the other remedies provided for DID, such as compensation and replacement land, might depend upon the property rights of the people concerned, alternative housing should be provided in the event of displacement or eviction regardless of the nature of tenure in question.[278] Hence, if DID has resulted in homelessness, it constitutes a violation of the right to housing since access to basic shelter is part of the minimum contents of the right. The inadequacy of housing caused by DID might be justified, particularly when it is temporary, if it falls under the limitation clause discussed before.

3.6.3 Discrimination in the Course of Displacement

In light of the norms of non-discrimination discussed before, the process and outcome of DID often involve differential treatment that has the effect of impairing the enjoyment of rights including the right to housing. Generally, as elucidated in the preceding chapter, DID often disproportionately affects marginalized and vulnerable groups

---

[273] Nevertheless, this is only applicable to retrogressive measures that lead to poorer housing conditions; a retrogressive measure that causes homelessness cannot be justified since it is part of the core contents of the right to housing.

[274] General Comment No. 3 (n 60) para 9; see also *Mohamed Ben Djazia and Naouel Bellili v. Spain* (n 100) para 17.6.

[275] *Mohamed Ben Djazia and Naouel Bellili v. Spain* (n 100) para 15.1.

[276] Ibid., para 15.2; see also UN CESCR 1997, para 16; see also African Commission on Human and Peoples' Rights 2011, para 79(u).

[277] *Mohamed Ben Djazia and Naouel Bellili v. Spain* (n 100) para 15.2.

[278] Ibid. (in this case, the Committee reiterated that states should provide alternative housing even for people evicted from rental accommodation for inability to pay rent if they could not afford to do so by themselves. It also noted that special attention should be given to evictions that involve vulnerable groups, such as women, children, and the elderly).

that are neither the participants nor the beneficiaries of the development project of which they are bearing the cost.[279] Similarly, interferences with the rights to property, housing, and work, such as dispossession of land, eviction, and loss of income, more severely affect these groups, such as indigenous peoples and women.[280] For instance, women are grossly underrepresented in land ownership, although they often rely on land for their livelihoods. Women constitute less than 20% of the number of landholders in the world.[281] The number of women landholders is even lower in developing countries; women make up less than 15% of landholders in sub-Saharan Africa and 5% of landholders in North Africa and West Asia.[282] By contrast, the number of women that depend on land for their livelihood is much higher than these figures. In developing countries, for instance, women constitute 43% of "the agricultural labour force".[283] In most cases, the determination of monetary and non-monetary compensation provided for expropriation or eviction is based on ownership.[284] In other words, the unfair distribution of resources, particularly land, and the interests of people who derive their income from the land in different ways are seldom taken into account. Thus, the eviction, expropriation, and loss of income that DID involves will disproportionately affect marginalized groups that are excluded from or not equally represented in property ownership, specifically landholding. In addition, certain vulnerable groups face distinct challenges in the course of DID due to their specific socio-economic status and historical and ongoing marginalization.

These disproportionate impacts can amount to (indirect) discrimination when they are the result of state measures and/or when the state has failed to take sufficient measures to address formal and substantive discrimination that has contributed to these differential impacts. As mentioned before, states have a human rights obligation to eliminate not only formal or direct discrimination but also substantive and indirect discrimination. This requires states to take corrective measures taking into account the special vulnerabilities and historical injustices to which certain groups have been subjected.[285] Hence, the disproportionate effect of DID on marginalized groups contravenes this obligation of states.

In some cases, the laws or practices of the state involve direct discrimination in the provision of compensation and resettlement for involuntary displacement.[286] For

279 Robinson 2003, p. 10; see also Mathur 1995, p. 21.

280 UN CESCR, para 10.

281 UN Women, Facts and Figures, available at https://www.unwomen.org/en/news/in-focus/commission-on-the-status-of-women-2012/facts-and-figures accessed 28 June 2025; see also UN CESCR 2022, para 13.

282 UN Women, Facts and Figures (n 281); see also Committee on Economic, Social and Cultural Rights, Concluding observations on the initial report of South Africa, 29 November 2018, E/C.12/ZAF/CO/1, para 61 (the Committee expressed concern in this concluding observation "that women own only 13 per cent of agricultural land and that they still face discrimination in access to land, owing to traditional inheritance practices.").

283 UN Women, Facts and Figures (n 281).

284 Thukral 1996, p. 1501.

285 UN CESCR 2009, para 8.

286 Stanley 2004, p. 15.

instance, some property ownership laws involve gender-based discrimination that disadvantages women when it comes to the entitlement to remedies for eviction or expropriation.[287] In other cases, involuntary displacement and the remedies provided thereof have the effect of perpetuating already existing inequalities and discriminatory practices. For instance, a study conducted on the Tehri Dam in India, which displaced more than 12,000 families,[288] found gender bias in the policy and process of resettlement.[289] The policy endows compensation to the "family" as a unit that will be represented by the head of the family "in whose name the land is entered in the revenue records".[290] Since male family members are usually vested with such status, women were systematically excluded from participation in the compensation process.[291] These kinds of practices that maintain the status quo in property ownership have the effect of perpetuating existing inequalities. Further, these discriminatory practices affect the income-earning capacity of the people concerned, which further exacerbate their marginalization.

Overall, discriminatory practices in the course of DID constitute a violation of the obligation of non-discrimination in conjunction with the right(s) concerned. Hence, the rights to housing as well as the other human rights covered in the subsequent chapters can be violated when the laws, policies, and practices of DID involve unjustified differential treatment that impedes the equal enjoyment of these rights. Violation can also occur when the interferences that DID results in, such as eviction, loss of housing or deterioration of housing conditions, expropriation, and loss or decrease of income, are targeted at or disproportionately affect protected groups. The duty of non-discrimination can also be violated if the state has failed to take positive measures to address structural inequalities and substantive discrimination, for instance in relation to land ownership and resource distribution, which marginalize certain groups.

3.7 Conclusion

Overall, the process and outcome of DID often interfere with and potentially violate the right to adequate housing. This chapter has identified instances where DID can potentially result in the violation of the right to housing, i.e. when it involves forced eviction, when it leads to homelessness or poorer housing conditions, and when it involves discrimination. Some of the interferences that DID involves, however, can be justified based on the limitation clauses under the ICESCR and other relevant human rights frameworks provided that all the conditions stipulated therein are cumulatively fulfilled. Accordingly, limitations on the right to housing can be justified if they are

[287] UN CESCR, para 10; see also Thukral 1996, p. 1500.

[288] International Rivers Network (IRN), Tehri Dam, IRN fact sheet, October 2002, 2.

[289] Bisht 2009, p. 313.

[290] Ibid.

[291] Ibid. This has also been a common practice in other systems, particularly in the past (see Colson 2008, p. 32).

prescribed by law, compatible with the nature of the right, and aimed at advancing the general welfare in a democratic society. As established above, the economic and social reasons that prompted the displacement can be legitimately used to limit rights as long as they are clearly defined and justified under the ‘general welfare’ doctrine. In addition, states should also provide short-term and long-term safeguards to prevent the infringement of rights and mitigate the socio-economic consequences of DID. Overall, the norms on the right to housing along with the pertinent interpretations of human rights bodies can and should be used to inform the process of DID and the safeguards that need to be put in place along the way.

References

African Commission on Human and Peoples’ Rights (2011) Principles and Guidelines on the Implementation of Economic, Social and Cultural Rights in the African Charter on Human and Peoples’ Rights, available at https://achpr.au.int/index.php/en/node/871, accessed 20 July 2025.

Alston P, Quinn G (1987) The Nature and Scope of States Parties’ Obligations under the International Covenant on Economic, Social and Cultural Rights. (1987) 9(2) Human Rights Quarterly 156–229.

Bisht T C (2009) Development-Induced Displacement and Women: The Case of the Tehri Dam, India. (2009) 10(4) The Asia Pacific Journal of Anthropology 301–317.

Colson E (2008) Gendering Those Uprooted by ‘Development’. In: Indra D (ed) Engendering Forced Migration: Theory and Practice. Berghahn Books, New York.

Geneva Academy of International Humanitarian Law and Human Rights (2016) Use of Force in Law Enforcement and the Right to Life: The Role of the Human Rights Council. Academy in Brief No. 6, Geneva.

Giacca G (2014) Economic, Social, and Cultural Rights in Armed Conflicts. Oxford University Press, Oxford.

Lane L (2018) The Horizontal Effect of International Human Rights Law in Practice. (2018) 5(1) European Journal of Comparative Law and Governance 5–88.

Langford M, Du Plessis J (2006) Dignity in Rubble? Forced Evictions and Human Rights Law. Centre on Housing Rights and Evictions, available at https://www.jus.uio.no/ior/english/people/aca/malcolml/dignity-in-the-rubble---human-rights-law-and-forced-evictions.pdf, accessed 20 July 2025.

Leckie S (1995) The Right to Housing. In: Eide A, Krause C, Rosas A (eds) Economic, Social and Cultural Rights: A Textbook, 1st edn. Martinus Nijhoff Publishers.

Mathur M H (1995) The Resettlement of People Displaced by Development Projects: Issues and Approaches. In: Mathur H M, Cernea M (eds) Development, Displacement and Resettlement: Focus on Asian Experience, 1st edn. Vikas Publishing House, New Delhi.

Monnheimer M (2021) Due Diligence Obligations in International Human Rights Law. Cambridge University Press, Cambridge.

Muller A (2009) Limitations to and Derogations from Economic, Social and Cultural Rights. (2009) 9(4) Human Rights Law Review 557–601.

Office of the High Commissioner for Human Rights (OHCHR) (2014) Forced Evictions, Fact Sheet No. 25/Rev.1, United Nations, New York/Geneva, 1 May 2014.

Reidel E, Giacca G, Golay C (2014) The Development of Economic, Social and Cultural Rights in International Law. In: Reidel E, Giacca G, Golay C (eds) Economic, Social and Cultural Rights in International Law: Contemporary Issues and Challenges. Oxford University Press, Oxford.

Robinson C (2003) Risks and Rights: The Causes, Consequences, and Challenges of Development-Induced Displacement. The Brookings Institution-SAIS Project on Internal Displacement, An Occasional Paper.

Saul B (2016) The International Covenant on Economic, Social and Cultural Rights: Travaux Préparatoires 1946–1966, Volume I. Oxford University Press, Oxford.

Saul B, Kinley D, Mowbray J (2014) The International Covenant on Economic, Social and Cultural Rights: Commentary, Cases, and Materials. Oxford University Press, Oxford.

Shelton D, Gould A (2013) Positive and Negative Obligations. In: Shelton D (ed) Oxford Handbook of International Human Rights Law. Oxford University Press.

Special Rapporteur on Adequate Housing (2007) Basic Principles and Guidelines on Development-based Evictions and Displacement, 5 February 2007, A/HRC/4/18.

Ssenyonjo M (2011) Reflections on State Obligations with Respect to Economic, Social and Cultural Rights in International Human Rights Law. (2011) 15(6) The International Journal of Human Rights 969–1012.

Stanley J (2004) Development-induced Displacement and Resettlement. Forced Migration Online.

Tadeg M A (2010) Defining the Minimum Core Obligations-Conundrums in International Human Rights Law and Lessons from the Constitutional Court of South Africa. (2010) 1(1) Mekelle University Law Journal.

Thiele B (2003) Litigating against Forced Evictions under the American Convention on Human Rights. (2003) 21(3) Netherlands Quarterly of Human Rights 463–478.

Thukral E G (1996) Development, Displacement and Rehabilitation: Locating Gender. (1996) 31(24) Economic and Political Weekly 1500–1503.

UN Committee on Economic, Social and Cultural Rights (UN CESCR) (1981) General Comment No. 1: Reporting by States Parties, 27 July 1981, E/1989/22.

UN Committee on Economic, Social and Cultural Rights (UN CESCR) (1990) General Comment No. 3: The Nature of States Parties' Obligations (Article 2, Para 1 of the Covenant), 14 December 1990, E/1991/23.

UN Committee on Economic, Social and Cultural Rights (UN CESCR) (1991) General Comment No. 4: The Right to Adequate Housing (Article 11(1) of the Covenant), 13 December 1991, E/1992/23.

UN Committee on Economic, Social and Cultural Rights (UN CESCR) (1997) General Comment No. 7: The right to adequate housing (Article 11.1): forced evictions, 20 May 1997, E/1998/22.

UN Committee on Economic, Social and Cultural Rights (UN CESCR) (2009) General Comment No. 20: Non-discrimination in economic, social and cultural rights (Article 2, para 2, of the International Covenant on Economic, Social and Cultural Rights), 2 July 2009, E/C.12/GC/20.

UN Committee on Economic, Social and Cultural Rights (UN CESCR) (2022) General Comment No. 26 (2022) on Land and Economic, Social and Cultural Rights, 22 December 2022, E/C.12/GC/26.

UN Human Rights Committee (UNHRC) (1988) General Comment No. 16: Article 17 (Right to Privacy), The Right to Respect of Privacy, Family, Home and Correspondence, and Protection of Honour and Reputation, 27 May 1988, HRI/GEN/1/Rev.9 (Vol. I).

UN Human Rights Committee (UNHRC) (2001) General Comment No. 29: Article 4: Derogations during a State of Emergency, 31 August 2001, CCPR/C/21/Rev.1/Add.11.

Van Hoof G J H (1984) The Legal Nature of Economic, Social and Cultural Rights: a Rebuttal of Some Traditional Views. In: Tomaševski K, Alston P (eds) The Right to Food. International Studies in Human Rights Series, Volume 4.

Walker S (2014) Human Rights Impact Assessments: Emerging Practice and Challenges. In: Riedel E, Giacca G, Golay C (eds) Economic, Social, and Cultural Rights in International Law: Contemporary Issues and Challenges. Oxford University Press, Oxford.

Chapter 4
The Right to Property

Contents

Abstract Another human right that is commonly interfered with and potentially violated in the course of development-induced displacement (DID) is the right to property. The acquisition of land, the (forced) eviction, and disruption of access to common resources often associated with DID ostensibly constitute interferences with the peaceful enjoyment of property. Studies also evince that DID often leads to landlessness or a decrease in landholding as well as homelessness, which contribute to the overall long-term impoverishment of the people affected that often follows displacement. Such interferences and adverse outcomes can breach the right to property when they are not justified and implemented in line with the relevant human rights standards. This chapter, therefore, examines the extent to which DID interferes with the right to property, how such interferences might be justified, and the rights-based safeguards that must be put in place to prevent violations.

Keywords Right to property · Expropriation · Land rights · Landlessness · Arbitrary deprivation of property · Forced eviction

© T.M.C. ASSER PRESS and the authors 2026

R. G. Teshome, *The Human Cost of Development*, Human Rights Research Series 104,
https://doi.org/10.1007/978-94-6265-751-9_4

4.1 Introduction

The right to property, recognized in a number of human rights frameworks, protects the peaceful enjoyment of one's property and offers safeguards against arbitrary deprivation of property. This right, which has both individual and collective aspect, is particularly important for the protection of land rights as these are not recognized as standalone rights in international human rights law. Development-induced displacement (DID) evidently interferes with the right to the peaceful enjoyment of property as it often involves the acquisition of land, eviction from housing, and disruption of access to common resources. These interferences may amount to arbitrary deprivation of property and, hence, constitute a violation if they are not justified by the relevant human rights standards and accompanied by the necessary rights-based safeguards. Against this background, the current chapter examines how the process and outcome of DID interfere with the right to property and the human rights standards states must comply with to justify these interferences and prevent violations.

To this end, the chapter begins by elucidating the recognition of the right to property in Sect. 4.2. It then identifies the subjects, objects, and substantive entitlements of the right in Sect. 4.3. Section 4.4 outlines the measures states are obliged to take in order to realize the right to property. In Sect. 4.5, the chapter explores the permissible limitations on the right and the standards that states need to meet to justify its restriction in the public interest. Subsequently, Sect. 4.6 examines how the entitlements the right to property entails are adversely affected by DID with reference to practical cases. The section also explores whether and how these adverse effects can be justified and outlines the rights-based safeguards states need to put in place to prevent the infringement of property rights.

4.2 The Recognition of the Right to Property

The right to property is recognized under Article 17 of the Universal Declaration of Human Rights (UDHR), which states that "everyone has the right to own property alone as well as in association with others," and that "no one shall be arbitrarily deprived of his property".[1] However, neither of the two Covenants that codify the rights recognized in the UDHR—the International Covenant on Civil and Political Rights (ICCPR) and the International Covenant on Economic, Social and Cultural Rights (ICESCR)—includes a provision explicitly protecting the right to property. This omission can be attributed to the ideological divide between the Western and Eastern blocs, as well as between states of the global North and global South, during

[1] UN General Assembly, Universal Declaration of Human Rights, 10 December 1948, 217 A (III) ('UDHR'), Article 17.

the negotiation process of the two Covenants.[2] The Communist states, led by the Soviet Union at the time, were not convinced that the right to property should be recognized as a human right. They further argued that, even if such a right were to be recognized, its scope and limitations should be determined by domestic law. Another group of states that opposed the inclusion of the right to property consisted of newly decolonized nations as they were concerned about the potential restrictions on their power of expropriation—restrictions that recognition of the right to property would necessarily entail.[3] A closer look at the travaux préparatoires suggests that the disagreement, which ultimately led to the non-inclusion of the right, mainly pertained to the scope of the acceptable limitations on the right to property rather than its recognition as a right.[4]

The UDHR is a soft law instrument that did not initially create binding obligations. In addition, the lack of recognition of the right to property in the two binding Covenants puts into question the normative status of the right to property at the universal level. There is, however, a compelling argument that the provisions of the UDHR in general and Article 17, which guarantees the right to own property and prohibits arbitrary deprivation of property, in particular, have obtained the status of customary international law.[5] As an integral part of the "International Bill of Human Rights",[6] the UDHR is widely accepted by states and most of its provisions reflect the rules of customary international law.[7] Some scholars even go as far as arguing that all provisions of the Declaration have such status, which makes the UDHR a binding instrument.[8]

When it comes to the right to property, specifically, the literature on the subject suggests that there is "generalized and consistent state practice" and a corresponding *opinio juris* that attest to the customary international law status of the right.[9] The right to property is explicitly recognized in most national constitutions and subsidiary

---

[2] Golay and Cismas 2010, p. 3; see also Sprankling 2014, p. 471. The Communist states led by the Soviet Union at the time were not convinced about the recognition of the right to property as a human right. They further contended that even if the right is recognized, the determination of its scope should be left to domestic laws. The other group of states that objected to the inclusion of the right to property were newly decolonized states that did not accept a limitation to their power of expropriation, which the right to property demands (see Sprankling 2014, pp. 471 and 472).

[3] Sprankling 2014, pp. 471 and 472; see also van Banning 2002, pp. 42–44, 47 and 49.

[4] Saul 2016, pp. 506–522 (see the drafting records UN Commission on Human Rights, UN Docs E/CN.4/599, E/CN.4/603, E/CN.4/614, E/CN.4/SR.232); Golay and Cismas 2010, p. 4; see also Jayawickrama 2017, p. 1076.

[5] Sprankling 2014, p. 496.

[6] The "International Bill of Human Rights" includes the UDHR and the two Covenants, i.e. ICCPR and ICESCR.

[7] Hannum 1998, pp. 145 and 148.

[8] Ibid., pp. 148 and 149.

[9] Golay and Cismas 2010, p. 10; see also Sprankling 2014, p. 474; see also General Assembly, Resolution 45/98 Respect for the right of everyone to own property alone as well as in association with others and its contribution to the economic and social development of Member States, 14 December 1990, A/RES/45/98.

laws; more specifically, 95% of states in the world have enshrined the right to property in their domestic laws, particularly within their constitutions.[10] This is also true for former communist countries and decolonized states that had previously opposed the incorporation of the right to property in the two Covenants.[11] There is particularly overwhelming agreement when it comes to the first paragraph of Article 17 of the UDHR, which guarantees the right to own property.[12] The most contentious aspect of this right concerns the definition and scope of "public interest" as a legitimate limitation, as well as the determination of appropriate remedies, such as compensation, in cases of expropriation.[13] Moreover, a significant majority of states in the world are parties to binding treaties that explicitly include the right to property, namely, specialized human rights instruments and regional human rights treaties discussed below.[14] This not only proves the existence of widespread state practice but also reflects the subjective element of *opinio juris*.[15] As the International Court of Justice (ICJ) indicated in *the North Sea Continental Shelf Cases*, "a very widespread and representative" acceptance of a treaty might be evidence that the state practice stemmed from the belief that it is required by international law.[16] This evidence of state practice and *opinio juris* tends to show that the right to property has obtained the status of customary international law, or, at the very least, is in the process of emerging as such.

Furthermore, contrary to the two Covenants, several specialized human rights treaties explicitly guarantee the right to property to the specific groups of persons they seek to protect. These include Articles 15 and 16 of the International Convention on the Elimination of All Forms of Discrimination against Women (CEDAW),[17] Article 15 of the International Convention on the Protection of Migrant Workers and Members of their Families,[18] and Article 12(5) of the Convention on the Rights of Persons with Disabilities (CRPD).[19] In addition, the instruments on indigenous

---

[10] Sprankling 2014, p. 484. (apart from evidencing the existence of general state practice and the move towards the formation of customary international law, this wide recognition of the right to property in domestic laws also arguably amounts to a general principle of law, which is another source of international law (see Sprankling 2014, pp. 484–488)).

[11] Ibid., p. 474.

[12] Golay and Cismas 2010, p. 10.

[13] Ibid.

[14] Sprankling 2014, p. 476 (Sprankling indicated in his article that more than two-thirds of states in the world, 132 states specifically, are parties to those regional treaties).

[15] Ibid., p. 496.

[16] *North Sea Continental Shelf Cases (Federal Republic of Germany v. Denmark; Federal Republic of Germany v. the Netherlands)*, Judgment, International Court of Justice (ICJ), 20 February 1969, para 73, see also Sprankling 2014, p. 496.

[17] UN General Assembly, Convention on the Elimination of All Forms of Discrimination Against Women, 18 December 1979, 1249 United Nations Treaty Series 13 ('CEDAW'), Articles 15 and 16.

[18] UN General Assembly, International Convention on the Protection of the Rights of All Migrant Workers and Members of their Families, 18 December 1990, A/RES/45/158, Article 15.

[19] UN General Assembly, Convention on the Rights of Persons with Disabilities: Resolution/adopted by the General Assembly, 24 January 2007, A/RES/61/106, Articles 5 and 30.

peoples rights, specifically the UN Declaration on the Rights of Indigenous Peoples and ILO Convention No. 169, recognize the property rights of the peoples concerned to the "land they traditionally occupy".[20] These instruments particularly provide protection against forced displacement or relocation,[21] which will be discussed in Chap. 7. Hence, based on the cumulative effect of these instruments and the emerging customary international law rule discussed above, it is safe to conclude that there is a right to property at the universal level that gives rise to binding state obligations.

Several regional human rights treaties also expressly recognize the right to property. Within the Council of Europe, although the European Convention on Human Rights (ECHR) did not include this right initially, the right to property was subsequently introduced by the first Additional Protocol to the Convention.[22] Article 1 of the Protocol guarantees the right to "peaceful enjoyment of [one's] possessions", the deprivation of which can only be justified based on "public interest and subject to the conditions provided for by law and by the general principles of international law."[23] Similarly, Article 21 of the American Convention on Human Rights (ACHR) recognizes the right to "use and enjoy" one's property.[24] Under this provision, deprivation of property is permissible only when it serves the public interest, is carried out in accordance with the law, and is accompanied by the payment of adequate compensation.[25] The African Charter on Human and Peoples' Rights likewise recognizes the right to property under Article 14, which provides: "the right to property shall be guaranteed. It may only be encroached upon in the interest of public need or in the general interest of the community and in accordance with the provisions of appropriate laws."[26] Apart from Article 14, which protects private property, the Charter also contains provisions that recognize rights to public or collective property, i.e. Article 13(3)—equal access to public property[27]—and Article 21—peoples' right to

[20] UN General Assembly, United Nations Declaration on the Rights of Indigenous Peoples: Resolution adopted by the General Assembly, 2 October 2007, A/RES/61/295 ('UNDRIP'), Article 10; see also International Labour Organization (ILO), Indigenous and Tribal Peoples Convention, C169, 27 June 1989, Articles 13–19.

[21] UNDRIP (n 20) Article 10; ILO Convention No. 169 (n 20) Article 16.

[22] Council of Europe, Protocol 1 to the European Convention for the Protection of Human Rights and Fundamental Freedoms, 20 March 1952, 9 ETS, Article 1.

[23] Ibid.

[24] Organization of American States (OAS), American Convention on Human Rights, 22 November 1969, 36 OAS Treaty Series ('American Convention on Human Rights'), Article 21(1).

[25] Ibid., Article 21(2).

[26] Organization of African Unity (OAU), African Charter on Human and Peoples' Rights, 27 June 1981, CAB/LEG/67/3 rev. 5, 21 I.L.M. 58 (1982) ('African Charter'), Article 14.

[27] Ibid., Article 13(3).

"freely dispose of their wealth and natural resources".[28] These provisions, specifically the latter, are particularly relevant in the African context given the continent's colonial history and its experiences of a "pattern of exploitation".[29]

Overall, the right to property is recognized in a number of international and regional human rights instruments. The subsequent sections will elucidate the normative content of the right to property and the corresponding state obligations.

4.3 Normative Content of the Right to Property

Within the UN human rights system, the jurisprudence concerning the general right to property is very limited, if not non-existent. Moreover, the right to property as a human right has not received substantial attention in academic literature. This normative underdevelopment renders a systematic analysis of the relevant legal norms focusing on the UN system, which this part of the book seeks to do, particularly challenging. To address this gap, this section will draw on general principles of law, norms developed in relation to other rights, and other fields of international law.

In contrast, the regional human rights systems have developed more extensive jurisprudence on the right to property. The normative content of the right, as well as the corresponding state obligations, have been clarified through case law and interpretative documents issued by regional human rights monitoring bodies. While these regional systems fall outside the primary focus of this chapter, the following sections will refer to them where appropriate to elucidate the applicable norms and concepts associated with the right to property.[30]

4.3.1 Subjects (Right-Holders) of the Right to Property[31]

The right to property is both an individual and a collective right. This is evident from the wording of Article 17 of the UDHR, which recognizes "the right to own

---

[28] Ibid., Article 21.

[29] Golay and Cismas 2010, p. 6; see also *Social and Economic Rights Action Center (SERAC) and Center for Economic and Social Rights (CESR) v. Nigeria*, Communication No. 155/96, 27 October 2001, African Commission on Human and Peoples' Rights, para 56.

[30] While the case law and interpretative documents of a given human rights monitoring body might not be formally used to interpret the human rights frameworks of a different system, they play a crucial role in the development of human rights norms across systems. This is also evident from the practices of several human rights monitoring bodies in different systems, which frequently refer to and draw inspiration from one another.

[31] As the subject of the right to property has different aspects and components that are also relevant in the DID discourse, it is important to discuss this more extensively in a separate section, unlike the other two rights covered in this part of the book.

property alone as well as in association with others".[32] The collective dimension of the right to property can take two forms. The first is when property rights are attached to a certain group identity as is the case for indigenous peoples. In these cases, the property claims of the members of the group are contingent on their identification as such. For instance, indigenous peoples are accorded special property rights to the land they traditionally occupy due to their indigenous status.[33] This is evident from the judgment of the African Commission in the *Endorois case*—a case concerning the removal of the people concerned from their ancestral land for development purposes[34]—and the judgment of the Inter-American Court in the *Awas Tingni case*.[35] After it identified the Endorois community as "indigenous people", the African Commission concluded that the Endorois people's rights to their ancestral land are protected under Article 14, which the state encroached upon by forcefully relocating them.[36] Similarly, the Inter-American Court recognized, in the *Awas Tingni case*, that indigenous peoples' collective rights to the land they traditionally occupy are protected under the right to property.[37] The other form of a collective right to property exists in relation to common properties. These include communal land, such as grazing land and forests, that communities use to sustain or support their livelihood.[38] This distinction is particularly relevant in the context of DID as several case studies have demonstrated that the latter aspect or form of collective right is not usually taken into account in the provision of compensation or resettlement.[39]

The other important feature of the right to property in relation to its subjects is that both natural and legal persons can be right-holders.[40] The first additional protocol to the ECHR explicitly mentions this aspect of the right to property; Article 1 of

[32] UDHR (n 1) Article 17.

[33] UNDRIP (n 20) Article 10; see also ILO Convention No. 169 (n 20) Articles 13–19.

[34] *Centre for Minority Rights Development (Kenya) and Minority Rights Group International on behalf of Endorois Welfare Council v. Kenya*, 276/2003, African Commission on Human and Peoples' Rights, 4 February 2010.

[35] *Case of the Mayagna (Sumo) Awas Tingni Community v Nicaragua*, Merit, Inter-American Court of Human Rights, 31 August 2001.

[36] *Endorois case* (n 34) paras 185–209.

[37] *Awas Tingni case* (n 35) paras 148 and 149 (the Court came to this decision regardless of the fact that the wording of Article 21 of the American Convention on Human Rights does not indicate the collective aspect of the right unlike Article 17 of the UDHR).

[38] *Doğan and Others v. Turkey*, Applications 8803-8811/02, 8813/02 and 8815-8819/02, Judgment, European Court of Human Rights, 29 June 2004, paras 138–139; see also *Endorois case* (n 34) para 189.

[39] Cernea 1995, p. 252.

[40] In principle, human rights are guaranteed to natural persons (individually or collectively), which is also evident from the main rationale of these rights, i.e. human dignity and equality, among others, and the way human rights frameworks are formulated. However, in some cases, the full realization of certain rights, such as freedom of religion, freedom of expression, and freedom of association, might necessitate the protection of legal persons under the human rights law regime. In these cases, some human rights monitoring bodies, particularly the ECtHR, have also extended their jurisdiction *ratione personae* to legal persons (see Tomuschat 2014, p. 117; see also *Sunday Times v United Kingdom*, Application No 6538/74, A/30, [1979] ECHR 1, (1979–80) 2 EHRR 245, (1979) 76 LSG 328, IHRL 21 (ECHR 1979), Judgment, European Court of Human Rights, 26 April 1979; see also

the Protocol states that "[e]very natural or legal person is entitled to the peaceful enjoyment of his possessions."[41] On the contrary, the UDHR and the other regional human rights frameworks do not clearly specify whether or not legal persons are entitled to this right; nor is this evident from the wording of the provisions concerned. However, by its very nature, the right to property is capable of being enjoyed by both natural and legal persons, although the existing norms or jurisprudence do not decisively show that this is accepted by all systems.

4.3.2 Objects of the Right to Property

The object of the right to property pertains to the tangible and intangible goods or interests that the right protects. While this is not explicitly stated in the relevant provisions of the universal and regional human rights frameworks mentioned above,[42] it can be inferred from the interpretations of human rights (quasi-)judicial bodies. It is widely accepted that the concept of property has an "autonomous meaning", which implies that its interpretation is not dependent on definitions provided in domestic legal systems.[43] Moreover, it covers movable and immovable assets,[44] ownership or possession of tangible things, and other pecuniary interests that form part of one's asset including "legitimate expectations" yet to be acquired.[45] For instance, contractual rights, entitlement to compensation and future income, among others, have been regarded as property in several cases.[46]

It is evident from the interpretive documents and case law of the human rights monitoring bodies that one of the principal objects of the right to property is land.[47]

Civil Liberties Organisation v Nigeria, communication 101/93, African Commission on Human and Peoples' Rights, 22 March 1995, para 17; see also *Article 19 v Eritrea*, communication 275/03, African Commission on Human and Peoples' Rights, 30 May 2007, para 107). However, the UN treaty bodies, particularly the Human Rights Committee, have not followed suit in recognizing legal persons as right-holders (see Tomuschat 2014, p. 117).

[41] Protocol 1 to the ECHR (n 22) Article 1.

[42] Golay and Cismas 2010, p. 11.

[43] *Iatridis v. Greece*, Application no. 31107/96, Judgment, European Court of Human Rights, 25 March 1999, para 54; see also *Awas Tingni case* (n 35) para 146.

[44] *Case of the Yakye Axa Indigenous Community v Paraguay*, Merits, Inter-American Court of Human Rights, 17 June 2005, para 137.

[45] *Doğan and Others v. Turkey*, n 38, paras 138–139; see also *Case of the "Five Pensioners" v. Peru*, Merits, Inter-American Court of Human Rights, 28 February 2003, para 84; see also African Commission on Human and Peoples' Rights 2011, para 53.

[46] *Malhous v. the Czech Republic*, Application no. 33071/96, Judgment, The European Court of Human Rights (the Grand Chamber), 13 December 2000; see also *Anheuser-Busch Inc. v. Portugal*, Application no. 73049/01, Judgment, The European Court of Human Rights (the Grand Chamber), 11 January 2007, para 64.

[47] Golay and Cismas 2010, p. 14; see also African Commission on Human and Peoples' Rights 2011, para 54; see also *Endorois case* (n 34); see also *Case of the Yakye Axa Indigenous Community v Paraguay* (n 44).

Land as an object of property rights is particularly important in the context of DID as it commonly involves expropriation of land and/or removal of the individuals or people(s) concerned from their land.

Although land rights are not explicitly recognized as standalone rights in general human rights instruments, they can be derived from the right to property and from several other rights whose effective enjoyment depends on access to and use of land.[48] More specifically, the realization of the right to an adequate standard of living, which includes the rights to food, water, and housing, is contingent on access to, utilization of, and control over land.[49] The right to food, for instance, entails access to the means of obtaining adequate food,[50] including the opportunity of "feeding oneself directly from productive land or other natural resources".[51] Thus, the right to food is interfered with and potentially violated when people that make a living from land are removed from such land without being provided with alternative means.[52] Similarly, the acquisition of land and/or denial of access to land could disrupt access to water sources, which is protected under the right to water.[53] Land rights also emanate from the right to adequate housing. First, access to and use of land are "the means by which the right to housing can be realized"[54] necessitating their protection under the right to housing regime. Second, the legal security of tenure, which requires protection against forced evictions and other arbitrary interferences,[55] is also applicable in the context of land. The definition of forced eviction also covers the involuntary removal of individuals or groups from their land without the provision of legal and other necessary safeguards.[56] Consequently, eviction from land should be provided by law, justified on the basis of the "general welfare", and accompanied by adequate safeguards discussed in the previous chapter in relation to the right to housing.

---

[48] OHCHR 2015, p. 3; African Commission on Human and Peoples' Rights 2011, para 54.

[49] OHCHR 2015, p. 19; see also UN CESCR 2022, paras 1 and 6–8; see also Kanosue 2015, pp. 652 and 653.

[50] UN CESCR 1999, para 6.

[51] Ibid., para 12.

[52] UN Committee on Economic, Social and Cultural Rights (CESCR), Consideration of reports submitted by States parties under Articles 16 and 17 of the Covenant: concluding observations of the Committee on Economic, Social and Cultural Rights: Madagascar, 16 December 2009, E/C.12/MDG/CO/2, para 12 (in this concluding observation, the Committee expressed its concern that the acquisition of "cultivable lands" compromises the realization of the right to food); see also Human Rights Council 2009; see also Kanosue 2015, p. 653; see also OHCHR 2015, p. 19.

[53] UN CESCR 2003, para 12; see also Kanosue 2015, p. 653. Even if water is not specifically mentioned under Article 11 of the CESCR, the Committee in its general comment affirmed that the right to water is part of the right to an adequate standard of living (see UN CESCR 2003, para 3).

[54] OHCHR 2015, p. 23; see also Human Rights Council 2008; see also UN CESCR 1991, para 8(e) (the Committee stressed that states' policies should aim to increase access to land, especially for socially and economically disadvantaged groups).

[55] UN CESCR 1991, para 8.

[56] UN CESCR 1997, para 3.

Cultural rights provided under the two Covenants and the relevant regional human rights frameworks also protect land.[57] This is based on the recognition that land is more than an economic asset and it has "cultural and spiritual significance",[58] particularly for indigenous peoples whose way of life is highly intertwined with the land they traditionally occupy.[59] Apart from these general human rights instruments, land rights are also recognized in specialized human rights frameworks with respect to the specific groups they protect, such as women, IDPs, indigenous peoples, and peasants.[60] Overall, the human right to land emanates from its pecuniary nature or value to which the right to property extends and its significance in the realization of other human rights. There is, however, a normative gap since most of the norms and the jurisprudence on land rights have been developed in relation to indigenous peoples,[61] and a general right to land is yet to be recognized as a standalone right.

The current chapter focuses on land rights from the perspective of the right to property for two reasons. First, the right to property formulates what land rights entail more comprehensively than the other rights that indirectly protect land. Second, since some of these other rights, such as the right to housing and the right to work, are discussed under separate chapters, their discussion in relation to land rights is not necessary here.

4.3.3 Substantive Entitlements of the Right to Property

One of the issues heavily debated during the drafting process of Article 17 of the UDHR was whether the right to property only protects existing property claims or whether it also entitles the right to own or have access to a minimum amount of property that is essential to meet one's basic needs.[62] One of the earlier drafts of the provision seems to support the latter; the draft reads, "[e]veryone has the right to own such property as meets the essential needs of decent living, that helps to maintain the dignity of the individual and of the home, and shall not be arbitrarily deprived of it."[63] This version of the draft was replaced by the current version, which protects existing

---

57 UN General Assembly, International Covenant on Economic, Social and Cultural Rights, 16 December 1966, 993 United Nations Treaty Series 3 ('ICESCR'), Article 15; see also UN General Assembly, International Covenant on Civil and Political Rights, 16 December 1966, 999 United Nations Treaty Series 171, Article 27; see also UDHR (n 1) Article 27.

58 Kanosue 2015, p. 643.

59 Charters 2018, p. 398.

60 OHCHR 2015, p. 3.

61 FIAN International 2017, p. 16.

62 van Banning 2002, pp. 35–38.

63 UN Economic and Social Council, Commission on Human Rights, Drafting Committee, Report of the Drafting Committee to the Commission on Human Rights, 21 May 1948, UN Doc E/CN.4/95.

property claims from arbitrary deprivation.[64] A similar approach was followed by the regional human rights frameworks that provide for the right to property. This individualistic formulation of the right and its potential in perpetuating income or wealth disparity remains one of the criticisms of the right to property as formulated in human rights instruments.[65] Against this background, the following are the main substantive entitlements the right to property guarantees.

The first entitlement is the right to peaceful enjoyment of property.[66] Peaceful enjoyment, first, involves undisrupted access to one's property.[67] Second, it guarantees the right to freely utilize one's property, which includes "the right to undisturbed possession, use and control of such property however the owner(s) deem fit".[68] This is not limited to a mere right to use the property in question, rather it entails effective control on or agency in decision-making concerning the property.[69]

The other entitlement the right to property provides is security of tenure. Security of tenure refers to protection against arbitrary deprivation of property. This is explicitly enshrined in the respective provisions of most of the universal and regional human rights instruments providing for this right.[70] Deprivation of property should not be construed narrowly as only meaning expropriation or acquisition of property; rather, it means interference with any of the entitlements that the right to property guarantees described above.[71] This includes denial of access, destruction, and expropriation of property.[72] As the term "arbitrary" implies, deprivation of property does not always constitute a violation. There are certain circumstances in which a state can use its eminent domain power to expropriate private property for public purposes in

[64] Some representatives during the negotiation strongly contested the new version (see UN General Assembly, The Third Committee, Summary Record of the Ninety-Third Meeting, 4 October 1948, UN Doc A/C.3/SR.93, paras 9–10).

[65] On the other hand, this shortcoming of the right to property is partly mitigated by the recognition of economic, social, and cultural rights, which envisage the provision of minimum essential goods and services, such as food, housing, health, and education, that are indispensable for a dignified life (see Glendon 1998, pp. 1164–1190).

[66] *Sudan Human Rights Organisation & Centre on Housing Rights and Evictions (COHRE) v. Sudan*, 279/03-296/05, African Commission on Human and Peoples' Rights, 27 May 2009, para 193.

[67] *Endorois case* (n 34) para 186.

[68] Ibid.; see also *African Commission on Human and Peoples' Rights v. Republic of Kenya*, Application No. 006/2012, African Court on Human and Peoples' Rights, 26 May 2017 ('*Ogiek case*'), para 124.

[69] *Endorois case* (n 34) para 206; see also *Case of the Saramaka People v Suriname*, Preliminary objections, merits, reparations and costs, IACHR Series C no. 172, IHRL 3046 (IACHR 2007), 28th November 2007 ('*Saramaka case*'), para 122.

[70] UDHR (n 1) Article 17(2); see also African Charter (n 26) Article 14; see also Protocol 1 to the ECHR (n 22) Article 1; see also American Convection on Human Rights (n 24) Article 21(2).

[71] Jayawickrama 2017, p. 1080.

[72] Ibid.

accordance with the law and international human rights norms.[73] These conditions will be further discussed below under the section on justified limitations on the right to property.

The legal status that guarantees the entitlements discussed above can take the form of ownership or possession. However, a formal title to the property concerned is not a necessary precondition for the right to property to exist or to be claimed.[74] This can be inferred, for instance, from the protection of indigenous peoples' land rights and the norms on legal security of tenure under the right to housing regime. Indigenous peoples are entitled to rights to their ancestral land irrespective of the existence or absence of a formal legal title.[75] Moreover, the legal security of tenure that the right to housing entails applies irrespective of the type of tenure.[76] This interpretation can be applied to the right to property by analogy as the underlying rationale of providing security of tenure in both cases is similar, i.e. protecting right-holders from arbitrary interference, and the two rights are highly interdependent. This principle was also affirmed by the African Commission in the case of *COHRE v. Sudan* where it found a violation of the right to property due to the destruction of victims' properties by state agents.[77] In this case, the Commission indicated that protection from arbitrary interference with the peaceful enjoyment of property does not depend on the existence of a formal title.[78] A similar principle is applied in the *Endorois case* where indigenous peoples' property right to their ancestral land was an issue. Indigenous peoples usually do not have formal titles to the land they traditionally occupy, which should not affect their entitlement to the land concerned.[79] The Inter-American Court of Human Rights had also affirmed this in the *case of Awas Tingni* where it stressed that "possession of the land should suffice for indigenous communities lacking real title to property of the land to obtain official recognition of that property."[80] Overall, the right to property guarantees the peaceful enjoyment of property and protection from arbitrary interference, regardless of whether a formal legal title to the property exists.

---

[73] *The Nubian Community in Kenya v. The Republic of Kenya*, Communication 317/2006, African Commission on Human and Peoples' Rights, 30 May 2016, para 153; see also *COHRE v. Sudan* (n 66) para 193.

[74] Jayawickrama 2017, p. 1082.

[75] UNDRIP (n 20) Article 10; see also ILO Convention No. 169 (n 20) Articles 13–19.

[76] UN CESCR 1991, para 8(a).

[77] *COHRE v. Sudan* (n 66) para 205.

[78] Ibid.

[79] *Endorois case* (n 34) paras 187–190 (The Commission also noted that possession is not a necessary precondition for the entitlements the right to property gives rise to, which is "indigenous land restitution rights" in this particular case, to exist.(see *Endorois case* (n 34) para 209).

[80] *Awas Tingni case* (n 35) para 151.

4.4 State Obligations Related to the Right to Property

The duty to respect the right to property obliges states to refrain from interfering with the peaceful enjoyment of property, for instance, through unjustified expropriation or destruction of property.[81] States also have a duty to protect the property rights of individuals or groups against interference by third parties. This includes putting in place legislative, judicial, and administrative measures in order to prevent violations and to provide remedies when violations happen.[82] The duty to fulfil, which is a positive obligation, requires states to facilitate and take necessary steps to enhance the realization of rights.[83] The scope of the duty to fulfil is the most contentious aspect of state obligations when it comes to the right to property,[84] since this right as currently formulated does not necessarily entail access to the minimum essential property. However, states are still obliged to support the efforts of individuals and groups in obtaining essential properties and to take necessary positive measures to improve the enjoyment of the right.[85] This positive obligation can be inferred, for instance, from the duties established under the rights to food and housing, which include facilitating access to property essential for the realization of these rights, such as land and housing.[86] Among the measures required under these positive obligations are providing registration services for immovable properties and taking "affirmative action to correct past inequalities".[87] This is particularly essential in relation to certain properties, such as housing and land.

More specifically, states are obliged to take various legal or policy and practical measures in order to protect the entitlements described above. One of these measures is providing security of tenure through legal and other necessary mechanisms.[88] This includes incorporating the right into domestic law; the law should also specify the circumstances and conditions in accordance with which acquisition of property or expropriation can be justified.[89] States are also required to take steps in order to provide formal titles to certain immovable properties, particularly land. For

---

[81] Golay and Cismas 2010, p. 21; see also van Banning 2002, pp. 224 and 225. In the case of *Malawi African Association and other v. Mauritania*, the African Commission found the violation of the right to property due to "the confiscation and looting of the property of Black Mauritanians and the expropriation or destruction of their land and houses" by state agents (see *Malawi African Association and Others v. Mauritania*, Communication Nos. 54/91, 61/91, 98/93, 164/97 à 196/97 and 210/98, African Commission on Human and Peoples' Rights, 11 May 2000, para 128).

[82] Golay and Cismas 2010, p. 21; see also van Banning 2002, p. 227; see also *SERAC v. Nigeria* (n 29) para 57 (In this case, the African Commission stressed that the Nigerian government contravened its duty to protect by giving a "green light" to private companies to engage in activities that interfered with the rights of Ogoni people and by facilitating their operation (see para 58)).

[83] African Commission on Human and Peoples' Rights 2011, para 10.

[84] van Banning 2002, p. 230.

[85] Ibid., pp. 230–232.

[86] UN CESCR 1991, paras 8(c) and 10; see also UN CESCR 1999, paras 13 and 26.

[87] van Banning 2002, p. 232.

[88] African Commission on Human and Peoples' Rights 2011, para 55(a).

[89] Ibid., para 55(b).

instance, in the case of the *Nubian Community in Kenya*, the African Commission dealt with the issue of whether or not the failure of the state to recognize the property rights of the community and the "dispossession of their property through forced evictions" amounted to a violation of the right to property.[90] In addressing this issue, the Commission stressed the state's obligation to guarantee security of tenure through appropriate means.[91] Failure of the state to comply with this obligation, which left the community concerned in "a precarious situation of insecurity and uncertainty", was one of the reasons a violation of the right to property was found in this case.[92] Moreover, this lack of security of tenure had led to the frequent forced evictions of the Nubian community from their homes and land.[93] Similarly, the Commission also indicated in the *Endorois case* that states should strive to give formal titles to communities that traditionally occupy land.[94] Lack of formal security of tenure, particularly in relation to land, puts right holders in "weak bargaining positions",[95] which in turn widens the expropriation power of the state. Overall, the right to property imposes a range of negative and positive obligations on states.

4.5 Limitations on the Right to Property

As is the case with most human rights, the right to property is not an absolute right. Legitimate limitations can be imposed by states on ownership or possession, control, and enjoyment of property. This also coincides with the eminent domain doctrine briefly discussed in Chap. 2. According to this doctrine, control over resources, particularly land, falls under the inherent power of the state, which, in turn, empowers a state to acquire private or communal properties for public purposes.[96] It is also a rule of customary international law that the state can expropriate private property for public purposes and with the payment of adequate compensation.[97]

This inherent power of states is also recognized in international human rights law through the limitation clauses of the provisions on the right to property and the interpretation of these clauses by human rights monitoring bodies. This is evident from the wording of the respective provisions of the UDHR and the regional human rights instruments providing for the right to property, which prohibit deprivation of

[90] *The Nubian Community in Kenya vs The Republic of Kenya* (n 73) para 154.

[91] Ibid., para 160.

[92] Ibid.

[93] Ibid., para 161.

[94] *Endorois case* (n 34) paras 196–199.

[95] Kanosue 2015, p. 648.

[96] Ramanathan 1996, p. 1488; see also United Nations Conference on Trade and Development, Expropriation, UNCTAD Series on Issues in International Investment Agreements II, 2013, 1.

[97] Waincymer 2009, pp. 290–292.

property when it is "arbitrary".[98] This indicates that deprivation of property can be justified when it is not arbitrary. As the African Commission, for instance, asserted in the case of *COHRE v. Sudan* and reiterated in subsequent cases, "states are in certain circumstances entitled, among other things, to control the use of property in accordance with the public or general interest, by enforcing such laws as they deem necessary for the purpose."[99] For example, measures intended to address structural inequalities and social injustices in the use and control of property, particularly land, can be justified as permissible limitations.[100] It is worth reiterating here that one of the shortcomings of the right to property is that it perpetuates economic inequalities and discriminatory practices since it usually protects already existing possessions. In other words, property rights can have the effect of maintaining the unfair distribution of wealth.[101] Hence, the limitation clause arguably gives a leeway for states to take measures that have a redistributive effect in favour of marginalized groups provided that they comply with the requirements stipulated therein.[102] This also corresponds with the social function of property discussed below.

The limitation on the right to property or deprivation of property needs to comply with certain conditions. First, the limitation must be prescribed by law, which needs to be specific, clear, and accessible.[103] Second, the limitation should be aimed at advancing the general public interest.[104] The limitation of property rights in the interest of the general public correlates with the notion of the "social function of property". This notion, which is one of the concepts extensively discussed during the drafting process of Article 17 of the UDHR, demands that private property should be accessed and used in a way that contributes to the collective wellbeing of society.[105] Moreover, while all persons have a right to peacefully enjoy their property, they also have an obligation not to do so in a manner that is harmful to others.[106] This, according to Van Banning, necessitates that "the rules regulating property are to be determined by the relationship between the needs of the individual and the needs of society in connection with the property concerned."[107] Thus, the social function of property encompasses two potentially competing aspects: property as an individual

---

[98] UDHR (n 1) Article 17; see also African Charter (n 26) Article 14; see also American Convention on Human Rights (n 24) Article 21(2).

[99] *COHRE v Sudan* (n 66) para 193; see also *The Nubian Community in Kenya v The Republic of Kenya* (n 73) para 153.

[100] OHCHR 2015, p. 53.

[101] Ibid. ("Measures aimed to rectify structural inequalities in access to, use of and control over land, such as land or agrarian reform or elimination of discrimination against women with regard to inheritance or ownership of land, may therefore limit the right to property of some.").

[102] OHCHR 2015, p. 53.

[103] Golay and Cismas 2010, p. 15; see also van Banning 2002, p. 93; see also *Lithgow v United Kingdom*, Applications Nos. 9006/80, 9262/81, 9263/81, 9265/81, 9266/81, 9313/81, 9405/81, Merits, European Court of Human Rights, 8 July 1986.

[104] van Banning 2002, p. 95.

[105] Foster 2011, pp. 102 and 103; see also van Banning 2002, p. 146.

[106] Foster 2011, p. 103; see also van Banning 2002, p. 146.

[107] van Banning 2002, p. 146.

entitlement and as a means to achieve the general welfare.[108] This necessitates a balancing exercise to be undertaken.

This balancing exercise is done using the principles of necessity and proportionality, which collectively form the third condition of limitation. A limitation should not only be necessary and the least intrusive alternative to achieve the general public interest sought but also be proportionate, a balance "which must exist between the means employed and the aim sought to be realized."[109] Overall, restrictions imposed on the right to property should strike a fair balance between the competing interests of advancing public interest and protecting individual rights.[110]

The fourth condition of limitation, which is specific to the right to property, is a provision of "adequate compensation".[111] While the requirement of "just compensation" was explicitly mentioned in the earlier draft of Article 17 of the UDHR,[112] it did not make it to the final draft. However, the obligation of states to make good the damage incurred by right holders as a result of interference with the enjoyment of the right to property, particularly for deprivation of property, reflects a general principle of law.[113] Similarly, compensation is not explicitly mentioned under Article 1 of the first Additional Protocol to the ECHR, which guarantees the right to property.[114] The jurisprudence of the ECtHR, however, clearly indicates that the right to property entails a provision of adequate compensation for deprivation of property.[115] According to the Court, "the protection of the right to property…would be largely illusory and ineffective" without the provision of compensation for deprivation of property.[116] The same reasoning can be employed to read the requirement of compensation into the UDHR and the other human rights frameworks that provide for the right to property. Moreover, arguably it is also a customary international law rule that deprivation of property entails payment of just compensation for the loss sustained.[117] The rationale behind this is that when the public interest justifies a deprivation of property "the loss should not fall upon the individual whose property

---

[108] Ibid., pp. 146 and 147.

[109] Golay and Cismas 2010, p. 15; see also van Banning 2002, p. 97.

[110] Jayawickrama 2017, p. 1084, see also Golay and Cismas 2010, p. 15; see also van Banning 2002, p. 97.

[111] Golay and Cismas 2010, p. 17.

[112] United Nations Economic and Social Council, Statement of Essential Human Rights Presented by the Delegation of Panama, E/HR/3, 26 April 1946, at 8. The first draft of the Article reads, "[e]veryone has the right to own property under general law. The state shall not deprive anyone of his property except for a public purpose and with just compensation" (see the statement, at 8).

[113] Golay and Cismas 2010, p. 10.

[114] Protocol 1 to the ECHR (n 22) Article 1.

[115] *James and others v. The United Kingdom*, Application no. 8793/79, Judgment, The European Court of Human Rights, 21 February 1986, para 54; see also Golay and Cismas 2010, pp. 16 and 17.

[116] *James and others v. The United Kingdom*, n 381, para 54; see also Golay and Cismas 2010, pp. 16 and 17.

[117] Golay and Cismas 2010, p. 10.

is taken but should be borne by the public as a whole."[118] Hence, limitation of property rights without the provision of compensation amounts to "arbitrary deprivation of property".

The other important and often controversial issue in relation to compensation is the determination of the type and the amount of compensation due. The standards used in the determination of compensation may vary from jurisdiction to jurisdiction. For instance, the ECtHR uses the market value of the property or "an amount reasonably related to [this] value" to determine whether the compensation provided by the state is adequate, although an amount lesser than this can be justified in exceptional cases.[119] The same approach is followed by the African human rights system. According to the African Commission, the market value of the property should be taken into account to determine the amount of compensation save for exceptional circumstances where a lesser amount can be justified.[120]

In relation to this, the general principle accepted in the law of remedies is that "[compensation should] aim to place an aggrieved party in the same position as he or she would have been had no injury occurred."[121] In this context, compensation encompasses both monetary and non-monetary remedies provided to redress the loss or damage incurred as the result of interference with property rights. In the *Chorzow Factory Case*,[122] the Permanent Court of International Justice (PCIJ) stressed that:

> [R]eparation must, as far as possible, wipe out all the consequences of the illegal act and reestablish the situation which would, in all probability, have existed if that act had not been committed. Restitution in kind, or, if this is not possible, payment of a sum corresponding to the value which a restitution in kind would bear; the award, if need be, of damages for loss sustained which would not be covered by restitution in kind or payment in place of it.[123]

Thus, as noted in this case and also affirmed in several human rights cases, restitution is the preferred remedy to make good the damage incurred by the victim.[124] Where restitution is not possible, monetary compensation and other specific non-monetary remedies, depending on the circumstances of the case, should be awarded.[125] It is

---

[118] Jayawickrama 2017, p. 1087; see also African Commission on Human and Peoples' Rights 2011, para 55(e).

[119] *Lithgow and Others v. the United Kingdom* (n 103) para 121; see also Golay and Cismas 2010, pp. 17 and 18 (the Court also leaves a wide margin of appreciation for states in the determination of compensation).

[120] African Commission on Human and Peoples' Rights 2011, para 55(e).

[121] Shelton 2015, p. 19.

[122] While this case relates to reparation for breach of international obligation in the context of inter-state obligations, the underlying principles it established can be employed to assess the adequacy of compensation in international human rights law, particularly in relation to the right to property. The principles established in this case concerning reparation had been accepted as general principles of international law and used in various fields of international law. These principles are particularly relevant in the context of expropriation of property to which the subject matter of the case relates.

[123] *Factory At Chorzów, Germany v Poland*, Judgment, Claim for Indemnity, Merits, Judgment No 13 (1928) PCIJ Series A No 17, ICGJ 255 (PCIJ 1928), 13th September 1928, 47.

[124] Shelton 2015, p. 298.

[125] Ibid., pp. 315 and 319.

important to note that the above case and the norms in the law of remedies relate to the provision of remedies after a violation or breach of obligation has occurred. In the context of the right to property, compensation needs to be provided as a part of the conditions of limitation in order to preclude violation. With this understanding, the underlying principles established in the law of remedies and the case cited above can inform the determination of "just compensation".

In the context of DID, restitution is hardly possible since the implementation of development projects commonly results in permanent relocation.[126] However, when restitution is not possible, non-monetary remedies that can redress the real property rights lost, i.e. replacement of real properties, should be prioritized.[127] This will be further discussed subsequently in relation to the expropriation of property for development purposes. Overall, limitations imposed on the right to property—including the acquisition of property for development purposes—need to be provided by law, promote public interest, and be accompanied by a provision of sufficient compensation.

4.6 Interference with the Right to Property in the Course of Development-Induced Displacement

In light of the substantive content of the right to property outlined above, the (forced) eviction and expropriation that DID involves inevitably interfere with the right to the peaceful enjoyment of property. These interferences might be caused by the process or the outcome of displacement. This section explores how DID interferes with the right to property with reference to practical cases as well as when and how these interferences can be justified as permissible limitations.

Generally, a violation of the right to property may occur when DID involves expropriation or land acquisition that is not justified under the relevant human rights norms, when it results in landlessness or a significant reduction in landholding, or when it entails forced eviction, which will be further elaborated in the following subsections. Additionally, the right to property can also be violated when DID involves direct or indirect discrimination. However, as the legal standards on non-discrimination are similar to those discussed under the right to housing (Chap. 3), this chapter will not address them in detail here.

[126] The Special Rapporteur on Adequate Housing 2007, para 64.

[127] Ibid., para 60.

4.6.1 Expropriation or Land Acquisition

Expropriation refers to the acquisition of private property by the state for public purposes.[128] This can take two forms: direct (de jure) expropriation where the state formally seizes private property or transfers the title to third parties and indirect (de facto) expropriation where there is no "formal transfer of title or outright seizure" but the measures taken by the state result in the deprivation of property rights.[129] In the former case, expropriation is often provided by law and the action taken by the state is clear.[130] In the latter case, expropriation might not be prescribed by law or be evident from the measure taken by the state and, thus, the effect of such a measure on the enjoyment of property rights needs to be assessed to determine whether or not there is expropriation. The widely accepted definition of indirect expropriation was articulated in the *Starrett Housing case*,[131] an investment arbitration decision, the relevant part of which reads:

> ....measures taken by a State can interfere with property rights to such an extent that these rights are rendered so useless that they must be deemed to have been expropriated, even though the State does not purport to have expropriated them and the legal title to the property formally remains with the original owner.[132]

The African Commission has also made a similar assertion in the case of *COHRE v. Sudan* where it stressed, "the fact that the victims cannot derive their livelihood from what they possessed for generations means they have been deprived of the use of their property..."[133] Hence, even if a state does not formally expropriate a particular property, its actions may still constitute expropriation or acquisition of property if they render the peaceful enjoyment—that is, the use and control—of the property impossible. This distinction between direct and indirect expropriation is also relevant in the context of DID. In some cases, development projects might have the effect of disrupting access to and use of property, although the state did not go

[128] In this work, the terms 'expropriation' and 'land acquisition' will be used interchangeably when the property in question is land.

[129] United Nations Conference on Trade and Development, Expropriation: UNCTAD Series on Issues in International Investment Agreements II (New York and Geneva: United Nations 2012) 6 and 7; see also Jayawickrama 2017, p. 1080.

[130] United Nations Conference on Trade and Development (n 129) 7.

[131] The Starrett Housing case is an investment arbitration case decided by the Iran-US Tribunal. In this case, the Tribunal dealt with the issue of whether or not the measure taken by Iran amounts to expropriation. The Tribunal decided that even if there is no formal law to that effect since the measures taken by the state had "deprived of the effective use, control and benefits of [the claimants'] property rights", it amounts to expropriation (see *Starrett Housing Corporation v Iran*, Case No. 24, Iran-US Claims Tribunal, Interlocutory Award (Award No. ITL 32-24-1), 19 December 1983, para 66 and 67). It has to be noted that this case is not decided by a human rights monitoring body and, hence, it cannot be directly used to interpret any of the human rights frameworks. However, it is an important source to understand what indirect expropriation constitutes.

[132] *Starrett Housing case* (n 131) para 66; see also United Nations Conference on Trade and Development (n 129) 7 and 8.

[133] *COHRE v Sudan* (n 66) para 205; see also *Dogan and Others v Turkey* (n 38) para 143.

through a formal expropriation procedure. Thus, the expropriation that DID entails and its interference with the right to property need to be seen in light of this broader understanding.

Generally, expropriation, whether de jure or de facto, interferes with the use and control of property, which the right to peaceful enjoyment of property guarantees. It amounts to arbitrary deprivation of property if it does not comply with the requirements of the limitation of the right discussed above, i.e. provided by law, aimed at promoting the public interest, necessary and proportionate, and followed by due compensation and other necessary remedies. One of the problems often witnessed in the process of DID is that the law providing for expropriation or land acquisition fails to clearly define what public purpose means. For instance, a study conducted on 30 countries from Africa and Asia evinced that only four of them provided a definition for the concept of public purpose in their respective domestic laws.[134] This opens the door for arbitrary decisions and abuse of power. Another study conducted on DID cases in several regions in India found that in many of these cases the public purpose requirement for land acquisition was neither clearly defined nor consistently complied with.[135] "Public purpose often serves as a façade for gentrification, whereby the urban poor are removed from coveted areas to make way for commercial ventures and high-income housing."[136] Thus, it is not sufficient that there is a law that permits expropriation of property for public purposes, but what public purpose entails needs to be clearly defined. Expropriation that is not justified under this condition amounts to arbitrary deprivation of property and, as such, constitutes a violation of the right to property.

Another recurrent issue in DID cases is the determination and adequacy of compensation for land acquisition. Often displaced persons rely on the land they inhabited to make a living,[137] and expropriation not only affects the property value of the land but also the income derived from it. Thus, the determination of compensation also needs to take this factor into account. In the case of DID, in-kind compensation—replacement housing and/or land—should be provided apart from monetary compensation for the income lost and other damages incurred.[138] As mentioned before in relation to the right to housing, the replacement of real properties is the preferred remedy in this context and, in principle, monetary compensation should not be used in lieu of that.[139] Not only do states need to provide replacement land or housing in-kind but they should also ensure that the replacement land or housing

[134] Tagliarino 2016, pp. 3 and 12.

[135] Internal Displacement Monitoring Centre (IDMC) 2016, p. 17.

[136] Ibid.

[137] Kanosue 2015, p. 648.

[138] The Special Rapporteur on Adequate Housing 2007, para 60; see also Randell 2016, pp. 385–400.

[139] The Special Rapporteur on Adequate Housing 2007, para 60.

provided is "of better or equal quality"[140] than what was expropriated in order to enable those affected to restore their livelihoods.

Moreover, adequate procedural safeguards should be put in place throughout the process of expropriation. These include meaningful participation of and consultation with all the pertinent stakeholders particularly the people whose properties are planned to be expropriated.[141] In cases where indigenous peoples' land is to be expropriated, states should obtain the "free, prior, and informed consent" of the people concerned as will be discussed in Chap. 7.[142] In any case, the people(s) affected by the expropriation should have a real opportunity to influence the decision and propose alternatives. States should also guarantee access to information and transparency in decision-making.[143] As mentioned above, the definition of forced eviction also encompasses arbitrary removal from land. Hence, the substantive and procedural safeguards that should be provided by states at all phases of expropriation, i.e. before, during, and after expropriation, can be informed by the rules on eviction elaborated in the preceding chapter.

4.6.2 Landlessness or Decrease of Landholding After Displacement

Expropriation of land that DID involves creates dispossession of land, which in turn often leads to landlessness or a decrease in landholding after displacement when adequate replacement land or compensation is not provided. For instance, a study conducted on the Kiambere Hydropower project in Kenya found that the landholdings of farmers displaced by this project decreased from 13 to 6 hectares on average after resettlement.[144] Similarly, another study revealed that the landholding of people displaced by the Saguling Dam in Indonesia decreased by 47% after displacement.[145] A study conducted on four development projects in the Tigray

---

[140] Ibid., para 16. This rule is particularly stressed in international instruments protecting the rights of indigenous peoples, i.e. ILO Convention No. 169 and the United Nations Declaration on the Rights of Indigenous Peoples. If relocation of these peoples is inevitable and justified in the circumstances of the case, they should be provided "with lands of quality and legal status at least equal to that of the lands previously occupied by them" (see ILO Convention No. 69 (n 20) Article 16(4); see also UNDRIP (n 20) Article 28(2)). This rule could also apply to other displaced people by analogy since its main purpose is to ensure that compensation provided for land acquisition should be adequate enough to improve or restore the economic wellbeing of the people affected. This is also affirmed by the Special Rapporteur on adequate housing.

[141] UN CESCR 1997, para 15; see also African Commission on Human and Peoples' Rights 2011, para 55(d).

[142] UNDRIP (n 20) Article 10.

[143] UN CESCR 1997, para 15; see also African Commission on Human and Peoples' Rights 2011, para 55(d).

[144] Mburugu 1994, p. 53; see also Cernea 2000, p. 3663.

[145] Hong et al. 2009, p. 228.

region of Ethiopia, similarly, documented a significant decrease—from 1.2 to 0.68 hectares—in average landholding of the people affected after relocation.[146] These few examples are not isolated cases. Several other studies have also demonstrated that DID and the involuntary resettlement it involves significantly affect the landholdings of displaced persons.[147]

As discussed in Chap. 2, landlessness or a decrease in landholding is the main cause of the economic impoverishment that DID results in. For instance, the study on the Kiambere Hydropower project also found that the decrease in landholding has significantly affected agricultural and livestock production, which the farmers concerned relied upon to make a living. This, in turn, decreased their family income by 82%.[148] According to Cernea, "[e]xpropriation of land removes the main foundation upon which people's productive systems, commercial activities, and livelihoods are constructed. This is the principal form of de-capitalisation and pauperisation of displaced people, as they lose both natural and [human-made] capital."[149] Particularly for people who derive their livelihoods from land, landlessness causes a special vulnerability.[150] Landlessness compromises their ability to meet their basic needs potentially affecting a range of human rights, such as the rights to an adequate standard of living and work, apart from the right to property.

Landlessness or a decrease in landholding is mainly attributable to the lack or inadequacy of the compensation and other remedies provided, which should not be limited to a lump-sum monetary compensation. In other words, both the kind of compensation selected and the amount provided should be adequate to restore the landholdings of the people displaced. Nevertheless, as several studies demonstrate, compensation provided for DID often falls short of this standard.[151] For instance, in the case of the Hirakud dam in India, persons whose lands had been acquired by the state for the construction of the dam were provided with monetary compensation, "which was much less than the market value".[152] Due to the inadequacy of the compensation provided and the failure of the state to provide replacement land, the people displaced by the project were unable to restore their landholdings, which eventually led to their impoverishment coupled with other socio-economic problems caused by the displacement.[153] The study conducted on four development projects in the Tigray region of Ethiopia mentioned above also attributes the decrease of landholding to the means and inadequacy of the remedies provided by the state.[154] The people displaced by these projects were not provided with replacement land.[155]

---

146 Gebreyesus and Tadesse 2019, p. 133.

147 See, for instance, Kahsay 2020, pp. 100 and 101.

148 Cernea 2000, p. 3663; see also Mburugu 1994, p. 53.

149 Cernea 2000, p. 3663; see also Robinson 2003, p. 11.

150 OHCHR 2015, p. 21; see also Downing 2002, p. 9.

151 George and Rajan 2015, p. 3.

152 Nayak 2013, p. 412.

153 Ibid., pp. 412 and 413.

154 Gebreyesus and Tadesse 2019, pp. 132 and 133.

155 Ibid., p. 132.

Rather, they were offered a lump-sum monetary compensation, which according to the study was neither sufficient nor effective to restore their landholdings.[156] Monetary compensation not only often fails to fully capture the value of real assets, such as land, but also it is often spent on immediate expenses rather than replacement of assets, thus exposing those affected to loss or decrease in landholding.[157] This is the principal reason why experts and relevant organizations recommend the replacement of real assets as the primary remedy for expropriation.[158] Hence, expropriation without adequate compensation that results in landlessness or a decrease in landholding amounts to arbitrary deprivation of property.

In other instances, a replacement land comparable in size to the expropriated land may be provided, but might be of poorer quality,[159] which will affect agricultural production. For instance, some of the resettlement sites provided for people displaced by the Sardar Sarovar Project in India were found to be unsuitable for irrigation.[160] Similarly, a study conducted on the Merowe Dam project in Sudan, which displaced approximately 50,000 individuals,[161] revealed that some of the people displaced by this project were resettled in desert areas where the land is of poor quality in terms of agricultural productivity compared to the fertile land from which they were displaced.[162] This all comes down to the adequacy of monetary and non-monetary compensation provided for land-acquisition, which also determines whether or not the right to property is encroached upon in the process of DID. Thus, as depicted before, the replacement land provided must be "of better or equal quality"[163] both in terms of size and productivity or cultivability.

In addition to its adverse effect on private landholding, displacement also affects access to communal lands, such as grazing and forest lands, which is also vital for the livelihood of the people concerned.[164] These communal resources are usually not taken into account in the determination of compensation and resettlement following displacement.[165] For instance, a study conducted on the Rengali Dam project in India found that only 23.7% of displaced households had access to common grazing land after resettlement while all of them had had such access before displacement.[166] These households did not receive compensation for loss of access to common resources and its adverse effect on their income.[167] This is another interference with the right to property.

---

[156] Ibid., p. 133.

[157] Ibid.

[158] The Special Rapporteur on Adequate Housing 2007, para 60.

[159] George and Rajan 2015, p. 3.

[160] Maitra 2009, p. 200.

[161] Ahmed 2019, p. 131.

[162] Ibid., pp. 148 and 149.

[163] Special Rapporteur on Adequate Housing 2007, para 16.

[164] Terminski 2015, pp. 44–45 and 75.

[165] Cernea 2000, p. 3665.

[166] Ibid., p. 3666; see also Pandey 1996.

[167] Cernea 2000, pp. 3665 and 3666; see also Pandey 1996.

4.6.3 Forced Eviction and Destruction of Property

As discussed in the preceding chapter, DID often involves forced eviction—eviction without the provision of adequate legal and other protections. Forced eviction constitutes not only the violation of the right to housing but also a violation of the right to property,[168] as it interferes with the use and control of one's property, i.e. housing and land in this context. This was affirmed by the African Commission in the case of *COHRE v. Sudan* in which it found a violation of the right to property due to unjustified evictions or destruction of houses by state agents.[169] Nevertheless, since the human rights norms on forced eviction are discussed in detail in Chap. 3, this brief remark here suffices to note that the forced eviction and the demolition of housing that DID might involve also violate the right to property.

4.7 Conclusion

The right to property, which protects the peaceful enjoyment of property and prohibits arbitrary deprivation thereof, is another right commonly interfered with and potentially violated in the course of DID. Arbitrary interference with or deprivation of property, particularly land, is one of the main reasons behind the economic impoverishment that often taints DID. Generally, the process and outcome of DID can interfere with or potentially violate the right to property in the three instances discussed above, i.e. when the expropriation of property or land acquisition that DID involves is not justified by pertinent human rights norms and principles; when DID involves forced eviction; and when DID leads to landlessness or a decrease in landholding. However, not all these interferences automatically constitute a violation of the right to property. The limitation of the right to property including for development purposes can be justified if all the necessary conditions provided in the relevant human rights frameworks are fulfilled. Accordingly, the limitation needs to be provided by a law of sufficient clarity and accessibility, pursue a clearly defined public purpose, be necessary and proportionate, and be accompanied by adequate compensation. In addition, states should also put in place the necessary procedural safeguards, such as access to information and meaningful participation, and substantive safeguards, such as in-kind and monetary compensation, to prevent or mitigate the adverse consequences of DID and protect the right to property of the people affected.

References

[168] *Akdivar and Others v. Turkey*, Application No. 99/1995/605/693, Judgment, European Court of Human Rights, 16 September 1996, para 88.

[169] *COHRE v. Sudan* (n 66) para 204.

African Commission on Human and Peoples' Rights (2011) Guidelines and Principles on Economic, Social and Cultural Rights in the African Charter on Human and Peoples' Rights, available at https://achpr.au.int/index.php/en/node/871, accessed 20 July 2025.
Ahmed I A I (2019) The Merowe Dam in Northern Sudan: A Case of Population Displacement and Impoverishment. In: Schmidt J D, Kimathi L, Owiso M O (eds) Refugees and Forced Migration in the Horn and Eastern Africa: Trends, Challenges and Opportunities. Springer.
Cernea M M (1995) Understanding and Preventing Impoverishment from Displacement: Reflections on the State of Knowledge. 8(3) Journal of Refugee Studies 245–264.
Cernea M M (2000) Risks, Safeguards and Reconstruction: A Model for Population Displacement and Resettlement. (2000) 35(41) Economic and Political Weekly 3659–3678.
Charters C (2018) Part IV Rights to Land and Territory, Natural Resources, and Environment, Ch.14 Indigenous Peoples' Rights to Lands, Territories, and Resources in the UNDRIP: Articles 10, 25, 26, and 27. In: Hohmann J, Weller M (eds) The UN Declaration on the Rights of Indigenous Peoples: A Commentary. Oxford University Press, Oxford.
Downing T E (2002) Avoiding New Poverty: Mining-Induced Displacement and Resettlement. (2002) 58 Mining, Minerals and Sustainable Development.
FIAN International (2017) The Human Right to Land: Position Paper. FIAN International Secretariat.
Foster S R (2011) The Social Function of Property: A Comparative Law Perspective. (2011) 80(3) Fordham Law Review 101–113.
Gebreyesus A, Tadesse S (2019) Livelihood Impacts of Development-Induced Displacements: an Investigation into Post-Project Livelihoods of PAPs. (2019) 35(1/2) Eastern Africa Social Science Research Review 123–151.
George A, Rajan I (2015) Changing Cities and Changing Lives: Development Induced Displacement in Kochi, Kerala. (2015) 1(1) International Journal on Urban Environments 1–18.
Glendon M A (1998) Knowing the Universal Declaration of Human Rights. (1998) 73(5) Notre Dame Law Review 1153–1190.
Golay C, Cismas I (2010) Legal Opinion: The Right to Property from a Human Rights Perspective. International Centre for Human Rights and Democratic Development.
Hannum H (1998) The UDHR in National and International Law. (1998) 3(2) Health and Human Rights 144–158.
Hong P Y P, Singh S, Ramic J (2009) Development-induced impoverishment among involuntarily displaced populations. (2009) 25(3) Journal of Comparative Social Welfare 221–238.
Human Rights Council (2008) Report of the Special Rapporteur on adequate housing as a component of the right to an adequate standard of living, Miloon Kothari, mission to Spain, 7 February 2008, A/HRC/7/16/Add.2.
Human Rights Council (2009) Report of the Special Rapporteur on the right to food, Olivier De Schutter, Large-Scale Land Acquisitions and Leases: A Set of Minimum Principles and Measures to Address the Human Rights Challenge, 28 December 2009, A/HRC/13/33/Add.2.
Internal Displacement Monitoring Centre (IDMC) (2016) Pushed Aside: Displaced for 'Development' in India, IDMC report, July 2016, available at http://www.internal-displacement.org/publications/pushed-aside-displaced-for-development-in-india, accessed 20 July 2025.
Jayawickrama N (2017) The Judicial Application of Human Rights Law: National, Regional and International Jurisprudence, 2nd edn. Cambridge University Press.
Kahsay B G (2020) Socio-cultural and economic impacts of development induced displacement on resettled people: The case of Welkayt Sugar Factory in Tigray Region, Ethiopia. (2020) 12(4) International Journal of Sociology and Anthropology 94–103.
Kanosue Y (2015) When Land is Taken Away: States Obligations under International Human Rights Law Concerning Large-Scale Projects Impacting Local Communities. (2015) 15(4) Human Rights Law Review 643–667.
Maitra S (2009) Compensation and Resettlement – Experiences from the Narmada Valley and Sardar Sarovar Project. (2009) 10(2) Japanese Journal of Political Science 191–211.

Mburugu E K (1994) Dislocation of Settled Communities in the Development Process: The Case of Kiambere Hydroelectric Project. In: Cook C C (ed) Involuntary Resettlement in Africa, World Bank Technical Paper No. 227. World Bank, Washington DC.

Nayak A K (2013) Development, Displacement and Justice in India: Study of Hirakud Dam. (2013) 43(3) Social Change 397–419.

Office of the United Nations High Commissioner for Human Rights (OHCHR) (2015) Land and Human Rights: Standards and Applications, HR/PUB/15/5/Add.1, 2015.

Pandey B (1996) Impoverishment Risks: A Case Study of Five Villages in Coal Mining Areas of Talcher, Orissa. Paper presented at the workshop on Involuntary Resettlement and Impoverishment Risks, New Delhi.

Ramanathan U (1996) Displacement and the Law. (1996) 31(24) Economic and Political Weekly 1486–1491.

Randell H (2016) The short-term impacts of development-induced displacement on wealth and subjective well-being in the Brazilian Amazon. (2016) 87 World Development 385–400.

Robinson C W (2003) Risks and Rights: The Causes, Consequences, and Challenges of Development-Induced Displacement. The Brookings Institution-SAIS Project on Internal Displacement, An Occasional Paper May 2003.

Saul B (2016) The International Covenant on Economic, Social and Cultural Rights: Travaux Préparatoires 1946–1966, Volume I. Oxford University Press, Oxford.

Shelton D (2015) Remedies in International Human Rights Law, 3rd edn. Oxford University Press, Oxford.

Special Rapporteur on Adequate Housing (2007) Basic Principles and Guidelines on Development-based Evictions and Displacement, 5 February 2007, A/HRC/4/18.

Sprankling J G (2014) The Global Right to Property. (2014) 52(2) Columbia Journal of Transnational Law 464–505.

Tagliarino N K (2016) Encroaching on Land and Livelihoods: How International Expropriation Laws Measure up to International Standards. Working Paper, World Resources Institute.

Terminski B (2015) Development-Induced Displacement and Resettlement: Causes, Consequences, and Socio-Legal Context. Ibidem-Verlag, Stuttgart.

Tomuschat C (2014) Human Rights: Between Idealism and Realism, 3rd edn. Oxford University Press, Oxford.

UN Committee on Economic, Social and Cultural Rights (UN CESCR) (1991) General Comment No. 4: The Right to Adequate Housing (Article 11 (1) of the Covenant), 13 December 1991, E/1992/23.

UN Committee on Economic, Social and Cultural Rights (UN CESCR) (1997) General Comment No. 7: The right to adequate housing (Article 11.1): forced evictions, 20 May 1997, E/1998/22.

UN Committee on Economic, Social and Cultural Rights (UN CESCR) (1999) General Comment No. 12: The Right to Adequate Food (Article 11 of the Covenant), 12 May 1999, E/C.12/1999/5.

UN Committee on Economic, Social and Cultural Rights (UN CESCR) (2003) General Comment No. 15: The Right to Water (Articles 11 and 12 of the Covenant), 20 January 2003, E/C.12/2002/11.

UN Committee on Economic, Social and Cultural Rights (UN CESCR) (2022) General Comment No. 26 (2022) on Land and Economic, Social and Cultural Rights, E/C.12/GC/26, 22 December 2022.

van Banning T R G (2002) The Human Right to Property. Intersentia.

Waincymer J (2009) Balancing Property Rights and Human Rights in Expropriation. In: Dupuy P M, Petersmann E-U, Francioni F (eds) Human Rights in International Investment Law and Arbitration. Oxford University Press, Oxford.

Chapter 5
The Right to Work

Contents

Abstract The process and outcome of development-induced displacement (DID) often interfere with, and in some cases violate, the right to work. These interferences can be caused by joblessness, loss of income, or a decrease in income to which DID often leads. Some of these interferences can be justified if they are necessary to promote public interest and comply with the other conditions of limitations. In addition, states need to put in place the necessary rights-based safeguards to restore and protect the incomes and income-generating activities of displaced persons. This chapter aims to elucidate the recognition and normative content of the right to work, examine how the process and consequences of DID can interfere with and potentially violate this right, and identify the procedural and substantive safeguards that states should implement to prevent such violations.

Keywords Right to work · Decent work · Joblessness · Loss of income · Decrease in income · Arbitrary deprivation of employment

© T.M.C. ASSER PRESS and the authors 2026

R. G. Teshome, *The Human Cost of Development*, Human Rights Research Series 104,
https://doi.org/10.1007/978-94-6265-751-9_5

5.1 Introduction

As established in Chap. 2, development-induced displacement (DID) often leads to loss or decrease of income and joblessness. These consequences directly interfere with the right to make a living through decent work and not to be unfairly deprived of such work, which the right to work protects. The human rights framework that recognizes this right obliges states, *inter alia*, to create a conducive environment to facilitate access to work, regulate conditions of work, and offer protection against arbitrary deprivation of employment. In the context of DID, the state is actively taking measures that directly or indirectly disrupt access to work or lead to deprivation of employment or loss of income. This arguably should heighten the obligations of states. Hence, states need to not only justify the measures that potentially lead to such unfavourable outcomes but also put in place rights-based safeguards to prevent or mitigate those outcomes and avoid the violation of the right to work. In light of this, the current chapter examines the application and interference of the right to work in the context of displacement prompted by development projects.

Similar to the previous chapters in this part of the book, the chapter begins by introducing the sources or recognition of the right to work (Sect. 5.2). It then explores the normative content of the right and the state obligations it entails as well as the norms on limitation of this right (Sects. 5.3, 5.4, and 5.5, respectively). Subsequently, the chapter examines, in Sect. 5.6, the interferences with the right to work stemming from the process and outcome of DID and the human rights safeguards required to justify those interferences and prevent a violation.

5.2 The Recognition of the Right to Work

The right to work is explicitly recognized in numerous global and regional human rights frameworks. Globally, it is recognized under Article 23(1) of the Universal Declaration of Human Rights (UDHR),[1] Articles 6, 7, and 8 of the International Covenant on Economic, Social and Cultural Rights (ICESCR),[2] and several other human rights instruments.[3] One of the normative elements of this right—prohibition of compulsory labour—is also recognized under Article 8(3) of the International

---

[1] UN General Assembly, Universal Declaration of Human Rights, 10 December 1948, 217 A (III) ('UDHR'), Article 23(1).

[2] UN General Assembly, International Covenant on Economic, Social and Cultural Rights, 16 December 1966, 993 United Nations Treaty Series 3 ('ICESCR'), Articles 6, 7, and 8.

[3] UN General Assembly, Convention on the Elimination of All Forms of Discrimination Against Women, 18 December 1979, 1249 United Nations Treaty Series 13 ('CEDAW'), Article 11(1)(a); see also UN General Assembly, International Convention on the Elimination of All Forms of Racial Discrimination, 21 December 1965, 660 United Nations Treaty Series 195, Article 5(e)(i); see also UN General Assembly, International Convention on the Protection of the Rights of All Migrant Workers and Members of their Families, 18 December 1990, A/RES/45/158, Articles 11, 25, 26, 40, 52, and 54.

Covenant on Civil and Political Rights (ICCPR).[4] In addition, a number of treaties adopted by the International Labour Organization (ILO) recognize different aspects of the right to work.[5] Similarly, the right to work is expressly provided under all the major regional human rights frameworks, i.e. Article 15 of the African Charter on Human and Peoples' Rights,[6] Article 6 of the San Salvador Protocol (the Additional Protocol to the American Convention on Human Rights),[7] and Articles 1–6 of the European Social Charter.[8]

These instruments recognize three interdependent aspects of the right: a general right to work, "just and favourable conditions of work", and a collective right to form and join trade unions, which are enshrined under Articles 6, 7, and 8 of the ICESCR, respectively.[9] This chapter primarily focuses on the first aspect since it is thematically more relevant in the context of DID as will be elucidated subsequently. However, as the Committee on Economic, Social and Cultural Rights (CESCR) has also stressed, these aspects are highly interdependent[10] and, hence, a reference to the other two aspects will be made where necessary. The following sections will explore the normative content of the right and the state obligations it entails mainly drawing on the ICESCR and the authoritative interpretation by the Committee.

---

[4] UN General Assembly, International Covenant on Civil and Political Rights, 16 December 1966, 999 United Nations Treaty Series 171, Article 8(3).

[5] International Labour Organization (ILO), Forced Labour Convention, C29, 28 June 1930; see also International Labour Organization (ILO), Abolition of Forced Labour Convention, C105, 25 June 1957; see also International Labour Organization (ILO), Discrimination (Employment and Occupation) Convention, C111, 25 June 1958; see also International Labour Organization (ILO), Convention Concerning Termination of Employment at the Initiative of the Employer, C158, 22 June 1982 see also International Labour Organization (ILO), Convention Concerning Employment Policy, C122, 9 July 1964.

[6] Organization of African Unity (OAU), African Charter on Human and Peoples' Rights, 27 June 1981, CAB/LEG/67/3 rev. 5, 21 I.L.M. 58 (1982) ('African Charter'), Article 15.

[7] Organization of American States (OAS), Additional Protocol to the American Convention on Human Rights in the Area of Economic, Social and Cultural Rights, 17 November 1988, 69 OAS Treaty Series ('Protocol of San Salvador'), Article 6. In addition, Article 6(2) of the American Convention on Human Rights prohibits compulsory labour (see Organization of American States (OAS), American Convention on Human Rights, 22 November 1969, 36 OAS Treaty Series ('American Convention on Human Rights'), Article 6(2)).

[8] Council of Europe, European Social Charter (Revised), 3 May 1996, 163 ETS ('European Social Charter (revised)'), Articles 1–6. Plus, Article 4(2) of the European Convention on Human Rights contains a prohibition of compulsory labour (see Council of Europe, European Convention for the Protection of Human Rights and Fundamental Freedoms, as amended by Protocols Nos. 11 and 14, 4 November 1950, 5 ETS, Article 4(2)).

[9] ICESCR (n 2) Articles 6, 7, 8; see also UN CESCR 2006, para 2.

[10] UN CESCR 2006, para 8; see also Saul et al. 2014, p. 273.

5.3 Normative Content of the Right to Work

The right to work provided under Article 6 of the Covenant guarantees the right to make a living through work one "freely chooses or accepts".[11] The first paragraph of the provision reads, "[t]he States Parties to the present Covenant recognize the right to work, which includes the right of everyone to the opportunity to gain his living by work which he freely chooses or accepts, and will take appropriate steps to safeguard this right."[12] As the Committee elaborated, "[t]he right to work should not be understood as an absolute and unconditional right to obtain employment."[13] Rather, it implies a right to have equal access to employment opportunities and a right to freely decide one's line of work.[14] Accordingly, the right to work embodies three fundamental normative elements, namely access to employment opportunities, the right "not to be unfairly deprived of employment", and the prohibition of compulsory labour.[15]

The first element, access to employment opportunities, is a broad notion that encompasses various conditions—availability, accessibility, acceptability, and quality.[16] The condition of availability requires states to take the necessary measures "to assist and support individuals in order to enable them to identify and find available employment".[17] Accessibility implies the prohibition of "discrimination in access to and maintenance of employment" based on any of the protected grounds enumerated under Article 2(2) of the Covenant,[18] physical accessibility, and access to relevant information.[19] Moreover, the right to work also pertains to the quality of the work; as the Committee contended:

> Work as specified in article 6 of the Covenant must be decent work. This is work that respects the fundamental rights of the human person as well as the rights of workers in terms of conditions of work safety and remuneration. It also provides an income allowing workers to support themselves and their families as highlighted in article 7 of the Covenant. These fundamental rights also include respect for the physical and mental integrity of the worker in the exercise of his/her employment.[20]

---

[11] ICESCR (n 2) Article 6(1).

[12] Ibid.

[13] UN CESCR 2006, para 6; see also Saul et al. 2014, p. 282.

[14] UN CESCR 2006, para 6; see also Ó Cinnéide 2015, p. 77; see also African Commission on Human and Peoples' Rights 2011, para 58.

[15] UN CESCR 2006, para 6.

[16] Ibid., para 12.

[17] Ibid., para 12(a).

[18] ICESCR (n 2) Article 2(2).

[19] UN CESCR 2006, para 12(b).

[20] Ibid., para 7; see also African Commission on Human and Peoples' Rights 2011, para 57.

Hence, the right to work not only guarantees equal access to employment but also regulates the quality of the work.[21] This brings into the picture the requirements of "just and favourable conditions of work" specified under Article 7 of the Covenant.[22] These conditions consist of, *inter alia*, "[f]air wages and equal remuneration for work of equal value without distinction of any kind" and "safe and healthy working conditions".[23] In a nutshell, the first normative element of the right to work—access to employment—requires states to create a conducive environment for individuals to have access to decent work in order to make a living.

The second normative element of the right, which is particularly important in the context of DID, protects individuals from unfair or arbitrary deprivation of employment.[24] The Covenant does not define what constitutes unfair deprivation of employment. However, Article 4 of the ILO Convention No. 158, which is also endorsed by the Committee,[25] provides that "[t]he employment of a worker shall not be terminated unless there is a valid reason for such termination connected with the capacity or conduct of the worker or based on the operational requirements of the undertaking, establishment or service."[26] The Convention contains a non-exhaustive list of grounds of termination that are not considered "valid reasons", which include membership in trade unions, taking maternity leave, and discriminatory grounds based on any of the protected grounds.[27] It further stipulates procedural and other safeguards that need to be put in place to preclude arbitrariness, such as adequate notice and compensation.[28] The deprivation of employment that DID causes does not equate to termination of employment per se. Rather, in the case of DID, the loss of employment or income is often the result of the difficulties created by physical relocation. The limitation clause of the ICESCR can also be employed to understand what constitutes arbitrary deprivation of employment.[29] Accordingly, a loss of employment or income that is not justified based on the conditions of limitations discussed below amounts to an arbitrary deprivation of employment.

[21] Ó Cinnéide 2015, p. 77.

[22] ICESCR (n 2) Article 7; see also UN CESCR 2006, para 7.

[23] ICESCR (n 2) Article 7; see also UN CESCR 2016, paras 7–49; see also African Commission on Human and Peoples' Rights 2011, para 57.

[24] UN CESCR 2006, para 6.

[25] Ibid., para 11; see also Saul et al. 2014, p. 349.

[26] ILO Convention No. 158 (n 5) Article 4.

[27] Ibid.

[28] Ibid., Articles 7–14; see also Saul et al. 2014, pp. 353–355.

[29] ICESCR (n 2) Article 4.

The jurisprudence of the African Commission also indicates that arbitrary deprivation of employment occurs when deprivation of employment or the measure that led to such an outcome is not justified by a legitimate cause and/or not undertaken in accordance with the law. For instance, in the case of *Zimbabwe Lawyers for Human Rights & Associated Newspapers of Zimbabwe v. Zimbabwe*, the Commission contended that the state's decision to close the applicants' offices should not only be supported by a legitimate cause but also meet the proportionality test.[30] "The principle of proportionality seeks to determine whether, by the action of the State, a fair balance has been struck between the protection of the rights and freedoms of the individual and the interests of the society as a whole."[31] Similarly, in the case of *Monim Elgak, Osman Hummeida and Amir Suliman v. Sudan*, the Commission reiterated that the state's closure of the applicant's business without a legitimate reason, which left the applicant and his staff without jobs, is an unjustified interference and, hence, amounts to an arbitrary deprivation of employment.[32] Thus, these cases can also inform the interpretation of the term "unfair or arbitrary deprivation of employment".

The other important normative element of the right to work is the prohibition of compulsory labour, which is mirrored in the phrase "…work which [one] freely chooses and accepts" under Article 6 of the Covenant.[33] According to the definition adopted by the ILO Conventions, which is also endorsed by the Committee,[34] compulsory or forced labour is "all work or service which is exacted from any person under the menace of any penalty and for which the said person has not offered himself voluntarily."[35] The prohibition of compulsory labour, on the one hand, entitles a person the right to freely choose the type of work they wish to engage in and, on the other hand, protects "the negative freedom not to work".[36] Overall, the right to work entitles individuals to equal access to decent work of their choice and protects them from being unfairly deprived of the ability to make a living through such work.

---

[30] *Zimbabwe Lawyers for Human Rights & Associated Newspapers of Zimbabwe v Republic of Zimbabwe*, Communication 284/03, African Commission on Human and Peoples' Rights, 3 April 2009, paras 175–176.

[31] Ibid., para 176.

[32] *Monim Elgak, Osman Hummeida and Amir Suliman (represented by FIDH and OMCT) v Sudan*, Communication 379/09, African Commission on Human and Peoples' Rights, 10 March 2015, paras 127–131.

[33] ICESCR (n 2) Article 6(1); see also Saul et al. 2014, p. 322.

[34] UN CESCR 2006, para 9.

[35] ILO Convention No. 29 (n 5) Article 2(1); see also ILO Convention No. 105 (n 5) Article 1; see also Saul et al. 2014, p. 323. The ILO Convention No. 29 allows certain exceptions to the rule of prohibition of compulsory labour, which include mandatory military service, compulsory labour as a result of a criminal conviction and emergency services, among others (see ILO Convention No. 29 (n 5) Article 2(2)). Similar exceptions are also enumerated under Article 8(3) of the ICCPR, a provision that prohibits compulsory labour (see ICCPR (n 4) Article 8(3); see also Saul et al. 2014, p. 332). Although the ICESCR does not expressly stipulate these exceptions, the limitation clause of the Covenant can be used to this effect provided that such exceptions comply with the conditions of limitation (see Saul et al. 2014, p. 333).

[36] Saul et al. 2014, p. 280.

5.4 State Obligations Related to the Right to Work

Generally, pursuant to Article 2(1) of the Covenant, states have an obligation to take necessary steps using the maximum of resources available at their disposal in order to progressively realize economic, social and cultural rights including the right to work.[37] Further, the principle of progressive realization prohibits states from taking retrogressive measures save for narrowly tailored exceptions.[38] In the context of the right to work, "…while there is no obligation on states to immediately guarantee full employment, states must adopt a national employment policy directed towards the progressive expansion of the quantity and quality of employment opportunities."[39] The three types of human rights obligations, i.e. the duty to respect, protect, and fulfil, are also applicable to the right to work.[40] As what these general obligations entail is extensively discussed in the chapter on the right to housing, this section briefly explicates the specific state obligations that the right to work demands.

States are required to take legislative and other necessary measures to prohibit compulsory labour and eliminate discrimination both in the public and private sectors as well as to ensure equal access to decent work.[41] Furthermore, states are obliged to undertake positive steps in order to provide the right "when individuals or groups are unable, for reasons beyond their control, to realize that right themselves"[42] and facilitate access to employment by creating technical and vocational education programs.[43] Moreover, similar to the other socio-economic rights, the right to work also involves minimum core obligations that have immediate effect and should be prioritized in the case of resource constraints.[44] These include "non-discrimination and equal protection of employment",[45] which particularly involve ensuring equal access to employment for vulnerable groups.[46] Overall, states are required not only to refrain from interfering with the enjoyment of the right to work but also to take proactive measures to ensure equal access to decent work.

---

[37] ICESCR (n 2) Article 2(1); see also UN CESCR 2006, para 18; see also African Commission on Human and Peoples' Rights 2011, para 2.

[38] UN CESCR 2006, para 21; see also UN CESCR 1990, para 9.

[39] Saul et al. 2014, p. 280; see also UN CESCR 2006, paras 19 and 20.

[40] UN CESCR 2006, para 22.

[41] Ibid., paras 24 and 25; see also Ó Cinnéide 2015, p. 78.

[42] UN CESCR 2006, para 26.

[43] Ibid., para 27; see also Ó Cinnéide 2015, p. 79.

[44] UN CESCR 2006, para 31.

[45] Ibid.

[46] Ibid., para 31(a); see also Ó Cinnéide 2015, p. 79.

5.5 Limitations on the Right to Work

The right to work is not an absolute right and it can be limited under exceptional circumstances. The ICESCR prescribes a general limitation clause under Article 4,[47] which is applicable to all rights stipulated therein. As discussed in Chap. 3, a restriction on the rights enshrined under the Covenant can only be imposed if it is provided by law, "…compatible with the nature of these rights" and aimed at "promoting the general welfare in a democratic society".[48] The last condition further encompasses the requirements of necessity and proportionality. In other words, the restriction must be necessary, or the most effective and least intrusive measure, to protect the public interest in question and proportionate to the interest pursued. Furthermore, economic and social development purposes can be used as legitimate reasons to limit rights as long as they comply with the prerequisites mentioned above. Since these norms were discussed in detail previously (Chap. 3), a brief remark here suffices to note that the general limitation clause under the Covenant also applies to the right to work. Accordingly, interferences to the right to work that DID involves, which will be discussed below, need to be justified based on these conditions.

5.6 Interference with the Right to Work in the Course of Development-Induced Displacement

In light of the normative content of the right discussed above, the process and outcome of DID often interfere with the enjoyment of and potentially violate the right to work. Generally, DID interferes with the right to work when displacement leads to joblessness or loss of income and when it causes a decrease in income, which will be discussed in the following sections with reference to practical cases. These sections will also explore how the permissible limitation clause can be employed to justify these interferences and preclude violations. In addition, the right to work can also be breached when DID involves direct or indirect discrimination as discussed in Chap. 3.

[47] ICESCR (n 2) Article 4.

[48] Ibid.

5.6.1 *Joblessness or Loss of Income*[49]

As established in Chap. 2, joblessness or loss of income is one of the main consequences of DID, which is also one of the principal causes of the economic impoverishment that DID often results in.[50] For people whose livelihoods depend on land, i.e. farmers and pastoralists, this is usually the immediate consequence of dispossession of land.[51] In these cases, if replacement land of equal or higher quality is not provided, the people affected will lose their main source of income.[52] The case studies mentioned in the chapter on the right to property concerning landlessness caused by DID are also relevant examples here.[53]

Physical displacement can also cause those employed in various sectors in both urban and rural areas to lose their jobs.[54] For instance, a case study conducted on urban (re)development projects in Ahmedabad, India, found that 14% of workers displaced by these projects remained unemployed years after relocation.[55] Another case study conducted on three development projects in Kerala, India, revealed that the percentage of working adults among the people displaced by these projects significantly decreased after displacement.[56] One of the reasons for this decline discovered in the study is the fact that some of the displaced persons had to take on new responsibilities created by the displacement, for instance, reconstructing their houses.[57] The other reasons forwarded in the study are relocation to sites that are distant from their workplaces and loss of land.[58]

Loss of income due to displacement also affects self-employed individuals and business owners, particularly small business owners.[59] Those businesses often rely

---

[49] The term "joblessness" in this context refers to a loss of employment or job in public and private sectors as a result of displacement and the term "loss of income" refers to a total loss of previous earnings or sources of income due to displacement. The author has opted to use both terms to indicate the different sources of income that are potentially affected by DID, i.e. agriculture, self-employment or business ownership, and employment in public and private sectors. This section does not cover a decrease of income caused by displacement as it will be discussed separately below. Although in the DID literature, a total loss of income and decrease of income are discussed in the same category of 'joblessness', the author has chosen to address them in separate sections since they might have different human rights implications, at least theoretically. A total loss of income or joblessness is a more severe interference with human rights than a decrease of income as will be described in the subsequent section.

[50] Cernea 2000a, p. 3664; see also Robinson 2003, p. 11.

[51] Terminski 2015, p. 74; see also Aboda et al. 2019, p. 103.

[52] Cernea 2000a, p. 3663.

[53] See Chap. 4 , Sect. 4.6.

[54] Cernea 2000a, p. 3664; see also Terminski 2015, p. 74; see also Hong et al. 2009, p. 224; see also Huang et al. 2018, p. 9.

[55] Patel et al. 2015, p. 242; see also Aboda et al. 2019, p. 104.

[56] Manjula et al. 2013, pp. 8–10.

[57] Ibid., p. 8.

[58] Ibid., p. 9.

[59] Cernea 2000a, p. 3664.

on close customer bases and relationships built over time, which will be disrupted by displacement.[60] Thus, the people affected often have a hard time rebuilding their businesses in the place to which they are relocated.

Joblessness might not always materialize immediately after displacement. In some cases, displaced persons are provided with "project-related jobs".[61] Those jobs, however, are usually short-term and cease to exist upon the completion of the project leaving the workers without jobs.[62] As the empirical evidence reveals, this is particularly the case in the context of dam constructions, which often create a temporary "employment boom".[63]

Moreover, joblessness or loss of income in all of the above instances often persist for a long time leading to the chronic impoverishment of those affected.[64] According to Cernea:

> The risk of losing wage employment is very high both in urban and rural displacements for those employed in enterprises, services, or agriculture. Yet, creating new jobs is difficult and requires substantial investment. Unemployment or underemployment among resettles often endures long after physical relocation has been completed.[65]

Joblessness or loss of income caused by DID directly interferes with one of the principal elements of the right to work, namely protection from unfair or arbitrary deprivation of employment. As discussed above, deprivation of employment can only be justified when it is supported by a legitimate cause and undertaken in accordance with the law and human rights norms including the principle of proportionality. In the context of DID, the reason for the deprivation is not related to "the capacity or conduct of the worker";[66] rather, it is a direct or indirect result of being uprooted from one's home or residence to make room for development projects. Moreover, in most cases, the deprivation of employment or loss of income is mainly attributable to the lack or inadequacy of remedies provided by the state concerned for taking away the sources of income of those affected. The fact that such adverse consequences can be avoided makes the deprivation hardly proportionate or justifiable.

Furthermore, the main entitlement that the right to work protects is the ability to make a living through decent work one "freely chooses or accepts".[67] Loss of land and employment or any other source of income caused by DID take away this ability. Besides, joblessness or loss of income attributable to actions and/or inactions of a state is a serious interference, which is seldom justified as a permissible limitation. Even if the development project in question is necessary to achieve an overriding general welfare and DID is justified as a last resort, depriving people of the ability to

---

[60] Robinson 2003, p. 12.

[61] Cernea 2000a, p. 3664.

[62] Ibid.

[63] Ibid.

[64] Ibid.; see also Robinson 2003, p. 11.

[65] Cernea 2000a, p. 3664; see also Cernea 1997, p. 1573.

[66] ILO Convention No 158 (n 5) Article 4.

[67] ICESCR (n 2) Article 6(1).

make a sustainable living is arguably not proportionate to the legitimate aim pursued. Although the Committee has not clarified the potential violation of the right to work vis-à-vis DID, its reasoning in the case of *Mohamed Ben Djazia and Naouel Bellili v. Spain* concerning homelessness and forced eviction can be analogously applied here. The Committee, in this case, stressed that even if eviction can be justified in exceptional circumstances, it should not leave those affected homeless or without the means to acquire replacement housing.[68] Similarly, DID should not leave those affected without jobs or sustainable sources of income. Moreover, these unfavourable outcomes will have a ripple effect on the enjoyment of other rights, such as the right to an adequate standard of living, the right to health, and the right to education, among others.

The state measure that prompted these adverse consequences can also amount to a retrogressive measure—a "measure that reduces the extent to which [a right] is guaranteed"[69]—which is considered a prima facie violation of the right to work. As discussed before in the chapter on the right to housing, deliberate retrogressive measures are only justified in exigent circumstances by taking into account "…the totality of the rights provided for in the Covenant and in the context of the full use of the maximum available resources."[70] Thus, the standard of justification for such measures is even higher.

It is important to reiterate here that, in the current context, the circumstance that caused joblessness or loss of income, i.e. DID, is pre-planned and foreseeable. Hence, the state can either prevent displacement by seeking other less intrusive alternatives or avoid these adverse consequences by providing adequate short-term and long-term safeguards to restore the livelihoods of the persons affected.

5.6.2 Decrease of Income

In some cases, displaced persons do not fully lose their jobs/income or are able to regain their income after displacement, but their income might significantly decrease due to displacement.[71] Decrease in income can be attributable to various factors, such as the inadequacy of monetary and non-monetary compensation provided or lack thereof, disruption of access to common resources, and lack or decrease of employment or business opportunities in the places of resettlement.

---

[68] *Mohamed Ben Djazia and Naouel Bellili v. Spain*, Communication No. 5/2015, adoption of views, UN Committee on Economic, Social and Cultural Rights (CESCR), 21 July 2017, E/C.12/61/D/5/2015, para 15.1–2.

[69] International Commission of Jurists, Maastricht Guidelines on Violations of Economic, Social and Cultural Rights, 26 January 1997, available at http://hrlibrary.umn.edu/instree/Maastrichtguidelines_.html, accessed 28 June 2025, para 14(e).

[70] UN CESCR 1990, para 9; see also *Mohamed Ben Djazia and Naouel Bellili v. Spain* (n 68) para 17.6.

[71] Randell 2016, p. 386.

As discussed in the preceding chapter in relation to the right to property, several empirical studies demonstrate that the landholdings of the people affected by DID significantly decreased after displacement due to the inadequacy of the replacement land provided in terms of size and value, which, in turn, have decreased their income. For instance, a study undertaken on the Kiambere Hydropower project in Kenya revealed that the landholdings of the farmers displaced by this project decreased from 13 to 6 hectares on average after resettlement.[72] This, in turn, decreased their family income by 82%.[73] Similarly, according to a study conducted on Upper Krishna Irrigation Project in Karnataka, India, which displaced approximately 5794 households, the people displaced by this project were merely provided with monetary compensation rather than replacement land.[74] Consequently, most of them were not able to replace their landholdings, which significantly decreased their income.[75] This particularly hit small landowners the hardest.[76] Another example is the notorious the Three Gorges dam in China, which is one of the largest hydroelectric dams in the world and responsible for the displacement of approximately 1.3 million persons.[77] A large number of the people displaced by this project, particularly the farmers, experienced a decrease in landholdings and income, among other adverse consequences, after relocation.[78] As studies demonstrate, these negative outcomes are again largely attributable to the lack or inadequacy of the compensation and rehabilitative measures provided by the state.[79]

In other cases, displaced persons are provided with replacement land of a lesser value in terms of cultivability,[80] which adversely affects crop and livestock production and consequently reduces the income derived therefrom. For instance, this was the case with the displacement caused by the Sardar Sarovar Project in India as mentioned in the previous chapter.[81]

Moreover, displaced persons who were employed in various sectors and lost their jobs due to displacement are forced to join the already competitive and scarce labour market and struggle to earn as much as they did before displacement. For instance, in

---

72 Hong et al. 2009, p. 228; see also Cernea 2000a, p. 3664.

73 Hong et al. 2009, p. 228; see also Cernea 2000a, p. 3664; see also Randell 2016, p. 386.

74 Hong et al. 2009, p. 229.

75 Ibid.

76 Ibid., p. 230.

77 Hwang et al. 2011, pp. 73 and 74; see also Wilmsen et al. 2011, pp. 356 and 358; see also Stein 1998, p. 8 (apart from the people originally displaced by the project, an additional two million people have been relocated at later stages of the construction of the dam due to environmental pollution and frequent landslides attributed to the project (see Hwang et al. 2011, p. 74)).

78 Hwang et al. 2011, p. 87; see also Wilmsen et al. 2011, pp. 363 and 364 and at 370–372; see also Randell 2016, p. 386; see also Stein 1998, pp. 8 and 9.

79 Wilmsen et al. 2011, p. 373 (for instance, monetary compensation was provided for the loss of past and future earnings but not for the value of the land itself, which changes with time and location. Moreover, the state did not offer technical assistance to rebuild the lives of the people affected in the resettlement sites); see also Aboda et al. 2019, p. 103; see also Stein 1998, p. 9.

80 George and Rajan 2015, p. 3.

81 Maitra 2009, p. 200.

the Upper Krishna Irrigation Project mentioned above, some of the landless individuals affected by displacement, who were agricultural workers before displacement, migrated to the cities to join "the already over-supplied construction labour force".[82] The others remained in the place of resettlement in poor socio-economic conditions.[83] In general, the income of these households also significantly decreased after displacement.[84]

A decrease in income can also be caused by loss or disruption of access to common resources, such as grazing lands, forests, and water sources, which the people concerned depend upon to support their income.[85] These common resources are often not taken into account in the determination of compensation and resettlement sites.[86] Furthermore, displaced persons have to compete with the host communities inhabiting the resettlement sites in accessing employment and business opportunities as well as using common resources.[87] These factors also put a strain on the income-earning capacity of the people concerned.

These instances of decrease in income caused by actions or inactions of the state clearly interfere with the right to work. Indeed, in exceptional circumstances, a decrease in income might be justified if it falls within the scope of permissible limitations. In these cases, the development project in question and the resulting displacement must be necessary to achieve general welfare, i.e. social and/or economic development in the context of DID. Besides, the decrease in income or the other adverse consequences potentially caused by the displacement must be proportionate to the general welfare pursued. Moreover, similar to the cases of joblessness or loss of income discussed above, the state measure that caused a decrease in income can also amount to a retrogressive measure, which demands a higher standard of justification.

5.7 Conclusion

The process and outcome of DID often interfere with and, in some cases, violate the right to work. This interference can be caused by the joblessness or loss of income and decrease in income to which DID often leads. Some of these interferences can be justified if they are compatible with the nature of the right to work, are necessary to promote the general welfare, and are proportionate to the aim pursued. In addition, states need to put in place necessary safeguards to protect the incomes and income-generating activities of displaced persons. As the case studies referred to above demonstrate, in most cases, the joblessness and decrease in income that

[82] Hong et al. 2009, p. 229.

[83] Ibid., p. 230.

[84] Ibid.

[85] Cernea 2000a, p. 3665; see also Terminski 2015, pp. 44–45 and 75; see also Robinson 2003, p. 12; see also Kibreab 2000, pp. 298 and 309; see also Aboda et al. 2019, pp. 103 and 104.

[86] Cernea 2000a, p. 3665; see also Kibreab 2000, pp. 313 and 314.

[87] Cernea 2000a, p. 3665.

DID causes and the resulting interference with the right to work are attributable to the lack or inadequacy of short-term and long-term remedies provided rather than to the mere fact of displacement. In other words, even if displacement inevitably interferes with the right to work, a violation can be precluded by the provision of adequate remedies that can effectively restore the livelihoods of those affected.[88] One of these remedies is "[s]ettling displaced people back on cultivatable land or in income generating employment".[89] Thus, states need to provide adequate procedural and substantive remedies to restore the incomes of the people affected by DID and improve their livelihoods. Overall, if displacement is justified based on the 'general welfare' requirement and adequate remedies are provided at all phases of displacement, the violation of the right to work can be avoided.

References

Aboda C, Mugagga F, Byakagaba P, Nabanoga G (2019) Development Induced Displacement: A Review of Risks Faced by Communities in Developing Countries. (2019) 7(2) Sociology and Anthropology 100–110.

African Commission on Human and Peoples' Rights (2011) Guidelines and Principles on Economic, Social and Cultural Rights in the African Charter on Human and Peoples' Rights, 2011, available at https://achpr.au.int/index.php/en/node/871, accessed 20 July 2025.

Cernea M M (1997) The Risks and Reconstruction Model for Resettling Displaced Populations. (1997) 25(10) World Development 1569–1587.

Cernea M M (2000a) Risks, Safeguards and Reconstruction: A Model for Population Displacement and Resettlement. (2000) 35(41) Economic and Political Weekly 3659–3678.

Cernea M M (2000b) Risks, safeguards, and reconstruction: a model for population displacement and resettlement. In: Cernea M M, McDowell C (eds) Risks and Reconstruction: Experiences of Resettlers and Refugees. The World Bank, Washington DC.

George A, Rajan I (2015) Changing Cities and Changing Lives: Development Induced Displacement in Kochi, Kerala. 1(1) International Journal on Urban Environments 1–18.

Hong P Y P, Singh S, Ramic J (2009) Development-induced impoverishment among involuntarily displaced populations. (2009) 25(3) Journal of Comparative Social Welfare 221–238.

Huang Y, Lin W, Li S, Ning Y (2018) Social Impacts of Dam-Induced Displacement and Resettlement: A Comparative Case Study in China. (2018) 10(11) Sustainability.

Hwang S-S, Cao Y, Xi Y (2011) The Short-Term Impact of Involuntary Migration in China's Three Gorges: A Prospective Study. (2011) 101(1) Social Indicators Research at 73–92.

International Commission of Jurists (ICJ) (1997) Maastricht Guidelines on Violations of Economic, Social and Cultural Rights, 26 January 1997, available at http://hrlibrary.umn.edu/instree/Maastrichtguidelines_.html, accessed 28 June 2025.

Kibreab G (2000) Common property resources and resettlement. In: Cernea M M, Christopher M (eds) Risks and Reconstruction Experiences of Resettlers and Refugees. The World Bank, Washington DC.

Maitra S (2009) Compensation and Resettlement – Experiences from the Narmada Valley and Sardar Sarovar Project. (2009) 10(2) Japanese Journal of Political Science 191–211.

Manjula K, Kumar T A, Aneesh K A (2013) Impact of Development-induced Displacement in Kerala, India (2013) 3(1) Journal of Internal Displacement 2–18.

[88] Cernea 2000b, p. 13.

[89] Ibid., p. 35.

Ó Cinnéide C (2015) The Right to Work in International Human Rights Law. In: Mantouvalou V (ed) The Right to Work: Legal and Philosophical Perspectives. Hart Publishing.

Patel S, Sliuzas R, Mathur N (2015) The risk of impoverishment in urban development-induced displacement and resettlement in Ahmedabad. (2015) 27(1) Environment & Urbanization 231–256.

Randell H (2016) The short-term impacts of development-induced displacement on wealth and subjective well-being in the Brazilian Amazon. (2016) 87 World Development 385–400.

Robinson C (2003) Risks and Rights: The Causes, Consequences, and Challenges of Development-Induced Displacement. The Brookings Institution-SAIS Project on Internal Displacement, An Occasional Paper May 2003.

Saul B, Kinley D, Mowbray J (2014) The International Covenant on Economic, Social and Cultural Rights: Commentary, Cases, and Materials. Oxford University Press, Oxford.

Stein M (1998) The Three Gorges Dam: the Unexamined Toll of Development-induced Displacement. 1 Forced Migration Review 7–9.

Terminski B (2015) Development-Induced Displacement and Resettlement: Causes, Consequences, and Socio-Legal Context. Ibidem-Verlag, Stuttgart.

UN Committee on Economic, Social and Cultural Rights (UN CESCR) (1990) General Comment No. 3: The Nature of States Parties' Obligations (Article 2, Para 1, of the Covenant), 14 December 1990, E/1991/23.

UN Committee on Economic, Social and Cultural Rights (UN CESCR) (2006) General Comment No. 18: The Right to Work (Article 6 of the Covenant), 6 February 2006, E/C.12/GC/18.

UN Committee on Economic, Social and Cultural Rights (UN CESCR) (2016) General Comment No.23: The right to just and favourable conditions of work (art 7 of the International Covenant on Economic, Social and Cultural Rights), 7 April 2016, E/C.12/GC/23.

Wilmsen B, Webber M, Duan Y (2011) Involuntary Rural Resettlement: Resources, Strategies, and Outcomes at the Three Gorges Dam, China. 20(4) Journal of Environment & Development 355–380.

Part III
Human Rights Safeguards in Specialized Human Rights Frameworks

Chapter 6
The Rights of Internally Displaced Persons in the Context of Development-Induced Displacement

Contents

Abstract The frameworks on the rights of internally displaced persons (IDPs), namely the UN Guiding Principles and the Kampala Convention, envisage normative standards and safeguards that apply at all phases of internal displacement. These norms include the right not to be arbitrarily displaced; meaningful participation in the decision-making and process of displacement; human rights protections during displacement; and the possibility of return, resettlement, and reintegration after displacement. As development is one of the prominent causes of internal displacement, these norms can inform the process of development-induced displacement (DID) and the safeguards that need to be provided along the way. Against this background, the current chapter examines the normative standards set out in these frameworks and their contextual application in cases of DID. It also assesses the adequacy of these standards in protecting the rights of persons displaced by development projects.

Keywords Internally displaced persons · Internal displacement · Guiding Principles on Internal Displacement · Kampala Convention · Protection against arbitrary displacement · Safeguards in the course of displacement

© T.M.C. ASSER PRESS and the authors 2026

R. G. Teshome, *The Human Cost of Development*, Human Rights Research Series 104,
https://doi.org/10.1007/978-94-6265-751-9_6

6.1 Introduction

In addition to the general human rights frameworks and norms discussed in the previous chapters, human rights protection for people affected by development-induced displacement (DID) can also be drawn from specialized frameworks that deal with specific issues relevant to DID or the specific groups of people affected thereby. One of these specialized frameworks is the set of instruments protecting the rights of internally displaced persons (IDPs). IDPs are persons "who have been forced…to leave their homes or places of habitual residence" due to various external factors and remain within their country of origin.[1] As described in Chap. 2, the two principal elements of this definition are the involuntary nature of the displacement and the fact that IDPs do not cross international borders.[2] IDPs account for almost two-thirds of the number of forced migrants in the world.[3] Internal displacement can be caused by a host of factors including conflicts, natural disasters, human rights abuses, and the implementation of development projects. Irrespective of the cause of displacement, IDPs face various risks and consequences, which necessitated their special protection under international law.[4] As mentioned in the preceding chapters, DID is one of the prominent causes of internal displacement.

Against this background, the current chapter seeks to identify and contextually analyse the human rights protections available to people displaced by DID and the corresponding obligations of states under the frameworks on internal displacement. Hence, the main question that this chapter seeks to answer is: to what extent do the safeguards and protections enunciated under the instruments on IDPs protect the rights of people(s) affected by DID? It explores this question through a systematic analysis of the normative standards envisaged under the UN Guiding Principles on Internal Displacement (hereinafter "the Guiding Principles")[5] and the African Union Convention on the Protection and Assistance of Internally Displaced Persons" (hereinafter the "Kampala Convention").[6] The chapter also comments on the adequacy of these standards in protecting the rights of persons displaced by DID.

---

[1] UN Commission on Human Rights, Guiding Principles on Internal Displacement, 11 February 1998, E/CN.4/1998/53/Add.2, Introduction: Scope and Purpose, para 2; see also African Union, African Union Convention for the Protection and Assistance of Internally Displaced Persons in Africa, 23 October 2009 ('Kampala Convention'), Article 1(k); see the discussion on the definition of IDPs in Chap. 2, Sect. 2.2.

[2] Kälin 2014, p. 617. Since the definition of IDPs and how it applies to persons displaced by development projects are discussed in Chap. 2, this section will not delve into the definition in detail.

[3] UNHCR, Global Trends: Forced Displacement in 2021, available at https://www.unhcr.org/global-trends-report-2024, accessed 20 July 2025, p. 2.

[4] Kälin 2008, pp. 4 and 5 (the instruments on IDPs do not confer a special legal status to IDPs, unlike those of refugees. Instead, IDPs are offered special protections due to the specific vulnerability that comes with being forcibly displaced).

[5] The Guiding Principles on Internal Displacement (n 1).

[6] Kampala Convention (n 1).

To this end, the chapter begins by introducing the recognition of the rights of IDPs in international law and the relevant instruments on which the analysis in this chapter draws in Sect. 6.2. Section 6.3 examines the human rights safeguards these instruments envisage and how they apply at all phases of DID—before, during, and after.

6.2 The Recognition of the Rights of Internally Displaced Persons

Until the last decade of the twentieth century, there was a "protection gap" in international law when it came to the rights of IDPs.[7] This gap emanated from the lack of a specific and comprehensive legal framework stipulating the protections that need to be provided to IDPs and an institutional mechanism mandated to provide assistance to this group of forced migrants.[8] The international refugee law regime is not applicable to forced migrants who did not cross international borders and organizations like the UN High Commissioner for Refugees (UNHCR) did not have direct mandates to assist IDPs.[9] Moreover, there was a pushback from states against the intervention of the international community on the issues of IDPs based on the claim of state sovereignty.[10] Indeed, IDPs remain entitled to similar rights and protections granted to everyone or citizens of a given country,[11] which is also affirmed by the Guiding Principles.[12] However, being uprooted from one's home or residence creates a special vulnerability that the existing norms did not adequately or specifically address.[13] Furthermore, IDPs remain "under the jurisdiction of their own governments, the very governments that may have caused their displacement in the first place and that are often unwilling or unable to provide for their wellbeing and security."[14] These factors, among others, necessitated the development of a specific normative framework for the protection of IDPs.

[7] Kälin 2005, p. 30; see also Maru 2014, p. 2.

[8] Cohen 2004, pp. 461 and 462; see also Maru 2014, p. 2.

[9] Cohen 2004, p. 590 (IDPs were not included in the 1951 Refugee Convention despite the plea of some states to extend refugee protection to "persons in refugee-like conditions in their own countries" or IDPs (see Cohen 2004, p. 590). The UNHCR Statute does not mention IDPs either, but later on, the organization has used Article 9 of the Statute, which allows the organization to undertake "additional activities" based on the direction from the General Assembly, to provide assistance to IDPs (see Cohen 2004, p. 601; see also UN General Assembly, Statute of the Office of the United Nations High Commissioner for Refugees, 14 December 1950, A/RES/428(V), Article 9); see also Cohen 2004, p. 459; see also Adeola 2016, pp. 91 and 92.

[10] Cohen 2004, p. 464.

[11] Kälin 2005, p. 28.

[12] The Guiding Principles on Internal Displacement (n 1) Principle 1.

[13] Maru 2014, pp. 2–5; see also Kälin 2005, p. 28; see also Cohen 2004, p. 593; see also Kälin 2008, pp. 4 and 5.

[14] Cohen 2004, p. 459; see also Kälin 1998, p. 557.

Particularly with the rampant increase of the number of IDPs in the 1990s due to, *inter alia*, internal conflicts and human rights abuses in different parts of the world,[15] the need for a normative framework for the protection of IDPs became more apparent.[16] During this period, a group of inter-governmental organizations and international NGOs highlighted the need for the development of normative standards and lobbied for the appointment of a special representative on IDPs to undertake this task.[17] The then Human Rights Commission positively responded to these campaigns by adopting a Resolution in 1992 calling for the UN Secretary-General to appoint a special representative.[18] In the same year, Francis M. Deng was appointed as a "Representative of the Secretary-General on the Human Rights of Internally Displaced Persons" and entrusted with a mandate to explore the protection of IDPs in the existing international law norms[19] and, later, to develop a set of standards.[20] The Special Representative formed and led a team of experts that undertook extensive research on the issue and developed a document, entitled "Compilation and Analysis of Legal Norms",[21] which was presented to the Commission in 1996.[22]

One of the main conclusions the team reached in this document was that the normative protections relevant to IDPs can be found scattered in different areas of international law, i.e. international human rights law, international humanitarian law (IHL), and refugee law, which can be employed analogously.[23] Nevertheless, these frameworks do not explicitly mention or address the specific situations of IDPs.[24] The documents particularly "identified seventeen areas of insufficient protection" for IDPs in the existing international law norms, which are attributable to either gaps or ambiguities in the law.[25] In order to fill this protection gap, the team concluded that "a restatement of the law would be needed to make it more relevant to IDPs and to clarify gaps and gray areas."[26] The decision to develop a set of guiding principles for the protection and assistance of IDPs was reached against this backdrop. Accordingly, the team of experts led by Francis M. Deng drafted the "Guiding Principles on Internal

---

[15] Studies depict that in 1982, only approximately 1.2 million IDPs were registered in eleven countries; this number soared to an estimated 20–25 million IDPs in 1995 spread across more than forty countries (see Cohen 2004, p. 460; see also Cohen and Deng 1998, pp. 3 and 32; see also Cohen 2004, p. 589).

[16] Cohen 2004, p. 460.

[17] Ibid., 462; see also Orchard 2010, p. 284.

[18] The UN Commission on Human Rights, Resolution 1992/73, Internally Displaced Persons, 5 March 1992, UN Doc. E/CN.4/RES/1992/73, para 2; see also Kälin 2014, p. 613.

[19] Resolution 1992/73 (n 18) para 2; see also Cohen 2004, p. 462; see also Kälin 2014, p. 613.

[20] UN Human Rights Commission, Resolution 1996/52, Internally Displaced Persons, 19 April 1996, UN Doc. E/CN.4/RES/1996/52, para 9.

[21] Deng 1998a; see also Deng 1998b.

[22] Cohen 2004, p. 463; see also Kälin 2014, p. 615.

[23] Cohen 2004, p. 463.

[24] Ibid., pp. 463 and 464; see also Kälin 2005, p. 28.

[25] Cohen 2004, p. 464; see also Kälin 2014, p. 615; see also Maru 2014, pp. 25–28; see also Kälin 1998, p. 560.

[26] Cohen 2004, p. 464; see also Kälin 2014, p. 621.

Displacement", which consist of thirty principles on the standards of protection for IDPs at all phases of displacement, and presented to the Commission in 1998.[27]

Indeed, the Guiding Principles are not legally binding norms. They were neither negotiated nor approved by states. Instead, they were drafted and adopted outside the regular inter-governmental procedure by a team of experts,[28] albeit in consultation with pertinent stakeholders.[29] In most cases, soft law documents prepared by experts are at some point negotiated, revised, and adopted by states, which was not the case for the Guiding Principles.[30] Thus, due to this peculiar drafting process, which some states termed as a "standard setting by the back door",[31] even their status as soft law has been objectionable.[32]

However, as mentioned before, the Guiding Principles reiterate already existing international law norms rather than create new ones per se.[33] For instance, the protection against arbitrary displacement espoused under Principle 6 of the Guiding Principles, while not explicitly mentioned in any binding treaty, is grounded in "the right to choose one's residence" under international human rights law and the prohibition of displacement during armed conflicts under IHL.[34] Similarly, Principle 15, which provides for the right of IDPs "to be protected against forcible return to or resettlement in any place where their life, safety, liberty and/or health would be at risk", is derived from the principle of non-refoulement under international refugee law and international human rights law.[35] This is also true for most of the normative standards enshrined under the Guiding Principles.[36] Furthermore, some of these principles reflect already established customary international law.[37] Overall, the Guiding

[27] The Guiding Principles on Internal Displacement (n 1); see also Cohen 2004, p. 465; see also Kälin 2014, p. 616.

[28] Cohen 2004, pp. 460 and 467; see also Kälin 2005, p. 29.

[29] Cohen 2004, p. 465; see also Kälin 2005, p. 29; see also Kälin 2014, p. 616.

[30] Cohen 2004, p. 473.

[31] Ibid.; see also Kälin 2014, p. 617; see also Bagshaw 1998, p. 551.

[32] Kälin 2005, p. 29.

[33] Ibid.; see also Kälin 2014, p. 617.

[34] Kälin 2005, p. 29.

[35] Maru 2014, p. 310; see also Phuong 2005, p. 61; see also Kälin 2005, p. 29; see also Kälin 1998, p. 561. The principle of non-refoulement prohibits states from returning individuals to a state or jurisdiction where they will face persecution, torture and other grave human rights threats. This principle is widely recognized in different areas of international law and it also has the status of customary international law (see OHCHR, The principle of non-refoulement under international human rights law, available at https://www.ohchr.org/Documents/Issues/Migration/GlobalCompactMigration/ThePrincipleNon-RefoulementUnderInternationalHumanRightsLaw.pdf, accessed 30 June 2025).

[36] For instance, Principles 10–23 on the protections that need to be provided for IDPs during displacement mostly restate the general human rights norms widely recognized in various treaties and customary law (see the Guiding Principles on Internal Displacement (n 1) Principles 10–23).

[37] Kälin 2005, pp. 29 and 30; see also Kälin 2014, p. 628; see also Henckaerts and Doswald-Beck 2005, p. 176 (this study shows that some of the IHL norms that the Guiding Principles draw from, such as the prohibition of the destruction of properties of IDPs and the humanitarian assistance that need to be provided for IDPs (Principle 7(2)), reflect customary international law).

Principles "are drafted in a way that carefully restate[s] existing international law with a view to making more general norms applicable to the specific situation of internal displacement."[38] Hence, they draw their authority from binding norms that had already been "negotiated and accepted by states".[39]

In addition, the Guiding Principles have been endorsed by several intergovernmental organizations including various organs of the UN.[40] The Guiding Principles have also been referred to by the UN treaty bodies including the Human Rights Committee and the Committee on Economic, Social, and Cultural Rights (CESCR), which in their respective concluding observations recommended states to apply the Principles.[41] Moreover, the Guiding Principles have received the support of the regional human rights bodies, particularly the Inter-American Commission on Human Rights and the African Commission on Human and Peoples' Rights,[42] and a number of international organizations and NGOs.[43]

More importantly, the Guiding Principles have also been widely accepted by states, some of which have even incorporated them into their national laws and policies on IDPs.[44] Even some states that at first strongly opposed the framework due to its peculiar drafting process, such as Mexico, Egypt, and Sudan, subsequently

---

[38] Kälin 2005, p. 30; see also Phuong 2005, p. 58.

[39] Cohen 2004, p. 467; see also Kälin 2005, p. 33; see also Kälin 1998, p. 562.

[40] For instance, during the World Summit in 2005, members of the General Assembly unanimously endorsed the Guiding Principles "...as an important international framework for the protection of [IDPs]" (see UN General Assembly, Resolution 60/1, 2005 World Summit Outcome, 24 October 2005, A/RES/60/1, para 132; see also Kälin 2014, p. 612). The then UN Secretary-General, Kofi Annan, also characterized the Guiding Principles as "the basic international norm for protection" of IDPs and urged member states to recognize them (see Report of the Secretary-General, In larger freedom: towards development, security and human rights for all, 21 March 2005, A/59/2005, para 210; see also Kälin 2005, p. 27; see also Cohen 2004, p. 469). Similarly, the Human Rights Commission and its successor the Human Rights Council had recognized the framework as "an important tool for dealing with situations of internal displacement" and encouraged states and other relevant stakeholders to apply the principles incorporated therein (UN Commission on Human Rights, Internally displaced persons, 14 April 2005, UN Doc. E/CN.4/2005/L.60, para 7; see also Human Rights Council, Resolution 6/32, Mandate of the Representative of the Secretary-General on the human rights of internally displaced persons, 14 December 2007, UN Doc. A/HRC/RES/6/32, para 5; see also Human Rights Council, Resolution 23/8, Mandate of the Special Rapporteur on the human rights of internally displaced persons, 20 June 2013, UN Doc. A/HRC/RES/23/8, para 12; see also Kälin 2005, p. 27; see also Cohen 2004, p. 469; see also Kälin 2014, p. 612).

[41] UN Human Rights Committee (HRC), Concluding observations of the Human Rights Committee: Chad, 11 August 2009, CCPR/C/TCD/CO/1, para 13; see also UN Committee on Economic, Social and Cultural Rights (CESCR), Document submitted by the United Nations Interim Administration Mission in Kosovo (UNMIK), Concluding Observations of the Committee on Economic, Social and Cultural Rights, 1 December 2008, E/C.12/UNK/CO/1, para 27; see also Kälin 2014, p. 625.

[42] Cohen 2004, pp. 469 and 470. The Inter-American Convention referred to the Guiding Principles in the case of the *Mapiripán Massacre* (see Case of the *Mapiripán Massacre vs Colombia*, Judgment, Inter-American Court of Human Rights, 15 September 2005, para 171; see also Kälin 2014, p. 626).

[43] Cohen 2004, p. 468.

[44] Kälin 2014, p. 623; see also Cohen 2004, p. 470; Kälin 2005, p. 33; see also Orchard 2010, pp. 294 and 295; see also Deng and Adeola 2021, pp. 63 and 64.

endorsed it.[45] Thus, due to all the factors elucidated above, the Guiding Principles have an authoritative nature irrespective of the non-involvement of states in the drafting process.[46] At the very least, they can be considered a subsidiary source of international law under Article 38 of the ICJ Statute as they were presumably drafted by "the most highly qualified publicists".[47] Hence, the Guiding Principles carry significant normative weight.

The African Union, on the other hand, took the route of a binding treaty to address the protection gap mentioned above. As Africa has the highest number of IDPs, the need for a standard of protection was more urgent.[48] Consequently, the Kampala Convention was adopted in October 2009 and came into force in December 2012.[49] The overarching objectives of the Convention are to prevent or reduce internal displacement by addressing the root causes of displacement, to establish a legal framework for the protection of IDPs, and to elucidate the roles and responsibilities of various actors involved in the displacement process, among others.[50] The Convention drew heavily on the standards of protection enumerated under the Guiding Principles[51] and, thereby, it also reflects existing international law norms.[52] Nonetheless, unlike the latter, the Convention creates binding rights and obligations for state parties.[53]

Conversely, the other two major regional human rights systems, i.e. the Inter-American and European human rights systems,[54] have yet to develop special frameworks for the protection of IDPs. Hence, the analysis in the subsequent sections will

---

[45] Cohen 2004, pp. 473 and 474.

[46] Ibid., p. 475; Kälin 2014, p. 628.

[47] United Nations, Statute of the International Court of Justice, 18 April 1946, Article 38(1)(d).

[48] Maru 2014, pp. 2 and 3; see also Duchatellier and Phuong 2014, p. 650. For instance, according to the data of the Internal Displacement Monitoring Center (IDMC), by the end of 2018, there were around 17.8 million IDPs in Africa, which accounts for 40% of IDPs in the world (see IDMC, Africa Report on Internal Displacement, 2019, available at https://www.internal-displacement.org/publications/africa-report-on-internal-displacement, accessed 30 June 2025).

[49] Kampala Convention (n 1); see also Maru 2014, p. 1; while the African Union had been making various efforts to fill the protection gap and address the alarming increase of the number of IDPs in the continent since the beginning of 1990s, the decision to develop a binding treaty was reached in 2004 (see Maru 2014, pp. 29–31). To date, the Convention has 33 state parties (see the list of states at https://au.int/en/treaties/african-union-convention-protection-and-assistance-internally-displaced-persons-africa, accessed 30 June 2025).

[50] Kampala Convention (n 1) Article 2; see also Maru 2014, pp. 141–145.

[51] Maru 2014, p. 5; see also Adeola 2018, p. 15; see also Duchatellier and Phuong 2014, p. 655; see also Deng and Adeola 2021, pp. 64–69.

[52] Adeola 2018, p. 15.

[53] Maru 2014, p. 5.

[54] In 2006, the Committee of Ministers of the Council of Europe adopted a recommendation that provides guidance to member states when dealing with internally displaced persons (see Council of Europe, Committee of Ministers, Recommendation Rec (2006) 6 of the Committee of Ministers to member states on internally displaced persons, 5 April 2006). The principles incorporated in the Recommendation are highly influenced by the Guiding Principles (see Kälin 2014, p. 624).

draw on the normative contents of the Guiding Principles and the Kampala Convention and elucidate their application in the context of DID. It is worth noting here that the procedural and substantive safeguards that need to be provided for people displaced by DID should not be limited to the standards of protection envisaged in those two instruments. As will be described further subsequently, the Guiding Principles and the Kampala Convention reflect the minimum standards of protection.[55] Moreover, as depicted in Chap. 2, DID is foreseeable, pre-planned, and caused by the state or with the direct involvement of the state unlike most of the other forms of internal displacement. These factors (should) heighten the obligations of states when displacement is carried out to make room for development projects. Hence, states need to go beyond the minimum standards and provide comprehensive safeguards at all phases of DID including the human rights protections illuminated in other parts of this book.

6.3 Normative Content of the Rights of Internally Displaced Persons

The Guiding Principles and the Kampala Convention contain a set of normative standards that apply at all stages of displacement: before, during, and after displacement. These standards "...provide protection against arbitrary displacement, offer a basis for protection and assistance during displacement, and set forth guarantees for safe return, resettlement and reintegration."[56] An exhaustive discussion of all these standards and their normative content in this section is not necessary as some are not (directly) applicable in the context of internal displacement prompted by development.[57] Thus, this section focuses on the standards that are thematically most relevant to DID. The following sub-sections will identify these pertinent standards and analyse their normative content under three categories pertaining to the three phases of displacement.

Before proceeding to the analysis of the normative content of these instruments, it is important to note that while the Kampala Convention mostly emulates the Guiding Principles in terms of its normative content, the two instruments also have several differences. One of these differences pertains to the way the standards stipulated in the respective frameworks are formulated. The Guiding Principles use rights-based language—they enumerate the rights of IDPs at all stages of displacement. Meanwhile, the Kampala Convention espouses the same standards from the perspective of

[55] Kälin 2005, p. 30.

[56] The Guiding Principles on Internal Displacement (n 1), introductory note by Francis M. Deng (it has to be noted that Deng made this statement concerning the Guiding Principles, but it is also true for the Kampala Convention since the latter heavily draws on the former).

[57] For instance, section III of the Guiding Principles (Principles 10–23) restates the general human rights guarantees, such as the right to life, prohibition of genocide, the right to adequate standard of living, and the right to family life, provided in the core human rights treaties (The Guiding Principles on Internal Displacement (n 1) Principles 10–23).

the obligations of states and other stakeholders.[58] In other words, to a larger extent, the Convention identifies the duty-bearers and stipulates what their duties are rather than listing the substantive rights of IDPs. These frameworks also have some more specific differences, which will be mentioned in the relevant parts below. Indeed, the two instruments also have distinct legal statuses in international law as mentioned before.

6.3.1 Before Displacement

The instruments on IDPs envisage a range of standards of protection and safeguards that states need to be put in place prior to displacement. These standards of protection have twin objectives: preventing displacement or protecting right-holders against (arbitrary) displacement and advancing the provision of adequate procedural and substantive safeguards in order to minimise, if not prevent, the adverse consequences of displacement.[59] These standards will be discussed subsequently.

6.3.1.1 Protection from Displacement

The Guiding Principles and the Kampala Convention explicitly recognize the right not to be arbitrarily displaced from one's home or habitual residence,[60] which is one of the main novelties of these instruments.[61] While it is implied in other rights, such as the right to housing and "freedom to choose [one's] residence",[62] the right to protection against arbitrary displacement is not expressly recognized as a standalone right in other human rights instruments.[63] Pursuant to Principle 6(1) of the Guiding Principles, "[e]very human being shall have the right to be protected against being arbitrarily displaced from his or her home or place of habitual residence."[64] A similar

[58] The Kampala Convention identifies state parties, international organizations, humanitarian agencies, and private actors as duty-bearers and stipulates their respective obligations in relation to the protection of the rights of IDPs (see Kampala Convention (n 1)).

[59] The Guiding Principles on Internal Displacement (n 1), introductory note by the Representative of the Secretary-General on IDPs Francis M. Deng; see also Kampala Convention (n 1) Article 2.

[60] The Guiding Principles on Internal Displacement (n 1) Principle 6(1).

[61] Phuong 2005, p. 56; see also Duchatellier and Phuong 2014, p. 657.

[62] UN General Assembly, International Covenant on Economic, Social and Cultural Rights, 16 December 1966, 993 United Nations Treaty Series 3, Article 11(1); see also UN General Assembly, International Covenant on Civil and Political Rights, 16 December 1966, 999 United Nations Treaty Series 171, Article 12.

[63] Duchatellier and Phuong 2014, p. 657.

[64] The Guiding Principles on Internal Displacement (n 1) Principle 6(1).

provision is provided under Article 4(4) of the Kampala Convention.[65] These provisions "... [frame] the discussion on internal displacement as [a] rights-based problem requiring rights-based solutions that touch on states' human rights commitments."[66]

The second paragraph of Principle 6 further elucidates what "arbitrary displacement" entails by listing cases, albeit not exhaustively, that constitute arbitrary displacement.[67] One of the instances mentioned is displacement prompted by "large-scale development projects, which are not justified by compelling and overriding public interests".[68] The requirement of "compelling and overriding public interests" under this Principle embodies the dual requirements of necessity and proportionality.[69] Thus, DID can only be justified if the development project concerned is necessary to achieve such a prevailing public interest and the ensuing displacement is proportionate to the interest pursued. This is also in line with permissible limitation clauses of the relevant human rights,[70] such as the right to housing and the right to property, described in the preceding chapters. From this and the other instances of arbitrary displacement listed under the principle, it can be deduced that one of the elements of the right not to be arbitrarily displaced is that displacement must be justified based on the relevant international law norms.[71] If not, it is considered arbitrary displacement.

Nevertheless, this principle only refers to large-scale development projects.[72] While it is not clear whether this was an intentional choice by the drafters, it gives the impression that displacement caused by small-scale development projects, which are not justified by the public interest requirement, is not considered arbitrary displacement.[73] In reality, DID can be caused by both small and large-scale development projects. Indeed, large-scale development projects have the potential to displace a large number of people and the magnitude of their social and environmental impact can be significantly higher than that of small-scale projects. However, persons uprooted from their homes or residences bear similar socio-economic risks regardless of the scale of the project. Moreover, displacement will inevitably interfere with their human rights. Hence, in order to justify displacement and the resulting human rights interferences, the project needs to be justified by an overriding public interest irrespective of its scale.

65 Kampala Convention (n 1) Article 4(4).

66 Adeola 2016, p. 93.

67 The Guiding Principles on Internal Displacement (n 1) Principle 6(2).

68 Ibid., Principle 6(2)(c).

69 Robinson 2003, pp. 51 and 52; see also Kälin 2008, pp. 32 and 33.

70 Kälin 2008, p. 33.

71 Deng and Adeola 2021, p. 66; see also Adeola 2016, p. 93. This list of cases of arbitrary displacement also hints that displacement can be justified in exceptional situations (see Kälin 2014, p. 618). However, there are cases where the prohibition of displacement is absolute and cannot be justified under any circumstances, for instance, displacement caused by Apartheid policies or ethnic cleansing (see The Guiding Principles on Internal Displacement (n 1) Principle 6(2)(a); see also Adeola 2016, p. 94).

72 The Guiding Principles on Internal Displacement (n 1) Principle 6(2).

73 Giustiniani 2011, p. 356.

The Kampala Convention also contains a similar list of cases of arbitrary displacement.[74] The major distinguishing factor between the two instruments in this regard is that arbitrary displacement caused by development projects that are not justified by an "overriding public interest" is not included in the list under the Kampala Convention. This was included in the earlier draft of the Convention.[75] However, the drafters subsequently opted for a more lenient formulation.[76] Consequently, Article 10(1) of the Convention stipulates that "States Parties, as much as possible, shall prevent displacement caused by projects carried out by public or private actors".[77] The condition of "compelling and overriding public interest" is only required when displacement affects "...communities with special attachment to, and dependency, on land due to their particular culture and spiritual values".[78] Thus, the Convention is less stringent in this regard compared to the Guiding Principles, which is also one of its shortcomings.[79] Indeed, involuntary displacement exposes those who have special ties to their land or those who depend on land for their livelihoods to severe socio-economic and cultural adversities. Nevertheless, involuntary displacement inherently interferes with a range of human rights irrespective of the level of dependence of the people affected on land. While the level of dependence on land of the people(s) affected partly determines the severity of the consequences of DID and is also an important factor in the assessment of whether or not there is a violation, displacement inherently interferes with a range of human rights. Hence, it needs to be justified by a compelling public interest for these interferences to be permissible.

Yet, it can be argued that the norms envisaged under the Kampala Convention should be construed in accordance with the other human rights frameworks in the continent, such as the African Charter on Human and Peoples' Rights. Several provisions of the Charter provide that limitations on the respective rights must be necessary to protect a higher public interest and proportionate to the interest pursued. For instance, the right to property, espoused under Article 14 of the Charter, can only be limited in the interest of the public and in accordance with relevant laws.[80] Since involuntary displacement inevitably interferes with some of these rights including the right to property, it has to be justified based on the public interest requirement. This interpretation is also supported by the Kampala Convention, which demands State Parties to respect their human rights obligations in the process of displacement.[81]

---

[74] Kampala Convention (n 1) Article 4(4).

[75] Adeola 2018, p. 16; see also Okello 2019, p. 375.

[76] This is the result of objections by some states, particularly Egypt, which expressed concern about the extent of obligations related to compensation that the original formulation might create (see Okello 2019, p. 375).

[77] Kampala Convention (n 1) Article 10(1); see also Maru 2014, pp. 177, 178 and 181.

[78] Kampala Convention (n 1), Article 4(5); see also Adeola 2018, p. 16; see also Maru 2014, p. 182.

[79] Maru 2014, p. 182.

[80] Organization of African Unity (OAU), African Charter on Human and Peoples' Rights, 27 June 1981, CAB/LEG/67/3 rev. 5, 21 I.L.M. 58 (1982), ('African Charter'), Article 14.

[81] Kampala Convention (n 1) Article 3(1)(d).

The Kampala Convention rectifies one of the shortcomings of the Guiding Principles mentioned above—only referring to large-scale development projects—by avoiding a distinction between small and large-scale projects.[82] Article 10 generally refers to "projects" irrespective of their scale when addressing DID.[83] In addition, the Kampala Convention urges states to provide heightened protection for people who depend on land for their socio-economic and cultural subsistence. Article 4(5) of the Convention enunciates that "States Parties shall endeavour to protect communities with special attachment to, and dependency, on land due to their particular culture and spiritual values from being displaced from such lands, except for compelling and overriding public interests".[84] This is particularly relevant in the context of DID as these groups are often susceptible to special challenges due to their dependence on land.

In any case, displacement should only be undertaken as a last resort and states need to explore "all feasible alternatives" in order to prevent or minimize displacement.[85] In the context of DID, this includes changing the site of the project or looking for ways in which the project can be implemented without causing displacement. In cases where displacement cannot be avoided, less severe or intrusive alternatives should be explored to minimize the adverse consequences of displacement. This includes carrying out socio-economic and human rights impact assessments prior to the displacement decision.[86] This is particularly vital in the context of DID.

6.3.1.2 Procedural and Substantive Safeguards

In cases where displacement is inevitable and justified based on the public interest condition, states are required to ensure that adequate procedural and substantive safeguards are put in place prior to displacement in order to mitigate the adverse impacts of involuntary displacement.[87] Principle 7(3) of the Guiding Principles envisages procedural safeguards applicable in cases where displacement is not caused by emergency situations, such as armed conflicts and disasters,[88] under which DID falls. These safeguards include, *inter alia*, access to all relevant information concerning the reasons and the process of displacement as well as the proposed remedies, meaningful participation of those potentially affected by displacement, and access to legal remedies.[89] The interpretation of these safeguards can be informed by the relevant

---

[82] Giustiniani 2011, p. 356.

[83] Kampala Convention (n 1) Article 10.

[84] Ibid., Article 4(5).

[85] The Guiding Principles on Internal Displacement (n 1) Principle 7(1); see also Kampala Convention (n 1) Article 10(2).

[86] Adeola 2016, p. 94.

[87] The Guiding Principles on Internal Displacement (n 1) Principle 7(1); see also Kälin 2008, p. 38.

[88] The Guiding Principles on Internal Displacement (n 1) Principle 7(3).

[89] Ibid.; see also Adeola 2016, pp. 95 and 96.

norms discussed in the preceding chapters in relation to forced eviction and expropriation. In a nutshell, those affected by displacement should have a say in the process of displacement and the safeguards provided therefor. They should also be given an opportunity to challenge the decision through judicial and other means if they choose to do so. The Principle also provides that "[t]he free and informed consent of those to be displaced shall be sought".[90] This, however, does not confer veto power on those to be displaced, unlike the instruments on the rights of indigenous peoples as will be elucidated in the next chapter, which is evident from the wording of the Principle. It instead obliges states to seek consent, which is arguably an obligation of conduct rather than an obligation of result.

The Kampala Convention also sets out certain procedural safeguards that states are required to put in place before displacement, which might vary depending on the cause of displacement.[91] In relation to DID, the Convention obliges states to provide relevant information and consult with the persons potentially affected by displacement in order to explore less intrusive alternatives.[92] With regard to private projects undertaken by non-state actors, the Convention requires states to ensure that such procedural safeguards are guaranteed by the actors concerned.[93] The Convention, unlike the Guiding Principles, does not include the requirement of informed consent.

The Guiding Principles further stipulate a set of substantive safeguards in the second paragraph of Principle 7, which reads:

> The authorities undertaking such displacement shall ensure, to the greatest practicable extent, that proper accommodation is provided to the displaced persons, that such displacements are effected in satisfactory conditions of safety, nutrition, health and hygiene, and that members of the same family are not separated.[94]

It is evident from this paragraph that these safeguards reflect the bare minimum standards or requirements, which are seemingly targeted to emergency situations. One of these requirements is the provision of "proper accommodation" to those displaced.[95] The principle does not define what constitutes "proper accommodation". Nonetheless, this can be informed by the requirements of adequate housing under the International Covenant on Economic, Social and Cultural Rights (ICESCR) and the corresponding interpretation of the Committee.[96] This is particularly true in the case of DID. Since DID is not a displacement prompted by an emergency situation and, rather, is pre-planned, the replacement accommodation provided should go beyond

[90] The Guiding Principles on Internal Displacement (n 1) Principle 7(3)(c).

[91] The Convention separately addresses conflict-induced displacement and DID, albeit it also includes general provisions that apply in all cases.

[92] Kampala Convention (n 1) Article 10(2); see also Maru 2014, p. 181. The earlier draft of this provision, which required states to obtain consent, was not accepted by states (see Okello 2019, p. 375).

[93] Kampala Convention (n 1) Article 10(2).

[94] The Guiding Principles on Internal Displacement (n 1) Principle 7(2).

[95] Ibid.

[96] ICESCR (n 62) Article 11(1); see also UN CESCR 1991, para 8.

the bare minimum of providing shelter and comply with the "adequacy" requirements outlined in Chap. 3.

The Guiding Principles also minimally refer to compensation under the requirement of access to information for those to be displaced.[97] Principle 7(3) requires that those potentially affected by displacement should be provided with full information on, among others, "compensation and relocation" if applicable.[98] It can be reasonably inferred from this that the provision of compensation is one of the substantive safeguards envisaged under the Guiding Principles. However, the Guiding Principles do not offer further normative standards on the conditions and determination of compensation. Nor do they stipulate other substantive safeguards that are necessary to restore and possibly improve the livelihoods of displaced persons, such as replacement land and other assets and measures to restore the income-earning capacity of those affected. These safeguards are particularly essential in the context of DID. Most of the standards enshrined under the Guiding Principles, thus, reflect minimum international standards and they seldom address issues particularly relevant to DID. Hence, it is safe to assume that the principles were drafted with persons displaced by emergency situations in mind.

The Kampala Convention, on the other hand, provides that states should offer "effective remedies" to persons affected by displacement.[99] One of the remedies espoused under the Convention is the provision of "just and fair compensation" to make good the damage incurred due to displacement.[100] While the Convention does not specify what constitutes "just and fair compensation", it suggests that this should be determined based on international standards.[101] Despite this provision and addressing DID as a separate category of displacement, the Kampala Convention also does not stipulate standards of protection that take into account the peculiar features of DID and provide adequate protection for persons displaced by this form of displacement.

The Guiding Principles and the Kampala Convention further urge states to protect those who rely on land for their socio-economic and cultural subsistence from displacement.[102] This is particularly pertinent in the context of DID. However, the relevant provisions do not clarify what protections and safeguards states need to provide for these groups. When it comes to indigenous peoples, the interpretation of these provisions can be informed by the norms on indigenous peoples' rights, which will be discussed in the next chapter.

In a nutshell, the notion of "arbitrariness" pertains to both the rationale and the process of displacement as well as the remedies or safeguards provided along the way. In other words, displacement would be arbitrary if it is not justified in light

[97] The Guiding Principles on Internal Displacement (n 1) Principle 7(3)(b).

[98] Ibid.

[99] Kampala Convention (n 1) Article 12(1).

[100] Ibid., Article 12(2).

[101] Ibid.

[102] The Guiding Principles on Internal Displacement (n 1) Principle 9; see also Kampala Convention (n 1) Article 4(5).

of the pertinent international law norms and/or undertaken without the provision of adequate procedural and substantive safeguards.

6.3.2 *During Displacement*

The standards of protection that need to be provided during displacement are enumerated under Principles 10–23 of the Guiding Principles.[103] These principles restate general human rights norms by contextualizing them to situations of internal displacement.[104] For instance, Principle 18 guarantees "the right to an adequate standard of living",[105] which is also provided under multiple human rights frameworks.[106] The Principle further provides that in the context of IDPs, this right entails, "at the minimum", the provision of "[e]ssential food and potable water; [b]asic shelter and housing; [a]ppropriate clothing; and [e]ssential medical services and sanitation."[107] Similarly, Principle 17, which provides for the right to family life, emphasizes the right of family members to remain together after displacement if they wish to do so, which is particularly important in the context of IDPs.[108] In short, the norms that apply during displacement mostly reiterate general human rights norms with some contextualization. Hence, a detailed analysis of these norms is not pertinent here.

In addition, states are required to provide humanitarian assistance to IDPs during displacement or until the durable solutions discussed below are realized. Indeed, the primary duty to provide protection and assistance to IDPs rests on states.[109] However, both the Guiding Principles and the Kampala Convention also stress the "right" of international organizations and other stakeholders to provide assistance to IDPs, especially when states are "unable or unwilling" to do so.[110] Principle 25(2) of the Guiding Principles reads:

> International humanitarian organizations and other appropriate actors have the right to offer their services in support of the internally displaced. Such an offer shall not be regarded as an unfriendly act or an interference in a State's internal affairs and shall be considered in

---

[103] The Guiding Principles on Internal Displacement (n 1) Principles 10–23.

[104] Kälin 1998, pp. 559 and 561; see also Kälin 2014, pp. 618 and 619.

[105] The Guiding Principles on Internal Displacement (n 1) Principle 18(1).

[106] ICESCR (n 62) Article 11; see also UN General Assembly, Universal Declaration of Human Rights, 10 December 1948, 217 A (III) ('UDHR'), Article 25.

[107] The Guiding Principles on Internal Displacement (n 1) Principle 18(2).

[108] Ibid., Principle 17; see also Kälin 1998, p. 561; see also Phuong 2005, p. 58.

[109] The Guiding Principles on Internal Displacement (n 1) Principle 3; see also Kampala Convention (n 1) Article 5(1); see also Cohen 2004, p. 595; see also Kälin 2014, p. 619.

[110] The Guiding Principles on Internal Displacement (n 1) Principle 25(2); Kampala Convention (n 1) Articles 6 and 8; see also Brookings-Bern Project on Internal Displacement, Addressing Internal Displacement: A Framework for National Responsibility, April 2005, available at https://www.brookings.edu/research/addressing-internal-displacement-a-framework-for-national-responsibility/, accessed 30 June 2025.

> good faith. Consent thereto shall not be arbitrarily withheld, particularly when authorities concerned are unable or unwilling to provide the required humanitarian assistance.[111]

The Kampala Convention particularly emphasizes the role of the African Union in this regard.[112] Overall, states should not arbitrarily decline humanitarian assistance from the international community particularly when they are not in a position to provide such assistance themselves. This challenges the traditional conception of state sovereignty that insists on excluding the international community from intervening in the issues of IDPs or national affairs and providing assistance.[113]

6.3.3 After Displacement: Durable Solutions

The Guiding Principles and the Kampala Convention also envisage a set of normative standards that apply after displacement. These norms focus on durable solutions or long-term remedies needed to address the predicament of internal displacement and its adverse consequences. "Durable solutions principally relate to the restoration of the ability of IDPs to earn their livelihood and re-establish their normal lives."[114] Accordingly, Principle 28 of the Guiding Principles and Article 11 of the Kampala Convention specify three long-term remedies that states need to provide or facilitate after displacement, namely return, resettlement, and reintegration.[115]

IDPs should be provided with an opportunity to return to their homes or habitual residences, which is the preferred alternative,[116] after the situation that necessitated their flight has ceased to exist or to resettle elsewhere if they wish to do so.[117] It is worth noting here that although return is the preferred remedy, it might not always be a viable alternative. For instance, as depicted in Chap. 2, DID often leads to permanent relocation of the persons affected. Thus, return is seldom possible in the context of DID, which makes resettlement the only feasible alternative.

As both the Guiding Principles and the Kampala Convention clearly state, return and resettlement have to be voluntary.[118] The IDPs concerned should be consulted and informed about their options as well as should be given a chance to participate

---

[111] The Guiding Principles on Internal Displacement (n 1) Principle 25(2).

[112] Kampala Convention (n 1) Article 8; see also Giustiniani 2011, p. 358.

[113] Cohen 2004, p. 600.

[114] Maru 2014, p. 296.

[115] The Guiding Principles on Internal Displacement (n 1) Principle 28; see also Kampala Convention (n 1) Article 11; see also Kälin 2008, p. 125. The durable solutions envisaged in these instruments draw on international refugee law standards.

[116] Bradley 2018, p. 220; see also Kälin 2008, p. 126.

[117] The Guiding Principles on Internal Displacement (n 1) Principle 28(1); see also Kampala Convention (n 1) Article 11(1).

[118] The Guiding Principles on Internal Displacement (n 1) Principle 28(1); see also Kampala Convention (n 1) Article 11(1).

"in the planning and management of their return or resettlement".[119] Hence, return or resettlement should be based on the informed consent of the IDPs concerned. More specifically, IDPs should not be compelled to return or resettle "in any place where their life, safety, liberty and/or health would be at risk",[120] which mirrors the principle of non-refoulement.[121]

The other durable solution envisaged under those instruments is a reintegration of IDPs in their place of return or resettlement.[122] This encompasses various measures including restitution of the properties "they left behind",[123] which is often not feasible in the case of DID, and access to common resources and public services.[124] Reintegration also includes measures aimed at "achieving peaceful and meaningful coexistence between IDPs and host communities",[125] particularly in the case of resettlement. As mentioned in Chap. 2, the adverse effects of DID also extend to host communities inhabiting the resettlement sites due to competition for resources and the socio-cultural clash that resettlement potentially results in. Hence, reintegration measures need to address these calamities.

6.4 Conclusion

As this chapter has established, there was a legal and institutional protection gap for IDPs in international law until the last decade of the twentieth century. The Guiding Principles and the Kampala Convention have aimed at filling this protection gap by setting out normative standards that apply before, during, and after displacement. These norms include the right not to be arbitrarily displaced, meaningful participation in the process, human rights protections in the course of displacement, and return or resettlement and reintegration after displacement. Further, these instruments also put correlative obligations on states that generally "...encompass preventing and avoiding conditions that might lead to displacement, providing assistance and protection to IDPs once they are uprooted and helping IDPs return home or resettle after the emergency is over."[126] Indeed, these normative standards inform the protection and assistance that needs to be provided to IDPs and provide guidance to states and

[119] The Guiding Principles on Internal Displacement (n 1) Principle 28(2); see also Kampala Convention (n 1) Article 11(2); see also Maru 2014, p. 298; see also Kälin 2014, p. 619.

[120] The Guiding Principles on Internal Displacement (n 1) Principle 15; see also Kampala Convention (n 1) Article 9(2)(e).

[121] Maru 2014, p. 310; see also Phuong 2005, p. 61; Orchard 2010, p. 298.

[122] The Guiding Principles on Internal Displacement (n 1) Principle 28; see also Kampala Convention (n 1) Article 11.

[123] The Guiding Principles on Internal Displacement (n 1) Principle 29; see also Phuong 2005, pp. 61 and 62.

[124] Maru 2014, pp. 309 and 310.

[125] Ibid., p. 310.

[126] Cohen 2004, p. 595.

other stakeholders working on issues of internal displacement. Thus, they go a long way towards filling the protection gap.

Nevertheless, since most of the norms incorporated in those instruments mainly reflect minimum standards that are seemingly more geared towards displacement caused by emergency situations, the protection gap still persists to some extent particularly when it comes to persons displaced by DID. As elucidated throughout this book, DID is foreseeable, pre-planned, and predominantly instigated by states, which heighten the obligations of states. The Guiding Principles and the Kampala Convention do not specify how these factors affect the extent of state obligations in different phases of displacement. Nor do they stipulate the specific short-term and long-term remedies that need to be provided by states for people uprooted from their homes or residences to make room for development projects. They also do not clarify what return or resettlement and reintegration entail in the context of DID. Hence, the minimum standards envisaged under those instruments fall short of adequately addressing the peculiar features of DID and protecting the rights of the people affected thereby.

References

Adeola R (2016) The right not to be arbitrarily displaced under the United Nations Guiding Principles on Internal Displacement. (2016) 16(1) African Human Rights Law Journal 83–98.

Adeola R (2018) The Kampala Convention and the right not to be arbitrarily displaced. (2018) 59 Forced Migration Review 15–17.

Bagshaw S (1998) Internally Displaced Persons at the Fifty-Fourth Session of the United Nations Commission on Human Rights. (1998) 10(3) International Journal of Refugee Law 548–556.

Bradley M (2018) Durable Solutions and the Right of Return for IDPs: Evolving Interpretations. (2018) 30(2) International Journal of Refugee Law 218–242.

Cohen R (2004) The Guiding Principles on Internal Displacement: An Innovation in International Standard Setting. (2004) 10(4) Global Governance 459–480.

Cohen R, Deng F M (1998) Masses in Flight: The Global Crisis of Internal Displacement. Brookings Institution Press, Washington DC.

Deng F M (1998a) Internally Displaced Persons. Office of the United Nations High Commissioner for Human Rights, Geneva.

Deng F M (1998b) Internally displaced persons: compilation and analysis of legal norms. United Nations, New York.

Deng F M, Adeola R (2021) The Normative Influence of the UN Guiding Principles on the Kampala Convention in the Protection of Internally Displaced Persons in Africa. 65(S1) Journal of African Law 59–72.

Duchatellier M, Phuong C (2014) The African Contribution to the protection of internally displaced persons: A commentary on the 2009 Kampala Convention. In: Chetail V, Bauloz C (eds) Research handbook on international law and migration. Edward Elgar Publishing, Cheltenham, UK.

Giustiniani F Z (2011) New hopes and challenges for the protection of IDPs in Africa: the Kampala Convention for the Protection and Assistance of Internally Displaced Persons in Africa. (2011) 39(2) Denver Journal of International Law and Policy 347–370.

Henckaerts J-M, Doswald-Beck L (2005) Customary International Humanitarian Law, Volume I: Rules. Cambridge University Press.

Kälin W (1998) The Guiding Principles on Internal Displacement—Introduction. (1998) 10(3) International Journal of Refugee Law 557–562.

Kälin W (2005) The Guiding Principles on Internal Displacement as International Minimum Standard and Protection Tool. (2005) 24(3) Refugee Survey Quarterly 27–36.

Kälin W (2008) Guiding Principles on Internal Displacement: Annotations. American Society of International Law. Studies in Transitional Legal Policy No. 38. The American Society of International Law and the Brookings Institution.

Kälin W (2014) The Guiding Principles on Internal Displacement and the search for a universal framework of protection for internally displaced persons. In: Chetail V, Bauloz C (eds) Research Handbook on International Law and Migration. Edward Elgar Publishing, Cheltenham, UK.

Maru M T (2014) The Kampala Convention and Its Contributions to International Law: Legal Analyses and Interpretations of the African Union Convention for the Protection and Assistance of Internally Displaced Persons. Eleven International Publishing, The Hague, The Netherlands.

Okello J M (2019) In Lieu of a Travaux Préparatoires: A Commentary on the Kampala Convention for IDPs. (2019) 31(2/3) International Journal of Refugee Law 349–378.

Orchard P (2010) Protection of internally displaced persons: soft law as a norm-generating mechanism. (2010) 36(2) Review of International Studies 281–303.

Phuong C (2005) The International Protection of Internally Displaced Persons. Cambridge University Press, Cambridge.

Robinson C W (2003) Risks and Rights: The Causes, Consequences, and Challenges of Development-Induced Displacement. The Brookings Institution-SAIS Project on Internal Displacement, An Occasional Paper.

UN Committee on Economic, Social and Cultural Rights (UN CESCR) (1991) General Comment No. 4: The Right to Adequate Housing (Article 11 (1) of the Covenant), 13 December 1991, E/ 1992/23.

Chapter 7
The Rights of Indigenous Peoples in the Context of Development-Induced Displacement

Contents

Abstract Indigenous peoples are disproportionately represented among those displaced by development-induced displacement (DID) and face unique challenges in the course of displacement due to their distinct cultural, spiritual, and economic ties to their ancestral lands. This special relationship with their land is also precisely why indigenous peoples are accorded specific rights under international human rights law. These rights, in particular, offer protection against involuntary displacement and impose heightened obligations on states when DID affects these groups. In light of this, the present chapter explores the rights of indigenous peoples and their application in the context of DID. Specifically, it examines the human rights protections that must be afforded to indigenous peoples in the course of DID by contextually analysing the rights enshrined in relevant universal and regional human rights frameworks as well as in pertinent case law.

Keywords Indigenous peoples · Declaration on the Rights of Indigenous Peoples · ILO Convention · Land rights · Free, prior and informed consent · Just and fair compensation

© T.M.C. ASSER PRESS and the authors 2026

R. G. Teshome, *The Human Cost of Development*, Human Rights Research Series 104,
https://doi.org/10.1007/978-94-6265-751-9_7

7.1 Introduction

As established in the preceding chapters, economically and socially marginalized groups are disproportionately and severely affected by DID, which further exacerbates their vulnerability and marginalization. Indigenous peoples are among these marginalized groups. Numerous studies have depicted that indigenous peoples bear the costs of development, particularly DID, at a relatively higher proportion. For instance, a study conducted on development projects undertaken in India from 1951 to 1991 showed that out of the total number of people displaced by these projects, 40% were indigenous peoples, even though they only made up 8 percent of the general population.[1] Besides, "over 60 percent of the world's natural resources are located on indigenous lands."[2] This implies that projects involving the extraction of natural resources, such as mining and oil extraction, most likely affect indigenous peoples. Furthermore, due to their special cultural, spiritual, and economic ties to their ancestral land, physical displacement has a greater impact on these peoples.[3] Overall, indigenous peoples are more vulnerable to the adverse consequences of DID and the potential violation of human rights it causes.

On the other hand, indigenous peoples are endowed with special rights under international human rights law for the very reason that they have special ties to the land they traditionally occupy. These rights particularly protect indigenous peoples from involuntary displacement, which, in turn, imposes heightened obligations on states when DID affects these groups of people. In light of this, the current chapter explores what these rights of indigenous peoples are and how they apply in the context of DID. Hence, the central question that this chapter seeks to answer is: what are the human rights protections states need to provide for indigenous peoples in the course of DID? It answers this question by contextually analysing the indigenous peoples' rights stipulated in the pertinent universal and regional human rights frameworks and case law.[4]

To this end, the chapter consists of three main section. Section 7.2 establishes the recognition of indigenous peoples' rights in international human rights law by drawing on the pertinent global and regional instruments and case law. Section 7.3 then engages with the concept of indigeneity in international law and outlines the common standards used to identify indigenous peoples. Subsequently, Sect. 7.4 examines the relevant rights of indigenous peoples, particularly those relates to land and forcible displacement, and their application in the context of DID.

---

[1] Rew et al. 2000, pp. 104 and 105. Other studies have also documented a similar trend (see, for instance, Patel et al. 2015, p. 248).

[2] Terminski 2015, p. 39.

[3] Stanley 2004, p. 14.

[4] Note: the discussion in this chapter will be based on the relevant frameworks and jurisprudence of the UN, the Inter-American, and African human rights systems. Since the European human rights system does not have significant normative standards on indigenous peoples' rights, it is not included in this part of the book.

7.2 The Recognition of Indigenous Peoples' Rights

In the UN human rights system, the earlier efforts to protect the rights of indigenous peoples focused on fighting discrimination.[5] As a part of this agenda, in 1971, the UN Economic and Social Council (ECOSOC) adopted a Resolution that authorized a study on the "Problem of Discrimination Against Indigenous Populations".[6] The study was undertaken by José Martínez Cobo who was appointed as a Special Rapporteur for this very purpose.[7] The results of this thirteen-year-long study were several research-based documents that highlighted the discrimination and marginalization of indigenous peoples around the world.[8] These documents remain important references in the indigenous peoples rights discourse.

The effort to promulgate a specific human rights instrument for the protection of indigenous peoples dates back to the 1980s, a period particularly characterized by widespread indigenous rights movements.[9] Following a recommendation of Martínez Cobo's study, the Working Group on Indigenous Populations (WGIP), composed of five independent experts, was established in 1982 under the auspices of the then UN Human Rights Commission.[10] The Working Group was endowed with the mandate of reviewing the existing human rights norms on indigenous peoples and developing a separate framework.[11] Consequently, the Working Group developed a set of normative standards and, after a long negotiation process, the UN Declaration on the Rights of Indigenous Peoples (UNDRIP) was adopted by the General Assembly in 2007.[12]

While the Declaration is not a legally binding instrument, the overwhelming majority of votes by which it was adopted[13] and the extensive participation of indigenous peoples and other stakeholders in the drafting process[14] support its authoritative status. Moreover, most of the rights espoused under the Declaration reflect rights already recognized under existing binding human rights frameworks, which accords

[5] Anaya and Rodríguez-Piñero 2018, pp. 42 and 43.

[6] UN Economic and Social Council, Resolution 1589(L), The problem of indigenous population, 21 May 1971, UN Doc E/5044, para 7; see also Anaya and Rodríguez-Piñero 2018, p. 43.

[7] UN Commission on Human Rights, Rights of persons belonging to national, ethnic, religious and linguistic minorities, 11 March 1981, E/CN.4/RES/22(XXXVII).

[8] Study of the Problem of Discrimination Against Indigenous Populations Final report submitted by the Special Rapporteur, Mr. José Martínez Cobo, available at https://www.un.org/development/desa/indigenouspeoples/publications/martinez-cobo-study.html, accessed 30 June 2025; Anaya and Rodríguez-Piñero 2018, p. 43; see also Mazel 2009, p. 145.

[9] Anaya and Rodríguez-Piñero 2018, p. 43.

[10] Ibid.

[11] Economic and Social Council Resolution 1982/34, Study of the problem of discrimination against indigenous populations, 7 May 1982; see also Anaya and Rodríguez-Piñero 2018, p. 43.

[12] UN General Assembly, United Nations Declaration on the Rights of Indigenous Peoples: resolution/adopted by the General Assembly, 2 October 2007, A/RES/61/295; see also Anaya and Rodríguez-Piñero 2018, pp. 49–60.

[13] 144 states voted in favour of the Declaration and only 4 states voted against it, while 11 states abstained (see Hohmann and Weller 2018, p. 1).

[14] Anaya and Rodríguez-Piñero 2018, p. 49; see also Mazel 2009, p. 145.

it a "significant normative weight".[15] There is also a strong argument that some of the norms incorporated therein have the status of customary international law or at least reflect a move in that direction.[16]

In addition, the International Labour Organization (ILO), presumably "the first intergovernmental institution to focus on [i]ndigenous peoples' issues",[17] has adopted a couple of frameworks on indigenous peoples. The first instrument is the ILO Convention No. 107, adopted in 1957.[18] This Convention was succeeded by the 1989's ILO Convention No. 169 (hereinafter the "ILO Convention"),[19] which introduced a few important revisions. The major departure of the Convention from its predecessor, which was grounded on the ideal of "promoting the assimilation of [i]ndigenous peoples into majority societies",[20] is its focus on the self-determination of indigenous peoples.[21] The Convention represents an important development in the protection of indigenous peoples' rights, although it has only been ratified by a relatively few states,[22] not only because it is binding but also because it is detailed and embodies the aspirations of these peoples.[23] Moreover, the Convention aided the adoption of the UNDRIP as it reflected the "baseline normative consensus" that informed subsequent discussions on the Declaration.[24]

Hence, the UNDRIP and the ILO Convention are the two most important universal frameworks on indigenous peoples' rights from which the norms discussed in this chapter are derived. Nevertheless, it goes without saying that indigenous peoples also benefit from the general human rights norms stipulated under other treaties

---

15 Anaya and Rodríguez-Piñero 2018, p. 62; see also OHCHR, Indigenous Peoples and the United Nations Human Rights System, Fact Sheet No. 9/Rev.2 (United Nations, 2013) 8.

16 Barnabas 2017, pp. 249–251; see also *Awas Tingni Mayagna (Sumo) Indigenous Community v Nicaragua*, Judgment, Inter-American Court of Human Rights, 31 August 2001, para 71; see also Nykolaishen 2012, pp. 126–128. These sources contend that particularly land rights of indigenous peoples arguably have attained the status of customary international law.

17 Castellino and Doyle 2018, p. 19.

18 International Labour Organization (ILO), Indigenous and Tribal Populations Convention, C107, 26 June 1957.

19 International Labour Organization (ILO), Indigenous and Tribal Peoples Convention, C169, 27 June 1989.

20 Anaya and Rodríguez-Piñero 2018, p. 44; see also Mazel 2009, p. 143; see also Diergarten 2019, p. 41.

21 Anaya and Rodríguez-Piñero 2018, p. 44; see also ILO Convention No. 169 (n 19) Preamble; see also Diergarten 2019, p. 42.

22 As of September 2022, only 24 states have ratified the Convention (see ILO, Ratifications of C169 - Indigenous and Tribal Peoples Convention, 1989 (No. 169), available at https://www.ilo.org/dyn/normlex/en/f?p=NORMLEXPUB:11300:0::NO::P11300_INSTRUMENT_ID:312314, accessed 30 June 2025).

23 Mazel 2009, p. 146. This is true despite the fact that indigenous peoples had not participated in the drafting process of the Convention, which was one of the major criticisms forwarded against the Convention (see Mazel 2009, p. 146; see also Anaya and Rodríguez-Piñero 2018, p. 44); see also Diergarten 2019, p. 42.

24 Anaya and Rodríguez-Piñero 2018, p. 45.

and soft law instruments. In fact, some of these norms, such as the right to self-determination and minority rights, have been particularly used to support indigenous peoples' claims.[25]

In the Inter-American human rights system, the jurisprudence of the Inter-American Court of Human Rights (IACtHR) has played an indispensable role in the development of norms on indigenous peoples' rights. The Court developed normative standards through its case law based on the rights recognized in the American Convention on Human Rights.[26] For instance, in its seminal judgment in the *Awas Tingni case*, the Court recognized the right of indigenous peoples to the land they traditionally occupy by applying the general right to property espoused in the Convention.[27] In this case, the Court extended the scope of the right to property to protect the informal land tenures of indigenous peoples.[28] The Court stressed that "[i]ndigenous groups, by the fact of their very existence, have the right to live freely on their own territory; the close ties of indigenous people with the land must be recognized."[29] These norms were subsequently crystallized in a separate instrument—the American Declaration on the Rights of Indigenous Peoples (hereinafter the "American Declaration")—adopted in 2016.[30]

Contrary to the UN and Inter-American human rights systems, there is no separate human rights framework that recognizes the rights of indigenous peoples in the African human rights system. However, one of the peculiar features of the African Charter on Human and Peoples' Rights is that it contains a set of collective rights, or "peoples' rights" as the Charter categorizes them.[31] These rights include self-determination,[32] peoples' right to "freely dispose of their wealth and natural resources",[33] and the right to development,[34] among others. Some of these rights are

---

[25] For instance, Article 1 of the ICCPR grants the right to self-determination to "all peoples", which is a collective right in nature. Moreover, Article 27 of the same Convention recognizes the rights of minorities "…to enjoy their own culture, to profess and practice their own religion, or to use their own language" (see UN General Assembly, International Covenant on Civil and Political Rights, 16 December 1966, 999 United Nations Treaty Series 171, Articles 1 and 27, respectively). Thus, these rights have been invoked by indigenous peoples in their collective rights claims (see Mazel 2009, p. 143).

[26] Anaya and Rodríguez-Piñero 2018, pp. 47 and 48.

[27] *Awas Tingni case* (n 16) para 149.

[28] Anaya and Rodríguez-Piñero (n 5) 47.

[29] *Awas Tingni case* (n 16) para 149.

[30] Organization of American States (OAS), American Declaration on the Rights of Indigenous Peoples, 15 June 2016, AG/RES 2888 (XLVI-O/16).

[31] Organization of African Unity (OAU), African Charter on Human and Peoples' Rights, 27 June 1981, CAB/LEG/67/3 rev. 5, 21 I.L.M. 58 (1982), ('African Charter'), Articles 19–24.

[32] Ibid., Article 20.

[33] Ibid., Article 21.

[34] Ibid., Article 22.

similar in both nature and normative content to some of the rights granted to indigenous peoples.[35] Nevertheless, the Charter does not define what the term "peoples" constitutes, which the drafters deliberately omitted,[36] and the peoples' rights incorporated therein are not tailored to the specific questions and interests of indigenous peoples. Hence, they lack the specificity and comprehensiveness of the instruments on indigenous peoples' rights.

However, the African Commission on Human and Peoples' Rights have made efforts to promote the rights of indigenous peoples in the continent. In 2001, it established a "Working Group of Experts on Indigenous Populations/Communities" with the mandate of exploring the notion of indigenousness in Africa and the rights recognized under the African Charter.[37] The report of the Working Group, "which proposes several avenues for the recognition and promotion of indigenous rights in Africa",[38] was adopted by the Commission in 2003.[39] Furthermore, the Commission adopted an Advisory Opinion endorsing the UNDRIP.[40] Despite the lack of a separate framework, important norms on indigenous peoples' rights have also been developed in the landmark cases of *Endorois and Ogiek* decided by the African Commission and the African Court on Human and Peoples' Rights, respectively.[41] Both cases concern the removal and relocation of indigenous peoples from their respective lands due to development projects, which is particularly relevant for this work. Hence, the normative discussions in the subsequent sections will draw on these cases and interpretative documents adopted by the Commission.

The recognition of indigenous peoples' rights in the European human rights system is relatively less developed.[42] The European Court of Human Rights and the European Commission of Human Rights, before it was dissolved, have addressed indigenous peoples' rights in a few cases, although most of these cases have not been decided on the merits.[43] In the case of *G. & E. v. Norway*, for instance, the

[35] For instance, the right to self-determination enshrined under Article 3 of the UNDRIP is similar to the right provided under Article 20(1) of the African Charter except for the difference in textual formulation (see UNDRIP (n 12) Article 3; see also African Charter (n 31) Article 20(1)).

[36] *Centre for Minority Rights Development (Kenya) and Minority Rights Group International on behalf of Endorois Welfare Council v. Kenya*, 276/2003, African Commission on Human and Peoples' Rights, 4 February 2010, para 147.

[37] African Commission on Human and Peoples' Rights, 51 Resolution on the Rights of Indigenous Peoples' Communities in Africa, 6 November 2000, ACHPR/Res.51(XXVIII)00; see also Gilbert 2011, p. 247.

[38] Gilbert 2011, p. 247.

[39] African Commission on Human and Peoples' Rights, Resolution on the Adoption of the Report of the African Commission's Working Group on Indigenous Populations/Communities, ACHPR/Res 51 (XXVII), 34th Ordinary Session, 20 November 2003.

[40] African Commission on Human and Peoples' Rights, Advisory Opinion on the UN Declaration on the Rights of Indigenous Peoples', May 2007; see also Gilbert 2011, p. 247.

[41] The *Endorois case* sets an important precedent since it is the first case in the region where the indigenous peoples' right to their traditional land is recognized (see Claridge 2010, p. 2).

[42] Kovacs 2016, p. 784.

[43] Ibid., p. 785; see also Koivurova 2011, p. 8. Almost all cases related to indigenous peoples' rights had been declared inadmissible (see, for instance, *G. & E. v Norway*, Application No 9278/

Commission asserted that the right to private and family life protects the specific lifestyle minorities or indigenous peoples lead, although the case was declared inadmissible.[44] The cases before the Court where indigenous peoples' right to property was an issue had also been declared inadmissible.[45] However, the Court's interpretation of the right to property in other cases not involving indigenous peoples, i.e. the right to property as not dependent on the existence of a formal title,[46] can be used to protect indigenous peoples' rights to land. In addition, the Council of Europe instruments on minority rights, specifically the European Charter for Regional or Minority Languages[47] and the Framework Convention for the National Minorities,[48] can be used to support indigenous peoples' claims.[49] As the name indicates, the Charter recognizes the rights of minorities to use and develop their culture and language.[50] The Framework Convention enunciates the rights to equality, culture, religion, and education, among others, as they apply to minorities.[51] Nevertheless, while some of these norms can be used to support indigenous peoples' claims, they do not address issues specifically relevant for indigenous peoples, for instance, the special ties these groups have to their ancestral land and natural resources and the rights that emanate from that. Generally, the European human rights system evidently has less developed jurisprudence on indigenous peoples' rights compared to the other two regional human rights systems—in particular, the Inter-American human rights system.[52] This is partly due to the fact that Europe does not have as many indigenous peoples as the other two regions and, hence, not many cases have reached the ECtHR.[53] In addition, a significant number of cases brought to the Court had been dismissed at the admissibility stage as mentioned above.[54] Due to these reasons, the

81 and 9415/81, decision on admissibility, European Commission on Human Rights, 3 October 1983; see also *HINGITAQ 53 v Denmark*, Application no. 18584/04, decision on admissibility, European Court of Human Rights, 12 January 2006; see also *CHAGOS ISLANDERS v United Kingdom*, Application no. 35622/04, decision on admissibility, European Court of Human Rights, 11 December 2012).

[44] *G. & E. v. Norway* (n 43) para 2 (the application was dismissed for being manifestly ill-founded); see also Koivurova 2011, p. 10.

[45] *HINGITAQ 53 v Denmark* (n 43); see also *CHAGOS ISLANDERS v UK* (n 43); see also Gismondi 2016, p. 52.

[46] See, for instance, *Doğan and Others v. Turkey*, Applications 8803-8811/02, 8813/02 and 8815-8819/02, Judgment, European Court of Human Rights, 29 June 2004, para 139; see the discussion in Chap. 4, Sect. 4.3.

[47] Council of Europe, European Charter for Regional or Minority Languages, 5 November 1992, 148 ETS.

[48] Council of Europe, Framework Convention for the Protection of National Minorities, 1 February 1998, 157 ETS.

[49] Kovacs 2016, pp. 802–804.

[50] European Charter for Regional or Minority Languages (n 47).

[51] Framework Convention (n 48) Articles 4, 5, 8, 12, and 13.

[52] Kovacs 2016, p. 784.

[53] Ibid., p. 785.

[54] Ibid.

analysis in the following sections will mainly draw on the frameworks and case law of the UN, Inter-American and African human rights systems.

7.3 The Right-Holders: Who Are Indigenous Peoples?

Before proceeding to the analysis of the substantive rights of indigenous peoples and the corresponding obligations of states, it is important to determine who the right-holders are or, in other words, who indigenous peoples are. The term "indigenous peoples" remains one of the most controversial notions in international law.[55] Over the years, various definitions have been adopted by the instruments and organizations dealing with indigenous peoples' rights. This section does not aim to extensively engage with these debates and exhaustively list all the proposed definitions. However, since the debate is still lingering and there is no universally accepted definition, it seeks to explore the common criteria that can be used to identify indigenous peoples based on some of the most widely accepted definitions or standards of identification.

The earlier definitions of indigenous peoples focused on the elements of "first occupancy" or "pre-colonial origin" and self-identification as standards of identification. For instance, according to the working definition proposed by Martinez Cobo:

> Indigenous communities, peoples and nations are those which, having a historical continuity with pre-invasion and pre-colonial societies that developed on their territories, consider themselves distinct from other sectors of the societies now prevailing on those territories, or parts of them. They form at present non-dominant sectors of society and are determined to preserve, develop and transmit to future generations their ancestral territories, and their ethnic identity, as the basis of their continued existence as peoples, in accordance with their own cultural patterns, social institutions, and legal system.[56]

This widely cited definition further provides that such historical continuity can emanate from several factors, such as "…occupation of ancestral lands, or at least of part of them; common ancestry with the original occupants of these lands;" and a distinct culture or language, among others.[57]

A similar approach is followed by the ILO Convention No. 169; pursuant to the definition provided under this Convention, indigenous peoples are:

> …peoples in independent countries who are regarded as indigenous on account of their descent from the populations which inhabited the country, or a geographical region to which the country belongs, at the time of conquest or colonisation or the establishment of present state boundaries and who, irrespective of their legal status, retain some or all of their own social, economic, cultural and political institutions.[58]

[55] Castellino and Doyle 2018, pp. 17–24; see also Mazel 2009, pp. 147 and 148.

[56] Cobo 1987, para 379.

[57] Ibid., para 380; see also Castellino and Doyle 2018, p. 18.

[58] ILO Convention No. 169 (n 19) Article 1(1)(b); this definition is a reiteration of the definition adopted by the ILO Convention No. 107, a predecessor of the current Convention, except for

The Convention further added self-identification as a definitional criterion stating that "[s]elf-identification as indigenous or tribal shall be regarded as a fundamental criterion for determining the groups to which the provisions of this Convention apply."[59]

However, these definitions have been highly criticized since the depiction of indigenous peoples as pre-colonial descents or first occupants is not representative of the indigenous population in different parts of the world.[60] This concern was also raised during the drafting process of the UNDRIP predominantly by representatives from African and Asian states.[61] In response to the definition proposed by the drafters, which emulated the approach of the definitions quoted above, the African group of experts contended that:

> ...in Africa, the term 'indigenous peoples or communities' is not aimed at protecting the rights of the 'first inhabitants that were invaded by foreigners'. Nor does the concept aim to create hierarchy among national communities or set aside special rights for certain people. On the contrary, within the African context the term 'indigenous peoples' aims to guarantee equal enjoyment of rights and freedoms to some communities that have been left behind.[62]

The African Commission also questioned the viability of this narrow understanding of indigenousness.[63] It suggested that the focus should rather be on the socio-cultural peculiarity and marginalization of these peoples as well as their special economic, cultural, and spiritual relationship to their land and the surrounding environment.[64] Similar concerns had been raised by representatives from other continents and scholars against the definition of indigenous peoples based on "first-occupancy and pre-colonial descents" approach.[65]

The contemporary definitions or criteria of identification mainly emphasize the connection of indigenous peoples to their lands and their socio-cultural distinctiveness from mainstream society. For instance, this approach is reflected in the

---

removing the category of "semi-tribal", replacing the term "population" with "peoples" and adding self-identification as a criterion.

[59] ILO Convention No. 169 (n 19) Article 1(2).

[60] Mazel 2009, p. 148; see also Gilbert 2011, p. 250.

[61] Gilbert 2011, pp. 250 and 251.

[62] Response Note to 'The Draft Aide Memoire of the African Group on the UN Declaration on the Rights of Indigenous Peoples', presented by an African group of experts, 21 March 2007; see also African Commission's Advisory Opinion (n 40); see also Resolution on the Adoption of the Report of the African Commission's Working Group on Indigenous Populations/Communities (n 39).

[63] Advisory Opinion of the African Commission (n 40), para 13.

[64] Montes and Cisneros 2009, p. 150; see also Advisory Opinion of the African Commission (n 40) para 13. As Regino Montes and Torres Cisnero summarized the position of the Commission, "[Indigenous peoples] are distinguished by their cultures, their social institutions and their religious systems. Their way of life differs considerably from that of the dominant society, and their culture is under threat, if not on the verge of extinction. A key feature of these peoples is that their specific means of subsistence depends directly on access and related rights to their traditional territories and the natural resources found therein" (Montes and Cisneros 2009, p. 150; see also Advisory Opinion of the African Commission (n 40), para 13).

[65] Anaya 2010, p. 30.

Operational Policy of the World Bank adopted in 2005.[66] The policy deliberately refrained from providing a definition due to the diverse and dynamic situations in which indigenous peoples around the world live and the lack of general agreement on the subject.[67] Instead, it stipulated certain criteria that can be used to identify these groups, i.e. self-identification, close attachment to their lands and territories, distinct cultural, socio-political and economic life, and a unique language.[68]

During the drafting of the UNDRIP, defining the right-holders or subjects of the Declaration was one of the issues that sparked heated debate.[69] The debates extended from whether or not the term "indigenous peoples" is even appropriate to what it constitutes.[70] As mentioned above, the proposed definition, which was based on the "first occupancy and pre-colonial descents" approach was rejected by a large number of states for its lack of representativeness.[71] It eventually became evident that a consensus would not be reached. Consequently, the Working Group opted not to include a definition in the final draft,[72] which was adopted by the General Assembly.

Nevertheless, although the Declaration does not explicitly define who indigenous peoples are, it contains certain elements that indicate who the right-holders are.[73] This is evident from the Preamble as well as some of the substantive provisions of the Declaration.[74] For instance, the principles of distinctiveness and self-identification are mirrored in the Preamble, which "[affirms] that indigenous peoples are equal to all other peoples, while recognizing the right of all peoples to be different, to consider themselves different, and to be respected as such …"[75] Furthermore, the Preamble also echoes the historical marginalization of indigenous peoples, which is considered

---

[66] World Bank, Operational Manual 4.10: Indigenous Peoples, adopted in July 2005 (the manual has been revised several times; the latest revision was revised in 2013).

[67] Ibid., para 3.

[68] Ibid., para 4.

[69] Castellino and Doyle 2018, p. 26.

[70] For instance, a member of the Working Group contended that the term "people" used in the UN Charter and other documents encompasses all groups of people and creating a separate category would serve nothing but confusion (see Daes 2009, p. 54).

[71] Gilbert 2011, pp. 250 and 251.

[72] Castellino and Doyle 2018, pp. 29 and 30. This practice of omitting a definition of a controversial term is not unique to the Declaration. In fact, a similar practice can be observed in other Declarations, such as the UN Declaration on the Elimination of All Forms of Racial Discrimination, which did not define what "racial discrimination" constitutes, and the Declaration on the Rights of Persons Belonging to National or Ethnic, Religious or Linguistic Minorities, which did not define who "minorities" are. Thus, in some cases where providing a clear-cut definition has the effect of compromising the acceptability and credibility of an instrument, the drafters have chosen to omit the definitional provisions. There are also instances where Declarations have failed to come into effect merely due to a lack of agreement on the definitions of controversial notions (see Castellino and Doyle 2018, pp. 30–32).

[73] Castellino and Doyle 2018; see also Anaya 2009b, pp. 190 and 191.

[74] Castellino and Doyle 2018, p. 32.

[75] UNDRIP (n 12) Preamble; see also Castellino and Doyle 2018, p. 33.

one of the standards of identification.[76] In addition, the substantive provisions on the use of land and other resources reflect the special connection these groups have to their land and environment.[77] Hence, certain standards of identification can be inferred from the texts of the Declaration.

The American Declaration followed a similar approach to that of the UNDRIP. It abstained from providing a definition for who the beneficiaries of the rights stipulated in the Declaration are; rather, it specified self-identification as a fundamental standard of identification.[78] Article 1(2) of the Declaration states that:

> Self-identification as indigenous peoples will be a fundamental criterion for determining to whom this Declaration applies. States shall respect the right to such self-identification as indigenous, whether individually or collectively, in keeping with the practices and institutions of each indigenous people.[79]

This is grounded in some of the seminal judgments of the IACtHR pertaining to indigenous peoples' rights. For instance, in the cases of *Moiwana v. Suriname* and *Saramaka v Suriname*, the Court used the criterion of self-identification.[80] The Court also highlighted the socio-cultural distinctiveness of this group, which is embedded in their land and environment, as a distinguishing factor.[81] In the words of the Court, "[t]he lands and resources of the Saramaka people are part of their social, ancestral, and spiritual essence."[82] In these two cases, the peoples concerned would not have been considered "indigenous" based on the first-occupancy theory.[83] However, the Court attributed to them similar rights as indigenous peoples due to their distinct relationship to their lands.[84]

In the African human rights system, the controversy surrounding the definition of indigenous peoples has another angle. It had been frequently contended, both by state representatives and scholars, that there are no special groups that can be considered

---

[76] UNDRIP (n 12) Preamble; see also Castellino and Doyle 2018, p. 34.

[77] Article 25 of the Declaration that accords Indigenous peoples a right to maintain their special relationship with their land is a good example here (see UNDRIP (n 12) Article 25).

[78] American Declaration (n 30) Article 1(2).

[79] Ibid.

[80] *Case of the Saramaka People v Suriname*, Preliminary objections, merits, reparations and costs, IACHR Series C no. 172, IHRL 3046 (IACHR 2007), 28th November 2007, para 79.

[81] Ibid., paras 82–84.

[82] Ibid., para 82; see also *Case of the Moiwana Community v. Suriname*, Preliminary Objections, Merits, Reparations and Cost, Inter-American Court of Human Rights, 15 June 2005, paras 132 and 133.

[83] *Saramaka v Suriname* (n 80) para 79; see also *Moiwana v. Suriname* (n 82) para 132 (in both cases, the peoples concerned were settled to the lands and territories they occupy now during the period of colonisation).

[84] *Saramaka v Suriname* (n 80) paras 79–84; see also *Moiwana v. Suriname* (n 82) paras 132 and 133 (despite not being the first occupants, these peoples are regarded as "indigenous" for all intents and purposes; the Court, however, used the term "tribal" to show this difference. Hence, these cases also show that the first-occupancy or pre-colonial approach is not inclusive of the realities of indigenous peoples around the world).

indigenous peoples for everyone in the continent is indigenous.[85] However, this was rejected by the African Commission that embraced the existence of special groups identified as "indigenous" and entitled to special rights.[86] In the *Endorois case*, the question of what makes certain peoples "indigenous" was one of the issues contested. The respondent state rejected the identification of Endorois as a "distinct community in need of special protection" while the applicants claimed otherwise.[87] In dealing with this issue, the Commission referred to and drew inspiration from the definitions proposed by the UN Working Group and ILO as well as IACtHR case law.[88] In this landmark decision, the Commission highlighted that the "Endorois culture, religion, and traditional way of life are intimately intertwined with their ancestral lands – Lake Bogoria and the surrounding area."[89] It also stressed the right of these peoples to determine and preserve their identity.[90] Furthermore, the Commission noted that Endorois peoples are or "consider themselves to be" distinct in terms of history, culture, and religion.[91] On the basis of these standards, the Commission identified the Endorois community as indigenous peoples. Similar criteria were employed by the African Court in the case of *Ogiek*,[92] although the Court did not deal with the issue of indigenousness as extensively as the Commission. As opposed to the Commission, the Court also used the criterion of first-occupancy along with the other standards of identification.[93]

Overall, four common criteria can be deduced from these definitions. The first criterion is that indigenous peoples have special cultural and economic ties to their ancestral land.[94] As the above definitions suggest, the identity and culture of indigenous peoples are highly linked to their ancestral land, which also lies at the heart of their claims. "They are indigenous because their ancestral roots are embedded in the lands on which they live, or would like to live…"[95] Such "sacred relationship to their land"[96] is what differentiates indigenous peoples from other groups of people.

Another distinguishing factor of indigenous peoples is their distinctiveness in terms of, *inter alia*, culture, religion, and socio-political structure. Self-identification is also another common criterion. As described above, self-identification is continuously endorsed by almost all definitions. From the working definition proposed by Martínez Cobo to the criterion incorporated in the very recent American Declaration,

---

85 Henriksen 2009, p. 79.

86 *Endorois case* (n 36) para 148.

87 Ibid., para 145.

88 Ibid., para 158.

89 Ibid., para 156; see also Gilbert 2011, p. 253.

90 *Endorois case* (n 36) para 157.

91 Ibid., para 162; see also Gilbert 2011, p. 253.

92 *African Commission on Human and Peoples' Rights v. Republic of Kenya*, Application No. 006/2012, African Court on Human and Peoples' Rights, 26 May 2017 ('*Ogiek case*'), para 107.

93 Ibid., paras 107–112.

94 *Endorois case*, n 36 para 154.

95 Anaya 2009a, p. 1; see also *Endorois case* (n 36) para 152.

96 *Endorois case* (n 36) para 157.

the significance of what these groups wish to identify as has been stressed. Another criterion is the historical and ongoing marginalization of these communities.[97] This marginalization might stem from their non-dominant position in a society vis-à-vis the mainstream population—in terms of demography or economic and political power—and the dispossession of their land and natural resources.[98]

Overall, these common criteria can be employed to identify indigenous peoples. Nevertheless, it has to be noted that the identification standards and their application need to take into account the special circumstances and the diverse backgrounds of indigenous peoples living in different countries. Hence, instead of adopting a rigid definition and standards, the identification should be undertaken on a case-by-case basis. The use of the term "indigenous peoples" in this work is based on this understanding.

7.4 Normative Content of the Rights of Indigenous Peoples

The UN Declaration and the other instruments mentioned above confer a range of individual and collective rights to indigenous peoples including the right to self-determination, the right to nationality, the "right to live in freedom, peace and security", and the right to practice their culture.[99] An exhaustive discussion of all these rights is neither feasible nor desirable in this work. Hence, this section mainly focuses on the rights that are thematically relevant to DID, particularly the rights pertaining to the land and natural resources of indigenous peoples.

7.4.1 Rights to Land and Other Resources

For indigenous peoples, a "spiritual connection" to their land is at the heart of their economic, social, and cultural life as well as an integral part of their very identity.[100] Their quest for self-determination is also embedded in this special connection.[101] Moreover, the historical and ongoing marginalization and vulnerability of indigenous peoples are mainly attributable to the dispossession of their lands or lack of protection of their land rights.[102] This is compounded by the fact that, in most cases, these groups

---

[97] Ibid., para 148.

[98] Castellino and Doyle 2018, p. 34.

[99] UNDRIP (n 12) Articles 3, 6, 7 and 11, respectively.

[100] Charters 2018, p. 396; see also Case of *Awas Tingni v. Nicaragua* (n 16) para 149; see also *Moiwana v. Suriname* (n 82) para 131; see also *Case of the Yakye Axa Indigenous Community v Paraguay*, Merits, Inter-American Court of Human Rights, 17 June 2005, para 135; see also *Daniel Billy et al. v Australia*, communication No. 3624/2019, adoption of views, UN Human Rights Committee, 22 September 2022, CCPR/C/135/D/3624/2019, para 8.13.

[101] Charters 2018, p. 396.

[102] Ibid., pp. 396 and 397.

do not have formal titles to the land they traditionally occupy,[103] which increases their susceptibility to land dispossession and other arbitrary interferences. These are the main reasons that necessitated the provision of special rights to land to indigenous peoples.

These rights are provided under Articles 26 and 14 of the UNDRIP and the ILO Convention, respectively.[104] Article 26(1) of the Declaration sets out a general entitlement of indigenous peoples to the lands or other resources they traditionally occupy.[105] The provision states that "[i]ndigenous peoples have the right to the lands, territories and resources which they have traditionally owned, occupied or otherwise used or acquired."[106] What this entitlement entails is further elucidated under paragraph two of the same provision, which provides that "[i]ndigenous peoples have the right to own, use, develop and control the lands, territories and resources that they possess by reason of traditional ownership or other traditional occupation or use, as well as those which they have otherwise acquired."[107] Thereby, indigenous peoples have the right to utilize their lands and other resources as they see fit and make decisions regarding their management.

It is not clear from this provision to what extent the rights stipulated therein apply to the lands and other resources no longer under the possession of the indigenous peoples concerned.[108] Conversely, Article 14(1) ILO Convention explicitly provides that "...measures shall be taken in appropriate cases to safeguard the right of the peoples concerned to use lands not exclusively occupied by them, but to which they have traditionally had access for their subsistence and traditional activities."[109] Hence, this provision extends the applicability of the land rights of indigenous peoples to lands no longer in their possession.[110] This is also the major difference between the two provisions. Nevertheless, from the drafting process and Article 28 of the Declaration, it can be deduced that possession is not a necessary prerequisite for indigenous peoples' rights to land to exist.[111] Article 28(1) provides that if indigenous peoples are arbitrarily dispossessed of their lands or lose access to their lands, they are entitled to restitution or compensation.[112] For instance, if the land is legally transferred to third parties in good faith, restitution might not be possible in which case compensation should be provided.[113] This interpretation is also in line with

[103] Gilbert 2011, p. 258.

[104] UNDRIP (n 12) Article 26; see also ILO Convention No. 169 (n 19) Article 14.

[105] UNDRIP (n 12) Article 26(1).

[106] Ibid.

[107] Ibid., Article 26(2).

[108] Charters 2018, p. 414.

[109] ILO Convention No. 169 (n 19) Article 14(1).

[110] Charters 2018, p. 414.

[111] UNDRIP (n 12) Article 28.

[112] UNDRIP (n 12) Article 28. During the negotiation process, some states strongly contended that indigenous peoples' rights to lands that they no longer have possession of could be limited to protect the interest of third parties who have lawfully obtained possession (Charters 2018, p. 415).

[113] *Endorois case* (n 36) para 209; see also Charters 2018, p. 417.

the interpretation of the two regional human rights systems,[114] as will be discussed below. Article 28(2) of the Declaration further provides that compensation can take various forms, namely replacement land of equivalent value, monetary redress, or other suitable remedies.[115]

One of the most important features of the above provisions of the Declaration and the ILO Convention is that they recognize the traditional or informal land tenures of indigenous peoples, which are not contingent on formal ownership or state recognition.[116] This is further solidified by Articles 26(3) and 14(2) of the Declaration and the ILO Convention, respectively, which require states to "give legal recognition and protection to [the] lands, territories and resources" of indigenous peoples.[117] Hence, the land rights of indigenous peoples entail not only a negative obligation to refrain from interfering in the enjoyment and control of such lands and resources, but also a positive obligation to take the necessary measures in order to recognize and protect those rights.

As mentioned above, the IACtHR jurisprudence on the right to land of indigenous peoples is based on the right to property recognized under Article 21 of the American Convention.[118] In the landmark case of *Awas Tingni*, the Court proclaimed that the close connection of indigenous peoples with their lands and territories upon which their cultural and economic lives depend must be recognized.[119] This is also reiterated in the case of *Sawhoyamaxa v. Paraguay* where the Court stated that "…the close ties the members of indigenous communities have with their traditional lands and the natural resources associated with their culture thereof, as well as the incorporeal elements deriving therefrom, must be secured under Article 21 of the American Convention."[120] Similarly, in the case of *Yakye Axa v. Paraguay*, the Court employed the right to property to uphold the "rights to lands, territories, and resources" of indigenous peoples.[121] Thus, the right to property envisaged under the Convention accommodates the collective rights of indigenous peoples to the lands and territories they traditionally occupy irrespective of the fact that they might not have formal titles

---

[114] *Endorois case* (n 36) para 209; see also *Case of the Sawhoyamaxa Indigenous Community v. Paraguay*, Merits, Reparations and Costs, Inter-American Court of Human Rights, 29 March 2006, para 128; see also Charters 2018, pp. 416 and 417.

[115] UNDRIP (n 12) Article 28(1); it has to be noted that the arbitrary deprivation of land under Article 28 is different from the potential removal of indigenous peoples from their lands envisaged under Article 10 of the Declaration, which will be discussed below. Article 28 applies ipso facto—after the indigenous peoples are deprived of their possession illegally. On the other hand, Article 10 is applicable before the fact—before dispossession takes place; in other words, Article 10 protects indigenous people from removal from their lands by stipulating certain safeguards. Consequently, the acquisition of land and relocation undertaken following the requirements of Article 10 are lawful and justified.

[116] Feiring 2013, p. 18; see also International Labour Organization 2013, p. 21.

[117] UNDRIP (n 12) Article 26(3); see also ILO Convention No. 169 (n 19) Article 14(2).

[118] Anaya and Williams 2001, p. 41.

[119] *Awas Tingni v. Nicaragua* (n 16) para 149.

[120] *Sawhoyamaxa v. Paraguay* (n 114) para 118 and 121.

[121] *Yakye Axa v. Paraguay* (n 100) paras 135–137; see also Charters 2018, p. 416.

to those properties.[122] These rights remain in effect even if indigenous community members are unlawfully removed from or dispossessed of their lands except in cases where those lands "have been lawfully transferred to third parties in good faith" in which cases they will be entitled to restitution or replacement lands of equivalent value.[123] Thus, indigenous peoples' land rights are not contingent on formal ownership or even possession.

Furthermore, the equivalent of Article 26 of the UNDRIP is found under Article 25 of the American Declaration,[124] which is an almost verbatim copy of the former.[125] The provision recognizes the rights of indigenous peoples "to own, use, develop and control" their traditional lands and obliges states to accord protection to such rights.[126] The normative content of this provision is similar to its counterpart in the UNDRIP. Hence, a brief remark here suffices to note that the American Declaration also recognizes the collective rights of indigenous peoples to the land they traditionally occupy.

Similarly, the African Commission has also used the right to property to endorse the rights to land, territory, and resources of indigenous peoples as illuminated in the *Endorois case*.[127] In this case, by contextually utilizing Article 14 of the African Charter, the Commission enumerated what the land rights of indigenous peoples are.[128] Accordingly, these rights include the following elements:

> (1) traditional possession of land by indigenous people has the equivalent effect as that of a state-granted full property title; (2) traditional possession entitles indigenous people to demand official recognition and registration of property title; (3) the members of indigenous peoples who have unwillingly left their traditional lands, or lost possession thereof, maintain property rights thereto, even though they lack legal title, unless the lands have been lawfully transferred to third parties in good faith; and (4) the members of indigenous peoples who have unwillingly lost possession of their lands, when those lands have been lawfully transferred to innocent third parties, are entitled to restitution thereof or to obtain other lands of equal extension and quality.[129]

Hence, the Commission, in this case, recognized the collective land rights of indigenous peoples as well as gave full effect to their informal or customary land tenures.[130]

---

[122] *Awas Tingni v. Nicaragua* (n 16) paras 149–151; see also Anaya and Williams 2001, p. 44.

[123] *Sawhoyamaxa v. Paraguay* (n 114) para 128.

[124] American Declaration (n 30) Article 25.

[125] The only visible difference between the two provisions is that Article 25 of the American Declaration stipulates the rights provided under three different provisions of the UNDRIP, Articles 25, 26, and 27, in a single provision.

[126] American Declaration (n 30) Article 25(2-4).

[127] *Endorois case* (n 36) para 209.

[128] Ibid., paras 186–187, 191, and 209; see also African Charter (n 31) Article 14.

[129] *Endorois case* (n 36) para 209; this conclusion is a verbatim copy of the conclusion of the IACtHR in the case of *Sawhoyamaxa v. Paraguay* (see *Sawhoyamaxa v. Paraguay* (n 114) para 128).

[130] Gilbert 2011, pp. 260 and 261; see also *Endorois case* (n 36) para 209.

Furthermore, the UNDRIP has informed the development of norms on indigenous peoples' rights in the two regional systems discussed above as their respective case law attests.[131] Moreover, as mentioned before, the African Commission has explicitly endorsed the Declaration through its Advisory Opinion.[132] Hence, there is a convergence of norms among the three human rights systems under consideration.

Overall, it is well established under all three systems that indigenous peoples have full property right—"the right to own, use, develop and control"[133]—to the lands and territories they customarily possess. This right is not limited to the landholdings of these peoples but also extends to their territories and other common resources, *inter alia*, religious sites, water sources, and grazing lands. "Thus, international law embraces the indigenous notion of 'territory' that perceives land, its environment and its natural resources as an inseparable totality."[134] This is particularly relevant in the DID discourse since, as elucidated in Chap. 2, one of the causes of the economic impoverishment that DID results in is disruption of access to common resources on which the people affected depend. For indigenous peoples, access to these resources has not only economic but also cultural and spiritual significance. Hence, the collective property rights of indigenous peoples encompass all these territories and resources.

7.4.2 Protection from Displacement

The provision that is particularly important in the context of DID is Article 10 of the Declaration, which prohibits the involuntary relocation of indigenous peoples.[135] The Article reads:

> Indigenous peoples shall not be forcibly removed from their lands or territories. No relocation shall take place without the free, prior and informed consent of the indigenous peoples concerned and after agreement on just and fair compensation and, where possible, with the option of return.[136]

Four elements can be derived from this provision: the prohibition of the involuntary removal or relocation of indigenous peoples, the principle of "free, prior and informed consent", the requirement of "just and fair compensation" and the option to return.[137] These elements form the protections that states are required to provide for indigenous peoples in the course of DID. Thus, they will be separately discussed below. A similar

---

[131] *Saramaka v Suriname* (n 80) para 131; see also Pasqualucci 2009, pp. 53 and 54.

[132] African Commission Advisory Opinion (n 40); see also *Endorois case* (n 36) para 204.

[133] UNDRIP (n 12) Article 26(2).

[134] Diergarten 2019, p. 44.

[135] UNDRIP (n 12) Article 10.

[136] Ibid.

[137] Ibid.

entitlement, albeit differently formulated, is enshrined under Article 16 of the ILO Convention;[138] the difference between the two provisions will be described later.

Surprisingly, the American Declaration does not include a general right that affords indigenous peoples protection against involuntary removal or relocation. However, in relation to the right to development envisaged under Article 29 of the Declaration, states are required to seek the "free and informed consent" of the indigenous peoples concerned before undertaking any development project that potentially affects their lands and other resources.[139] The provision reads:

> States shall consult and cooperate in good faith with the indigenous peoples concerned through their own representative institutions in order to obtain their free and informed consent prior to the approval of any project affecting their lands or territories and other resources, particularly in connection with the development, utilization or exploitation of mineral, water, or other resources.[140]

Unlike the Article of the UNDRIP quoted before, this provision of the American Declaration does not generally and conclusively prohibit the forceful removal of indigenous peoples from their land. Nor does it concretely oblige states to obtain the consent of the peoples concerned before relocation. Rather, the above Article only applies to cases where relocation or any other adverse effect to the lands of indigenous peoples is caused by development projects and it requires states to "consult and cooperate in good faith" with these peoples to solicit their consent. Thus, compared to Article 10 of the UNDRIP, Article 25(4) of the American Declaration is framed in less absolute and concrete terms.

Nevertheless, the case law of the IACtHR is more concrete in this regard. In the case of *Saramaka v. Suriname*, the Court established three safeguards that states are required to put in place before undertaking development projects—extraction of natural resources in this particular case—that interfere with the property rights of indigenous peoples.[141] These safeguards are: ensuring the effective participation of the people affected, making sure that they "receive a reasonable benefit" from the project, and conducting "prior environmental and social impact assessment".[142] Further, the Court dictated that in these instances, a mere consultation is not sufficient; rather, states need to obtain the "free, prior, and informed consent" of the peoples affected.[143] According to the Court, the second safeguard stems from the requirement of "just compensation" stipulated under the limitation clause of the right to property.[144] In a nutshell, states are required to obtain the full consent of the indigenous

[138] ILO Convention No. 169 (n 19) Article 16.

[139] American Declaration (n 30) Article 29(4).

[140] Ibid.; a similar provision can be found under Article 32 of the UNDRIP, a general provision on the obligation of states when they undertake projects that can potentially affect the lands and territories of indigenous peoples. But the UNDRIP has a separate provision concerning the removal or relocation of indigenous peoples, as stated above, which is not found under the American Declaration.

[141] *Saramaka v. Suriname* (n 80) para 129.

[142] Ibid.

[143] Ibid., para 134; see also Diergarten 2019, p. 45.

[144] *Saramaka v. Suriname* (n 80) paras 138 and 139.

peoples concerned and provide adequate compensation before undertaking development activities that interfere with their property rights including removal from their land.

In the *Endorois case*, the African Commission assessed the removal of the indigenous peoples concerned from their lands based on the limitation clause of the right to property. The Commission noted that interference with the right to property can only be justified if it is necessitated by a public interest, proportionate to the interest pursued, and undertaken "in accordance with appropriate laws".[145] Further, it stressed that in cases where indigenous peoples are involved, the threshold of meeting these requirements is even higher.[146] Pursuant to the interpretation of the Commission the term "in accordance with the law" particularly entails "the requirements of consultation and compensation."[147] When it comes to indigenous peoples' lands, the requirement of consultation constitutes obtaining the consent of the peoples concerned.[148] Hence, the lands of indigenous peoples can only be expropriated for public interest after their consent is obtained and adequate compensation is paid.

Overall, the two regional human rights systems have also endorsed the four elements identified above. Nonetheless, they have yet to develop detailed rules on how these elements apply;[149] the literature on the subject is also quite limited. Thus, the four elements will be discussed below mainly based on the norms developed under the UNDRIP and the ILO Convention. Moreover, given the influence these universal frameworks, particularly the UNDRIP, have on the development of norms in the two regional systems, it is safe to assume that the interpretation of these elements will not be that different.

7.4.2.1 The Prohibition of Forcible Removal from Land

The Declaration conclusively prohibits the forcible removal of indigenous peoples from their land.[150] This rule is absolute and not subject to any exceptions.[151] In this regard, the text of the Declaration is more stringent than its counterpart in the ILO Convention. Article 16 of the ILO Convention allows the forcible removal or relocation of indigenous peoples in exceptional circumstances.[152] However, as the wording of the provision signals, this exception should be construed narrowly and

---

[145] *Endorois case* (n 36) para 211; see also African Charter (n 31) Article 14.

[146] *Endorois case* (n 36) para 212.

[147] Ibid., para 225.

[148] Ibid., para 226.

[149] For instance, although the IACtHR has a rich jurisprudence on indigenous peoples' land rights in general, it dealt with the issue of free and informed consent only in the case of *Saramaka v. Suriname*. In the African human rights system, the jurisprudence of the Commission and the Court regarding indigenous peoples' rights is still at an infant stage.

[150] UNDRIP (n 12) Article 10.

[151] Charters 2018, p. 409.

[152] ILO Convention No. 169 (n 19) Article 16.

applied with adequate procedural safeguards including meaningful consultation with the peoples concerned.[153]

Hence, pursuant to the UNDRIP, "development" or any other public purpose cannot be used to remove indigenous people from their land without their full consent. This negates the eminent domain doctrine.[154] As discussed in the preceding chapters, the eminent domain doctrine dictates that states have an inherent power to acquire private property including land for public purposes. International human rights law also leaves room for states to exercise this power as can be inferred from the permissible limitation clause of the right to property, which justifies interference with the right to property including the acquisition of property in exceptional cases. This does not, however, hold water when it comes to indigenous peoples' lands. In such cases, the only legitimate course of action for a state is to obtain "the free, prior and informed consent"[155] of the indigenous peoples concerned.

7.4.2.2 Free, Prior and Informed Consent

The principle of. "free, prior and informed consent" consists of several requirements. First, the term "free" implies that the consent should be given willingly without any "coercion, intimidation or manipulation".[156] Second, the term "prior" entails that the consent must be obtained prior to the approval and commencement of any project that potentially results in the relocation of indigenous peoples.[157] Moreover, sufficient time must be allocated to ensure meaningful consultation with these peoples and to enable them to reach a consensus.[158] Third, the term "informed" requires that the indigenous peoples concerned should have access to full information about the project, the activities it involves, and its social and environmental impacts. They should also receive information as to the removal and relocation process, if they have consented to it, as well as the remedies with which they will be provided. Furthermore, this information should be not only accurate but also accessible in terms of language and context.[159] These requirements further illuminate that consent is a process that involves meaningful consultation and extensive participation of the indigenous peoples concerned.[160]

Fourth, as the term "consent" indicates, states need to seek and obtain the consent of the indigenous peoples concerned before relocating them from their land. There is a divergent opinion on whether the requirement of consent gives a "veto power"

---

[153] Ibid; see also Charters 2018, p. 409.

[154] Diergarten 2019, p. 44.

[155] UNDRIP (n 12) Article 10.

[156] Barelli 2012, p. 2; see also Human Rights Council 2018, para 20.

[157] Barelli 2012, p. 2; see also Human Rights Council 2018, para 21.

[158] Barelli 2012, p. 2.

[159] Barelli 2012, p. 2; see also Human Rights Council 2018, para 22.

[160] Barelli 2012, p. 2.

to the peoples concerned or whether it simply implies meaningful consultation.[161] However, the wording of the Declaration is unequivocally clear when it comes to the relocation of indigenous peoples from their ancestral land; "[n]o relocation shall take place without the free, prior and informed consent of the indigenous peoples concerned".[162] As mentioned before, the Declaration does not include any exception to this rule unlike the ILO Convention No. 169.[163] The latter purports that "[w]here…consent cannot be obtained, such relocation shall take place only following appropriate procedures established by national laws and regulations".[164] The wording of Article 10 of the Declaration, which was adopted later than the ILO Convention, indicates that consent equates to a decision-making or veto power when it comes to relocation.[165] Moreover, the Declaration treats measures that potentially lead to the removal of indigenous peoples from their ancestral land differently than other measures or projects that may affect indigenous peoples but not involve relocation. Generally, according to Articles 19 and 32 of the Declaration, states are required to consult in "good faith" with indigenous peoples concerned to obtain their consent when taking measures or undertaking projects that affect them.[166] Thus, it appears that Article 10 of the Declaration, which deals with relocation, is *lex specialis* to this general rule. The degree of decision-making power it confers on the peoples concerned also differentiates the requirement of consent under the Declaration from mere meaningful participation or consultation required in other instruments, for instance, under the instruments on IDPs and the right to development discussed in the other chapters in this part of the book. While the latter allows the people(s) concerned to participate in and influence decision-making, the former transfers the decision making-power to the indigenous peoples concerned. Hence, it is safe to conclude that the requirement of "free, prior and informed consent" under Article 10 of the Declaration confers a collective decision-making power on indigenous peoples.[167]

---

[161] Kanosue 2015, p. 644.

[162] UNDRIP (n 12) Article 10.

[163] Charters 2018, p. 409.

[164] ILO Convention No. 169 (n 19) Article 16.

[165] MacInnes et al. 2017, p. 155.

[166] UNDRIP (n 12) Articles 19 and 32.

[167] "[Consent] does not necessarily mean that every single member must agree, but rather that the consent process will be undertaken through procedures and institutions determined by indigenous peoples themselves. Indigenous peoples should specify which representative institutions are entitled to express consent on behalf of the affected peoples or communities" (see OHCHR, 'Free, Prior and Informed Consent of Indigenous Peoples', September 2013, available at https://www.ohchr.org/sites/default/files/Documents/Issues/IPeoples/FreePriorandInformedConsent.pdf, accessed 1 July 2025, at 2).

7.4.2.3 Just and Fair Compensation

Articles 10 and 16 of the Declaration and the ILO Convention, respectively, further require that even in cases where the consent of the indigenous peoples concerned is obtained, relocation can only take place "after agreement on just and fair compensation" has been reached.[168] Two requirements are mirrored in this phrase, i.e. the indigenous peoples concerned should agree on the proposed compensation and the compensation has to be just and fair. One could argue that what is "just and fair" is subjective and depends on the perception of the indigenous peoples concerned. Thus, obtaining their agreement on the amount of compensation should be enough to fulfil the requirement of the above provisions. Nevertheless, this interpretation opens the door for states (and even private actors) to take advantage of the weak bargaining power of indigenous peoples. Hence, the requirement of "just and fair" stands alone and there has to be a set of objective standards, although some degree of subjectivity is to be expected, against which justice and fairness are assessed.

The Declaration and the ILO Convention do not specify what "just and fair compensation" entails. However, the interpretation of this phrase can be informed by the case law and interpretative documents of the universal and regional human rights bodies in relation to other rights. The analysis in the preceding chapters regarding the determination and provision of compensation for eviction and expropriation serves as an important reference, which is why a similar analysis is not needed here. Yet, it has to be noted that the term "compensation" should be construed broadly to include both monetary and non-monetary remedies.[169] Monetary compensation needs to be provided to redress any material or moral damage the indigenous peoples have incurred or will potentially incur. However, it is worth reiterating here that as the Special Rapporteur on the right to adequate housing stressed, monetary compensation should not be used in lieu of real property replacements.[170] The indigenous peoples removed from their lands should be provided with replacement "land[s] commensurate in quality, size and value, or better".[171] Moreover, states need to follow-up on the situations of those relocated and provide long-term assistance to rehabilitate them.[172] While these interpretations cannot be directly employed to interpret the Declaration or the ILO Convention, they can be used analogously to understand some of the concepts incorporated therein. Moreover, given the weight given to the land rights of indigenous peoples, it is plausible to assume that the threshold used to determine "just and fair compensation" cannot and should not be lower, if not higher, than the standards used in other instruments.

---

[168] UNDRIP (n 12) Article 10.

[169] This can also be inferred from Article 28 of the Declaration, although the subject matters of the two provisions are different as described before.

[170] The Special Rapporteur on Adequate Housing 2007, para 60.

[171] Ibid.; see also African Commission on Human and Peoples' Rights 2011, para 79(gg); see also UN CESCR 1997, para 16; see also Feiring 2013, p. 21.

[172] The Special Rapporteur on Adequate Housing Guidelines (n 170) para 68 and 69.

7.4.2.4 The Option to Return

Indigenous peoples should also be provided with the option to return to their lands and territories once the reason that necessitated their removal or relocation has ceased to exist.[173] Nevertheless, this option is only offered if it is feasible under the circumstances of the case. Internal displacement prompted by development projects usually results in the permanent relocation of the people affected, which is one of the factors that distinguish it from other forms of internal displacement, as discussed in Chap. 2. Hence, providing an option to return in these cases is seldom possible.

7.4.3 The Right to Maintain Their Relationship with Their Lands

Apart from the above provisions, the UNDRIP and the ILO Convention also recognize the special connection of indigenous peoples with their lands and their right to maintain that relationship in separate provisions.[174] Article 25 of the Declaration states that:

> Indigenous peoples have the right to maintain and strengthen their distinctive spiritual relationship with their traditionally owned or otherwise occupied and used lands, territories, waters and coastal seas and other resources and to uphold their responsibilities to future generations in this regard.[175]

What differentiates this provision from its counterpart under the ILO Convention, Article 13, is that it treats the special relationship of indigenous peoples with their land as "a stand-alone right".[176] Conversely, Article 13 of the ILO Convention conceives this connection as a theoretical foundation against which the rights to lands and other resources enshrined under the Convention are interpreted.[177] The Article obliges states to "respect the special importance for the cultures and spiritual values of the peoples concerned of their relationship with the lands or territories…" in implementing the land rights enshrined under the Convention.[178] Nonetheless, both instruments are in agreement as to the weight that needs to be given to the spiritual connection these peoples have with their lands.

The "right to maintain and strengthen" their special ties to their land and territories recognized under the provisions quoted above also applies to land and territories no longer under the possession of the indigenous peoples concerned.[179] According to Charters:

---

[173] Feiring 2013, p. 21.

[174] UNDRIP (n 12) Article 25; see also ILO Convention No. 169 (n 19) Article 13.

[175] UNDRIP (n 12) Article 25.

[176] Charters 2018, p. 410.

[177] Ibid; ILO Convention No. 169 (n 19) Article 13.

[178] ILO Convention No. 169 (n 19) Article 13.

[179] UNDRIP (n 12) Article 25; see also Charters 2018, p. 411.

> It is clear that under Article 25 [i]ndigenous peoples have the right to maintain and strengthen their spiritual relationship with lands, territories, and resources no longer in their possession, but which they owned, occupied, and used in the past, even where those lands, territories, and resources are now owned, occupied, or used by others.[180]

This is also evident from the text of the provision, which uses a past tense,[181] as well as its object and purpose.

This normative standard is particularly important in the context of DID, which involves the removal of indigenous peoples from their lands and territories. Even in cases where DID is justified, i.e. undertaken with the consent of the peoples concerned and with the payment of adequate compensation, indigenous peoples should be given a chance to continue their relationship with the land or territory in question. Hence, access to these sites should be taken into account in the determination of resettlement sites.

A similar provision can be found under Article 25(1) of the American Declaration, which recognizes the right of indigenous peoples to preserve their special ties to their lands and territories as a stand-alone right.[182] The IACtHR has also affirmed this right in the case of *Saramaka v. Suriname*.[183]

The African Commission has also upheld this special relationship of indigenous peoples with their lands not only as a standard of identification of these peoples but also as an indispensable element of their rights to religion and culture. In the *Endorois case*, the Commission recognized that the religious and cultural practices of the Endorois people are closely connected to lake Bogoria and their ancestral land.[184] Hence, the denial of access to such sites by the state violated their freedom of religion and cultural rights recognized under Articles 8 and 17 of the African Charter, respectively.[185] Overall, indigenous peoples should be provided with an opportunity to maintain their spiritual relationship with their lands and territories even after they are relocated therefrom.

7.5 Conclusion

As depicted throughout this chapter, for indigenous peoples, land is more than an economic resource or corporeal property. It is also at the heart of their cultural and spiritual life since their very identity and way of life are closely intertwined with their ancestral land. The development of norms on indigenous peoples' rights in international law is also based on the recognition of this special relationship. Thus, indigenous peoples are accorded special rights to the lands and territories they

---

180 Charters 2018, p. 411.

181 Ibid.; see also UNDRIP (n 12) Article 25.

182 American Declaration (n 30) Article 25(1).

183 *Saramaka v. Suriname* (n 80) para 95; see also Pasqualucci 2009, p. 57.

184 *Endorois case* (n 36) paras 163–168.

185 Ibid., paras 173 and 239–251.

traditionally occupy. These rights include, *inter alia*, the right to control and use their lands and other resources as they see fit, the right not to be removed from their lands or relocated without their full consent, and the right to maintain their spiritual connection with their lands or territories. These also put heightened obligations on states to refrain from interfering with and to take proactive measures to recognize these rights.

Overall, if a state wishes to acquire the lands of indigenous peoples for development purposes, it has to comply with a set of stringent requirements enshrined under pertinent human rights instruments. The obligation of the state starts from recognizing that indigenous peoples have full property rights to the lands and territories they traditionally occupy. Any proposal to remove them from their lands and relocate them elsewhere can only be executed with their full consent. This requires states to seek the consent of the indigenous peoples concerned by conducting extensive consultations and providing all relevant information. The final say or veto power rests with the indigenous peoples concerned. The obligation of the state does not end at obtaining consent; it should also provide adequate compensation—a set of monetary and non-monetary remedies—to restore the livelihoods of the peoples affected and make good the damage they have (potentially) incurred. The compensation needs to be not only fair and just in terms of means and amount but also agreed upon by the peoples concerned. Furthermore, the state needs to facilitate a condition where the indigenous peoples concerned can still preserve their spiritual connection to their lands and territories after displacement. These are the safeguards states are required to put in place to protect the rights of indigenous peoples in the course of DID.

References

African Commission on Human and Peoples' Rights (2011) Principles and Guidelines on the Implementation of Economic, Social and Cultural Rights in the African Charter on Human and Peoples' Rights, available at https://achpr.au.int/index.php/en/node/871, accessed 20 July 2025.

Anaya S J (2009a) International Human Rights and Indigenous Peoples. Aspen Publishers.

Anaya S J (2009b) The Right of Indigenous Peoples to Self-Determination in the Post- Declaration Era. In: Charters C, Stavenhagen R (eds) Making the Declaration Work: The United Nations Declaration on the Rights of Indigenous Peoples. IWGIA, Copenhagen.

Anaya S J (2010) International Human Rights and Indigenous Peoples. Wolters Kluwer Law & Business.

Anaya S J, Rodríguez-Piñero L (2018) Part I The UNDRIP's Relationship to Existing International Law: the Making of the UNDRIP. In: Hohmann J, Weller M (eds) The UN Declaration on the Rights of Indigenous Peoples: A Commentary. Oxford University Press, Oxford.

Anaya S J, Williams R A Jr (2001) The Protection of Indigenous Peoples' Rights over Lands and Natural Resources under the Inter-American Human Rights System. (2001) 14 Harvard Human Rights Journal 33–86.

Barelli M (2012) Free, prior and informed consent in the aftermath of the UN Declaration on the Rights of Indigenous Peoples: developments and challenges ahead. (2012) 16(1) The International Journal of Human Rights 1–24.

Barnabas S G (2017) The Legal Status of the United Nations Declaration on the Rights of Indigenous Peoples in Contemporary International Human Rights Law. (2017) 6 International Human Rights Law Review 242–261.

Castellino J, Doyle C (2018) Part I The UNDRIP's Relationship to Existing International Law, Ch.1 Who Are 'Indigenous Peoples'?: An Examination of Concepts Concerning Group Membership in the UNDRIP. In: Hohmann J, Weller M (eds) The UN Declaration on the Rights of Indigenous Peoples: A Commentary. Oxford University Press, Oxford.

Charters C (2018) Part IV Rights to Land and Territory, Natural Resources, and Environment, Ch.14 Indigenous Peoples' Rights to Lands, Territories, and Resources in the UNDRIP: Articles 10, 25, 26, and 27. In: Hohmann J, Weller M (eds) The UN Declaration on the Rights of Indigenous Peoples: A Commentary. Oxford University Press, Oxford.

Claridge L (2010) Landmark ruling provides major victory to Kenya's indigenous Endorois. Minority Rights Groups International briefing, 26 August 2010, available at https://minorityrights.org/publications/landmark-ruling-provides-major-victory-to-kenyas-indigenous-endorois-august-2010/, accessed 1 July 2025.

Cobo J M (1987) Special Rapporteur of the UN Sub-Commission on Prevention of Discrimination and Protection of Minorities, Study on the Problem of Discrimination against Indigenous Populations. March 1987, UN Doc E/CN.4/Sub.2/1986/Add.4.

Daes E-I A (2009) The Contribution of the Working Group on Indigenous Populations to the Genesis and Evolution of the UN Declaration on the Rights of Indigenous Peoples. In: Charters C, Stavenhagen R (eds) Making the Declaration Work: The United Nations Declaration on the Rights of Indigenous Peoples. IWGIA, Copenhagen.

Diergarten Y (2019) Indigenous or Out of Scope? Large-scale Land Acquisitions in Developing Countries, International Human Rights Law and the Current Deficiencies in Land Rights Protection. (2019) 19(1) Human Rights Law Review 37–52.

Feiring B (2013) Indigenous peoples' rights to lands, territories, and resources. ILC, Rome.

Gilbert J (2011) Indigenous peoples' human rights in Africa: the pragmatic revolution of the African Commission on Human and Peoples' Rights. (2011) 60(1) The International and Comparative Law Quarterly 245–270.

Gismondi G (2016) Denial of Justice: The Latest Indigenous Land Disputes Before the European Court of Human Rights and the Need for an Expansive Interpretation of Protocol 1. (2016) 18 Yale Human Rights & Development Law Journal 1–58.

Henriksen J B (2009) The UN Declaration on the Rights of Indigenous Peoples: Some Key Issues and Events in the Process. In: Charters C, Stavenhagen R (eds) Making the Declaration Work: The United Nations Declaration on the Rights of Indigenous Peoples. IWGIA, Copenhagen.

Hohmann J, Weller M (2018) Introduction. In: Hohmann J, Weller M (eds) The UN Declaration on the Rights of Indigenous Peoples: A Commentary. Oxford University Press, Oxford.

Human Rights Council (2018) Free, prior and informed consent: a human rights-based Approach, Study of the Expert Mechanism on the Rights of Indigenous Peoples, 10 August 2018, A/HRC/39/62.

International Labour Organization (2013) Understanding the Indigenous and Tribal Peoples Convention, 1989 (No. 169): Handbook for ILO Tripartite Constituents. International Labour Office, Geneva.

Kanosue Y (2015) When Land is Taken Away: States Obligations under International Human Rights Law Concerning Large-Scale Projects Impacting Local Communities. (2015) 15(4) Human Rights Law Review 643–667.

Koivurova T (2011) Jurisprudence of the European Court of Human Rights Regarding Indigenous Peoples: Retrospect and Prospects. (2011) 18 International Journal on Minority and Group Rights 1–37.

Kovacs P (2016) Indigenous Issues under the European Convention of Human Rights, Reflected in an Inter-American Mirror. (2016) 48(4) The George Washington International Law Review 781–806.

MacInnes A, Colchester M, Whitmore A (2017) Free, prior and informed consent: how to rectify the devastating consequences of harmful mining for indigenous peoples. (2017) 15 Perspectives in Ecology and Conservation 152–160.

Mazel O (2009) The Evolution of Rights: Indigenous Peoples and International Law. (2009) 13(1) Australian Indigenous Law Review 140–158.

Montes A R, Cisneros G T (2009) The United Nations Declaration on the Rights of Indigenous Peoples: The Foundation of a New Relationship between Indigenous Peoples, States and Societies. In: Charters C, Stavenhagen R (eds) Making the Declaration Work: The United Nations Declaration on the Rights of Indigenous Peoples. IWGIA, Copenhagen.

Nykolaishen S (2012) Customary International Law and the Declaration on the Rights of Indigenous Peoples. (2012) 17(1) Appeal 111–128.

Pasqualucci J M (2009) International Indigenous Land Rights: A Critique of the Jurisprudence of the Inter-American Court of Human Rights in Light of the United Nations Declaration on the Rights of Indigenous Peoples. (2009) 27(1) Wisconsin International Law Journal 51–98.

Patel S, Sliuzas R, Mathur N (2015) The risk of impoverishment in urban development-induced displacement and resettlement in Ahmedabad. (2015) 27(1) Environment & Urbanization 231–256.

Rew A, Fisher E, Pande B (2000) Addressing Policy Constraints and Improving Outcomes in Development-Induced Resettlement Projects. Refugee Studies Centre, Oxford.

Special Rapporteur on Adequate Housing (2007) Basic Principles and Guidelines on Development-based Evictions and Displacement, 5 February 2007, A/HRC/4/18, available at https://www.ohchr.org/en/documents/thematic-reports/basic-principles-and-guidelines-development-based-evictions-and, accessed 1 July 2025.

Stanley J (2004) Development-induced Displacement and Resettlement. (2004) Forced Migration Online.

Terminski B (2015) Development-Induced Displacement and Resettlement: Causes, Consequences, and Socio-Legal Context. Ibidem-Verlag, Stuttgart.

UN Committee on Economic, Social and Cultural Rights (UN CESCR) (1997) General Comment No. 7: The right to adequate housing (Article 11.1): forced evictions, 20 May 1997, E/1998/22.

Chapter 8
The Right to Development in the Context of Development-Induced Displacement

Contents

Abstract The other specialized human rights regime relevant to development-induced displacement (DID) pertains to the frameworks and norms governing the right to development. While the right to development does not directly address displacement or DID, it establishes important norms concerning the concept, process, and outcome of development. Since "development" is often invoked as a justification for DID, it is imperative to analyse these norms. The norms on the right to development can inform the approval process of development projects that potentially cause displacement, the execution of such displacement, and the safeguards that need to be provided along the way. Accordingly, this chapter explores the normative content of the right to development as envisaged under the relevant frameworks and examines its application in the context of DID.

Keywords Right to development · Public participation · Self-determination · UN Declaration on the Right to Development · African Charter on Human and Peoples' Rights · *Endorois* case

Note: Some parts of this chapter have been published as a journal article (see Teshome 2022).

© T.M.C. ASSER PRESS and the authors 2026
R. G. Teshome, *The Human Cost of Development*, Human Rights Research Series 104,
https://doi.org/10.1007/978-94-6265-751-9_8

8.1 Introduction

The right to development, recognized under the UN Declaration on the Right to Development and the African Charter on Human and Peoples' Rights, obliges states to take the necessary measures to facilitate the realization of economic, social, cultural, and political development. At the same time, it entitles "all persons and peoples" to the right to participate in the process of development and to equitably share its benefits. While the norms on the right to development do not directly address development-induced displacement (DID), they provide normative standards that can inform and guide both the decision-making process and the outcomes of DID. In light of this, this chapter seeks to answer the following questions: To what extent does the right to development inform the process of DID and the rights-based safeguards that need to be provided along the way? How can the relevant norms apply in the context of displacement prompted by development projects?

To this end, the chapter comprises three main sections. Section 8.2 introduces the emergence and recognition of the right to development in international law. The normative content of the right to development, including the conception of development, the nature of the right to development and the entitlements it contains, will be covered in Sect. 8.3. Section 8.4 then explores the state obligations the right to development entails. In all these sections, the analysis will be contextualized with regard to DID.

8.2 The Recognition of the Right to Development

Development and human rights had been regarded as isolated, sometimes even as competing, subjects.[1] While some international instruments including the United Nations Charter have urged the simultaneous promotion of both development and human rights,[2] this had not been positively welcomed for a long time. The past few decades, however, have witnessed an increasing acceptance of the inherent interdependence between the two subjects. The right to development and the human rights-based approach to development (HRBAD) were born from the recognition of this interdependence.[3]

The efforts to recognize the right to development as a human right date back to the early 1970s when Justin Keba M'baye, the former vice-president of the International

---

[1] Uvin 2007, p. 597.

[2] United Nations, *Charter of the United Nations*, 24 October 1945, 1 UNTS XVI, Article 55; see also Alston and Robinson 2005, pp. 1–3; see also United Nations, Final Act of the International Conference on Human Rights (The Proclamation of Teheran), 1968, UN doc. A/CONF.32/41, para 13.

[3] Uvin 2007, p. 597.

Court of Justice, coined the term.[4] However, the early efforts did not bear fruit mainly due to the ideological divide during the cold war.[5] In 1979, the UN Secretary-General concluded in a report, which laid the foundation for the subsequent development of the Declaration, that the right to development as a human right can be inferred from existing norms and principles of international law recognized under numerous hard law and soft law frameworks.[6] Subsequently, the Human Rights Commission established a Working Group with the mandate of drafting the UN Declaration on the Right to Development, which was adopted in 1986.[7] The Declaration was adopted with the overwhelming support of states.[8] This does not, however, imply a consensus as to the legal status, the justiciability, and the normative content of the right to development.[9]

The legal status of the right to development as a human right had given rise to a considerable debate.[10] These debates range from its significance as a legal right to whether or not it is a legal right in the first place. "The debate on the legal significance of the right ranges from hailing it as a major breakthrough in the history of human rights to debunking it as a distracting—if not dangerous—ideological initiative."[11] Some commentators expressed reservations that the recognition of the right to development might have the effect of "[diverting] attention from the pressing issues of human dignity and freedom".[12] A consensus as to the status was finally reached with the adoption of the Vienna Declaration, which affirmed that "the right to development, as established in the Declaration on the Right to Development, [is] a universal and inalienable right and an integral part of fundamental human rights."[13] This is further reiterated in a plethora of soft-law documents adopted subsequently,[14] such

---

[4] Sengupta 2000, p. 555; see also Lindroos 1999, pp. 1 and 4. The emergence of development as a human right is rooted in the decolonization process and the call of the newly independent states for a "new international economic order" (see Lindroos 1999, p. 3).

[5] Sengupta 2010, p. 13; see also Sengupta 2000, p. 555.

[6] Sengupta 2000, p. 555; see also Lindroos 1999, p. 4.

[7] UN General Assembly, Declaration on the Right to Development: resolution/adopted by the General Assembly, 4 December 1986, A/RES/41/128; see also Sengupta 2000, p. 555.

[8] Sengupta 2010, p. 13. The Declaration was adopted by 146 votes, 1 vote against and 8 abstentions (see Lindroos 1999, p. 5).

[9] Sengupta 2000, p. 555; see also Arts and Tamo 2016, pp. 222 and 230; see also Lindroos 1999, pp. 6 and 7.

[10] Sengupta 2000, p. 556.

[11] Bunn 2000, p. 1426.

[12] Ghai 1989, pp. 5–6; see also Bunn 2000, p. 1426.

[13] UN General Assembly, *Vienna Declaration and Programme of Action*, 12 July 1993, A/CONF.157/2, para 10; see also Sengupta 2000, pp. 555–557; see also Sengupta 2010, p. 13; see also Lindroos 1999, p. 6. The Declaration was adopted by a consensus of the representatives of 171 states present at World Conference on Human Rights, held in June 1993 (see World Conference on Human Rights, 14–25 June 1993, Vienna, Austria, available at https://www.ohchr.org/EN/ABOUTUS/Pages/ViennaWC.aspx, accessed 1 July 2025).

[14] Sengupta 2000, pp. 555 and 556; see also Sengupta 2010, p. 14.

as the Rio Declaration on Environment and Development,[15] the Cairo Declaration of the International Conference on Population and Development,[16] and the Copenhagen Declaration of Social Development.[17] Hence, it is safe to conclude that, currently, the status of the right to development as a human rights is widely accepted.

The other debate on the right to development pertains to its justiciability[18]—whether or not it can be claimed and enforced judicially. Some commentators, particularly positivists, argue that the right to development is not legally enforceable and, hence, cannot be considered a human right.[19] Proponents of the right to development as a human right, however, contend that, on the one hand, the status or normative value of rights in general and the right to development in particular is not contingent on the possibility of judicial enforcement and, on the other hand, the right to development can, in fact, be judicially enforced as the experiences of some jurisdictions attest. For instance, Arjun Sengupta, the former UN Independent Expert on the Right to Development,[20] argues that "[the above positivist view] confuses human rights with legal rights: human rights precede law and are derived not from law but from the concept of human dignity. There is nothing in principle to prevent a right [from] being an internationally recognized human right even if it is not individually justified."[21] Amartya Sen also argues that the existence and effectiveness of a right are not solely based on justiciability or "coercive legislation".[22] "[J]usticiability is only one of the ways of making a human right effective."[23] There are other enforcement tools that can be equally effective under the circumstances, such as "social and political activism".[24] Hence, the lack of justiciability alone does not deprive a right of its normative value or render it ineffective.

In addition, as can be deduced from the case law of the monitoring bodies of the African human rights system and some national courts, the right to development can

---

[15] UN General Assembly, Rio Declaration on Environment and Development, 12 August 1992, A/CONF.151/26 (Vol. I), Principle 3.

[16] UN Population Fund (UNFPA), *Report of the International Conference on Population and Development: Cairo, 5–13 September 1994*, A/CONF.171/13/Rev.1 (New York: United Nations, 1995), Principle 3.

[17] United Nations World Summit for Social Development, Copenhagen Declaration on Social Development, 14 March 1995, A/CONF.166/9.

[18] Sen 2010, pp. 4 and 5.

[19] Sengupta 2000, p. 558.

[20] The Independent Expert was appointed by the Human Rights Commission to follow up on the implementation of the Declaration (see The UN Commission on Human Rights, Resolution 1998/72 the Right to Development, 22 April 1998, ESCOR Supp. (No. 3) at 229 U.N. Doc. E/CN.4/1998/72). The mandate of the expert extended from 1998 to 2004.

[21] Sengupta 2000, p. 558.

[22] Sen 2010, p. 8.

[23] Ibid.

[24] Ibid.

indeed be enforced judicially. In the *Endorois*[25] and *Ogiek*[26] cases decided by the African Commission and the African Court, respectively, the right to development had been invoked and applied. Moreover, progressive cases decided by some national courts, particularly in South Africa and Colombia,[27] have also affirmed that judicial enforcement of the right to development is possible. Despite the potential challenges of judicially enforcing rights that have the nature of progressive realization and a collective aspect,[28] the right to development and other ESC rights are not categorically nonjusticiable.[29] They can indeed be invoked and enforced judicially as these cases demonstrate.

Furthermore, the normative content of the right to development and the state obligations it entails have also been—and still remain—contentious.[30] These debates particularly pertain to the duty of international cooperation and the means of implementation of the right.[31] Developed countries fear that the right to development could be deemed as "the right to everything" and used by developing countries to demand resource transfer.[32] Moreover, the text of the Declaration has been criticized for being vague and inconsistent.[33] Overall, there has been a debate as to the status, justiciability, and normative content of the right to development.

Despite the overwhelming support by which it was adopted and the subsequent consensus as to the status of the right to development, the Declaration is not legally binding. However, as mentioned before, the right to development is inextricably linked to other human rights, particularly economic, social and cultural rights, that are recognized in binding treaties.[34] Hence, the Declaration has a significant normative weight. At the beginning of 2020, the Working Group on the Right to Development prepared a "Draft Convention on the Right to Development" on the basis of the

---

[25] *Centre for Minority Rights Development (Kenya) and Minority Rights Group International on behalf of Endorois Welfare Council v. Kenya*, 276/2003, African Commission on Human and Peoples' Rights, 4 February 2010.

[26] *African Commission on Human and Peoples' Rights v. Republic of Kenya*, Application No. 006/2012, African Court on Human and Peoples' Rights, 26 May 2017 (*Ogiek case*).

[27] Liebenberg 2010, pp. 209–244; see also *Republic of South Africa v. Grootboom*, Case No. CCT 11/00. 2000 (11) BCLR 1169, Constitutional Court of South Africa, 4 October 2000 and *Minister of Health v. Treatment Action Campaign*, Case No. CCT 8/02, Constitutional Court of South Africa, 5 July 2002; see also *Minister of Health and Others v Treatment Action Campaign and Others (TAC case)* (No. 2), CCT8/02) [2002] ZACC 15; 2002 (5) SA 721; 2002 (10) BCLR 1033, 5 July 2002; see also Sentencia C-175/09, Colombia: Corte Constitucional, 18 March 2009.

[28] Sen 2010, p. 8.

[29] UN CESCR 1998, para 10; see also UN CESCR 1990, para 5.

[30] Sengupta 2010, p. 14.

[31] Arts and Tamo 2016, p. 224.

[32] Kerchmeier 2006, p. 12.

[33] Lindroos 1999, p. 5.

[34] OHCHR 2016, pp. 5–7; see also Committee on Economic, Social and Cultural Rights, Statement on the importance and relevance of the right to development, adopted on the occasion of the twenty-fifth anniversary of the Declaration on the Right to Development, 12 July 2011, E/C.12/2011/2.

mandate accorded to it by the Human Rights Council.[35] The draft, while it draws on the norms incorporated under the Declaration, has also introduced several important amendments and additions. The draft is expected to go through a long discussion and negotiation process given the controversial nature of the norms on the right to development. If the draft receives sufficient support from states and is ultimately adopted, the right to development will have a binding effect for state parties at the universal level.

At the regional level, the right to development is provided under Article 22 of the African Charter on Human and Peoples' Rights,[36] which is the first and the only binding treaty that recognizes this right. In the subsequent sections, the normative content of the right to development as they apply to DID will be elucidated based on the UN Declaration and the African Charter coupled with the case law of the African Commission and Court on Human and Peoples' Rights.

8.3 Normative Content of the Right to Development

8.3.1 What Is "Development"?

Before proceeding to the substantive elements of the right to development and the state obligations it entails, it is imperative to briefly look into what "development" as envisaged under the Declaration and the African Charter means. This is particularly relevant in the DID discourse as development is the principal justification invoked for displacing people to make room for development projects.

Development has long been a highly contested notion. The understanding of development, particularly in the UN system, has undergone three distinct stages.[37] In the early days, development was solely associated with economic growth or an increase in Gross National Product (GNP).[38] For instance, in the 1960s, the terms "development", "economic development", and "growth" were attributed a similar meaning and used interchangeably.[39] This "straightforward view of development as

[35] Human Rights Council, Working Group on the Right to Development, Revised Draft Convention on the Right to Development, 6 April 2022, A/HRC/WG.2/23/2; see also Human Rights Council, Resolution 39/9, The Right to Development, 25 September 2018, A/HRC/39/L.12; see also Human Rights Council, Resolution 42/23, The Right to Development, 20 September 2019, A/HRC/42/L.36.

[36] Organization of African Unity (OAU), African Charter on Human and Peoples' Rights, 27 June 1981, CAB/LEG/67/3 rev. 5, 21 I.L.M. 58 (1982), ('African Charter'), Article 22.

[37] Lindroos 1999, p. 40.

[38] Ibid.

[39] UN Secretary-General 2013, p. 7; see also Lindroos 1999, p. 40.

an upward climb",[40] however, resulted in neither a "...fair distribution of growth nor an appreciation of the non-material facets of human development."[41]

In the 1970s, the focus shifted to human welfare as it became evident that mere economic growth does not guarantee development.[42] Accordingly, the ultimate end of development should be the continuous improvement of "the well-being of the entire population" who should also be the main participants and beneficiaries of development.[43] This human-centred approach challenges the traditional conception that equates development with mere economic growth. This approach is also reflected in the Declaration as will be discussed below.

In the 1990s, a new approach or conception of development emerged, i.e. sustainable development, due to the need to accommodate environmental and social justice concerns.[44] Pursuant to the popular definition of the concept adopted by the World Commission on Environment and Development[45] in its report, "Our Common Future", "[s]ustainable development is development which meets the needs of the present without compromising the ability of future generations to meet their own needs."[46] Thus, sustainable development aims to achieve "intergenerational equity" in the pursuit of development.[47] This abstract concept was further dissected in subsequent frameworks and academic works. Overall, sustainable development encompasses three "interdependent and mutually reinforcing" components, i.e. economic, environmental and social sustainability, commonly referred to as "the three pillars of sustainable development".[48] This conception of development was also reiterated in the Sustainable Development Goals (SDGs), which contain 17 goals geared towards achieving economic, social, and environmental sustainability.[49]

The Declaration defines what development means in the Preamble, which reflects the human-centred or "anthropocentric" approach.[50] The relevant paragraph of the Preamble reads:

---

[40] Harris 2000, p. 5.

[41] Lindroos 1999, p. 40.

[42] Ibid.

[43] Ibid., pp. 40 and 41.

[44] Ibid., p. 41; see also Harris 2000, p. 5.

[45] World Commission on Environment and Development, also called "Brundtland Commission" after its chair, the then Prime Minister of Norway Gro Harlem Brundtland, was established by the UN General Assembly in 1882. The Commission, which constituted members from developed and developing countries, worked to harmonize development needs and environmental concerns, which resulted in the publication of the famous document—Our Common Heritage—in 1887.

[46] World Commission on Environment and Development 1987.

[47] Kates et al. 2005, pp. 10 and 11.

[48] The Johannesburg Declaration on Sustainable Development, 4 September 2002, para 5; The Declaration was adopted during the 2002 World Summit on Sustainable Development.

[49] UN General Assembly, Transforming our world: the 2030 Agenda for Sustainable Development, 21 October 2015, A/RES/70/1 (Adopted by the UN General Assembly in 2015, SDGs are development goals and agendas set to be achieved by 2030).

[50] Arts and Tamo 2016, p. 231; see also Lindroos 1999, p. 41.

> ...development is a comprehensive economic, social, cultural and political process, which aims at the constant improvement of the well-being of the entire population and of all individuals on the basis of their active, free and meaningful participation in development and in the fair distribution of benefits resulting therefrom[.][51]

Hence, this definition coupled with Article 1 of the Declaration indicates what development should achieve—improvement of well-being and the realization of human rights—and how that should be achieved—with the participation of the persons or people concerned in the process of development and the fruits therefrom.[52] According to the Independent Expert on the Right to Development, "well-being" in this context should be construed broadly and it "...extends well beyond the conventional notions of economic growth to the expansion of opportunities and capabilities to enjoy those opportunities."[53] Moreover, development comprises social, cultural, and political development in addition to the traditionally recognized economic growth.[54] A similar approach is adopted in Article 22 of the African Charter.[55] The African Commission has also affirmed this in the *Endorois* case underscoring that the outcome of development should be empowering and improving the capabilities and choices of the people involved.[56] This interpretation closely aligns with the Nobel Laureate Amartya Sen's capability approach, which significantly shaped the contemporary understanding of development.[57] According to this approach, development should be measured by its effect in expanding individual capabilities—"a person's freedom to choose between different ways of living."[58]

Nevertheless, neither the Declaration nor the Charter prescribes a specific development model; "[the right to development] is the right of individuals and peoples to pursue their development as they perceive it."[59] This also coincides with the principle of self-determination, which will be discussed below. In a nutshell, development as envisaged under the Declaration and the Charter refers to the pursuit of economic, social, and political progress that aims to improve the well-being of the population and advance the realization of human rights.

This human well-being and rights-based definition of development puts into question the legitimacy of displacement for development purposes. The conception of

---

[51] The Declaration on the Right to Development (n 7) Preamble.

[52] Ibid., Preamble and Article 1.

[53] The UN Commission on Human Rights, Study on the current state of progress in the implementation of the right to development submitted by Mr. Arjun K. Sengupta, independent expert, pursuant to Commission resolution 1998/72 and General Assembly resolution 53/155, 27 July 1999, E/CN.4/1999/WG.18/2 ('report 1 of the independent expert'), para 47; see also UN General Assembly, Report of the Independent Expert on the Right to Development, 17 August 2002, A/55/306 ('report 2 of the independent expert'), para 22.

[54] The Declaration on the Right to Development (n 7) Preamble and Article 1; see also Lindroos 1999, p. 41; see also Sengupta 2010, p. 16.

[55] African Charter (n 36) Article 22.

[56] *Endorois case* (n 25) para 283.

[57] Sen's capability approach was later used by the Intendent Expert to interpret the Declaration.

[58] Sen 1989, p. 44.

[59] Lindroos 1999, p. 47; see also the UN Secretary-General 2013, p. 8.

development as mere economic growth in the past "… has propounded the belief, though contestable, that all national development projects are in the public interest."[60] However, the understanding of development as a process aimed at improving human well-being will help to see the issue of "public interest" in a different light. In other words, this contemporary conception of development can and should inform the decision-making process at all stages of DID, particularly the determination of public interest. Does the development project in question contribute to the improvement of the well-being and the realization of the rights of the general population, particularly those affected by the project? Do the people affected by the project participate in the process of development and equitably share its benefits? These questions should guide the determination of whether or not a given project and the resulting displacement are necessary for the public interest. Hence, the definition or approach of development envisaged under the Declaration can be utilized to understand the public interest requirement discussed in the previous parts of this book in relation to forced eviction, expropriation, and internal displacement.

8.3.2 The Nature of the Right to Development

The declaratory statement of the Declaration stipulated under Article 1 sets out the main features of the right to development and the underlying premises on which it is based.[61] The provision reads:

> The right to development is an inalienable human right by virtue of which every human person and all peoples are entitled to participate in, contribute to, and enjoy economic, social, cultural and political development, in which all human rights and fundamental freedoms can be fully realized.[62]

As is evident from the wording of this provision, the right to development is both an individual and a collective right.[63] The determination of the subjects of the right is one of the issues intensely debated during the adoption of the Declaration mainly due to the divergence of views between the North and the South on the issue.[64] The compromise reached was to recognize the right both as an individual and a collective right—a right granted to "…every human person and all peoples".[65] Conversely, the African Charter recognizes this right only as a collective right; the subjects of the right, according to Article 22(1), are "peoples".[66] What the term "peoples" constitutes

---

60 Juma 2013, p. 212.

61 Report 1 of the Independent Expert (n 53) para 36.

62 The Declaration on the Right to Development (n 7) Article 1.

63 Ibid.; African Charter (n 36) Article 22.

64 Lindroos 1999, p. 30; the Global North states believed that human rights, including the right to development, are individual rights. On the other hand, the Global South states argued that the right to development is collective in nature.

65 The Declaration on the Right to Development (n 7) Article 1; see also Lindroos 1999, p. 30.

66 African Charter (n 36) Article 22(1); see also Lindroos 1999, p. 33.

for the purpose of the right to development has not been clarified in the Declaration or in the African Charter.

In the *Endorois* case, the African Commission gave an indication of the collective characteristics groups should possess to be regarded as "peoples", which are:

> ...a common historical tradition, racial or ethnic identity, cultural homogeneity, linguistic unity, religious and ideological affinities, territorial connection, and a common economic life or other bonds, identities and affinities they collectively enjoy – especially rights enumerated under Articles 19 to 24 of the African Charter – or suffer collectively from the deprivation of such rights.[67]

The African Court, on the other hand, gave a more simplistic and abstract definition in the *Ogiek* case.[68] Accordingly, the term "peoples" envisaged under the Charter "comprises all populations as a constitutive element of a state" including "sub-state ethnic groups and communities" forming the population.[69] Overall, based on these definitions, the term "peoples" denotes a group of individuals who share certain common traits, such as territory, language, and culture. It should be construed more broadly than the term "indigenous peoples" elucidated in the preceding chapter.

The other important feature of the right to development is that it applies to both the process and the outcome of development.[70] As mentioned before, the outcome of development should be an improvement of the well-being of the general population and this should be achieved with their participation in the process and proceeds of development. In other words, the right to development aspires to make both the process and the outcome of development equitable. In the *Endorois* case, the African Commission affirmed these procedural and substantive aspects of the right stating:

> ...the right to development is a two-pronged test, that it is both constitutive and instrumental, or useful as both a means and an end. A violation of either the procedural or substantive element constitutes a violation of the right to development. Fulfilling only one of the two prongs will not satisfy the right to development.[71]

What these aspects specifically entail will be discussed below. Nonetheless, it is important to note that this feature of the right to development is particularly relevant in the context of DID. As discussed in the previous chapters, several case studies depict that the process of DID in many cases falls short of guaranteeing equitable participation in the process and benefits of the development project concerned. Often, the people that bear the costs of development are neither the participants nor the beneficiaries of the development project concerned.[72] Rather, DID often results in the deterioration of the well-being of the persons or people affected and interferes with or potentially violates a number of human rights. Thus, in light of the understanding of the right to development both as process and outcome, the pursuit of economic

[67] *Endorois* case (n 25) para 151; see also Feyter 2013, p. 21.

[68] *Ogiek case* (n 26) paras 196–199 and 208.

[69] Ibid., paras 196–199 and 208.

[70] Sengupta 2010, p. 23.

[71] *Endorois* case (n 25) para 277.

[72] Robinson 2003, p. 10; see also Mathur 1995, p. 21.

growth or an increase in some economic growth indicators alone arguably does not justify the deprivation of rights or the worsening of social, economic, and cultural well-being. This is particularly true when those affected have not been given a chance to participate in the process.

The right to development also recognizes human rights both as a means and an end to development.[73] The operational definition of the right to development advanced by the Independent Expert on the right to development rightly captures this feature of the right. The definition reads:

> The right to development is the right to a process of development, consisting of a progressive and phased realization of all the recognized human rights, such as civil and political rights, and economic, social and cultural rights (other rights admitted in international law) as well as the process of economic growth consistent with human rights standards.[74]

Hence, on the one hand, the result or outcome of development should be progressing the realization of all sets of rights, from civil and political rights to economic, social, and cultural rights.[75] Comprehensive and inclusive development is an essential precondition for the protection of human rights as the realization of most rights is contingent upon the availability of resources.[76] On the other hand, development has to be carried out in accordance with human rights standards.[77] Overall, human rights have both "substantive and instrumental value" in the attainment of development.[78]

As mentioned before, the Declaration follows a human-centred approach. This is also evident from Article 2(1), which embraces the principle of putting humans at the centre of development.[79] The provision states that "[t]he human person is the central subject of development and should be the active participant and beneficiary of the right to development."[80] The draft Convention moves beyond this human-centred approach and addresses environmental concerns by adopting sustainable development as one of the guiding principles of the right to development.[81]

These features of the right to development also coincide with the features of the HRBAD.[82] Simply put, the HRBAD envisages that development programs and

---

[73] The Declaration on the Right to Development (n 7) Article 1.

[74] Sengupta 2010, p. 20; see also Report 1 of the Independent Expert (n 53) para 47; see also Report 2 of the Independent Expert (n 53) para 16.

[75] Sengupta 2010, p. 23.

[76] Ibid., p. 24; see also Beetham 2010, p. 102.

[77] Sengupta 2010, p. 23.

[78] Ibid., p. 24; see also Beetham 2010, pp. 103 and 104.

[79] The Declaration on the Right to Development (n 7) Article 2(1).

[80] Ibid., Article 2(1) and Preamble; see also Arts and Tamo 2016, p. 231.

[81] The Revised Draft Convention on the Right to Development (n 35) Article 3(g) (this provision provides that "development must be achieved in its three dimensions, namely, economic, social and environmental, in a balanced and integrated manner and in harmony with nature. The right to development must be fulfilled so as to equitably meet developmental and environmental needs of present and future generations; and the right to development cannot be realized if development is unsustainable").

[82] Sengupta 2010, p. 16.

projects should be undertaken in accordance with human rights standards.[83] It urges states and other stakeholders to integrate human rights norms in the planning and implementation of development programs.[84] The HRBAD champions the protection and promotion of human rights both as a tool and end result of development. To this end, "[i]t seeks to analyse inequalities which lie at the heart of development problems and redress discriminatory practices and unjust distributions of power that impede development progress."[85] This approach embodies the principles of access to information, public participation, accountability, transparency, non-discrimination, and do-no-harm.[86] These principles and values of the HRBAD are embedded in the norms of the right to development. Overall, these features of the right to development are important in the DID discourse as they can inform the decision-making process at all stages of displacement.

8.3.3 Substantive Elements of the Right to Development

The right to development contains three main substantive elements or entitlements, namely meaningful participation, an equitable share in the benefits of development, and self-determination.[87] One of the substantive elements of the right to development is popular participation.[88] Several Articles of the Declaration stipulate that "active, free and meaningful participation" is an integral part of the right.[89] The question is whether the participation requirement confers a collective decision-making power on the people concerned or whether mere consultation is sufficient.[90] This is not evident from the wording of the provision. However, arguably, participation would not be "meaningful" if it does not potentially influence decision-making.

In the *Endorois* case, the African Commission indicated that participation should go beyond merely informing the persons or people concerned and provide them with a chance to influence decision-making.[91] In this case, the Commission found the participation provided by the state inadequate because the "... community members

---

[83] Report 2 of the Independent Expert (n 53) para 19; see also Office of the UN High Commissioner for Human Rights, Principles and Guidelines for a Human Rights Approach to Development, 2006, HR/PUB/06/12, para 16.

[84] Piovesan 2013, p. 103.

[85] Boesen and Sano 2010, p. 50.

[86] OHCHR 2004, pp. 16–18; see also Report 2 of the Independent Expert (n 53) para 19; see also Boesen and Sano 2010, pp. 51 and 52.

[87] The Declaration on the Right to Development (n 7) Article 1.

[88] Lindroos 1999, p. 45.

[89] The Declaration on the Right to Development (n 7) Articles 2(3), 1(1), and 8(2); see also Lindroos 1999, p. 45.

[90] Lindroos 1999, pp. 46 and 47.

[91] *Endorois* case (n 25) para 281.

were informed of the impending project as a *fait accompli*, and not given an opportunity to shape the policies or their role in the game reserve."[92] The Commission also noted that the indigenous people, in this case, were not in an equal bargaining position due to lack of education and their "different understanding of property use and ownership".[93] Adequate participation needs to take these factors into account, which the state failed to do in this case.[94] While this case involves indigenous people, "free, active and meaningful participation" is generally accepted as an integral part of the right to development by the Commission, irrespective of the identity of the people involved.[95]

In the context of DID, the people affected by DID should be given a chance to participate and potentially shape decision-making at all stages of displacement—from the approval of the project to the determination of compensation or other remedies for displacement.[96] This is also complementary to the participation requirement of the frameworks on forced eviction, expropriation, and internal displacement elucidated in the previous chapters of this book.

The right to participate in the development process that the right to development entails, however, is not equivalent to the right to free and informed consent accorded to indigenous peoples as discussed in the preceding chapter.[97] The right to development does not prohibit states from taking development measures contrary to the will of the persons or people concerned. Nevertheless, even in those cases, right-holders—individuals and peoples—should benefit from development, which brings into the picture the other important substantive element of the right to development.

The right to development guarantees an equitable share in the benefits of development.[98] This entails, according to Article 8 of the Declaration, "…equality of opportunity for all in their access to basic resources, education, health services, food, housing, employment and the fair distribution of income."[99] In other words, fair distribution of the benefits of development is expressed in equal access to public services, such as health care, education, and social security as well as the ability to make a living through decent work. Further, this ultimate end would not be achieved without the participation of vulnerable and marginalized groups in the process and

[92] Ibid. (see also paras 289–291 and 297).

[93] Ibid., para 282.

[94] Ibid.

[95] Ibid., para 183; the Commission particularly endorsed the relevant provision of the UN Declaration on the Right to Development (Article 2(3)) regarding participation. Participation as an integral part of the right to development is also reiterated by the African Court in the *Ogiek* case—a similar case involving the eviction of indigenous people from the land they traditionally occupy (see *Ogiek* case (n 26) paras 209 and 210).

[96] van der Ploeg and Vanclay 2017, p. 40.

[97] UN General Assembly, United Nations Declaration on the Rights of Indigenous Peoples: resolution/adopted by the General Assembly, 2 October 2007, A/RES/61/295, Article 10; see also International Labour Organization (ILO), Indigenous and Tribal Peoples Convention, C169, 27 June 1989, Article 16(2).

[98] The Declaration on the Right to Development (n 7) Articles 1 and 2(1).

[99] Ibid., Article 8; see also Report 1 of the Independent Expert (n 53) para 39.

the proceeds of development and the "[eradication of] all social injustices."[100] Thus, states should strive to address economic and social inequalities that side-line some from participating in the development process and hinder equal enjoyment of rights.

This norm of fair distribution of the benefits of development is grounded on the principles of social justice, particularly fair (re)distribution of resources.[101] Social justice, according to John Rawls' theory of justice, constitutes two major principles, i.e. equality and distributive justice.[102] The principle of equality, or "the principle of equal liberty" in Rawls' terms, demands the provision of equal rights and liberties for everyone, which also embodies the principle of non-discrimination.[103] The second principle, namely "the difference principle", envisages that social and economic inequalities are acceptable only if they are "to the greatest benefit of the least advantaged persons"[104] and "attached to offices and positions open to all."[105] Thus, while in principle, rights and socio-economic opportunities—the benefits of development in this case—should be distributed equally, inequalities, or differential treatment in human rights terminology, can be justified when it is for the good of those that are disadvantaged, i.e. distributive justice.[106] Hence, social justice embodies the principles of equality and non-discrimination as well as the need to address the economic and social marginalization of disadvantaged groups.[107] The norms incorporated in the Declaration reflect these principles of social justice.

In the context of DID, participating in the benefits of development entails, *inter alia*, adequate compensation and replacement of real properties as well as rehabilitation measures to restore the well-being of the people affected.[108] In the *Endorois* case, the African Commission found that the lack of sufficient compensation and access to grazing land coupled with the inadequacy of participation discussed above indicate that the Endorois people were "left out of the development process or benefits."[109] Moreover, the direct and indirect discrimination that the process of DID often involves and practices that have the effect of perpetuating inequalities, which are elaborated in the preceding chapters, go against the principle of equitable distribution of the benefits of development.

The other important element of the right to development is self-determination.[110] As the Declaration also refers to, the right to self-determination is recognized in both Covenants; Articles 1 of both the ICCPR and ICESCR recognise peoples' right to

---

[100] The Declaration on the Right to Development (n 7) Article 8; see also Report 1 of the Independent Expert (n 53) para 39.

[101] Lindroos 1999, p. 47; see also report 2 of the Independent Expert (n 53) para 17.

[102] Rawls 1999, pp. 52 and 53.

[103] Ibid., p. 53.

[104] Rawls 1971, p. 302.

[105] Rawls 1999, p. 53.

[106] Ibid.

[107] Piovesan 2013, p. 104.

[108] *Endorois* case (n 25) paras 294 and 295.

[109] Ibid., para 298.

[110] The Declaration on the Right to Development (n 7) Article 1(2).

"freely determine their political status and freely pursue their economic, social and cultural development" and "freely dispose of their natural wealth and resources".[111] Based on these provisions, Article 1(2) of the Declaration stipulates:

> The human right to development also implies the full realization of the right of peoples to self-determination, which includes, subject to the relevant provisions of both International Covenants on Human Rights, the exercise of their inalienable right to full sovereignty over all their natural wealth and resources.[112]

As the provision also indicates, the right to self-determination in this context particularly involves the principle of sovereignty over natural resources, which entitles states and peoples to have control over the management and utilization of their natural resources.[113] This principle is rooted in the decolonization process and the quest of newly independent states to gain economic independence and control over their natural resources.[114] Thus, sovereignty over natural resources has both interstate and intrastate aspects or applications. The right to self-determination is also reflected in the right to free and meaningful participation discussed above. Overall, the right to self-determination demands that peoples should have a say in the utilization of their resources in general and development programs in particular. This should also guide the approval and implementation of DID. In other words, appropriate procedural and substantive safeguards should be provided in the course of DID to ensure that the people affected have participated in and benefited from the utilization of their resources.

8.4 State Obligations Related to the Right to Development

One of the salient features of the right to development, as envisaged in the Declaration, is the nature of the state obligations it entails. Unlike most human rights norms that put sole responsibility on states, the obligation to ensure the realization of the right to development is borne by all concerned stakeholders, i.e. individuals, states, and the international community.[115] Accordingly, the duty bearers of the right to development include "all human beings" who, pursuant to the Declaration:

---

[111] UN General Assembly, International Covenant on Economic, Social and Cultural Rights, 16 December 1966, 993 United Nations Treaty Series 3, Article 1; see also UN General Assembly, International Covenant on Economic, Social and Cultural Rights, 16 December 1966, 993 United Nations Treaty Series 3, Article 1.

[112] The Declaration on the Right to Development (n 7) Article 1(2).

[113] Schrijver 2013, p. 96. This principle is further elaborated in the Declaration on the Permanent Sovereignty over Natural Resources, which attributes this entitlement to both peoples and nations as well as enumerates the basic principles of this concept (UN General Assembly, Resolution 1720 (XVI), Permanent sovereignty over Natural Resources, 19 December 1961, A/RES/1720).

[114] Schrijver 2013, pp. 95–97.

[115] Sengupta 2000, pp. 563 and 564.

> …have a responsibility for development, individually and collectively, taking into account the need for full respect for their human rights and fundamental freedoms as well as their duties to the community…and they should therefore promote and protect an appropriate political, social and economic order for development.[116]

Hence, individuals privately as well as collectively as members of the community bear a responsibility for development, which requires them to actively take part in development activities and maintain the protection of fundamental rights along the way.[117] This is more of a moral responsibility than a legal obligation.

The primary duty to take necessary steps in order to realize the right, however, rests on states.[118] The obligation of states under the Declaration is formulated as "complementary" to individuals' efforts.[119] States are obliged to create a conducive environment for the realization of the right rather than actually realizing it per se as this can only be achieved by individuals themselves.[120] Accordingly, the obligations of states include, *inter alia*, formulating appropriate national and international development policies,[121] facilitating popular participation,[122] and promoting the realization of all human rights.[123] Nevertheless, the Declaration is quite vague and abstract in its formulation of state obligations, among others.[124] Consequently, they do not "… necessarily translate easily into concrete implementation obligations."[125]

In addition to their obligations at the domestic level, states also have a duty to cooperate as members of the international community in order to facilitate the realization of the right.[126] The Declaration particularly underlines the importance of "effective international co-operation" in complementing the development endeavours of developing countries.[127] This is based on the conviction that "…national development efforts in which human rights can be realized require an international enabling environment."[128] The international community particularly needs to cooperate in technology transfer, investment, and access to markets, among others.[129]

---

[116] The Declaration on the Right to Development (n 7) Article 2(2); see also Arts and Tamo 2016, p. 232.

[117] The Declaration on the Right to Development (n 7) Article 2(2); see also Sengupta 2000, p. 563.

[118] Arts and Tamo 2016, p. 232.

[119] Report 1 of the Independent Expert (n 53) para 41.

[120] Ibid.

[121] The Declaration on the Right to Development (n 7) Articles 2(3) and 4(1).

[122] Ibid., Article 2(3).

[123] Ibid., Article 6.

[124] Arts and Tamo 2016, p. 232.

[125] Ibid.

[126] The Declaration on the Right to Development (n 7) Article 4(1).

[127] Ibid., Article 4(2).

[128] Salomon 2010, pp. 122 and 123.

[129] Sengupta 2010, pp. 40 and 41.

This is usually facilitated by bilateral and multilateral processes and agreements,[130] which are political in nature. This international cooperation must be undertaken by giving due regard to the overriding principles of international relations, i.e. sovereign equality, interdependence, and mutual interest.[131] The duty to cooperate, although not novel to the Declaration,[132] is one of the highly controversial norms of the Declaration.[133] It is yet to be regarded as a concrete legal obligation as it is contingent on states' political willingness and diplomatic relationships.

Overall, the right to development obliges states to take the necessary steps and cooperate to ensure economic, social, cultural, and political development that will improve the well-being of the general public. One could rightly argue that the obligations of states include undertaking development projects that are essential to provide public services and foster economic growth. The implementation of these projects might inevitably involve human costs or adverse consequences including DID. While this, in principle, is true, as mentioned before, the people particularly those bearing the costs of development should be given a chance to participate in the process of development and equitably share the fruits of development. Moreover, the ultimate aim of development should be to improve the well-being and the realization of the rights of the people concerned. To this end, both the process and outcome of development including DID should be in line with human rights standards. Hence, even if displacement can be justified, the well-being of the people affected should not deteriorate, but rather improve, after displacement. The utilitarian view of "sacrifice of a few for the greater good of the majority" is seldom justified in the context of the right to development.

8.5 Conclusion

The right to development recognized under the UN Declaration and the African Charter obliges states to take the necessary measures to facilitate the realization of economic, social, cultural, and political development. Meanwhile, it entitles all persons and peoples the right to participate in the process of development and equitably share the benefits. Moreover, the right to development urges that development measures must be undertaken in accordance with human rights standards and ultimately lead to the improvement of the well-being of the right-holders and the realization of all sets of rights. Despite the persisting debate as to the justiciability and content of the right as well as the vagueness of the provisions in the Declaration,

[130] Ibid., p. 41; for instance, in 2002's World Summit on Sustainable Development, developed countries vowed to give 0.7% of their GNP to development assistance, albeit they rarely meet that (see Salomon 2010, pp. 123 and 124; see also Sengupta 2010, p. 41).

[131] Declaration on the Right to Development (n 7) Articles 3(3).

[132] The duty to cooperate is also recognized in several other international frameworks including the UN Charter and the ICESCR (see UN Charter (n 2) Articles 55 and 56; see also ICESCR (n 111) Article 2(1); see also Arts and Tamo 2016, p. 234).

[133] Arts and Tamo 2016, p. 234.

the right to development provides important guidance to understand what the human rights-based process and outcome of development should look like.

The principles and norms of the right to development elucidated in this chapter are also pertinent in the DID discourse. While not many concrete norms that might be used to regulate DID can be derived from this right, the underlying principles of the right to development, such as the human-centred approach, the HRBAD, equitable process and outcome of development, and social justice, can and should be used as guiding principles at all stages of DID. More specifically, the determination of the public interest requirement before the approval of DID as well as the process and outcome of the development project in question can be guided by the norms of the right to development. Moreover, the specific norms that the right to development constitutes, particularly "free, active and meaningful participation" in the development process, fair share in the benefits therefrom, and self-determination in the governance of resources, are relevant for DID.

References

Alston P, Robinson M (2005) Human Rights and Development: Towards Mutual Reinforcement. Oxford University Press, Oxford.

Arts K, Tamo A (2016) The Right to Development in International Law: New Momentum Thirty Years Down the Line? (2016) 63(3) Netherlands International Law Review at 221–249.

Beetham D (2010) The Right to Development and its Corresponding Obligations. In: Andreassen B-A, Marks S P (eds) Development as a Human Right, 2nd edn. Intersentia, Antwerp.

Boesen J K, Sano H-O (2010) The Implications and Value-Added of a Human Rights-Based Approach. In: Bard V. Andreassen, Marks S P (eds) Development as a Human Right: Legal, Political and Economic Dimensions, 2nd edn. Intersentia, Antwerp.

Bunn I D (2000) The Right to Development: Implications for International Economic Law. (2000) 15(6) American University International Law Review 1425–1467.

Feyter K D (2013) The Declaration on the Right to Development Revisited. (2013) 1(1) Journal of National Law University 15–32.

Harris J M (2000) Basic Principles of Sustainable Development. (2000) Global Development and Environment Institute Working Paper No. 00-04.

Ghai Y P (1989) Whose Human Right to Development? Human Rights Unit Occasional Paper.

Juma L (2013) Protection of development-induced internally displaced persons under the African Charter: the case of the Endorois community of Northern Kenya. (2013) 46(2) The Comparative and International Law Journal of Southern Africa 211–233.

Kates R W, Parris T M, Leiserowitz A A (2005) What is Sustainable Development? Goals, Indicators, Values, and Practice. (2005) 47(3) Environment: Science and Policy for Sustainable Development 8–21.

Kerchmeier F (2006) The right to development - where do we stand: the state of the debate on the right to development. (2006) Dialogue on Globalization, occasional paper No. 23.

Liebenberg S (2010) Masking a Difference: Human Rights and Development - Reflecting on the South African Experience. In: Andreassen B-A, Marks S P (eds) Development as a Human Right, 2nd edn. Intersentia, Antwerp.

Lindroos A (1999) The Right to Development. Faculty of Law, University of Helsinki, Helsinki.

Mathur H M (1995) The Resettlement of People Displaced by Development Projects: Issues and Approaches. In: Mathur H M, Cernea M M (eds) Development, Displacement and Resettlement: Focus on Asian Experience. Vikas Publishing House, New Delhi.

Office of the UN High Commissioner for Human Rights (OHCHR) (2004) Human Rights and Poverty Reduction: A Conceptual Framework. United Nations, New York/Geneva.

Office of the UN High Commissioner for Human Rights (OHCHR) (2016) Frequently Asked Questions on the Right to Development, Fact Sheet No. 37. United Nations, New York/Geneva.

Piovesan F (2013) Active, free and meaningful participation in development. In: United Nations (author) Realizing the Right to Development - Essays in Commemoration of 25 Years of the United Nations Declaration on the Right to Development. United Nations Publications, New York/Geneva, HR/PUB/12/4, December 2013, available at https://www.un-ilibrary.org/economic-and-social-development/realizing-the-right-to-development_49006c2a-en, accessed 1 July 2025.

Rawls J (1971) A Theory of Social Justice. Harvard University Press.

Rawls J (1999) A Theory of Social Justice, rev. edn. Harvard University Press.

Robinson R (2003) Risks and Rights: The Causes, Consequences, and Challenges of Development-Induced Displacement. The Brookings Institution-SAIS Project on Internal Displacement, An Occasional Paper.

Salomon M E (2010) International Human Rights Obligations in Context: Structural Obstacles and the Demands of Global Justice. In: Andreassen B-A, Marks S P (eds) Development as a Human Right, 2nd edn. Intersentia, Antwerp.

Schrijver N (2013) Self-determination of Peoples and Sovereignty over Natural Wealth and Resources. In: United Nations (author) Realizing the Right to Development - Essays in Commemoration of 25 Years of the United Nations Declaration on the Right to Development. United Nations Publications, New York/Geneva, HR/PUB/12/4, December 2013, available at https://www.un-ilibrary.org/economic-and-social-development/realizing-the-right-to-development_49006c2a-en, accessed 1 July 2025.

Sen A (1989) Development as Capability Expansion. (1989) 19 Journal of Development Planning 3–16.

Sen A (2010) Human Rights and Development. In: Andreassen B-A, Marks S P (eds) Development as a Human Right, 2nd edn. Intersentia, Antwerp.

Sengupta A (2000) Realizing the Right to Development. (2000) 31(3) Development and Change 553–578.

Sengupta A (2010) The Human Right to Development. In: Andreassen B-A, Marks S P (eds) Development as a Human Right, 2nd edn. Intersentia, Antwerp.

Teshome R G (2022) The Draft Convention on the Right to Development: A New Dawn to the Recognition of the Right to Development as a Human Right? (2022) 22(2) Human Rights Law Review.

UN Committee on Economic, Social and Cultural Rights (UN CESCR) (1990) General Comment No.3: The Nature of States Parties' Obligations (Art. 2, Para. 1, of the Covenant), 14 December 1990, E/1991/23.

UN Committee on Economic, Social and Cultural Rights (UN CESCR) (1998) General Comment No.9: The domestic application of the Covenant, 3 December 1998, E/C.12/1998/24.

UN Secretary-General (2013) The emergence of the right to development. In: United Nations (author) Realizing the Right to Development - Essays in Commemoration of 25 Years of the United Nations Declaration on the Right to Development. United Nations Publications, New York/Geneva, HR/PUB/12/4, December 2013, available at https://www.un-ilibrary.org/economic-and-social-development/realizing-the-right-to-development_49006c2a-en, accessed 1 July 2025.

Uvin P (2007) From the right to development to the rights-based approach: how 'human rights' entered development. (2007) 17(4/5) Development in Practice 597–606.

Van der Ploeg L, Vanclay F (2017) A Human Rights-based Approach to Project Induced Displacement and Resettlement. (2017) 35(1) Impact Assessment and Project Appraisal 34–52.

World Commission on Environment and Development (1987) Our Common Future. Oxford University Press, Oxford/New York.

Part IV
Beyond International Human Rights Law

Chapter 9
The Role of International Financial Institutions in Protecting the Rights of People(s) Affected by Development-Induced Displacement

Contents

Abstract International financial institutions (IFIs) are important actors in the context of development-induced displacement (DID) as they finance development projects that potentially cause displacement and have policy standards on involuntary displacement or resettlement in place. This chapter engages with these policy standards and examines to what extent they advance the human rights of the people(s) affected by DID. The overarching objective of these policy frameworks is to avoid displacement, if feasible, and prevent or mitigate the adverse impacts of displacement when it is unavoidable. To these ends, the policies envisage various procedural and substantive safeguards that apply at all phases of displacement and resettlement. These include meaningful consultation with those affected, the provision of in-kind and monetary compensation, relocation assistance, and rehabilitation measures. While these policies go a long way in providing guidance for states concerning involuntary displacement prompted by development projects, they are not impervious to limitations. These shortcomings have contributed to a reality in which displacement caused by development projects financed by IFIs often results in impoverishment, contrary to the policy objectives stated above. Accordingly, the chapter also critically engages with these limitations with a view to assessing whether and to what extent they contribute to the human rights violations occurring in the course of displacement.

© T.M.C. ASSER PRESS and the authors 2026

R. G. Teshome, *The Human Cost of Development*, Human Rights Research Series 104,
https://doi.org/10.1007/978-94-6265-751-9_9

Keywords International financial institutions · World Bank · African Development Bank · Asian Development Bank · Inter-American Development Bank · Resettlement policies

9.1 Introduction

The mandates and activities of international financial institutions (IFIs), on the one hand, and the promotion of human rights, on the other hand, have traditionally been viewed as divergent, if not as competing, pursuits. This is also evident in the lack of or inadequate integration of human rights norms and principles as well as the deliberate avoidance of a human rights language in the policies and practices of these institutions. IFIs, particularly the World Bank, have been heavily criticized for being directly or indirectly involved in human rights violations, financially supporting countries with poor human rights records, and failing to systematically integrate human rights norms and principles in their operations. This raises the question of whether and to what extent these institutions have human rights obligations or responsibilities in international law. This question can be approached from two perspectives: the indirect approach—through the human rights obligations of their member states—and the direct human rights obligations of international organizations, or IFIs in this context. Both approaches, particularly the latter, have been subject to considerable debate and there is currently prevailing uncertainty on the issue.

One of the areas where the human rights impacts of the activities of these institutions is evident is development-induced displacement (DID). IFIs are important actors in the DID discourse as they financially support development projects that potentially cause involuntary displacement. They also have operational policies on involuntary displacement or resettlement[1] that stipulate guidelines for states concerning the measures they need to take to prevent DID and/or mitigate its adverse consequences. These frameworks are neither considered human rights instruments nor form part of international law per se. However, apart from providing guidance for states, these policy frameworks can also potentially inform the academic and legal discourse on the subject and the development of human rights norms. Hence, it is imperative to explore the policies and practices of these institutions concerning DID, which this chapter aims to do. The main questions that this chapter seeks to answer are: whether and to what extent these institutions have human rights obligations in international law; what policy safeguards they have in place to mitigate the human rights impacts of their activities—involuntary displacement in this context; and to what extent these safeguards protect the rights and wellbeing of the people affected by DID or to what extent these safeguards guarantee and promote human rights.

[1] International financial institutions use the term ‘involuntary resettlement’ to refer to the process of involuntary displacement and resettlement caused by development projects. Thus, for the purpose of this chapter, the terms “DID” and “involuntary resettlement” will be used interchangeably depending on the context.

The term IFIs is an umbrella term that includes the Bretton Woods institutions, i.e. the World Bank and the International Monetary Fund (IMF), regional development banks, and other inter-governmental aid or funding institutions. As the mandate of the IMF makes its direct involvement in DID fairly minimal, if not non-existent,[2] this chapter does not cover the policies and practices of the IMF. Hence, for the purpose of this chapter, this term is used to refer to international and regional development banks, which provide funding for development projects that can potentially cause DID. Thus, the terms "IFIs" and "development banks" will be used interchangeably throughout this chapter based on this understanding. The chapter will cover four development banks: the World Bank, the African Development Bank (AfDB), the Inter-American Development Bank (IADB), and the Asian Development Bank (ADB). Nevertheless, it will mainly focus on the policy frameworks and practices of the World Bank not only because the relevant sources and literature on the Bank are extensive and readily available but also because the Bank's involvement in DID is significantly more profound as it is the largest lending institution.[3] The policies of the Bank have also heavily influenced those of regional development banks. Therefore, a comprehensive and in-depth analysis of the policies and practices of all development banks under a single chapter is neither necessary nor feasible. Thus, the chapter only marginally refers to the regional development banks.

This chapter has five main sections apart from this introduction and the conclusion. It commences by briefly introducing the organizational structures and mandates of the IFIs covered in Sect. 9.2. Section 9.3 offers a theoretical background by exploring the role, or lack thereof, of IFIs in advancing human rights and the controversies surrounding it. The section particularly focuses on the extent human rights are integrated into the activities of these institutions and the legal constraints to integration. Section 9.4 explores the human rights obligations, if any, of international organizations in general and IFIs in particular under international law. This section is needed to situate the issues discussed in this chapter in the overall normative scope of this book, i.e. international human rights law. Moreover, this section offers a conceptual background to the analysis provided in the subsequent sections on the extent to which the policies of IFIs on involuntary resettlement protect the rights of the people(s) affected by DID or promote human rights. As this chapter also assesses whether or not these policy standards are in line with relevant human rights norms and principles, it is important to examine to what extent IFIs have obligations to respect and promote these human rights norms in the first place. The fourth and principal section, Sect. 9.5, explores the substantive content of the operational policies on involuntary displacement or resettlement adopted by the development banks covered under this chapter and analyses the safeguards they provide for displaced

[2] The IMF is mandated to oversee and stabilize the international monetary system and it provides loans and grants for states in times of financial crises and other related circumstances. But it does not finance specific development projects (see The International Monetary Fund (IMF), Articles of Agreement, July 1944 (amended in January 2016)).

[3] Sarfaty 2012, p. 1. "Since 1947, the World Bank has funded over 12,000 development projects, via traditional loans, interest-free credits, and grants" (see the World Bank organizational information, available at https://www.worldbank.org/en/what-we-do, accessed 1 July 2025).

persons. This section also comments on the extent to which these policies protect the rights of people affected by DID with reference to the relevant international human rights law norms. Section 9.6 critically engages with the limitations of these policy frameworks, mainly that of the World Bank, and the reasons for the prevalent gap between policy and practice.

9.2 A Brief Introduction to Selected International Financial Institutions

Before proceeding to the substantive issues this chapter seeks to cover, it is imperative to briefly introduce the organizational structure and mandates of the financial institutions covered in this chapter. The World Bank was established in 1944 with the initial purpose of supporting the reconstruction and economic recovery of post-World War II Europe.[4] The mandate of the Bank was subsequently extended to include alleviating poverty and promoting economic development around the World.[5] The World Bank consists of two institutions, namely the International Bank for Reconstruction and Development (IBRD) and the International Development Association (IDA).[6] While the IBRD, which is the original institution of the Bank, "lends to governments of middle-income and creditworthy low-income countries",[7] the IDA "provides interest-free loans-called credits- and grants to governments of the poorest countries".[8] The World Bank is one of the specialized agencies of the United Nations,[9] which entails a relationship of cooperation rather than that of direct accountability.[10]

[4] World Bank 2011a, p. 12.

[5] Sarfaty 2012, p. 4.

[6] World Bank 2011a, p. 10; see also Bradlow 2010, p. 9. It is important to distinguish the terms "World Bank" and "World Bank Group". While the former refers to the IBRD and the IDP, the World Bank Group is comprised of five institutions, i.e. the two institutions mentioned above (IBRD and IDA) and the International Finance Corporation (IFC), the Multilateral Investment Guarantee Agency (MIGA), and the International Centre for Settlement of Investment Disputes (ICSID). The other three institutions work on investment-related issues with the private sector (World Bank 2011a, pp. 2 and 10). Thus, since only the first two institutions are relevant for this research, a reference to the World Bank under this chapter relates to these institutions.

[7] World Bank 2011a, pp. 2 and 11; see also Bradlow 2010, p. 10.

[8] World Bank 2011a, pp. 2 and 11; see also Bradlow 2010, p. 10.

[9] Specialized agencies enter into a special agreement with the UN as per Article 63 of the UN Charter to cooperate and work together (see United Nations, Charter of the United Nations, 24 October 1945, 1 United Nations Treaty Series XVI, Articles 57 and 63). The Bank entered into such an agreement in 1948 (see International Bank for Reconstruction and Development and United Nations, Protocol concerning the entry into force of the Agreement between the United Nations and the International Bank for Reconstruction and Development, 15 April 1948, 16 United Nations Treaty Series 341).

[10] One of the areas of cooperation, for instance, is when the Security Council imposes economic embargos, which the Bank is expected to back (see UN and the World Bank Relationship Agreement (n 9) Article VI).

In other words, the Bank is not one of the organs of the UN and maintains institutional independence.[11]

The World Bank, currently, has 189 member states that are also the shareholders of the capital of the Bank.[12] These member states "…are represented by a Board of Governors, who are the ultimate policymakers at the [Bank]."[13] Each member state has one representative on the Board.[14] However, members do not have equal votes; voting power in the Board of Governors is determined based on the capital contribution or shares of member states.[15] The US, for instance, is the largest shareholder with close to 17 shares and, hence, has the highest number of votes.[16] Thus, voting power at the Bank directly correlates with the economic capacity of states. The Board of Governors delegates specific management responsibilities to the Board of Executive Directors, which consists of 25 experts based at the Headquarters of which five are appointed by the largest shareholders,[17] and the rest are elected by the other member country groups.[18] The Directors oversee the overall operation of the Bank and make general policy and financial decisions.[19] Similar to the Board of Governors, the voting power of the Executive Directors is also determined based on the capital shares of the country or country groups they represent.[20] The day-to-day activities of the Bank are managed by the President (who is elected by the Executive Directors), vice presidents of different sectors, and other management staff.[21]

Established in 1959, the IADB is the first multilateral regional development bank.[22] The main objective of the Bank is to support economic development and poverty reduction in the region by providing grants, loans, and technical assistance.[23] The Bank has 48 member states, both from within and outside the American

[11] Skogly 2003, p. 48.

[12] World Bank, Organization, available at https://www.worldbank.org/en/about/leadership, accessed 1 July 2025; see also World Bank 2011a, p. 7.

[13] World Bank, Organization, available at https://www.worldbank.org/en/about/leadership, accessed 1 July 2025.

[14] World Bank 2011a, p. 7.

[15] World Bank, Voting Powers, available at https://www.worldbank.org/en/about/leadership/voting powers, accessed 1 July 2025.

[16] World Bank, Voting Powers, available at https://www.worldbank.org/en/about/leadership/voting powers (see the capital subscription and voting powers of each country), accessed 1 July 2025.

[17] World Bank 2011a, pp. 8 and 9.The five largest shareholders of the Bank are USA, Japan, Germany, UK, and France (see World Bank 2011a, pp. 9 and 10).

[18] World Bank 2011a, p. 9 (Member countries form groups based on geographic proximity or other factors to elect Directors).

[19] Ibid.; see also World Bank, Organization, available at https://www.worldbank.org/en/about/lea dership, accessed 1 July 2025.

[20] World Bank 2011a, p. 9 (however, the Board of Directors often makes decisions by consensus).

[21] World Bank 2011a, pp. 9 and 10.

[22] Inter-American Development Bank, About Us, https://www.iadb.org/en/about-us/overview, accessed 1 July 2025.

[23] Ibid.

region.[24] These states are represented in the Board of Governors with voting powers proportional to their capital subscriptions similar to the World Bank.[25] The Board elects 14 Executive Directors to whom it delegates general policy and financial decision-making mandates.[26] Further, the day-to-day decision-making and governance responsibilities are entrusted to the President, Vice-Presidents, and other managerial staff.[27]

The AfDB was established in 1963 when 23 newly independent states signed the constitutive instrument, the Articles of Agreement of the Bank, which entered into force the following year.[28] "The overall objective of the [Bank] is to support the economic development and social progress of African countries individually and collectively, by promoting investment of public and private capital in projects and programs designed to reduce poverty and improve living conditions."[29] Subscription to the capital of the Bank was initially limited to African countries, which changed in 1982 when it was opened to non-African states.[30] Currently, the Bank has 54 African states and 28 non-African or non-regional states as members or shareholders.[31] This differentiates regional multilateral Banks from inter-governmental political organizations, such as the Africa Union and the Organization of American States, in which membership is limited to states in the region. Member countries are represented in the Board of Governors, which is the highest decision-making body of the Bank.[32] The Board of Governors elects 20 Executive Directors, 13 of which represent African member countries and the remaining 7 represent non-regional members.[33] The Board of Executive Directors oversees the general operations of the Bank.[34] The Board of Governors also elects the President of the Bank who manages the daily business of the Bank along with the other management staff.[35]

The ADB was established in 1966 with the aim of fostering economic development and eradicating poverty in the region.[36] The Bank currently has 48 regional and

---

[24] Inter-American Development Bank, Organization, https://www.iadb.org/en/about-us/how-are-we-organized, accessed 1 July 2025.

[25] Ibid.

[26] Ibid.

[27] Ibid.

[28] AfDB 2013, p. 7. The Bank has two affiliate institutions, i.e. the African Development Fund (ADF) and the Nigerian Trust Fund (NTF), that make up the African Development Bank Group together with the parent institution (see AfDB 2013, pp. 6–8).

[29] AfDB 2013, p. 8.

[30] Ibid., p. 7.

[31] African Development Bank Group, Member countries, available at https://www.afdb.org/en/about-us/corporate-information/members, accessed 1 July 2025; see also AfDB 2013, pp. 8 and 9.

[32] AfDB 2013, p. 12.

[33] Ibid.

[34] Ibid.

[35] Ibid., p. 13.

[36] Asian Development Bank, About ADB, available at https://www.adb.org/who-we-are/about, accessed 1 July 2025.

19 non-regional member states.[37] Similar to the other multilateral Banks discussed above, the Bank is governed by the Board of Governors, which is composed of representatives of member states, and the Board of Directors—12 Directors elected by the former—along with the president, vice-presidents, and other management staff.[38] Overall, the mandates or objectives and the organizational structures of the IFIs covered in this chapter are mostly similar. The principal difference these institutions have—at least in terms of decision-making—with other inter-governmental organizations, such as the United Nations, African Union, and Organization of American States in which members have equal votes, is their voting system, which correlates voting power with capital contributions or shares.

9.3 Human Rights and International Financial Institutions

The role—or lack thereof—of IFIs in advancing human rights has received considerable attention from scholars and human rights experts.[39] These institutions, particularly the World Bank, have been criticized for being reluctant to actively engage in human rights or to adequately take into account human rights issues in their decision-making.[40] Accordingly, several human rights concerns have been raised against the activities of development banks.[41] One of these concerns pertains to the direct or indirect involvement of these institutions in human rights violations through their activities, for instance, by funding development projects that cause displacement and potentially violate human rights.[42] The World Bank, for instance, has been heavily criticized for turning a blind eye to the human rights impacts of its activities or not taking adequate preventive and remedial measures to rectify the potential human rights violations caused by its activities.[43]

The other human rights concern raised against these banks relates to the provision of financial support to governments that are infamous for "gross and systemic human rights violations".[44] The World Bank, for instance, seldom takes into account the human rights records or situations of states in its loan decision-making.[45] Particularly in its early days, the Bank firmly opposed using human rights considerations in decision-making. For instance, in the 1960s, the General Assembly adopted a set of Resolutions recommending financial institutions to impose financial sanctions

---

[37] Ibid.

[38] Asian Development Bank, Organization, available at https://www.adb.org/who-we-are/organization, accessed 1 July 2025.

[39] See, for instance, Sarfaty 2012; see also Clark 2002; see also Mcbeth 2006.

[40] Sarfaty 2012, p. 2.

[41] Ibid.

[42] Clark 2002, p. 206; see also Sarfaty 2012, p. 2.

[43] Zhou 2012, p. 823; see also Clark 2002, pp. 207, 209–210, 215–216; see also Evans 2013, p. 299.

[44] Sarfaty 2012, p. 2; see also Clark 2002, p. 206.

[45] Ciorciari 2000, pp. 332–333 and 335–336.

on South Africa and Portugal for their apartheid policies.[46] The Bank ignored the recommendation and refused to cease loans to these countries citing its policy of non-interference in the internal political affairs of states.[47] Similarly, in recent years, concerns have been raised by experts that financial assistance to governments responsible for gross human rights violations might have the effect of facilitating further violations and consolidation of power by these regimes.[48] Meanwhile, there is a legitimate concern that economic sanctions affect people more than governments. As will be discussed below, the apolitical character of the Bank set forth in its constitution has been used to justify not taking into account the human rights records of states in funding decision-making.[49]

The other human rights concern relates to the lack of adequate and systematic mainstreaming or integration of human rights in the activities of these institutions.[50] Despite constant pressure from UN organs, academics, and human rights activists, the World Bank, for instance, is yet to adopt a human rights agenda or a comprehensive operational policy on human rights.[51] While the Bank has numerous policy frameworks that address human rights issues in one way or another, such as its policies on environmental and social issues, it does not have a general and comprehensive policy framework on human rights.[52] Even those policy frameworks that deal with human rights issues only marginally refer to human rights.[53] One does not have to look further than the involuntary displacement or resettlement policy of the World Bank to understand this.[54] Despite dealing with evidently human rights-sensitive issues, not once does the policy mention the term "human rights"; nor does it refer to the relevant human rights instruments.

---

[46] UN General Assembly, Resolution 2184 (XXI), Questions of Territories under Portuguese Administration, 12 December 1966, A/RES/2184, para 9; see also UN General Assembly, Resolution 2270 (XXII), Questions of Territories under Portuguese Administration, 3 November 1967, A/RES/2270 (XXII), para 13; see also UN General Assembly, Resolution 2202 (XXI), The policies of apartheid of the Government of the Republic of South Africa, 16 December 1966, A/RES/2202, para 6(d); overview of these Resolutions can be found at UN General Assembly, The Politics of Apartheid of the Republic of South-Africa & Question of Territories under Portuguese Administration – Consultation with the International Bank for Reconstruction and Development, Report of the Secretary-General, U.N. Doc. A/6825, 15 September 1967.

[47] Zhou 2012, p. 829; see also 'Memorandum of the Legal Department of the IBRD', A/6825 (5 May 1967) Annex II in United Nations, *Juridical Yearbook 1997: Part Two: Legal activities of the United Nations and related inter-governmental organizations* (United Nations, 1997) 121.

[48] Human Rights Council 2014.

[49] Sarfaty 2012, pp. 58 and 659; see also Clark 2002, p. 208.

[50] Sarfaty 2012, p. 2; see also Zhou 2012, p. 826; see also Byrnes 2011, p. 8.

[51] Sarfaty 2009, pp. 649 and 656.

[52] Sarfaty 2012, p. 2 and p. 83; see also Sarfaty 2009, p. 648.

[53] Alston 2015, para 32. Most of these policies do not explicitly mention human rights save for the operational policy on indigenous peoples and the Environmental and Social Framework. Even the reference to human rights in these policies is very minimal.

[54] World Bank, Operational Manual OP 4.12 - Involuntary Resettlement, December 2001 ('the World Bank resettlement policy').

The most progressive policy of the Bank in this regard is its 2017 Environmental and Social Framework,[55] which acknowledges the Bank's role in supporting the realization of rights stipulated under the UDHR as one of its underlying objectives.[56] The relevant paragraph of the Framework reads:

> …the World Bank's activities support the realization of human rights expressed in the Universal Declaration of Human Rights. Through the projects it finances, and in a manner consistent with its Articles of Agreement, the World Bank seeks to avoid adverse impacts and will continue to support its member countries as they strive to progressively achieve their human rights commitments.[57]

Thus, the Framework indicates that the Bank can support states in fulfilling their human rights obligations provided that it is done in a way that is consistent with its Articles of Agreement,[58] a document that has been used to preclude the Bank from engaging in human rights issues as will be elucidated below. Besides, it is not clear whether the reference to progressive realization in the paragraph quoted above indicates the preservation of the Bank's long-held position that economic, social, and cultural rights are consistent with the mandate of the Bank as opposed to civil and political rights that, according to Bank, are inherently political as will be further discussed subsequently.[59] In any case, this endorsement of the role of the Bank in the promotion of human rights did not translate into the substantive content of the Framework, which hardly refers to human rights norms.

In addition to the absence of systematic integration of human rights into the policies of the Bank, human rights are neither sufficiently taken into account in the decision-making nor systematically integrated into the activities of the Bank.[60] In fact, critics allege that "[t]he issue of human rights has been and continues to be a taboo at the institution",[61] albeit this is slowly changing.[62] As Philip Alston, the former Special Rapporteur on extreme poverty and human rights, concluded in his report, "…the existing approach taken by the Bank to human rights is incoherent, counterproductive and unsustainable. For most purposes, the World Bank is a human rights-free zone."[63] On the other hand, the official view at the Bank is that there is

---

55 The World Bank, Environmental and Social Framework (ESF), 2017, available at https://documents1.worldbank.org/curated/en/383011492423734099/pdf/The-World-Bank-Environmental-and-Social-Framework.pdf, accessed 1 July 2025 ('the World Bank Environmental and Social Framework'). The Framework includes a set of policy standards on various issues relevant to the operation of the Bank, such as land acquisition, environmental issues, labour, and indigenous peoples, that are aimed at fostering sustainable development.

56 The World Bank Environmental and Social Framework (n 55) 1 and 2.

57 Ibid.

58 International Bank for Reconstruction and Development (IBRD), Articles of Agreement (As amended effective June 27, 2012); see also International Development Association (IDA), Articles of Agreement (effective 24 September 1960).

59 World Bank 1994a, p. 53; see also Clark 2002, pp. 207 and 208.

60 Sarfaty 2012, p. 2.

61 Ibid., 108.

62 Ibid.

63 Alston 2015, p. 2.

an apparent substantive overlap between the works of the Bank and human rights and, thus, the Bank is doing human rights work without explicitly using human rights language, which would have politicized the works of the Bank.[64] Hence, the argument is the mandate and the work of the Bank directly or indirectly advance human rights without the need to adopt a rights-based language.

Similarly, none of the regional development banks covered in this chapter have a specific human rights policy or agenda. Nor do their operational policies on environmental, social, and other issues adequately refer to human rights.[65] In some instances, these institutions have remarked that they seek to respect human rights norms and principles, particularly economic, social and cultural rights, in their operations.[66] For instance, the AfDB's stated that it "...views economic and social rights as an integral part of human rights, and accordingly affirms that it respects the principles and values of human rights as set out in the UN Charter and the African Charter of Human and Peoples' Rights."[67] The Bank has also encouraged states to respect their human rights obligations.[68] However, their policies rarely refer to human rights or explicitly integrate human rights norms and values. For instance, none of the resettlement policies of the regional development banks covered in this chapter refer to human rights. One of the only departures in this regard is the IADB's safeguard policy on indigenous peoples, which enunciates that the bank will take into account the rights of indigenous peoples including those recognised in international human rights frameworks.[69] Overall, although there is insufficient literature on the integration of human rights into the activities of these regional institutions, it is safe to assume that human rights have a marginal place in their decision-making and operations due to their apolitical character[70]—at least in theory—and lack of reference to human rights in their policies.

---

64 Clapham 2006, pp. 139 and 140; see also Cisse 2012, p. 74; see also Mclnerney-Lankford and Sano 2010, pp. 5 and 6; see also Mclnerney-Lankford 2009, p. 53; see also World Bank, Development and human rights: the role of the World Bank, 1998, available at https://documents.worldbank.org/en/publication/documents-reports/documentdetail/820031468767358922/development-and-human-rights-the-role-of-the-world-bank, accessed 1 July 2025; see also Byrnes 2011, p. 9 (this view is also shared by the management of the ADP).

65 See, for instance, African Development Bank Group's Policy on the Environment, February 2004; see also Inter-American Development Bank, Environmental and Safeguards Compliance Policy, 19 January 2006 (none of these policies mention human rights).

66 African Development Bank Group's Integrated Safeguards System: Policy statement and operational safeguard, Safeguards and Sustainability Series, Volume 1 - Issue 1, December 2013, Preamble.

67 Ibid (despite these remarks in the preamble none of the operational policies incorporated in this document refer to human rights).

68 Ibid.

69 Inter-American Development Bank, Operational Policy on Indigenous Peoples and Strategy for Indigenous Development, July 2006, 8 and 5.

70 As will be discussed below, the Articles of Agreements of these institutions prevent them from taking into account political considerations, which are often understood as including human rights considerations, particularly civil and political rights (see Bøås 1998, p. 118; see also Byrnes 2011, p. 8).

One of the principal reasons for these institutions' limited engagement with human rights or the marginality of human rights in their operations is the legal constraints imposed by their constitutions or articles of agreement, which explicitly prohibit them from interfering in the political affairs of states or from considering political factors in their decision-making.[71] This is particularly true for the World Bank, which was designed to be an apolitical institution from its inception.[72] This apolitical nature of the Bank is reflected under two of the provisions of its Articles of Agreement. Article III, Section 5(b) of the Articles of Agreement of the IBRD provides that:

> The Bank shall make arrangements to ensure that the proceeds of any loan are used only for the purposes for which the loan was granted, with due attention to considerations of economy and efficiency and without regard to political or other non-economic influences or considerations.[73]

Article IV, Section 10 further enunciates that:

> The Bank and its officers shall not interfere in the political affairs of any member; nor shall they be influenced in their decisions by the political character of the member or members concerned. Only economic considerations shall be relevant to their decisions, and these considerations shall be weighed impartially in order to achieve the purposes stated in Article I.[74]

The Articles of Agreement of the IDA also include comparable rules under Article V, Section 1(g) and Section 6, respectively.[75] These provisions oblige the Bank to make decisions solely based on economic considerations and refrain from interfering in the political affairs of states or using political considerations in its decision-making. This has been conservatively interpreted by the Bank to limit its involvement in human rights issues or preclude it from taking into account human rights concerns in its decision-making.[76] The Bank has also used these provisions to draw a distinction between economic, social and cultural rights and civil and political rights—the former as directly relevant to further its mandate and the latter as inherently political matters that fall outside the scope of its mandate.[77] This interpretation not only maintains the outdated categorization of human rights but also overlooks the inherent interdependence and indivisibility of human rights.[78]

---

[71] Sarfaty 2012, p. 51.

[72] During the establishment of the post-war international institutions, the United Nations was designed to be a political institution while the Bretton Woods Institutions were designed to focus solely on economic and financial matters mainly reflecting the worldview and interests of the powerful states that took the lead in the establishment of these institutions. According to Pahuja, "...the separation of the political from the economic specific to capitalism was built into the institutional structure of international law" (see Pahuja 2011, p. 22; see also Sarfaty 2012, p. 58).

[73] Articles of Agreement of the IBRD (n 58) Article III, Section 5(b).

[74] Articles of Agreement of the IBRD (n 58) Article IV, Section 10.

[75] Articles of Agreement of the IDA (n 58) Article V, Section 1(g) and Section 6.

[76] Sarfaty 2009, p. 659; see also Clark 2002, p. 208; see also Clapham 2006, p. 142; see also McInerney-Lankford 2009, p. 55.

[77] World Bank 1994a, p. 53; see also Clark 2002, pp. 207 and 208; see also Sarfaty 2012, p. 58.

[78] UN General Assembly, Vienna Declaration and Programme of Action, 12 July 1993, A/CONF.157/23, para 5.

Some commentators, including those affiliated with the Bank, have been challenging the above narrow interpretation of the Bank's mandate and the hard line drawn between what is an economic and what is a political consideration. Critics particularly emphasize the inherent interdependence between human rights and the principal mandate of the Bank, i.e. promoting development and alleviating poverty. For instance, Shihata, the Bank's former General Counsel, recognized that human rights are and should be an integral part of the Bank's activities, albeit he maintained the categorization of rights vis-à-vis the Bank's mandate elucidated above.[79] His successor, Roberto Danino, even argued that "…the Articles of Agreement permit, and in some cases require, the Bank to recognize the human rights dimensions of its development policies and activities since it is now evident that human rights are an intrinsic part of the Bank's mission."[80] This can be inferred, according to Danino, from the inextricable link between development and all human rights—he rejected the categorization of rights maintained by his predecessor—and the evolving understanding of what "development" constitutes.[81] As elucidated in the preceding chapter, the contemporary conception of development goes beyond economic growth and encompasses the expansion or advancement of human capabilities in economic, social, and political aspects and the realization of all rights.[82] Danino contends that the mandate of the Bank should be interpreted using this evolving conception of development.[83] In stark contrast to the mainstream position at the Bank, he even went as far as arguing that in some cases, the human rights record or situation of a country should be taken into account in decision-making.[84] Andrew Clapham has also argued that the rationale behind the provisions quoted above is to ensure the impartiality of the Bank in the face of global ideological divides and divergent political systems.[85] This does not and should not hinder the Bank from considering the human rights impacts of its activities; nor does it imply that the Bank does not have human rights obligations.[86] These challenges from experts coupled with the pressure

[79] Sarfaty 2012, p. 63; Sarfaty 2009, pp. 663 and 664.

[80] Danino 2006, para 25. As much as it is a consequential document, the legal authority of this legal opinion is uncertain as official legal opinions or interpretations of the Articles of Agreement are commonly prepared by the Legal Counsel upon request by the Board and are subsequently endorsed by the Board (see Sarfaty 2012, p. 71). This legal opinion, on the other hand, is prepared by Danino's own initiative who resigned from his post on the same day he sent out the opinion to the legal department (Sarfaty 2012, pp. 62 and 63).

[81] Danino 2006, paras 6–8.

[82] UN General Assembly, Declaration on the Right to Development: resolution/adopted by the General Assembly, 4 December 1986, A/RES/41/128, Preamble; see also UN General Assembly, Report of the Independent Expert on the Right to Development, 17 August 2000, A/55/306, para 22.

[83] Danino 2006, paras 6–8; see also Sarfaty 2012, p. 63.

[84] Danino 2006, paras 18–22; see also Sarfaty 2012, p. 63.

[85] Clapham 2006, p. 143.

[86] Ibid., pp. 143 and 144.

from international human rights organizations and NGOs are partly responsible for the Bank's increased engagement with human rights.[87]

Consequently, in the past few decades, the Bank's interpretation of its mandate and perception of its role in advancing human rights have evolved considerably.[88] Accordingly, the Bank has been increasingly engaging in matters that are traditionally considered political, such as the rule of law, corruption, and governance.[89] This increased engagement of the Bank in human rights issues and change of perception is also reflected in its recently adopted Environmental and Social Framework, which makes an explicit reference to the UDHR as noted above.[90] In 2009, the World Bank established the Nordic Trust Fund for the purpose of "[supporting] a knowledge and learning program for World Bank staff and management focusing on how human rights relate to the Bank's core mission of promoting economic growth and poverty reduction".[91] Moreover, the Bank has taken a few other initiatives to foster human rights knowledge among its staff and, to a certain extent, integrate human rights into its work.[92] The line between what is political and what is economic is not always unequivocally clear and there is often some overlap. The Bank's mandate of development and poverty reduction intrinsically involves human rights considerations. There seems to be an increasing acceptance of these facts at the Bank.

The regional development banks covered in this chapter are mostly modelled after the World Bank maintaining an apolitical character. Thus, their respective constituent instruments or Articles of Agreements also preclude them from interfering in the political affairs of their member states and taking into account political considerations in their decision-making. This is stipulated under Article 38(2), Article 36(2), and Article 8, Section 5(f) of the Articles of Agreements of the African, the Asian, and the Inter-American development banks, respectively,[93] which are almost verbatim copies of Article IV, Section 10 of the IBRD Articles of Agreement quoted above.[94]

Another legal constraint underlying the Banks' limited or marginal involvement in human rights stems from the prevailing uncertainty regarding their obligations under international human rights law.[95] As will be discussed further in the next section, there is uncertainty as to whether and to what extent IFIs have human rights

[87] Sarfaty 2012, p. 65.

[88] Ibid 59; see also Zhou 2012, p. 829.

[89] Clark 2002, p. 208.

[90] The World Bank Environmental and Social Framework (n 55) 1 and 2.

[91] World Bank 2011b, p. 3; see also Cisse 2012, p. 74.

[92] OHCHR 2019.

[93] Agreement Establishing the African Development Bank, 2016 edition, Article 38(2), available at https://www.afdb.org/en/documents/agreement-establishing-african-development-fund-2016-edition, accessed 1 July 2025; see also Agreement Establishing the Asian Development Bank, December 1965, Article 36(2), available at https://www.adb.org/documents/agreement-establishing-asian-development-bank-adb-charter, accessed 1 July 2025; see also Agreement Establishing the Inter-American Development Bank, entered into force on 30 December 1959, last amended 31 December 1987, Article 8, Section 5(f).

[94] Articles of Agreement of the IBRD (n 58) Article IV, Section 10.

[95] Sarfaty 2012, p. 56.

obligations under international law. This uncertainty creates what some scholars call "a legal blackhole"[96] that hinders the possibility of invoking the human rights responsibilities of these institutions.

9.4 Human Rights Obligations of International Financial Institutions

The human rights obligations of IFIs can be understood from two perspectives, i.e. through the human rights obligations of their member states, an indirect approach, and the direct human rights obligations of these institutions, if any. The following sections will briefly elucidate these two perspectives and the debates surrounding them.

9.4.1 Indirect Approach: Human Rights Obligations of Member States

International organizations including the IFIs under consideration are composed of states, which are the principal duty bearers in international human rights law.[97] This entails that states need to respect their human rights obligations in their engagements with or within these institutions.[98] As the Maastricht Guidelines confirmed in the context of economic, social, and cultural rights:

> The obligations of States to protect economic, social and cultural rights extend also to their participation in international organizations, where they act collectively. It is particularly important for States to use their influence to ensure that violations do not result from the programmes and policies of the organizations of which they are members.[99]

Domestically, states are required to give due regard to their human rights obligations when they enter into agreements or plan and implement projects with IFIs.[100] States also need to ensure that international organizations operating in their territories respect human rights,[101] which is what the duty to protect demands. Moreover, "[states] are obliged to respect human rights, not only domestically, but also

---

[96] Van Den Meerssche 2021, p. 84.

[97] Skogly 2003, p. 49.

[98] Ibid.; see also Byrnes 2011, p. 11.

[99] International Commission of Jurists (ICJ), Maastricht Guidelines on Violations of Economic, Social and Cultural Rights, 26 January 1997, para 19.

[100] Skogly 2003, p. 58.

[101] Verdirame 2011, p. 87.

when they are acting internationally."[102] This extraterritorial obligation of states also extends to their conduct as members of international organizations or IFIs.[103]

Hence, as members of IFIs, states need to respect their human rights obligations in their dealings with and within these institutions. The Committee on Economic, Social, and Cultural Rights (CESCR) has also affirmed this in its General Comment on the right to education.[104] The relevant paragraph of the General Comment enunciates, "...state parties have an obligation to ensure that their actions as members of international organizations, including international financial institutions, take due account of the right to education."[105] The Committee has made similar remarks in its general comments on the right to health and the right to work, among others.[106] Moreover, the Committee has reiterated this in several of its concluding observations in which it has firmly recommended both donor and borrower states to take into account their human rights obligations when they engage with these institutions.[107]

In addition, mere compliance with the operational policies and standards of development banks does not relieve a state of its human rights obligations. For instance, in relation to DID, besides complying with the resettlement policy of the bank financing the project, a state also has to make sure that the displacement and resettlement process complies with human rights standards. Overall, the direct human rights obligations of IFIs, or lack thereof, do not preclude states' human rights obligations in relation to the activities of these institutions.

Overall, one way in which the question of whether or not IFIs have human rights obligations can be approached is through the human rights obligations of their member states. However, as autonomous entities, international organizations including IFIs have independent existence and legal personality separate from their member states.[108] In other words, they are not merely a collection of states. Consequently, the human rights obligations of states are not directly transferable to international organizations of which they are members.[109] Hence, it is imperative to explore the direct human rights obligations, if any, of these institutions under international law.

---

[102] Fujita 2013, p. 5; see also Verdirame 2011, pp. 86 and 87.

[103] Maastricht Principles on Extraterritorial Obligations of States in the Area of Economic, Social and Cultural Rights, September 2011, para 15.

[104] UN CESCR 1999, para 56.

[105] Ibid.

[106] UN CESCR 2000, para 39; see also UN CESCR 2006, para 33.

[107] Committee on Economic, Social and Cultural Rights, Concluding Observation of Committee on Economic, Social and Cultural Rights: Egypt, 23 May 2000, E/C.12/1/Add/44, para 28; see also Committee on Economic, Social and Cultural Rights, Concluding Observation of Committee on Economic, Social and Cultural Rights: Italy, 23 May 2000, E/C.12/1/Add.43, para 20; see also Committee on Economic, Social and Cultural Rights, Concluding Observation of Committee on Economic, Social and Cultural Rights: Belgium, 1 December 2000, E/C.12/1/Add.54, para 31; see also Fujita 2013, pp. 6 and 7.

[108] Skogly 2003, p. 46; see also Van Den Meerssche 2021, pp. 82 and 85; see also Sarfaty 2012, pp. 56 and 57; see also Byrnes 2011, p. 11.

[109] Skogly 2001, p. 109; see also Fujita 2013, p. 5.

9.4.2 Direct Human Rights Obligations of International Financial Institutions

Whether and to what extent international organizations, IFIs in this context, have direct human rights obligations in international law has been a contentious subject. As international organizations, it is well established that these institutions have international legal personality,[110] a separate personality from their founding states.[111] This is also evident from the Articles of Agreements of these institutions, which grant them independence from their member states, the legal capacity to enter into agreements, and certain privileges and immunities in their operations.[112] International legal personality entails that development banks have certain obligations under international law, for instance, those emanating from their constitutions, international agreements they are party to, and, possibly, customary international law.[113] What is questionable is whether and to what extent they have human rights obligations. As international human rights law is inherently state-centric, international organizations including development banks often cannot become parties to and, hence, are "not directly bound by human rights treaties".[114] The draft Convention on the Right to Development departs from this general nature of human rights treaties by allowing international organizations to be parties to the Convention.[115] The draft also explicitly outlines obligations of international organizations.[116] Accordingly, "international organizations…have the obligation to refrain from conduct that aids, assists, directs, controls or coerces, with knowledge of the circumstances of the act, a State or another

---

[110] Van Den Meerssche 2021, pp. 82 and 85; see also Sarfaty 2012, pp. 56 and 57; see also Crippa 2010, p. 537; see also International Court of Justice, Reparation for Injuries Suffered in the Service of the United Nations, Advisory Opinion of 11 April 1949, (1949) ICJ report 174, 179 (in this Advisory Opinion where it was asked to comment on whether or not the UN as an international organization can bring an international claim, the ICJ concluded that the organizations have an international legal personality. This entails "…that it is subject of international law and capable of possessing international rights and duties, and that it has capacity to maintain its rights by bringing international claims."); see also International Court of Justice, Interpretation of the Agreement of 25 March 1951 between the WHO and Egypt, Advisory Opinion of 20 December 1980, (1980) ICJ report at 73, para 37.

[111] Skogly 2003, p. 46.

[112] Ibid.

[113] Advisory Opinion on the Interpretation of the Agreement of 25 March 1951 between the WHO and Egypt, n 110, para 37 (In this advisory opinion the Court noted that "[i]nternational organizations are subjects of international law and, as such, are bound by any obligations incumbent upon them under general rules of international law, under their constitutions or under international agreements to which they are parties."); see also Verdirame 2011, p. 71; see also Sarfaty 2012, p. 57; see also Van Den Meerssche 2021, p. 85; see also Sarfaty 2009, p. 657.

[114] Sarfaty 2012, p. 57. While international organizations can become parties to some international law treaties, human rights treaties do not offer this option yet.

[115] Human Rights Council, Working Group on the Right to Development, Draft Convention on the Right to Development, 17 January 2020, A/HRC/WG.2/21/2, Articles 28 and 29.

[116] Ibid., Article 9.

international organization to breach" their obligations.[117] Apart from this new development, there is yet to exist a human rights treaty that creates binding obligations for international organizations, or IFIs in this case.

There is, however, a compelling argument that they are bound by human rights obligations that emanate from customary international law.[118] As the former UN Independent Expert on the Promotion of a Democratic and Equitable International Order, Alfred de Zayas, contended, "...in the twenty-first century there are no "human rights-free zones", that all States, international organizations and non-State actors must respect the customary international law of human rights...".[119] This, in turn, implies that human rights treaties and norms that have obtained the status of customary international law, for instance, most of the norms of the UDHR or their aspects, have a binding effect on these institutions.[120]

Moreover, as one of the specialized agencies of the UN, the World Bank is obliged to respect the overarching objectives and principles of the organization enunciated under the UN Charter and the decisions of the Security Council including those related to human rights.[121] However, a similar argument cannot be made about the regional development banks as they do not form part of the inter-governmental organizations of their respective regions.

Nevertheless, the question remains whether the human rights obligations of these institutions, if any, are limited to refraining from directly interfering with the enjoyment of rights—the duty to respect—or that they are expected to actively work to protect and fulfil rights. There is a divergent view among scholars regarding this. According to some commentators, in the current state-centric international human rights law system, non-state actors including IFIs only have a duty to respect and, perhaps, a limited duty to protect.[122] Thus, they cannot reasonably be expected to undertake positive obligations required under the duty to fulfil.[123] On the other hand,

---

117 Ibid.

118 Van Den Meerssche 2021, p. 86; see also Fujita 2013, p. 8; see also Fujita 2011, p. 374; see also Zhou 2012, p. 833. This view is also supported by the European Court of Justice, which found in several cases that the EU and EC are bound by customary international law (see Verdirame 2011, p. 72).

119 Human Rights Council 2017, para 2.

120 Skogly 2003, p. 51.

121 Sarfaty 2012, p. 58; see also Van Den Meerssche 2021, pp. 86 and 87; see also Sarfaty 2009, p. 658; see also Fujita 2013, p. 9. One of the objectives of the UN, as stipulated under Article 55 of the Charter, is promoting "...universal respect for, and observance of, human rights and fundamental freedoms..." (United Nations Charter (n 9) Article 55). Thus, scholars contend that the Bank should integrate and promote human rights in its activities.

122 Fujita 2013, p. 8; see also Skogly 2003, pp. 54–56 (Skogly argues that IFIs may have a duty to protect to the extent that they are able to control or influence the actions of third parties).

123 Fujita 2013, p. 8; see also Skogly 2003, p. 57. According to Skogly, the duty to fulfil often emanates from treaties to which these institutions are not parties. Hence, this positive obligation would not apply to them in most cases. But in exceptional cases where customary international law or general principles of law entail a duty to fulfil, international financial institutions can have this obligation.

other scholars contend that the human rights obligations of these institutions are rather broader; Andrew Clapham, for instance, argues that:

> … if the entity has sufficient legal capacity to be the bearer of international obligations, the relevant obligations include multiple aspects of the appropriate customary international law of human rights. The international financial institutions can therefore be said to have obligations, not only to respect human rights, but also to protect and even fulfil human rights in appropriate circumstances.[124]

Similarly, the former UN Special Rapporteur on the right to food, Jean Ziegler, stressed in his report that international organizations, particularly IFIs, have obligations to respect, protect, and "support the fulfilment" of the right to food.[125] According to the report:

> The obligation to respect is a minimum obligation, which requires international organizations to ensure that their advice, policies and practices do not lead to violations of the right to food. This means that, at least with regard to the World Bank and the IMF, international organizations should have minimum negative obligations to respect or not to do harm in relation to the realization of the right to food. The prohibition against doing harm seems to be universally recognized. This means that these organizations should not promote "development" projects that would result in forced displacement or the destruction of sources of livelihood, especially in cases without proper compensation and rehabilitation for the affected populations.[126]

Further, the duty to protect, according to the Special Rapporteur, obliges these institutions to ensure that the states and non-state actors they work with do not violate the right to food in relation to the projects in which they are involved.[127] Meanwhile, "the duty to support the fulfilment" of the right—not akin to the duty to fulfil[128]—requires financial institutions "to facilitate the realization of the right to food and to provide necessary assistance when required for all people, indigenous, minorities and vulnerable groups".[129] However, this extensive interpretation of the human rights obligations of IFIs is not always accepted.

On the other end of the spectrum, others argue that the acceptance of a legal personality of international organizations, i.e. autonomous entities separate from states, means that they "…can pursue their own political projects independently"[130]

---

[124] Clapham 2006, p. 151; see also Darrow 2003, pp. 132 and 133; see also Fujita 2013, pp. 8 and 9.

[125] UN Commission on Human Rights 2006, paras 43–45.

[126] Ibid., para 43.

[127] Ibid., para 44.

[128] The duty to fulfil requires states to take the necessary positive steps including the provision of essential services to realize rights (see Maastricht Guidelines (n 99) para 6). The phrase "the duty to support the fulfilment" used by the Special Rapporteur seems to be premised on the assumption that the primary duty to fulfil the right to food rests on states and international financial institutions should step in when the state is unable to do so. It does not necessarily put the onus on these institutions.

[129] UN Commission on Human Rights 2006, para 45.

[130] Van Den Meerssche 2021, pp. 87 and 88; see also d'Aspremont 2011; see also Verdirame 2011, p. 59.

without being bound by the international legal order created for states.[131] Hence, there is no positive law basis for the existence of human rights obligations of international organizations save for those that emanate from their own constitutions and international agreements to which they are parties.

The other important issue is whether and to what extent the human rights obligations of IFIs can be inferred from the rules on international responsibility of international organizations for internationally wrongful acts. The relevant framework in this regard is the "ILC draft articles on the responsibility of international organizations".[132] The draft is largely similar to the ILC draft articles on state responsibility in formulation and substance.[133] Generally, international organizations can be held responsible for committing an internationally wrongful act,[134] i.e. an action or omission that, "(a) is attributable to that organization under international law; and (b) constitutes a breach of an international obligation of that organization."[135] The draft articles further stipulate that the responsibility of an international organization will be engaged if it assists or directs or controls or coerces states or other international organizations to commit an internationally wrongful act.[136] This is provided that "the…organization does so with knowledge of the circumstances of the internationally wrongful act" and "the act would be internationally wrongful if committed by that organization."[137] Hence, international organizations are responsible not only for breaching their obligations under international law but also for assisting states and other non-state actors to breach those obligations.

Accordingly, the development banks covered in this chapter will be internationally responsible if they assist states in violating their human rights obligations—for example, by funding projects that violate human rights—"with the knowledge of the circumstances" and if those human rights obligations also apply to the Banks,[138] which seems the most important caveat. Given the uncertainty of the human rights obligations of these institutions, it would be challenging to hold them internationally responsible for human rights violations committed by states and in which they played some part. Moreover, the draft articles do not specify what the obligations of international organizations are or indicate where they emanate from. Rather, they specify

---

[131] Van Den Meerssche 2021, pp. 87 and 88; see also Fujita 2013, p. 10.

[132] The International Law Commission, Draft Articles on the Responsibility of International Organizations, Yearbook of the International Law Commission, 2011, vol. II, Part Two, A/CN.4/SER.A/2011/Add.1.(par.2), 87. Indeed, this framework is not binding. However, it has been endorsed by various UN organs and yields significant support from states and international organizations. Moreover, the draft articles are drafted by renowned publicists. Hence, serve as a subsidiary source of international law as per Article 38 of the ICJ Statute. Thus, they carry significant normative weight.

[133] International Law Commission, Draft Articles on Responsibility of States for Internationally Wrongful Acts, November 2001, Supplement No. 10 (A/56/10), chp.IV.E.1.

[134] Draft Articles on the responsibility of international organizations (n 132) Article 3.

[135] Ibid., Article 4.

[136] Ibid., Articles 14–16.

[137] Ibid.

[138] Ibid.

how the breach of those obligations can give rise to the responsibility of the international organization concerned. Hence, the human rights obligations of international organizations cannot be inferred from this instrument.

Overall, while a strong argument can be made for the existence of human rights obligations of international organizations, the scope of these obligations—beyond a minimum level of duty to respect—is still contentious.

9.5 Policies on Involuntary Displacement or Resettlement

IFIs or the development banks covered in this chapter finance a range of development projects, particularly in developing countries, through loans and grants. A significant portion of these development projects also causes involuntary displacement and resettlement.[139] For instance, studies show that around 20% of the development projects financed by the World Bank involve land acquisition and, hence, cause displacement.[140] Given the scale of the projects financed by the Bank, as it is the largest lending institution, these displacements affect a significantly large number of people. Studies also show that at any given point in time, approximately more than one million people are affected by involuntary displacement and resettlement caused by active development projects financed by the World Bank.[141] As established in Chap. 2, involuntary displacement, in turn, results in a number of adverse economic, social, and cultural consequences the effect of which might linger for an extended period. As the World Bank also acknowledged:

> ...involuntary resettlement under development projects, if unmitigated, often gives rise to severe economic, social, and environmental risks: production systems are dismantled; people face impoverishment when their productive assets or income sources are lost; people are relocated to environments where their productive skills may be less applicable and the competition for resources greater; community institutions and social networks are weakened; kin groups are dispersed; and cultural identity, traditional authority, and the potential for mutual help are diminished or lost.[142]

In order to prevent or mitigate these adverse consequences, the development banks covered in this chapter have adopted policy frameworks that lay down resettlement

---

[139] Robinson 2003, p. 28.

[140] Ibid. According to a study undertaken by the Bank's Social Development Department on the involuntary resettlement policy and practice of the Bank, among the projects financed by the Bank from a January 1990 to 30 June 2012, 1423 projects—or 21% of all projects financed by the Bank—led to involuntary resettlement the majority of which are in East Asian and African countries (see World Bank Social Development Department, Involuntary Resettlement Portfolio Review: Phase I, Inventory of Bank-financed Projects Triggering the Involuntary Resettlement Policy (1990–2010), May 2012, 12 and 13).

[141] IDI et al. 2013, para 4.

[142] The World Bank resettlement policy (n 54) para 1. This Operational Policy, which was the first of its kind, was adopted in February 1980 and last revised in December 2001.

guidelines for borrower states undertaking projects that involve involuntary displacement.[143] These policies are grounded on the premise that despite the inherent risks involved in DID, "[w]ell-designed and well-implemented resettlement can…turn involuntary resettlement into a development opportunity."[144] Hence, these policy frameworks stipulate various procedural and substantive safeguards that apply at all stages of displacement and resettlement.

The current section seeks to elucidate the substantive content of these policy frameworks and explore to what extent the safeguards stipulated therein protect the rights of people affected by DID with reference to the relevant human rights norms. This does not, however, imply that these human rights norms are directly applicable to IFIs or that IFIs are bound by these norms. Rather, it is based on the assumption that the integration of human rights norms in resettlement policies and practices can lead to a better outcome in protecting the rights of people affected thereby and achieving the very objectives of these policies. Moreover, this also helps to situate this chapter in the overall scope and theoretical framework of this book, i.e. the human rights-based approach. Hence, the assessment of the resettlement policies of the development banks under consideration in light of the pertinent human rights norms in the subsequent sections should be understood based on these premises.

Compared to the policies of the regional development banks, the World Bank resettlement policy is not only the oldest,[145] but also relatively the most detailed and comprehensive particularly regarding the procedural and substantive safeguards that need to be provided for displaced persons. The Bank also has a Sourcebook, which is a detailed guideline on the interpretation and application of these safeguards coupled with best practices that can be emulated under various circumstances.[146] Moreover, the resettlement policies of the regional development banks heavily draw on the policy of the World Bank.[147] Thus, the analysis in the subsequent sections will primarily focus on the policy of the World Bank and only refer to the respective policies of the regional development banks when necessary.

9.5.1 The Scope and Objectives of the Policy Frameworks

The scope of the resettlement policies of the development banks under consideration extends to the (direct) economic and social impacts of the projects they finance

[143] The World Bank resettlement policy (n 54); see also the African Development Bank Involuntary Resettlement Policy, November 2003; see also Asian Development Bank Involuntary Resettlement Policy, August 1995; see also Inter-American Development Bank, Operational Policy on Involuntary Resettlement, OP-710, October 1998.

[144] World Bank 2004, p. xvii.

[145] Terminski 2015, p. 88; see also Robinson 2003, p. 28.

[146] World Bank 2004.

[147] Robinson 2003, p. 33.

that emanate from two project-related causes.[148] The first cause is the involuntary acquisition of land, which affects the assets, income, and access to housing of those affected, and the second cause is the disruption of access to common resources that adversely impact the livelihood of those affected.[149] Thus, the policies cover both physical and economic displacement,[150] although the standards and safeguards applicable in each case might differ as will be elaborated on subsequently. In other words, these policies apply even if the people affected by the project are not physically displaced from their homes or residences provided that the restriction of access to common resources caused by the project negatively affects their socio-economic well-being.[151] The scope of these policies, however, does not cover cases where development projects do not involve land acquisition or the disruption of access to common resources but create unfavourable social and environmental situations that force people to move.[152] In such cases, the good practice the World Bank Sourcebook recommends is for states to include land acquisition as part of the project design and resettle the people affected.[153] Nonetheless, formally, these policies do not cover instances where displacement is caused by such "externalities" despite the fact that the socio-economic and human rights risks they impose are comparable to displacement directly caused by the project.[154]

Moreover, the World Bank policy applies only to "direct" socio-economic impacts of the projects, which "…means any consequence immediately related to the taking of a parcel of land or to restrictions in the use of legally designated parks or protected areas."[155] The construction of large-scale development projects can significantly alter market competition, the culture of consumption, and other economic factors that potentially affect the income of those living in the area.[156] The scope of the policy, nevertheless, does not extend to these indirect economic impacts.[157] Critics contend that, "[t]his artificial distinction between direct and indirect impacts contradicts the objective of the policy by precluding the possibility of conceiving and executing

---

148 The World Bank resettlement policy (n 54) para 3; see also World Bank 2004, pp. 3–5; see also African Development Bank resettlement policy (n 143) para 3.4.1 (Although this paragraph is almost similar to that of the World Bank's on the scope of the policy (para 3), it does not include the term 'direct'. In other words, the policy of the African development bank does not specifically require that the adverse socio-economic impact of the project has to be direct for the policy to apply.).

149 The World Bank resettlement policy (n 54) para 3; see also World Bank 2004, pp. 3–5; see also African Development Bank resettlement policy (n 143) para 3.4.1.

150 In the context of these policies, "The term "displaced persons" is synonymous with "project-affected persons" and is not limited to those subjected to physical displacement" (see World Bank 2004, p. 5).

151 World Bank 2004, p. 5.

152 IDI et al. 2013, para 20.

153 World Bank 2004, p. 19; see also IDI et al. 2013, para 21.

154 IDI et al. 2013, para 22.

155 World Bank 2004, p. 4.

156 Ibid., pp. 18 and 19.

157 Ibid.

resettlement activities as sustainable development programs."[158] It is hardly possible to sustainably restore and improve the livelihoods of those affected, which is the main objective of the policy, without taking into account the overall impacts of the project, be it direct or indirect.[159] Moreover, the distinction between direct and indirect impacts appears to be an arbitrary distinction devoid of objective standards. This opens a door for states to misrepresent the impacts of the projects they are proposing.[160] Theodore Downing, for instance, proposed a broader approach based on a *sine qua non* test to rectify this; accordingly, "[t]he correct, economic litmus test should be: if the costs would not have accrued without the project, then they are project costs and must be factored in."[161]

In a nutshell, the policy safeguards that will be discussed in the subsequent sections apply to development projects that involve the acquisition of land or disruption of access to common resources, which impose (direct) socio-economic adversities on those affected.

These policy frameworks have three underlying objectives. The first objective is prevention— "[i]nvoluntary resettlement should be avoided where feasible, or minimized, exploring all viable alternative project designs".[162] Since DID is inherently disruptive and poses immense socio-economic risks as established above, it should be used only as a last resort when other less restrictive alternatives—for instance, project sites "with little or no population"—are not available.[163] States not only need to use DID as a last resort but also need to attempt to minimize its magnitude in terms of the number of people affected and the amount of land taken.[164] The resettlement policies of the African and Inter-American development banks specifically enumerate some of the important considerations that need to be taken into account to determine the necessity of the involuntary displacement in question.[165] The relevant paragraphs read:

> Particular attention must be given to socio-cultural considerations, such as cultural or religious significance of land, the vulnerability of the affected population, or the availability of in-kind replacement for assets, especially when they have important intangible implications. When a large number of people or a significant portion of the affected population would be subject to relocation or would suffer from impacts that are difficult to quantify and to

---

[158] IDI et al. 2013, para 23; see also Kangave 2012, p. 385.

[159] IDI et al. 2013, para 23; see also Kangave 2012, p. 385.

[160] Downing 2012, p. 14; see also Kangave 2012, p. 385.

[161] Downing 2012, p. 14; see also IDI et al. 2013, para 24.

[162] The World Bank resettlement policy (n 54) para 2(a); see also the African Development Bank resettlement policy (n 143) para 3.2; see also Asian Development Bank resettlement policy, n 143, paras 33 and 34(i) and (ii); see also the Inter-American Development Bank resettlement policy (n 143) para III(1).

[163] World Bank 2004, p. 6.

[164] Ibid.

[165] African Development Bank resettlement policy (n 143) para 3.2; see also the Inter-American Development Bank resettlement policy (n 143) para III(1).

> compensate, the alternative of not going ahead with the project should be given a serious consideration[.][166]

Overall, states should explore all viable alternatives to avoid, or at least minimize, the adverse impacts of involuntary displacement. This also corresponds with the principles of necessity and proportionality under human rights law. As discussed in the preceding chapters, any interference with human rights, for instance, the forced eviction and acquisition of property that DID involves, must be necessary to achieve a legitimate objective and proportionate to the objective pursued.[167]

Nevertheless, these policies do not specifically require the development project itself to be necessary or justified based on the principle of general welfare or public interest. It appears that the safeguards provided therein only come into play after the development project has been approved. In other words, the resettlement policies under consideration only require states to justify and use involuntary displacement as a last resort but do not expect states to justify the necessity of the project that caused the displacement.[168] Even if that is indirectly implied, the policies do not provide explicit or clear standards of assessment that can be used by states. As elucidated in part II of this book, the eviction and expropriation that DID involves—or the development projects that cause these unfavourable outcomes—are only justified if they are necessary to promote the general welfare or public interest.[169] The policy frameworks covered in this chapter, however, do not include a comparable policy standard.

In cases where involuntary displacement or resettlement cannot be avoided, the second underlying objective of these policies seeks to make the process of DID sustainable, participatory, and beneficial to the people affected.[170] According to the World Bank Policy:

> ...resettlement activities should be conceived and executed as sustainable development programs, providing sufficient investment resources to enable the persons displaced by the project to share in project benefits. Displaced persons should be meaningfully consulted and should have opportunities to participate in planning and implementing resettlement programs.[171]

The third objective is that resettlement programs should restore and preferably improve the livelihood or well-being of those affected to the level it was at prior

---

[166] African Development Bank resettlement policy (n 143) para 3.2; see also the Inter-American Development Bank resettlement policy (n 143) para III(1). These paragraphs reflect a human rights language, particularly of the human rights norms on indigenous peoples rights.

[167] UN General Assembly, International Covenant on Economic, Social and Cultural Rights, 16 December 1966, 993 United Nations Treaty Series 3, Article 4.

[168] IDI et al. 2013, para 35.

[169] ICESCR (n 167) Article 4.

[170] The World Bank resettlement policy (n 54) para 2(b); see also African Development Bank resettlement policy (n 143) para 3.2.

[171] The World Bank resettlement policy (n 54) para 2(b).

to displacement.[172] To this end, adequate assistance should be provided to displaced persons not only before and during displacement but also after relocation to restore or improve their standard of living.

Accordingly, borrower states are required to submit a "resettlement plan" detailing the resettlement process and the substantive and procedural safeguards they have in place to avoid or mitigate the adverse impacts of involuntary resettlement.[173] The Banks will assess whether or not the resettlement plan satisfies the policy standards of their respective resettlement policies before approving funds for the project.[174] The safeguards that need to be put in place by borrower states at different phases of displacement and resettlement will be elaborated on in the subsequent sections.

9.5.2 *Procedural and Substantive Safeguards*

The resettlement policies of the development banks under consideration demand states to put in place various procedural and substantive safeguards at all phases of displacement and resettlement. The following sections will classify these safeguards into three categories depending on the stage at which they need to be provided, i.e. before, during, and after displacement, and elucidate their substantive content.

9.5.2.1 Safeguards Before Displacement

According to the resettlement policies, states need to provide a range of procedural and substantive safeguards before displacement or relocation in order to achieve the objectives identified in the preceding section.

A. **Procedural Safeguards**

One of the objectives of the operational policies as discussed above is to ensure that "[d]isplaced persons [are] meaningfully consulted and…have opportunities to participate in planning and implementing resettlement programs".[175] This entails that, first, displaced persons should be duly "informed about their options and rights pertaining to resettlement".[176] Borrower states need to provide those affected by the project

[172] Ibid., para 2(c); see also African Development Bank resettlement policy (n 143) paras 3.2 and 3.3.(a); see also Asian Development Bank resettlement policy (n 143) para 33; see also the Inter-American Development Bank resettlement policy (n 143) para III(2).

[173] The World Bank resettlement policy (n 54) para 6; see also African Development Bank resettlement policy (n 143) paras 3.4.4.-3.4.10; see also Asian Development Bank resettlement policy (n 143) paras 38–40; see also the Inter-American Development Bank resettlement policy (n 143) para V.

[174] The World Bank resettlement policy (n 54) paras 22 and 25.

[175] The World Bank resettlement policy (n 54) para 2(b).

[176] Ibid., para 6(a)(i) and para 13(a); see also African Development Bank resettlement policy (n 143) para 3.3(b); see also Asian Development Bank resettlement policy (n 143) para 34(v).

with timely and accurate information about the project and its potential impacts, the proposed resettlement plan, and the choices they have.[177] Second, displaced persons should be "consulted on, offered choices among, and provided with technically and economically feasible resettlement alternatives".[178] Accordingly, they should be given an opportunity to weigh in on the proposed resettlement plan, propose new alternatives, and influence decision-making in general.[179] "The magnitude of implications of involuntary resettlement on the lives of people displaced is of such high order that it would be manifestly unjust and unconscionable to exclude affected people from enjoying a significant degree of control over decision making."[180] This is what "meaningful" participation demands. As the World Bank also explained in its Sourcebook—a guideline on the interpretation and implementation of its resettlement policy:

> Effective participation provides people with an opportunity to express their interests and concerns and suggest alternatives and options. Current measures of participation, however, are typically formal and minimal: they emphasize the numbers of meetings and participants, instead of the quality, content, and impact of interaction. Participation should not become just one more thing to check off on the list of things to do.[181]

Consultation and participation should ensue at the earliest possible time of the displacement or resettlement process.[182] Moreover, the format and details of the consultation need to take into account the local context, language, and culture of the affected communities as well as the scale and nature of the project.[183] States particularly need to take the necessary measures to make the consultation process more inclusive to vulnerable groups.[184] These rules are in line with the pertinent human rights norms and standards elaborated in the preceding chapters.

The consultation and participation rules and standards espoused in these policies, however, only apply to the resettlement process. The policies do not explicitly require that displaced persons should be consulted and have a say in the development project itself. It appears that the state decides the necessity of the project and

---

177 The World Bank resettlement policy (n 54) para 6(a)(i) and para 13(a); see also World Bank 2004, pp. 124 and 128; see also African Development Bank resettlement policy (n 143) para 3.3(b).

178 The World Bank resettlement policy (n 54) para 6(a)(ii) and para 13(a); see also African Development Bank resettlement policy (n 143) para 3.3(b); see also Asian Development Bank resettlement policy (n 143) para 34(v); see also the Inter-American Development Bank resettlement policy (n 143) para V(2).

179 World Bank 2004, p. 124.

180 IDI et al. 2013, para 54.

181 World Bank 2004, p. 127.

182 Ibid., p. 128; see also African Development Bank resettlement policy (n 143) para 3.3(b).

183 World Bank 2004, pp. 128–129 and 130–132 (for instance, in large-scale projects that affect a large number of people, conducting the consultation in small groups might be necessary to make sure that all voices are represented); see also African Development Bank resettlement policy (n 143) para 3.3(b).

184 World Bank 2004, p. 128; see also African Development Bank resettlement policy (n 143) para 3.3(b); see also Asian Development Bank resettlement policy (n 143) para 34(v); see also the Inter-American Development Bank resettlement policy (n 143) para V(2).

the resulting involuntary displacement and consult those affected merely about the resettlement plan and alternatives. The World Bank also only advises states "…to have the initial information campaign describe and justify the project, explain why resettlement is necessary, give a preliminary assessment of its impacts…"[185] but not necessarily consult with those potentially affected about the necessity of the project before it is approved. This is apparently lower than the threshold of participation and consultation set under general human rights norms or the interpretation of those norms by the relevant monitoring bodies or special procedures. As elucidated in the previous chapters in relation to the rights to housing, property, and development, when a certain development project involves displacement—or eviction and expropriation depending on the context—, states should consult with those affected about the necessity of the project for "public interest".[186] Those individuals or groups should be given a chance to propose other alternatives and influence the decision-making before the project is approved. The resettlement policies of the IFIs under consideration do not appear to recognize this aspect of public participation.

B. **Substantive Safeguards**

The World Bank resettlement policy envisages three types of remedies to restore and preferably improve the livelihoods of those displaced by development projects, namely the replacement of real assets—land and housing—(in-kind compensation), monetary compensation, and (long-term) rehabilitation measures.[187] The first two remedies, which will be discussed in this section, need to be provided before displacement or relocation takes place. The policy specifically demands that the "…[acquisition] of land and related assets may take place only after compensation has been paid and, where applicable, resettlement sites and moving allowances have been provided to the displaced persons."[188] Rehabilitation measures, on the other hand, entail follow-up and long-term assistance provided after displacement to ensure that the livelihoods of those displaced are restored and, hence, they will be discussed subsequently under the relevant section.

The policy of the AfDB does not specifically enumerate the different types of remedies that need to be provided for displaced persons. It rather stresses that borrower states need to provide assistance to displaced persons before, during, and after displacement, which is aimed at improving the "…former living standards, income earning capacity, and production levels."[189] Further, the policy stipulates that displaced persons should be provided with a commensurate amount of compensation for the losses they have incurred before relocation takes place.[190] The policy,

---

[185] World Bank 2004, p. 128.

[186] UN CESCR 1997, para 15; see also Special Rapporteur on Adequate Housing 2007, paras 37 and 38; see also Declaration on the Right to Development (n 82) Articles 2(3), 1(1), and 8(2) (it should be recalled that "meaningful participation" is one of the substantive elements of the right to development); see also van der Ploeg and Vanclay 2017, p. 40.

[187] World Bank 2004, p. 51.

[188] The World Bank resettlement policy (n 54) para 10.

[189] African Development Bank resettlement policy (n 143) para 3.3(a).

[190] Ibid., para 3.3(e).

nonetheless, does not specify whether in-kind compensation (replacement of assets) is required or that monetary compensation alone is sufficient. The policy of the ADB envisages three types of remedies, i.e. compensation, relocation assistance, and rehabilitation, aimed at achieving "…at least the same level of wellbeing with the project as without it".[191] However, it also does not differentiate between in-kind and monetary compensation. Similarly, the policy of the IADB sets out compensation and rehabilitation as required remedies,[192] without specifying if and when an in-kind remedy should be provided save for cases where indigenous peoples are concerned,[193] as will be discussed below.

For projects involving the acquisition of land, the principal remedy, according to the World Bank's resettlement policy, is the provision of replacement land.[194] Replacement land, which the policy calls "land-based resettlement strategy", is particularly the preferable remedy for people whose livelihoods depend on land.[195] Accordingly, this strategy includes:

> …resettlement on public land…, or on private land acquired or purchased for resettlement. Whenever replacement land is offered, resettlers are provided with land for which a combination of productive potential, locational advantages, and other factors is at least equivalent to the advantages of the land taken.[196]

As is evident from this paragraph, the policy also sets a standard for the quality of the land. Not only should borrower states provide replacement land but also the replacement land provided should be of a comparable or higher quality than the expropriated land in terms of location, cultivability, and other relevant factors.

In addition, the World Bank policy recognizes that for indigenous peoples, land is more than an economic asset and it is closely linked to "…their identity and cultural survival".[197] In order to preserve this special relationship, the physical displacement of these groups should be avoided if other viable alternatives are available.[198] If not, priority should be given to "land-based resettlement strategies" that need to be prepared and implemented in consultation with the affected people.[199] Nevertheless, it is not clear from the policy whether or not this consultation confers a veto power to the indigenous people concerned. The policy does not specifically adopt the principle of "free, prior, and informed consent" envisaged under the relevant frameworks on

---

[191] Asian Development Bank resettlement policy (n 143) para 34.

[192] The Inter-American Development Bank resettlement policy (n 143) paras III(2) and V(3).

[193] Ibid., para IV(4) (the policy requires that for indigenous peoples, land-based resettlement options, among other remedies, should be made available).

[194] The World Bank resettlement policy (n 54) para 11.

[195] The World Bank resettlement policy (n 54) para 11.

[196] Ibid; see also World Bank 2004, p. 64.

[197] The World Bank resettlement policy (n 54) para 9.

[198] Ibid.

[199] Ibid; see also World Bank 2004, pp. 79–80.

indigenous peoples rights explored in Chap. 7.[200] In fact, the policy does not appear to provide heightened protection or safeguards for indigenous peoples compared to other groups whose livelihoods depend on land, albeit it recognizes the special relationship of these peoples with their ancestral land. This might be traced back to the economic factors-focused nature of the Bank. On the other hand, by extending the land-based resettlement strategy to all groups that rely on land for their livelihoods—farmers or peasants and indigenous people alike—the policy can potentially fill the prevalent gap in international human rights law regarding the general protection of land rights as discussed in Chap. 4.

Meanwhile, the World Bank operational policy on indigenous peoples espouses that when the proposed project affects indigenous peoples, it has to go through "a process of free, prior, and informed consultation with the affected Indigenous Peoples' communities at each stage of the project, and particularly during project preparation, to fully identify their views and ascertain their broad community support for the project".[201] This is again not akin to requiring states to obtain the "free, prior, and informed consent" of the people concerned despite the misleading language since, while consent gives autonomy of choice or decision-making power, consultation only indicates participation in the process. In other words, similar to its resettlement policy, the policy of the Bank on indigenous peoples does not explicitly confer a decision-making power on the indigenous peoples concerned.

On the other hand, the Environmental and Social Framework of the Bank, in effect since 2018, has taken progressive steps in this regard. The framework explicitly requires states to obtain the "free, prior, and informed consent" of indigenous peoples in certain circumstances where the project adversely affects this group of people.[202] One of these circumstances is when the project involves the displacement of indigenous peoples from their ancestral land or the land they traditionally occupy.[203] In these cases, the project can only proceed with the full consent of the indigenous peoples concerned.[204] Moreover, the Framework contains detailed rules on what free, prior, and informed consent entails and how it should be obtained.[205] These progressive developments address the shortcoming of the resettlement policy in this respect.

---

[200] UN General Assembly, United Nations Declaration on the Rights of Indigenous Peoples: resolution/adopted by the General Assembly, 2 October 2007, A/RES/61/295, Article 10; see also Chap. 7, Sect. 7.4 of this book; see also IDI et al. 2013, para 62.

[201] The World Bank Operational Manual OP 4.10 - Indigenous Peoples, July 2005 (revised April 2013), par.6(c).

[202] The World Bank, Indigenous Peoples/Sub-Saharan African Historically Underserved Traditional Local Communities (hereinafter "World Bank indigenous peoples framework"), in the Environmental and Social Framework, p. 75, 2017, para 24.

[203] The World Bank indigenous peoples framework (n 202) para 24. In relation to indigenous peoples, the Framework also espouses that a development process should promote the human rights, cultural identity, and dignity of these peoples, which is one of the very few times that "human rights" is mentioned in the Framework (see World Bank indigenous peoples framework (n 202) para 5).

[204] World Bank indigenous peoples framework (n 202) para 31.

[205] Ibid., paras 24–27.

Out of the three regional development banks covered in this chapter, only the resettlement policy of the IADB deals with the rights of indigenous peoples vis-à-vis project-induced land acquisition. Accordingly, the bank will only finance development projects that potentially cause the displacement of indigenous peoples if the peoples concerned "have given their informed consent to the resettlement and compensation measures", land-based resettlement options have been made available, traditional rights to land are recognized and fully compensated, and those affected can benefit from the project.[206] These safeguards are evidently more consistent with the relevant human rights standards—particularly in relation to the principle of informed consent—than those of the World Bank's resettlement policy.

In cases where the replacement of land is not possible, the World Bank policy requires that "…non-land-based options built around opportunities for employment or self-employment should be provided in addition to cash compensation for land and other assets lost".[207] This again shows that the main objective of the safeguards proposed under the policy is restoring the income or livelihoods of the people displaced.

Monetary compensation for land acquisition or expropriation can be a viable option under three circumstances. First, when the livelihood of those displaced is not based on land.[208] Second, even if it is, when the land acquired for the project is only a small fraction that does not significantly affect their livelihood.[209] Third, when "active markets for land, housing, and labor exist, displaced persons [can] use such markets, and there is sufficient supply of land and housing".[210] The monetary compensation "…should be sufficient to replace the lost land and other assets at full replacement cost in local markets".[211] The policy, thus, envisages a "replacement cost" standard of assessment to determine the amount of compensation. Accordingly, a replacement cost is equivalent to the current actual market price of the asset plus transaction costs, for instance, administrative fees.[212] This differs from the "registered market-value" standard of assessment used by many countries, which does not fully replace the assets taken.[213]

Both the African and Inter-American development banks also adopt the "replacement cost" standard as a standard of assessment of compensation.[214] The AfDB policy, however, specifically postulates that non-economic factors, such as "…the social, health, environmental and psychological impacts of the project and the

[206] The Inter-American Development Bank resettlement policy (n 143) para IV(4).

[207] The World Bank resettlement policy (n 54) para 11.

[208] Ibid., para 12.

[209] Ibid.

[210] Ibid.

[211] Ibid.

[212] World Bank 2004, pp. 52 and 53.

[213] Ibid., p. 52 ("In many countries, legal compensation criteria are based on a registered "market value" that underestimates actual market value, so landowners are unable to replace their assets.").

[214] African Development Bank resettlement policy (n 143) para 3.3(e); see also the Inter-American Development Bank resettlement policy (n 143) para V(3).

displacement, which may disrupt productivity and social integration", also need to be taken into account in the calculation of compensation.[215] This appears to be more progressive than the World Bank policy that solely focuses on economic factors. The policy of the ADB, on the other hand, does not put forward a specific standard of assessment of compensation; it only indicates that compensation should address the loss of assets, livelihoods, and income.[216]

Meanwhile, reliance on monetary compensation as a primary means of remedy in most cases overlooks the fact that this form of remedy often causes impoverishment as it is not sustainable in the long run and often not fully compensatory.[217] One of the alternatives proposed by scholars to rectify this is putting in place project benefit-sharing schemes; in other words, giving those bearing the costs of development, or displaced by the project in this context, an opportunity to share the benefits therefrom.[218] Benefit-sharing as a safeguard in the context of DID can also be inferred from one of the normative elements of the right to development, i.e. the right of individuals and groups to equitably share the proceeds of development, as discussed in the previous chapter.[219] While the World Bank policy envisages benefit-sharing as one of the policy objectives, it does not enumerate specific ways in which this can be achieved.[220]

None of the policy frameworks of the development banks under consideration include an explicit prohibition of forced eviction, which is a *prima facie* violation of the right to housing as per the relevant human rights norms discussed in Chap. 3,[221] or any policy standard on eviction for that matter. The only exception is the recent Environmental and Social Framework of the World Bank, which discourages borrower states from resorting to forced eviction.[222] A number of case studies, however, demonstrate that development projects financed by these banks often involve (forced) eviction as land acquisition and eviction often go hand in hand.[223] The only relevant policy standard on the right to housing is the provision in the World Bank policy that requires states to provide displaced persons with "residential housing, or housing sites".[224]

---

215 African Development Bank resettlement policy (n 143) para 3.3(f).

216 Asian Development Bank resettlement policy (n 143) para 34.

217 IDI et al. 2013, para 79; see also Downing 2012, p. 14; see also Kangave 2012, p. 378.

218 Cernea 2008, pp. 48–56; see also IDI et al. 2013, paras 78–83; see also Koenig 2020, pp. 417 and 418. Project benefit-sharing includes using the proceeds of development to develop infrastructure, create jobs, and provide public services, among others, for those affected (see Koenig 2020, pp. 418–420).

219 See the discussion in Chap. 8, Sect. 8.3.

220 IDI et al. 2013, para 83; World Bank resettlement policy (n 54) para 2(b).

221 UN CESCR 1991, para 18.

222 The World Bank, Land Acquisition, Restrictions on Land Use and Involuntary Resettlement, in the Environmental and Social Framework, p. 53, 2017, para 31. The definition of "forced eviction" adopted by the Framework is also mostly similar to the one proposed by the UN Committee on Economic, Social and Cultural Rights in its general comments as discussed in Chap. 3. The Framework, however, does not refer to the right to housing and the relevant human rights instruments.

223 IDI et al. 2013, para 33; see also Clark 2002, pp. 211 and 212.

224 The World Bank resettlement policy (n 54) para 6(b)(ii).

In situations where this is not viable, adequate monetary compensation calculated based on the replacement cost standard elucidated above should be provided in lieu of replacement housing.[225] The policy, nevertheless, does not specifically demand states to provide replacement housing as a preferred remedy as it does with land. According to the human rights norms on the rights to housing and property discussed in Chaps. 3 and 4, in-kind compensation should be given the utmost priority when real properties, or housing and land, are expropriated.[226] The policy does not explicitly recognize this. The policies of the regional development banks covered in this chapter are rather silent on this issue.

As the World Bank's resettlement policy espouses, eligibility for the remedies or entitlements described above is determined based on two criteria: the type of land tenure and the severity of the impact.[227] The policy classifies displaced persons into three groups based on the type of tenure they possess, namely:

> (a) those who have formal legal rights to land (including customary and traditional rights recognized under the laws of the country);
> (b) those who do not have formal legal rights to land at the time the census begins but have a claim to such land or assets–provided that such claims are recognized under the laws of the country or become recognized through a process identified in the resettlement plan…
> (c) those who have no recognizable legal right or claim to the land they are occupying.[228]

Consequently, the first and the second groups—displaced persons who have formal rights, which include traditional ownership, or legitimate claims to the expropriated land—are eligible for in-kind and monetary compensations and other applicable assistances elucidated above.[229] On the other hand, those who fall under the third category or do not have a legal right or claim to the land they occupy, such as tenants and squatters, are only eligible for resettlement assistance,[230] which includes, for instance, moving assistance and allowance.[231] The policy does not, however, require states to provide this group with accommodation or housing options. Thus, individuals or households that fall under this group run the risk of homelessness. This falls short of meeting the minimum core content of the right to housing. As discussed in Chap. 3, eviction should not render those affected homeless regardless of the type of tenure they possess.[232]

The policy of the AfDB also maintains this classification of displaced persons based on their type of land tenure.[233] Accordingly, those who have formal rights or legitimate claims to the land they occupy are eligible for compensation, while

[225] Ibid., para 12.

[226] The Special Rapporteur on Adequate Housing 2007, para 60.

[227] The World Bank resettlement policy (n 54) para 15; see also World Bank 2004, p. 35.

[228] The World Bank resettlement policy (n 54) para 15; see also World Bank 2004, p. 35.

[229] The World Bank resettlement policy (n 54) para 16.

[230] Ibid.

[231] World Bank 2004, pp. 37 and 38.

[232] UN CESCR 1997, para 16.

[233] African Development Bank resettlement policy (n 143) paras 3.4.2 and 3.4.3.

those who have no recognizable right or claim are only eligible for resettlement assistance.[234] The policy of the ADB, however, does not espouse specific eligibility criteria for compensation. Rather, it only indicates that "[t]he absence of formal legal title to land by some affected groups should not be a bar to compensation."[235] It is not clear whether this only applies to those who have traditional rights to the land they occupy, for instance, indigenous peoples, or whether it also includes other legitimate claims to land and a simple occupancy without legal rights or claims. The policy of the IADB is rather silent on the issue of land tenure.

The second criterion, the severity of the impact, pertains to the amount of land expropriated and its impact on the livelihoods of those affected. The general rule, according to the World Bank's Sourcebook, is that if land acquisition affects less than 20% of a family's income-generating asset or productive land, as discussed before, monetary compensation in lieu of replacement of real asset or land is a viable option.[236] Nevertheless, this should be evaluated and flexibly applied on a case-by-case basis by taking different circumstances into account since even a 20% or less of land acquisition can have a significant impact on the income of households with small landholdings.[237] If land acquisition affects more than 20% of the productive land, on the other hand, replacement of land should be the preferred remedy.[238] When it comes to residential and business landholdings, "...necessity of relocation is often used to determine severity of impact".[239] If the land acquisition affects residential and business structures and necessitates the relocation of the affected residents or businesses, it is regarded as severe impact or vice versa.[240] In case of a severe impact, replacement of land and monetary compensation for reconstruction and loss of income, if applicable, need to be provided.[241] In other cases, monetary compensation for the portion of land affected can be sufficient.[242] For displaced persons who are employees, the severity of the impact and, in turn, the commensurate amount of compensation is determined based on the duration of joblessness and the income lost.[243] In any case, borrowing states should make an effort to provide employment opportunities, if possible, and assist displaced persons in restoring and improving their earnings.[244] Overall, the severity of the impact of displacement on the persons affected, which should be assessed taking into account different factors,

---

234 Ibid., paras 3.4.2 and 3.4.3.

235 Asian Development Bank resettlement policy (n 143) para 34(vii).

236 World Bank 2004, pp. 38 and 40–41; see also The World Bank resettlement policy (n 54) para 12.

237 World Bank 2004, p. 38.

238 Ibid., p. 41; see also The World Bank resettlement policy (n 54) para 11.

239 World Bank 2004, p. 43.

240 Ibid., pp. 43 and 44.

241 Ibid.

242 Ibid.

243 Ibid., p. 44.

244 Ibid.

partly determines the type and amount of redress to which displaced persons are entitled.

From the discussion above it is evident that the resettlement policies of the development banks under consideration put a greater emphasis on land particularly as a means of production or source of income. As a result, most of the substantive safeguards envisaged therein also revolve around preserving this income source. This also correlates with the mandates of these banks, which mainly focus on economic issues, and their perception of their role. While land is one of the most, if not the most, important factors in the DID discourse, it is not the sole determinant of the socio-economic wellbeing of displaced persons. Other factors, such as access to adequate housing, access to public services, and maintaining social and cultural ties, are also important, if not indispensable, to achieve the overarching objective of these safeguards, i.e. restoring or improving the livelihoods of displaced persons. The safeguards espoused under the policies of development banks overlook or do not duly appreciate these factors.

9.5.2.2 Safeguards During Displacement

Safeguards during displacement relate to the financial, technical, and other assistance that needs to be provided for displaced persons during the actual relocation to ensure safe and convenient transfer to the resettlement site. The World Bank policy obliges borrowing states to provide necessary assistance, such as logistics and moving allowances, to displaced persons during physical relocation in order to facilitate their transition.[245] Similar rules are reiterated in the policies of the regional development banks.[246] This section will not delve into these further as they appear fairly straightforward.

9.5.2.3 Safeguards After Displacement

As discussed throughout this book, DID often results in long-term socio-economic adversities, which potentially cause the chronic impoverishment of those affected. In some cases, the adverse consequences of DID only materialize after a significant time lapse. In order to prevent or mitigate these long-term consequences, the World Bank policy enunciates that displaced persons should be "offered support after displacement, for a transition period, based on a reasonable estimate of the time likely to be needed to restore their livelihood and standards of living."[247] Accordingly, apart from the replacement of real properties and/or monetary compensation discussed

---

[245] The World Bank resettlement policy (n 54) para 6(b)(i); see also World Bank 2004, p. 260.

[246] African Development Bank resettlement policy (n 143) para 3.3(a); see also Inter-American Development Bank resettlement policy (n 143); see also Asian Development Bank resettlement policy (n 143) para 34.

[247] The World Bank resettlement policy (n 54) para 6(c)(i).

above, states need to provide development assistance, "such as land preparation, credit facilities, training, or job opportunities", to displaced persons or people.[248] While the policies of the regional development banks do not contain comparable provisions, they recognize that all necessary safeguards need to be provided at all phases of displacement and resettlement to sustainably restore or improve the livelihoods of displaced persons.[249] Overall, borrower states need to put in place pertinent rehabilitation measures after relocation.

The nature of the rehabilitation measures varies depending on, *inter alia*, the type of income-generating activities the displaced persons are engaged in and their culture and way of life. In any case, these measures should aim to restore, and possibly improve, the livelihoods of those affected. The World Bank has particularly endorsed the Impoverishment Risk and Reconstruction (IRR) model developed by Michael Cernea after the extensive research he conducted under the auspices of the Bank.[250] By drawing on empirical case studies of projects, the IRR model identified eight common and interdependent adverse consequences of DID, namely landlessness, joblessness, homelessness, marginalization, food insecurity, increased morbidity and mortality, social disarticulation, and loss of access to common resources, and recommended that resettlement measures should be specifically planned to prevent or mitigate these risks.[251]

One of the rehabilitation measures the policy promotes is providing displaced persons with stable or fairly long-term employment opportunities.[252] Temporary jobs, for instance, short-term project-related jobs that do not allow these individuals to restore their livelihoods are not considered adequate measures.[253] As the World Bank also stressed, "[t]emporary employment in project construction and temporary living support, for example, may be desirable forms of short-term assistance, but they do not constitute long-term income restoration."[254] Hence, states should provide sustainable employment opportunities or put place measures that can sustainably restore the income-earning capacity of those uprooted from their homes and residences for development purposes. Overall, after relocation takes place, states need to continue providing assistance and opportunities for displaced persons to improve their livelihoods and to turn involuntary resettlement into a development opportunity as these policies aspire to do.

In a nutshell, a state seeking to obtain funding from IFIs needs to submit a resettlement plan detailing the scope and impacts of the involuntary displacement potentially caused by the given project as well as the safeguards they have in place to avert or

---

[248] Ibid., para 6(c)(ii)and(iii).

[249] African Development Bank resettlement policy (n 143) para 3.3(a); see also Asian Development Bank resettlement policy (n 143) paras 33 and 44; see also Inter-American Development Bank resettlement policy (n 143) para 2.

[250] World Bank 2004, p. 163; see also Cernea 1997; see also Cernea 2000.

[251] World Bank 2004, pp. 163 and 164; see also Cernea 1995, pp. 245–264.

[252] World Bank 2004, p. 69.

[253] Ibid.

[254] Ibid., p. 155.

mitigate the adverse impacts of the involuntary resettlement.[255] This is one of the documents states need to submit as a part of project appraisal. A state seeking funding from these banks needs to demonstrate that the resettlement plan complies with the policy standards on involuntary resettlement discussed above.[256] The IFI concerned assesses whether or not the resettlement plan complies with its policy standards. The banks may decide not to finance the project or negotiate the details of the project with the state concerned if the resettlement plan falls short of meeting their policy standards.[257] There are several cases where the development banks under consideration refused to finance development projects for non-compliance with their policies. This, however, does not always result in the amendment of the resettlement plan or the discontinuation of the project by the state concerned. In some cases, states obtain alternative sources of funding from other countries or institutions. For instance, this was the case with the Gilgel Gibe III dam project in Ethiopia mentioned in Chap. 1 of this book. The Dam was funded by the loan obtained from the financial institutions of China and the local banks after the World Bank and the AfDB refused to finance the project for a lack of compliance with their policies.[258] The existence of these alternative funding sources is not always a negative thing as it gives states more options and increases the likelihoods of obtaining funding. However, some of these alternative funding sources do not have extensive policy standards on social and environmental issues, and rarely require states to comply with standards on, for instance, involuntary displacement before approving funding.[259] Hence, the potential adverse consequences of the project concerned are not often taken into account as a condition of loan.

---

[255] World Bank Resettlement Policy (n 54) paras 17 and 21; see also World Bank 2004, p. 27; see also African Development Bank resettlement policy (n 143) para 3.4.4; see also Asian Development Bank Resettlement Policy (n 143) para 38.

[256] World Bank Resettlement Policy (n 54) para 22.

[257] World Bank 2011a, p. 91.

[258] The Economist, Ethiopia opens Africa's tallest and most controversial dam, available at https://www.economist.com/middle-east-and-africa/2016/12/21/ethiopia-opens-africas-tallest-and-most-controversial-dam, accessed 1 July 2025; see also Sean Avery, Fears over Ethiopian dam's costly impact on environment, people, available at https://theconversation.com/fears-over-ethiopian-dams-costly-impact-on-environment-people-80757, accessed 1 July 2025; see also The Oakland Institute 2019, pp. 8 and 9. This is not an isolated incident; several other projects initially rejected by the World Bank or other IFIs, in particular, projects in low-income countries, have been funded by Chinese lending institutions. In fact, over the past couple of decades, China has emerged as "one of the largest creditors" globally (see World Bank, International Debt Statistics 2022, available at https://openknowledge.worldbank.org/entities/publication/47f55cbf-ee14-531a-8acb-8e2406f4354d, accessed 26 July 2025, 8 and 9; see also Kai Wang, 'China: Is it burdening poor countries with unsustainable debt?', BBC, 6 January 2022, available at https://www.bbc.com/news/59585507, accessed 1 July 2025; see also Chen 2020, pp. 436 and 437).

[259] Avery (n 258).

9.6 Policy Limitations: The Gap Between Policy and Practice

The policy frameworks discussed above provide important normative standards to inform and guide the process of involuntary displacement prompted by development projects, particularly in light of the absence of a specific and comprehensive legal framework on DID in international law. However, these frameworks also exhibit certain shortcomings or limitations. Some of these have already been addressed in relation to the corresponding policy standards. This section identifies and examines some of the main general policy limitations.

The World Bank policy on involuntary resettlement is considered to be one of the most comprehensive resettlement policies.[260] It contains important safeguards aimed at preventing displacement and improving or restoring the livelihoods of those affected when displacement is inevitable as elucidated above. The policy has also offered states and other stakeholders a much-needed guidance in planning and implementing involuntary resettlement. Particularly in countries where there are no legal or policy frameworks on involuntary displacement or resettlement, the policy has helped to improve the protection of the rights of displaced persons.[261] The policy has also significantly shaped legal and policy developments, both nationally and internationally. For instance, the "Basic Principles and Guidelines on Development-based Evictions and Displacement", advanced by the UN Special Rapporteur on Adequate Housing and discussed in part II of this book, were heavily influenced by the resettlement policy of the World Bank.[262] Moreover, to a certain extent, the policy can also fill the "protection gap"[263] in international law given the lack of a comprehensive and specific hard law or soft law framework on DID. Besides, while the discrepancies identified in the preceding sections cannot be overlooked, significant portions of the substantive and procedural safeguards envisaged under the policy are in line with relevant human rights norms and standards despite not explicitly mentioning human rights or referring to human rights frameworks. In some cases, they are even more comprehensive and specific—for instance, the rules related to land rights.

However, a significant portion of the involuntary displacements caused by the development projects financed by the World Bank falls short of upholding the main objective of the policy, i.e. improving or at least restoring the livelihoods of displaced persons.[264] In fact, several studies have depicted that a large number of development

---

[260] Clark 2002, p. 205.

[261] Kangave 2012, p. 376.

[262] Bugalski 2016, p. 8; see also The Special Rapporteur on Adequate Housing 2007.

[263] As mentioned in Chap. 6, the instruments on internal displacement, i.e. UN Guiding Principles on IDPs and Kampala Convention, only marginally deal with internal displacement caused by development projects. While the human rights protections of the people affected by DID can be found scattered in different general and special human rights frameworks, there is no comprehensive instrument in international law that specifically addresses the socio-economic and human rights risks DID poses and provides guidance on resettlement.

[264] Clark 2002, p. 212.

projects financed by the Bank have instead resulted in the chronic impoverishment and marginalization of the people displaced to make room for these development projects.[265] For instance, a study conducted on selected dams financed by the Bank found that the resettlement programs in most of these projects have not succeeded in restoring, much less improving, the livelihoods of those affected.[266] This coupled with the fact that DID often affects those who are politically and economically marginalized ostensibly goes against the very mandate of the Bank, i.e. alleviating poverty and promoting development.[267] Overall, "evidence suggests that the policy often fails to achieve its core objective of avoiding or mitigating adverse impacts of displacement and that Bank projects have frequently caused violations of human rights."[268] Hence, there is a prevalent gap between policy and practice. One of the factors that contributed to this gap is the shortcomings of the policies themselves with which this section engages.

This section primarily focuses on the World Bank for pragmatic reasons. As it is the largest lending institution, particularly for developing countries, there is relatively more data and literature to assess the long-term effects of the projects it finances and the effectiveness of its policies. While the regional development banks also share some of the challenges and limitations discussed below, there is insufficient and inconclusive data to draw general conclusions. Thus, the following section will elucidate the main reasons for the prevalent gap between policy and practice in relation to the World Bank's resettlement policy.

9.6.1 Failure to Embrace a Human Rights-Based Approach

As discussed in relation to the right to development in the previous chapter, a human rights-based approach entails integrating human rights norms and principles—both as means and end goals—in development activities. In the context of DID, it requires framing the socio-economic and cultural impacts of involuntary displacement or resettlement as human rights issues, which imply rights and obligations, and seeking rights-based solutions to address those adverse impacts. To this end, the process of DID—from the approval of the development project concerned to the planning and implementation of resettlement plans—should be evaluated and implemented in accordance with human rights standards. Moreover, the success of a resettlement plan should be measured based on the extent to which it has protected or advanced the rights of those involuntarily displaced. Since DID interferes with and potentially

[265] Ibid., pp. 212 and 213; see also Baird et al. 2015, pp. 1080 and 1081; see also Clark 1997, p. 215.

[266] Picciotto et al. 2017, pp. 9–12. The Bank's own review conducted on the projects it financed between 1986 and 1993 had also reached the same conclusion- "[U]nsatisfactory performance in reestablishing resettlers at an equal or better level of living" (see World Bank 1994b, p. 110; see also Clark 1997, p. 219). This is the last extensive review the Bank has undertaken on the resettlement practices of the projects it finances.

[267] Clark 2002, pp. 213 and 214; see also Downing 2012, p. 14.

[268] IDI et al. 2013, para 4.

violates a range of human rights as has been established in the preceding chapters, an involuntary resettlement approach that does not recognize and address these human rights impacts is ostensibly inadequate.

The World Bank has failed to systematically and consistently embrace this approach in its resettlement policy and practice. The lack of a human rights-based approach to involuntary displacement in the Bank's resettlement policy is evident in several areas. As discussed before, there is no mention of human rights or a reference to human rights norms or treaties in the operational policy despite the inherent connection between the subject matters the policy deals with and human rights. Human rights norms are not adequately integrated into the language, formulation, and substance of the relevant policies of the Bank. As Natalie Bugalski argued, "…the failure to ground the policy in human rights law and fully integrate human rights standards into policy language means that requirements and entitlements can be both strengthened and diluted in response to the political vagaries influencing the Bank."[269] Some of the normative deficiencies or inconsistencies of the policy identified in the preceding sections are also partly attributable to this lack of mainstreaming of human rights norms in policy standards.

In addition, the World Bank resettlement policy does not require states to conduct human rights impact assessments for development projects that cause involuntary displacement; nor does it have a separate policy on that. While the merits of undertaking a human rights impact assessment for all development and investment activities that can potentially impact the enjoyment of rights is widely accepted, even for business corporations,[270] the Bank is yet to adopt a policy standard acknowledging and requiring that. Particularly given the wide range of human rights risk that DID poses, human rights impact assessment of the projects that cause involuntary displacement is indispensable to avoid or mitigate those risks.[271] As several NGOs working on issues related to displacement stressed in their joint report:

> Undertaking human rights impact assessments is a precondition for ensuring that the Bank is not complicit in human rights violations as a result of displacement caused by its projects. It is also an essential foundation for designing Resettlement Plans…that effectively achieve policy objectives, including conceiving and executing resettlement as a sustainable development program and improving the livelihoods and standards of living of those resettled.[272]

The Environmental and Social Framework of the Bank only requires borrower states to undertake "environmental and social assessment" of proposed projects,[273] which "will inform the design of the project, and be used to identify mitigation

[269] Bugalski 2016, p. 9.

[270] The Guiding Principles on Business and Human Rights: Implementing the United Nations "Protect, Respect and Remedy" Framework, 2011, HR/PUB/11/04.

[271] IDI et al. 2013, para 46.

[272] Ibid.

[273] The World Bank, Assessment and Management of Environmental and Social Risks and Impacts (hereinafter "environmental and social assessment policy"), in the Environmental and Social Framework, 2017, paras 3, 15, and 23. "The term 'environmental and social assessment' is a generic term that describes the process of analysis and planning used by the Borrower to ensure the environmental

measures and actions and to improve decision making".[274] The assessment needs to identify the potential direct and indirect environmental and social risks of the project and explore alternatives and measures to avoid and/or mitigate these risks.[275] Among the social risks listed under the Framework that need to be covered by the assessment are the "negative economic and social impacts relating to the involuntary taking of land or restrictions on land use".[276] The framework does not explicitly mention human rights risks among the risks that need to be addressed by the assessment. Overall, borrower states need to conduct a risk assessment of the involuntary displacements potentially caused by the projects they are proposing as part of the general environmental and social assessment required for the projects financed by the Bank.

A human rights impact assessment, however, is wider in scope than the social and environmental impact assessments required by the World Bank policies. "[It] looks not only at current assets, living standards, and incomes of affected households and communities, as currently required by the policy, but…also covers the potential for lost resources and opportunities for self-development to which they would have otherwise had access."[277] A human rights impact assessment also covers the effect of the project on all rights, not only on those related to the economic well-being of the people affected. Moreover, a human rights impact assessment should not only be conducted before the project commences but also undertaken regularly *ex post facto* or after resettlement to ensure that the rights of those affected are fully realized and the objectives of the policy are being met.[278] On the contrary, the policy discussed above only requires states to undertake a socio-economic impact assessment before the project begins, although, in practice, even this is not fully complied with by states.[279]

Overall, its failure to embrace or adopt a human rights-based approach in its resettlement policy and practice is one of the shortcomings of the World Bank that has contributed to the prevalent gap between policy and practice.

---

and social impacts and risks of a project are identified, avoided, minimized, reduced or mitigated" (see Environmental and social assessment policy (n 273) para 1).

[274] Environmental and social assessment policy (n 273) para 3.

[275] Ibid., paras 24–27.

[276] Ibid., para 28.

[277] IDI et al. 2013, para 47.

[278] Ibid., para 50.

[279] For instance, a comprehensive review of projects financed by the Bank undertaken by Michael Carnea in 1994 revealed that only 45% of the active projects over the past eight years prior to study undertaken impact assessments (see IDI et al. 2013, para 52). In more recent cases, the Inspection Panel has also dealt with several cases where adequate socio-economic impact assessments are not undertaken and how that adversely affected the restoration of livelihoods or exacerbated the risk of impoverishment (see IDI et al. 2013, para 52; see also World Bank Inspection Panel, Investigation Report, Ghana: West African Gas Pipeline Project, IDA Guarantee No. B-006-0-GH, 2008, available at https://documents.worldbank.org/en/publication/documents-reports/documentdetail/664021468003035202/ghana-west-african-gas-pipeline-project-inspection-panel-request-for-inspection, accessed 1 July 2025).

9.6.2 *Inadequate Monitoring and Follow-Up Mechanisms*

The World Bank does not have systematic and comprehensive monitoring and follow-up mechanisms in place to ensure that borrower states have complied with its resettlement policy and fully implemented the resettlement plan they proposed. The obligation not only to prepare and implement but also to monitor the implementation of the resettlement plan—the main framework governing involuntary resettlement in a given project—rests on states.[280] The borrower is expected to inform the Bank about the progress of the implementation of the resettlement plan and the Bank's supervision is essentially based on information received from the borrower.[281] The policy does not require the Bank to undertake independent supervisions.

One of the main problems recurrently identified by the studies undertaken on Bank-financed projects that caused displacement is the absence of sufficient supervision and monitoring by the Bank of resettlement processes and outcomes.[282] The Inspection Panel, a body of the World Bank mandated to receive complaints related to the policies of the Bank as will be discussed below, has also found in its report that, on several occasions, the management of the Bank has failed to follow up on the restoration and improvement of the livelihoods of those affected after relocation.[283] For instance, in the case of "Cambodia Land Management and Administration Project", the Panel found that the management of the Bank had not been aware of the adverse impacts of the displacement caused by the project due to a lack of adequate monitoring and follow-up.[284]

Similarly, the responsibility to implement, monitor, and assess the performance or the implementation of the environmental and social assessment is also primarily left to states,[285] with little oversight from the Bank. States are required to submit regular reports to the Bank and facilitate field visits by the Bank officials when necessary.[286] The Bank's monitoring and supervision are mainly dependent on the information provided by states. Reports also show that the Bank does not duly consider the success of the project in addressing the social and environmental concerns including involuntary resettlement as a part of the development outcome.[287] In other words, resettlement outcomes are not adequately and systematically monitored and evaluated. The Independent Evaluation Group (IEG), for instance, suggests that the Bank should put

---

280 The World Bank resettlement policy (n 54) para 18; see also Kangave 2012, p. 358.

281 The World Bank resettlement policy (n 54) paras 23 and 24.

282 Bugalski 2016, p. 28.

283 World Bank Inspection Panel 2016, p. 17; see also Kangave 2012, p. 357.

284 World Bank Inspection Panel 2016, p. 17.

285 Environmental and social assessment policy (n 273) para 45.

286 Ibid., paras 47 and 49.

287 IDI et al. 2013, para 92.

in place performance indicators to evaluate resettlement outcomes and systematically collect data and monitor the implementation of its policy safeguards.[288]

Moreover, accurate and timely information about the process and performance of resettlement programs are not publicly available.[289] This hinders NGOs and other stakeholders from actively following up on resettlement outcomes. Overall, a lack of adequate follow-up and monitoring mechanisms is one of the policy limitations that has contributed to the poor implementation of the resettlement policy of the Bank.

9.6.3 Lack of Effective Remedy or Accountability Procedures

The other limitation of the involuntary resettlement policy of the World Bank is the lack of adequate accountability and remedial procedures for non-compliance with the Bank's policy.[290] The World Bank resettlement policy does not include a right to effective remedy or a specific complaint procedure for violations and harm caused by the projects financed by the Bank.[291]

Generally, complaints related to the resettlement policy of the Bank can be submitted to the Inspection Panel—a quasi-judicial and permanent body of the Bank originally established by the Board of Executive Directors in 1993 with the mandate of receiving complaints about breaches of the policies of the Bank.[292] The Panel

---

[288] The Independent Evaluation Group (IEG) 2010, p. 105 (The Independent Evaluation Group (IEG) is an independent group within the World Bank that evaluates the activities of the Bank); see also IDI et al. 2013, para 93.

[289] IDI et al. 2013, para 89.

[290] It is important to note that this book mainly focuses on the analysis of existing norms, not the effectiveness of the enforcement of those norms. In the context of IFIs, however, it is important to discuss the enforcement mechanisms for two reasons. First, IFIs have the leverage to demand states to comply with their policies as states rely on their financial support. Second, it is important to look into whether or not the policies of IFIs put in place sufficient remedial or enforcement mechanisms in order to answer the central question this chapter poses, i.e. to what extent IFIs protect the rights of people(s) affected by DID.

[291] IDI et al. 2013, para 98.

[292] International Bank for Reconstruction and Development and International Development Association, Resolution No. IBRD 93-10 and Resolution No. IDA 93-6 (1993); see also Clark 2002, pp. 217 and 218. The Resolution establishing the Panel has been recently revised with some amendments (see International Bank for Reconstruction and Development and International Development Association, Resolution No. IBRD 2020-0004 and Resolution No. IDA 2020-0003, The World Bank Inspection Panel, September 8, 2020). This revision was part of the recent restructuring accountability procedures at the Bank. In September 2020, the Board of the Bank established an Accountability Mechanism (AM), which consists of the Inspection Panel and the dispute Resolution Service (DRS) (see International Bank for Reconstruction and Development and International Development Association, Resolution No. IBRD 2020-0005 and Resolution No. IDA 2020-0004, The World Bank Accountability Mechanism September 8, 2020). The DRS facilitates voluntary dispute resolution efforts between complainants and borrowers as a part of the Inspection Panel Procedure (see Resolution No. IBRD 2020-0005 Resolution No. IDA 2020-0004, para 9). It does

consists of three members from different member states of the Bank who are nominated by the President and appointed by the Executive Directors of the Bank.[293] Members of the Panel serve in their individual capacity but are considered officials of the Bank and are, therefore, bound by the rules and obligations applicable to Bank officials.[294] Among the complaints received by the inspection panel, issues related to involuntary displacement have been the third most cited subject matters,[295] which also shows the gravity of the problem.

A group of individuals or people living in project-affected areas or adversely affected by Bank-financed projects or their representatives can directly submit complaints to the Inspection Panel after exhausting other remedies within the Bank—for instance, raising their concern to the management of the Bank.[296] "The Panel provides a forum where local people can voice their concerns at the highest level of the institution."[297] The complainants, or "requesters" as they are formally known,[298] can request the Inspection Panel to conduct an independent investigation into the role of the Bank in the project concerned and its alleged adverse impacts.[299] It is important to note that the Panel is only mandated to investigate actions or omissions of the Bank rather than those of the borrower state.[300] Generally, "…the Panel evaluates the extent to which a project is in compliance with Bank policies, and the harm, if any, suffered by the claimants as a result of policy violations."[301] To this end, the Panel also considers the written response of the management of the Bank,[302]

---

not provide independent remedies per se; hence, the discussion in this section will only focus on the Inspection Panel.

293 Resolution No. IBRD 2020-0004 and Resolution No. IDA 2020-0003 (n 292) para 3.

294 Ibid., para 11.

295 IDI et al. 2013, para 4; see also Robinson 2003, p. 31; see also Zvobgo and Graham 2020, pp. 425, 427.

296 Resolution No. IBRD 2020-0004 and Resolution No. IDA 2020-0003 (n 292) paras 13 and 14; see also Clark 2002, p. 218. The Panel's operating procedures require that complaints need to be submitted by two or more individuals or their local representatives; non-local representatives can only submit complaints in exceptional cases (see The Inspection Panel at the World Bank, Operating Procedures, April 2014, available at https://www.inspectionpanel.org/about-us/panel-mandate-and-procedures, accessed 1 July 2025, para 10).

297 Clark 2002, pp. 217 and 218.

298 The Inspection Panel Operating Procedures (n 296) para 1; the newly revised draft of the Operating Procedures has been prepared by the Bank and is awaiting final adoption.

299 Resolution No. IBRD 2020-0004 and Resolution No. IDA 2020-0003 (n 292) para 17; see also Resolution No. IBRD 2020-0005 and Resolution No. IDA 2020-0004 (n 292) para 7.

300 Resolution No. IBRD 2020-0004 and Resolution No. IDA 2020-0003 (n 292) para 15; see also Clark 2002, p. 218.

301 Clark 2002, p. 218.

302 Resolution No. IBRD 2020-0004 and Resolution No. IDA 2020-0003 (n 292) paras 19–21; see also Clark 2002, p. 218. The management of the bank for the purpose of this procedure refers to the institutions and offices of the Bank involved in the project appraisal or implementation (see The Inspection Panel Operating Procedures (n 296) 9).

and recommends the Executive Directors as to whether or not an independent investigation is necessary.[303] If the Executive directors approve the investigation,[304] the Panel will conduct the investigation using relevant methods including interviews and field visits.[305] Finally, the Panel prepares a report on its findings and submits its recommendations to the Board of Executive Directors of the Bank.[306] Then the management of the Bank is expected to come up with an action plan to implement the recommendations of the Panel and propose remedies that need to be taken to rectify the harm caused by the breach of the policy, if any, which need to be approved by the Board of Executive Directors.[307] The management is responsible for implementing and monitoring the implementation of these remedies.[308]

Hence, even in cases where the Panel decides that there has been a breach of the Bank's policy, which, in turn, has caused harm to those affected, there are no remedial procedures in place to make the damage good or redress the harm. The discretion to decide the action that needs to be taken to rectify the damage is left to the Board and management of the Bank.[309] The Panel is not empowered to evaluate the adequacy of the remedial plan proposed by the management or monitor its implementation.[310] There is no guarantee that the management and the Board will act in the interest of the people affected by the Bank's projects and there is no oversight to ensure that. As Dana Clark pointed out:

> Herein lies the weak link in the process: the Inspection Panel does not have oversight authority over the implementation of those remedial measures; nor is it able to provide the Board with an assessment of whether Management's proposed remedial measures would satisfy the concerns of the claimants and/or bring the project into compliance with Bank policy. The lack of independent oversight has meant that remedial action plans do not always lead to satisfactory remedies or action.[311]

Hence, not only the necessity of an independent investigation but also the remedies that need to be taken to rectify the violations found in the investigation is determined by the Executive Directors of the Bank. In other words, the remedial procedure for non-compliance of the Bank with its own policies is effectively controlled by the management and Executive Directors. This is where the accountability gap lies.

There are, however, cases where the Inspection Panel procedure has led to the provision of effective remedies. In a few cases, the management of the Bank, for

---

303 Resolution No. IBRD 2020-0004 and Resolution No. IDA 2020-0003 (n 292) paras 22–27.

304 Ibid., para 29.

305 Ibid., paras 34 and 35; see also The Inspection Panel Operating Procedures (n 296) para 54; see also Clark 2002, p. 218.

306 Resolution No. IBRD 2020-0004 and Resolution No. IDA 2020-0003 (n 292) para 36; see also Clark 2002, p. 218.

307 Resolution No. IBRD 2020-0004 and Resolution No. IDA 2020-0003 (n 292) paras 40 and 41; see also Clark 2002, p. 218.

308 Resolution No. IBRD 2020-0004 and Resolution No. IDA 2020-0003 (n 292) para 47. The management is also required to submit progress reports to the Board.

309 IDI et al. 2013, para 98.

310 Bugalski 2016, p. 35.

311 Clark 2002, pp. 218 and 219; see also Robinson 2003, p. 32.

instance, has decided to cease the involvement of the Bank in projects that fail to comply with its policies based on the investigation of the Panel.[312]

In any case, whether or not the people affected by the projects financed by the Bank get effective remedies is left in the hands of the Board and the management of the Bank without any oversight. "This fundamental accountability gap threatens to render the safeguard policies and Inspection Panel meaningless for people who are harmed as a result of Bank-supported operations."[313] The recent amendment of the Resolution that establishes and sets out the mandates of the Inspection Panel did not address this accountability gap. Hence, the lack of effective remedial procedures for non-compliance with the Bank's policies is one of the limitations of the resettlement policy of the World Bank.

9.7 Conclusion

As they finance development projects that potentially cause involuntary displacement, IFIs play a vital role in setting policies and guiding resettlement practices around the world. This chapter has set out to elucidate the substantive contents of the involuntary resettlement policies adopted by these institutions and assess their role and adequacy in protecting the rights of people affected by DID particularly focusing on the policies and practices of the World Bank.

The chapter commenced by analysing the role, or lack thereof, of these development banks in advancing human rights, which has induced strong criticisms from human rights experts and scholars. IFIs particularly the World Bank have been heavily criticized for not adequately addressing the human rights impacts of their activities, supporting countries with poor human rights records, and failing to systematically integrate human rights norms and principles into their operations. Generally, critics agree that human rights have a marginal place—are even considered a taboo—in the policies and practices of these institutions. This marginality of human rights is partly attributable to the legal constraints arising from their constitutions and the prevailing uncertainty in international law as to their human rights obligations. The development banks covered in this chapter were designed to be apolitical institutions and refrain from taking into account political considerations in their decision-making, which has been conservatively construed to preclude them from engaging in human rights issues. Moreover, whether and to what extent international organizations, development banks in this context, have human rights obligations in international law remains contentious. However, it is widely accepted that these institutions are bound by human rights obligations emanating from customary international law, their constitutions,

[312] Clark 2002, p. 219. For instance, in the Arun Dam Project case in Nepal, the Bank decided to terminate its financial support after the panel found non-compliance with the resettlement policy of the Bank (see Robinson 2003, p. 31). Similarly, in the Mumbai Urban Transport Project case, the Bank decided to cease funding after the investigation of the Panel disclosed non-compliance with the Bank's policies (see Bugalski 2016, p. 36).

[313] IDI et al. 2013, para 98.

and international agreements they are a party to and that they have a duty to, at least, respect human rights. The interpretation of the Articles of Agreement of the World Bank is also evolving and the Bank has been increasingly engaging in human rights and other issues that are traditionally considered political. Nevertheless, despite this progress, the attitude of the Bank towards human rights and its active efforts to advance human rights leave much to be desired.

One of the areas of operations of these banks where the protection of human rights is at stake is the financing of development projects that cause involuntary displacement and resettlement. As this chapter has elucidated, a significant portion of the development projects financed by these banks, particularly the World Bank as it is the largest lending institution, lead to involuntary displacement. Consequently, the development banks covered under this chapter have developed involuntary resettlement policies that provide guidance for borrower states in designing, approving, and implementing involuntary resettlements caused by development projects. The overarching objective of these policies is to avoid displacement, if feasible, and prevent or mitigate the adverse impacts of displacement when it is inevitable. To these ends, the policies have put in place various procedural and substantive safeguards that apply at all phases of displacement and resettlement. These include, *inter alia*, meaningful consultation with those affected, provision of in-kind and monetary compensation, relocation assistance, and rehabilitation measures. These safeguards primarily aim at restoring and preferably improving the livelihoods of displaced persons. Most of these safeguards are in line with the relevant human rights standards, although they do not explicitly mention human rights norms or refer to human rights frameworks. In some respects, the policies also envisage progressive standards—for instance, extending land rights to those who rely on land for their livelihoods regardless of their identity—that can potentially fill the gaps in international law. As pointed out in this chapter, however, some of these safeguards fall short of meeting the standards set by the pertinent human rights norms. For instance, the policies neither require development projects that potentially cause displacement to be justified based on a public interest requirement nor the people affected by the project to be consulted about the necessity of the project. The other shortcomings relate to a lack of policy guidance on eviction or protection of the right to housing and a lack of special protection of indigenous peoples' land rights.

These policy safeguards, however, do not always translate into equitable practices that turn involuntary displacement into development opportunities as they aim to achieve. As several studies attest, people displaced by the projects financed by these banks, particularly the World Bank, often face a range of socio-economic and human rights risks. Involuntary resettlements in many cases have resulted in the chronic impoverishment of those affected, which contradicts the Banks' overall mandate. Hence, while these resettlement policies offer much-needed guidance for states in designing and implementing involuntary resettlement, there is a prevalent gap between policy and practice. As the chapter has demonstrated using the World Bank policy and practices, this is partly attributable to the limitations of the policy. Apart from the specific shortcomings mentioned above, the policy grapples with some general limitations. These limitations include a lack of adequate integration of human rights norms into the policies and practices of the Bank, a lack of adequate follow-up procedures on the implementation of resettlement plans, and a lack of effective remedies and accountability procedures for violation of the Bank's policies. Hence, it is imperative to address these shortcomings to create a resettlement policy and practice that is responsive to the needs of displaced persons and, indeed, can turn resettlement into a development opportunity.

References

African Development Bank (AfDB) (2013) AfDB in Brief. African Development Bank.

Alston P (2015), Report of the Special Rapporteur on extreme poverty and human rights, 4 August 2015, A/70/274.

Baird I G, Shoemaker B P, Manorom K (2015) The People and their River, the World Bank and its Dam: Revisiting the Xe Bang Fai River in Laos. (2015) 46(5) Development and Change 1080–1105.

Bøås M (1998) Governance as multilateral development bank policy: The cases of the African development bank and the Asian development bank. (1998) 10(2) The European Journal of Development Research 117–134.

Bradlow D D (2010) International Law and the Operations of the International Financial Institutions. In: Bradlow D D, Hunter D B (eds) International Financial Institutions and International Law. Kluwer Law International.

Bugalski N (2016) The Demise of Accountability at the World Bank. (2016) 31(1) American University International Law Review 1–56.

Byrnes A (2011) The Asian Development Bank and the Role of Human Rights in the Pursuit of Just and Sustainable Development in the Asia-Pacific Region: An Advocacy Role for Australia? (2011) 18 Australian International Law Journal 1–21.

Cernea M M (1995) Understanding and Preventing Impoverishment from Displacement: Reflections on the state of Knowledge. (1995) 8(3) Journal of Refugee Studies 245–264.

Cernea M M (1997) The Risks and Reconstruction Model for Resettling Displaced Populations. (1997) 25(10) World Development 1569–1587.

Cernea M M (2000) Risks, safeguards, and reconstruction: a model for population displacement and resettlement. In: Cernea M M, McDowell C (eds) Risks and Reconstruction: Experiences of Resettlers and Refugees. The World Bank, Washington DC.

Cernea M M (2008) Compensation and Investment in Resettlement: Theory, Practice, Pitfalls, and Needed Policy Reform. In: Cernea M, Mathur H M (eds) Can Compensation Prevent Impoverishment? Reforming Resettlement through Investments. Oxford University Press, Oxford.

Chen M (2020) Beyond Donation: China's Policy Banks and the Reshaping of Development Finance. (2020) 55 Studies in Comparative International Development 436–459.

Ciorciari J D (2000) The Lawful Scope of Human Rights Criteria in World Bank Credit Decisions: An Interpretive Analysis of the IBRD and IDA Articles of Agreement. (2000) 33(2) Cornell International Law Journal 331–371.

Cisse H (2012) Should the Political Prohibition in Charters of International Financial Institutions Be Revisited: The Case of the World Bank. (2012) 3 World Bank Legal Review 59–92.

Clapham A (2006) Human Rights Obligations of Non-State Actors. Oxford University Press, Oxford.

Clark D (1997) The World Bank and Development-Induced Displacement in South Asia. (1997) 4(2) The Brown Journal of World Affairs 215–231.

Clark D L (2002) The World Bank and Human Rights: The Need for Greater Accountability. (2002) 15 Harvard Human Rights Journal 205–226.
Crippa L A (2010) Multilateral Development Banks and Human Rights Responsibility. (2010) 25(3) American University International Law Review 531–577.
Danino R (2006) Legal Opinion on Human Rights and the Work of the World Bank. 27 January 2006.
Darrow M (2003) Between Light and Shadow: The World Bank, The International Monetary Fund and International Human Rights Law. Hart Publishing.
d'Aspremont J (2011) The Multifaceted Concept of the Autonomy of International Organizations and International Legal Discourse. In: Collins R, White N D (eds) International Organizations and the Idea of Autonomy. Routledge Publishing.
Downing T E (2012) Creating Poverty: the Flawed Economic Logic of the World Bank's Revised Involuntary Resettlement Policy. 12 Forced Migration Review 13–14.
Evans J (2013) Abuse-Free Development: How the World Bank Should Safeguard Against Human Rights Violations. (2013) 107 Proceedings of the Annual Meeting- American Society of International Law (International Law in a Multipolar World) 298–302.
Fujita S (2011) The challenges of mainstreaming human rights in the World Bank. (2011) 15(3) The International Journal of Human Rights 374–396.
Fujita S (2013) The World Bank, Asian Development Bank and Human Rights: Developing Standards of Transparency, Participation and Accountability. Edward Elgar Publishing.
Human Rights Council (2014) Report of the Independent Expert on the effects of foreign debt and other related international financial obligations of States on the full enjoyment of all human rights, particularly economic, social and cultural rights, Juan Pablo Bohoslavsky, 22 December 2014, A/HRC/28/59.
Human Rights Council (2017) Report of the Independent Expert on the promotion of a democratic and equitable international order, 20 July 2017, A/HRC/36/40.
Inclusive Development International (IDI), International Accountability Project (IAP), Bank Information Center (BIC), Habitat International Coalition- Housing and Land Rights Network (HIC-HLRN) (2013) Reforming the World Bank Policy on Involuntary Resettlement, Submission to the World Bank Safeguards Review, April 2013.
Independent Evaluation Group (IEG) (2010) Safeguards and Sustainability Policies in a Changing World: An Independent Evaluation of the World Bank Group Experience. The World Bank, Washington DC.
Inspection Panel (2016) Involuntary Resettlement, Emerging Lessons Series No. 1. The World Bank.
Kangave J (2012) Investigating the failure of resettlement and rehabilitation in development projects: a critical analysis of the World Bank's policy on involuntary resettlement using lessons from Uganda's Bujagali hydroelectric project. (2012) 45(2) University of British Columbia Law Review 329–392.
Koenig D (2020) Advantages and obstacles to retrofitting benefit-sharing after development-induced displacement and resettlement. (2020) 39(5) Impact Assessment and Project Appraisal 417–428.
Mcbeth A (2006) Breaching the Vacuum: A Consideration of the Role of International Human Rights Law in the Operations of the International Financial Institutions. (2006) 10(4) The International Journal of Human Rights 385–404.
Mclnerney-Lankford S (2009) Human Rights and Development: A Comment on Challenges and Opportunities from a Legal Perspective. (2009) 1(1) Journal of Human Rights Practice 51–82.
Mclnerney-Lankford S, Sano H-O (2010) Human Rights Indicators in Development: An Introduction. The World Bank, Washington DC.
Oakland Institute (2019) "How They Tricked Us": Living with the Gibe III Dam and Sugarcane Plantations in Southwest Ethiopia. The Oakland Institute.

OHCHR (2019) Human Rights and Development Trust Fund Launch: Statement by UN High Commissioner for Human Rights, Michelle Bachelet, 12 April 2019, available at https://www.ohchr.org/en/newsevents/pages/DisplayNews.aspx?NewsID=24487&LangID=E, accessed 1 July 2025.

Pahuja S (2011) Decolonizing International Law: Development, Economic Growth and the Politics of Universality. Cambridge University Press, Cambridge.

Picciotto R, Van Wicklin W, Rice E (eds) (2017) Involuntary Resettlement Comparative Perspectives, World Bank Series on Evaluation and Development Volume 2, 2nd edn. Routledge, New York.

Robinson C W (2003) Risks and Rights: The Causes, Consequences, and Challenges of Development-Induced Displacement. The Brookings Institution-SAIS Project on Internal Displacement, An Occasional Paper.

Sarfaty G A (2009) Why Culture Matters in International Institutions: The Marginality of Human Rights at the World Bank. (2009) 103(4) American Journal of International Law 647–683.

Sarfaty G A (2012) Values in Translation: Human Rights and the Culture of the World Bank. Stanford University Press, Stanford, California.

Skogly S (2001) The Human Rights Obligations of the World Bank and the International Monetary Fund. Cavendish Publishing.

Skogly S I (2003) The Human Rights Obligations of the World Bank and the International Monetary Fund. In: Van Genugten W, Hunt P, Mathews S (eds) World Bank, IMF, and Human Rights. Wolf Legal Publishers, Nijmegen.

Special Rapporteur on Adequate Housing (2007) Basic Principles and Guidelines on Development-based Evictions and Displacement, 05 February 2007, A/HRC/4/18.

Terminski B (2015) Development-Induced Displacement and Resettlement: Causes, Consequences, and Socio-Legal Context. Ibidem-Verlag, Stuttgart.

UN Committee on Economic, Social and Cultural Rights (UN CESCR) (1991) General Comment No. 4: The Right to Adequate Housing (Article 11 (1) of the Covenant), 13 December 1991, E/1992/23.

UN Committee on Economic, Social and Cultural Rights (UN CESCR) (1997) General Comment No. 7: The right to adequate housing (Article 11.1): forced evictions, 20 May 1997, E/1998/22.

UN Committee on Economic, Social and Cultural Rights (UN CESCR) (1999) General Comment No. 13: The Right to Education (Article 13 of the Covenant), 8 December 1999, E/C.12/1999/10.

UN Committee on Economic, Social and Cultural Rights (UN CESCR) (2000) General Comment No. 14: The Right to the Highest Attainable Standard of Health (Article 12), 11 August 2000, E/C.12/2000/4.

UN Committee on Economic, Social and Cultural Rights (UN CESCR) (2006) General Comment No. 18: The Right to Work (Article 6 of the Covenant), 6 February 2006, E/C.12/GC/18.

UN Commission on Human Rights (2006) The right to food. Report of the Special Rapporteur on the right to food, Jean Ziegler, 20 March 2006, E/CN.4/2006/44.

van Den Meerssche D (2021) A Legal Black Hole in the Cosmos of Virtue—The Politics of Human Rights Critique Against the World Bank. (2021) 21(1) Human Rights Law Review 80–107.

van der Ploeg L, Vanclay F (2017) A Human Rights-based Approach to Project Induced Displacement and Resettlement. (2017) 35(1) Impact Assessment and Project Appraisal 34–52.

Verdirame G (2011) The UN and Human Rights: Who Guards the Guardians? Cambridge University Press, Cambridge.

World Bank (1994a) Governance: the World Bank Experience. The World Bank.

World Bank (1994b) Resettlement and Development: The Bankwide Review of Projects Involving Involuntary Resettlement 1986–1993. World Bank.

World Bank (1998) Recent Experience With Involuntary Resettlement China Shuikou (and Yantan). Report No. 17539, 2 June 1998.

World Bank (2004) Involuntary Resettlement Sourcebook: Planning and Implementation in Development Projects. The World Bank.

World Bank (2011a) A Guide to the World Bank, 3rd edn. The World Bank, Washington DC.
World Bank (2011b) Knowledge and Learning for Human Rights and Development: Nordic Trust Fund Progress Report November 2010–October 2011. World Bank.
World Bank Inspection Panel (2016) Involuntary Resettlement, Emerging Lessons Series No. 1. The World Bank.
Zhou S (2012) Reassessing the Prospects of Human Rights Safeguard Policy at the World Bank. (2012) 15(3) Journal of International Economic Law 823–841.
Zvobgo K, Graham B A T (2020) The World Bank as an enforcer of human rights. (2020) 19(4) Journal of Human Rights 425–448.

Part V
The Way Forward

Chapter 10
A Guiding Framework for a Human Rights-Based Approach to Development-Induced Displacement

Contents

Abstract Drawing on the doctrinal analysis presented in the preceding chapters, this concluding chapter proposes a human rights-based guiding framework that can inform and guide the process of development-induced displacement (DID). Applying a human rights-based approach (HRBA) to DID entails (re)framing the adverse consequences of displacement as human rights issues and seeking rights-based solutions to address them. The first step in implementing the HRBA involves framing DID as an interference with human rights and assessing whether such interference can be justified based on the permissible limitations in human rights law. If the interference is deemed justified, the state must put in place various procedural safeguards, such as access to information, public participation, and access to judicial remedies, and substantive safeguards, such as the replacement of real property, compensation, and rehabilitation, to prevent or mitigate the adverse consequences of DID. Furthermore, states need to avoid direct and indirect discrimination in the process and/or outcome of DID and take positive measures to address structural problems that marginalize certain groups. In addition to outlining the safeguards necessary to prevent or mitigate the adverse impacts of DID, this chapter also examines the gaps and limitations in international human rights law in relation to DID.

© T.M.C. ASSER PRESS and the authors 2026

R. G. Teshome, *The Human Cost of Development*, Human Rights Research Series 104,
https://doi.org/10.1007/978-94-6265-751-9_10

Keywords Human rights-based approach · Due diligence · Non-discrimination · Justifying displacement · Procedural safeguards · Substantive safeguards · Land rights

10.1 Introduction

This book commenced by asking *how and to what extent international human rights law protects the rights of people(s) affected by development-induced displacement (DID).* To this end, it has sought to identify and map out the relevant human rights norms, analyse their application in the context of DID, and assess their adequacy in addressing the legal and practical issues associated with DID.

DID is a form of internal displacement where individuals or groups are involuntarily moved from their homes or residences to make room for development projects. Displacement, in this context, occurs when the implementation of development projects involves the acquisition of land and eviction or results in unbearable living conditions that force people to flee their homes. Similar to other forms of internal displacement, the two main elements of this definition are the involuntary nature of the displacement and the fact that displaced persons remain within the national borders of the state. DID, however, is pre-planned, foreseeable, prompted by the state or with the blessing and/or support of the state, and often leads to the permanent relocation of those displaced. These factors distinguish DID from other forms of internal displacement that are often caused by unforeseeable emergency situations over which states have little or no control, such as natural disasters and conflict. As this book has established, these distinguishing factors are important considerations in the determination of the necessary safeguards that need to be provided for people affected by displacement and the corresponding obligations of states. States should have heightened obligations when they themselves are planning and instigating displacement. In the context of DID, states need to go beyond providing humanitarian assistance, which might satisfy their obligations in emergency situations, and take appropriate steps to effectively re-establish the livelihoods of displaced persons.

Against this backdrop, the current work has set out to explore the human rights safeguards states need to provide in the course of DID. The book uses the human rights-based approach (HRBA) as a theoretical framework to understand and analyse DID and its adverse consequences. This involves (re)framing the socio-economic and cultural impacts of DID as human rights issues and seeking rights-based solutions to address those issues. The preceding chapters have elucidated how the process and outcome of DID interfere with and potentially violate human rights, thus, framing the adverse consequences of DID as human rights problems. They have also identified the general and specialized human rights frameworks and norms applicable to DID. Drawing on the doctrinal analysis provided in the previous chapters, this concluding chapter presents the main findings of this research by proposing a rights-based guiding framework that can and should inform and guide the process and outcome of development in general and of DID in particular.

This is predicated on the assumption that using HRBA not only gives the process of DID legitimacy but also leads to a better outcome—in terms of restoring the livelihoods and protecting the rights of those affected. While DID is inherently disruptive, most of its adverse consequences are attributable to the lack or inadequacy of the procedural and substantive safeguards put in place by states as established throughout this book. Based on this premise, the current chapter provides a general overview of what human rights law offers to avoid or at least mitigate these consequences or, in other words, to ensure the provision of adequate safeguards. In doing so, it aims to offer a guiding framework for a justified process of DID that is based on human rights norms and principles. In other words, it offers a checklist of the steps states need to take and the safeguards they need to provide in order to implement DID in accordance with human rights law (Sect. 10.2).

The current chapter also provides an overview of the gaps and limitations in international human rights law vis-à-vis DID based on the findings of the book (Sect. 10.3). As established in the previous chapters, there is no specific treaty or soft-law instrument that specifically and comprehensively deals with this form of displacement. While the human rights protections for people affected by DID can be found scattered in various human rights instruments, there are some normative gaps in certain areas. Hence, in the theme of framing DID as a human rights issue and finding rights-based solutions to address its adverse impacts, this chapter engages with the areas where international human rights law, as it stands today, falls short of offering a solution or normative guidance. The chapter will also propose possible solutions to address these gaps and normative underdevelopment.

10.2 Human Rights-Based Approach to Development-Induced Displacement

The HRBA is born from the recognition of the inextricable link between development and human rights and, as mentioned in the preceding chapters, it entails integrating human rights norms and principles into the process of development, or DID in this context. This approach recognizes human rights both as a means and an end of development. In other words, human rights norms and principles should guide the process of development and the outcome of development should advance the realization of rights.[1] This also coincides with the contemporary conception of "development" discussed in Chap. 8, which views development as more than a pursuit of economic growth and, rather, as a process aimed at improving human capabilities in different aspects and advancing the realization of all human rights. While the HRBA is a fluid and flexible concept that can be customized to fit the issue or sector to which it is applied,[2] it contains certain core principles, i.e. equality and non-discrimination, participation, transparency, accountability, empowerment, and the principle of "do

[1] Boesen and Sano 2010, p. 51; see also OHCHR 2006, p. 15.

[2] Braniff and Hainsworth 2015, p. 41.

no harm".[3] These core principles are rooted in human rights norms and standards recognized in human rights treaties, customary law, and other sources.[4] The subsequent sections will elucidate how these core principles apply in the context of DID using the concrete human rights norms in which they are rooted.

The HRBA—the integration of human rights norms and values in the process of development—has several advantages or added values. One of these advantages is that it offers legal authority and legitimacy by grounding development policies and practices in human rights law.[5] As states are bound by human rights treaties they have ratified and by customary international law, reframing development in human rights terms creates a legal effect.[6] The other advantage of the HRBA is that it links development policies and practices to concrete rights and duties. As Uvin puts it, the rights-based approach represents "the move from needs to rights, and from charity to duties".[7] Redefining development or the specific undertakings it requires as rights entails that the state has corresponding obligations to deliver.[8] The other added value of the HRBA, which also follows from the above two advantages, is that it fosters accountability by creating a system where right-holders can claim their rights using appropriate mechanisms and duty-bearers can be held accountable for failing to fulfil their obligations.[9] As the right to effective remedies lies at the heart of all human rights entitlements,[10] international human rights law provides avenues where violations of human rights can be remedied. Hence, the HRBA integrates these remedial norms and mechanisms into development policies and practices.

Against this background, in the context of DID, the HRBA entails reframing the socio-economic consequences of DID as human rights issues and integrating human rights norms and principles into the process of displacement and resettlement to address these issues. The following sections will give a general overview of the relevant human rights norms and principles that can inform the process of DID.

---

[3] Gready 2008, p. 736; see also Braniff and Hainsworth 2015, p. 42.

[4] OHCHR 2006, p. 23.

[5] Gready 2008, pp. 737–740; see also Osmani 2005, p. 8.

[6] Hamm 2001, p. 1013.

[7] Uvin 2007, p. 602; see also OHCHR 2006, p. 15.

[8] Gready 2008, p. 740; see also Boesen and Sano 2010, p. 52.

[9] Gready 2008, p. 741; Boesen and Sano 2010, p. 52; see also Osmani 2005, p. 9; see also OHCHR 2006, p. 17.

[10] Gready 2008, p. 741.

10.2.1 *Justifying Displacement: Development-Induced Displacement as a (Permissible) Limitation on Human Rights*

One of the specific questions this book asked was: *to what extent do the economic, social, and cultural consequences of DID interfere with and potentially violate human rights?*

As the preceding chapters have established, being forcibly ousted from one's home or residence comes with a plethora of economic, social, and cultural consequences. Some of the common consequences of DID include, *inter alia*, landlessness or decrease in landholdings, loss or decrease in income, homelessness or deterioration of housing conditions, loss of access to common resources, and disruption of social and cultural practices. Most of these consequences have long-term effects that potentially lead to the chronic impoverishment and marginalization of those affected. These adverse consequences interfere with and potentially violate a range of human rights. This book has demonstrated how DID can interfere with and potentially violate human rights by closely looking into three rights that are commonly affected in the course of DID, i.e. the rights to housing, property, and work (part II). The forced eviction that DID involves and the homelessness or deterioration of housing conditions it often results in clearly interfere with the right to adequate housing recognized in the relevant human rights frameworks. Similarly, the expropriation of private property, disruption of access to common property, and eviction that accompany DID interfere with the right to peaceful enjoyment of property. The right to work is also interfered with in the course of DID when involuntary displacement leads to the deprivation of employment and a decrease or loss of income.

However, most human rights are not absolute and not all interferences constitute a violation. Indeed, states have to implement development projects to pursue economic, social, and political progress. States also have human rights obligations to undertake development activities that are aimed at maximization of the resources of the state or the provision of public services as this is essential for the realization of most human rights. These development endeavours can inevitably have adverse consequences that potentially interfere with human rights. This calls for reconciliation of the benefits of these development undertakings, on the one hand, and their adverse consequences, on the other, which requires a balancing exercise. This balancing exercise is what is needed to address the dilemma pointed out at the beginning of this book, i.e. the paradox between development as a socio-economic advancement and displacement as a source of various adversities.

International human rights law leaves room for states to restrict rights in certain circumstances in order to protect a higher individual or public interest. This is provided under the specific limitation clauses of the rights concerned or the general limitation clauses of some treaties as is the case for the International Covenant on Economic, Social and Cultural Rights (ICESCR).[11] As can be deduced from these

[11] UN General Assembly, International Covenant on Economic, Social and Cultural Rights, 16 December 1966, 993 United Nations Treaty Series at 3 ('ICESCR'), Article 4; see also UN General

pertinent provisions, limitations of human rights have to comply with certain conditions. Generally, there are three cumulative conditions for a justified limitation to be imposed, namely legality, legitimacy, and necessity and proportionality, although the language and specifics might differ depending on the treaty or the right.

These conditions should inform the approval processes of the development project that caused the displacement, the displacement itself, and the interferences it involves, such as eviction and land acquisition. In other words, DID and the interferences to human rights it results in should be justified based on the conditions of limitation. Hence, the first step of applying the HRBA to DID involves reframing DID as an interference with human rights and exploring the ways this interference can be justified. The following sections will elucidate what the conditions of limitation entail and how they can be applied to justify displacement and its consequences.

10.2.1.1 Legality: Prescribed by Law

The condition of legality demands that the limitation has to be prescribed in a pre-existing "national law of general application".[12] Not only does there need to be a law but the law should also have certain qualities. The law providing for limitations needs to be clear, accessible, reasonable, and consistent with the human rights treaty concerned.[13] The law should also be sufficiently specific and foreseeable to allow its subjects to regulate their conduct accordingly and prevent arbitrariness.[14] As the Human Rights Committee stressed, "[t]he laws authorizing the application of restrictions should use precise criteria and may not confer unfettered discretion on those charged with their execution."[15] In addition, the law needs to put in place effective remedies and safeguards to prevent and/or rectify a potential abuse of law.[16]

In the context of DID, the specific interferences that DID involves, such as eviction and expropriation of private and communal property, need to be provided for by law. The law should also specifically prescribe and clearly define the legitimate aims that can warrant those interferences and the procedural and substantive safeguards that need to be provided for those affected. Hence, a state can only displace people to

---

Assembly, Universal Declaration of Human Rights, 10 December 1948, 217 A (III) ('UDHR'), Article 29(2).

[12] UN Commission on Human Rights, The Siracusa Principles on the Limitation and Derogation Provisions in the International Covenant on Civil and Political Rights, 28 September 1984, E/CN.4/1985/4 ('Siracusa Principles'), para 15; see also UN Commission on Human Rights, Note verbale dated 5 December 1986 from the Permanent Mission of the Netherlands to the United Nations Office at Geneva addressed to the Centre for Human Rights, 8 January 1987, E/CN.4/1987/17 ('Limburg Principles'), para 48.

[13] Siracusa Principles (n 12) paras 15–18; see also Limburg Principles (n 12) paras 48–50; see also Muller 2009, pp. 578 and 579; see also Sommario 2018, p. 100.

[14] Muller 2009, pp. 578 and 579; see also Sommario 2018, pp. 100 and 101.

[15] UN CCPR 1999, para 13; see also Muller 2009, p. 579.

[16] Siracusa Principles (n 12) para 18; see also Limburg Principles (n 12) para 51.

make room for development projects based on a domestic law that meets the criteria discussed above.

10.2.1.2 Legitimacy: Legitimate Aim

Limitations to human rights can only be imposed to protect or advance one or more of the legitimate aims enumerated under the specific or general limitation clauses concerned. In relation to economic, social and cultural rights, the sole legitimate aim provided for by Article 4 of the ICESCR is the promotion of "general welfare",[17] which denotes "...the wellbeing of the people as a whole" as discussed in Chap. 3.[18] The specific limitation clauses under the ICCPR, on the other hand, enunciate several legitimate aims that the limitation can pursue, *inter alia*, public order, national security, health, and the rights and freedoms of others.[19]

The interference in the context of DID often aims to advance a public interest, which can be, for instance, economic development and a provision of public services. These public interests can qualify, depending on the circumstances, as general welfare purposes if the rights at stake are economic, social, and cultural (ESC) rights. Nonetheless, these broad objectives have to be clearly defined and their relevance in achieving general welfare has to be established.[20] When it comes to civil and political rights, the public interest that DID pursues can fall under the legitimate aim of "protecting the rights and freedoms of others".[21] For instance, being forcibly ousted from one's home or residence and involuntarily resettled interferes with the freedom to choose one's residence recognized under Article 12 of the ICCPR.[22] Nonetheless, justified limitations can be imposed on this right to protect, among others, "the rights and freedoms of others",[23] which can be used in the context of DID. To this end, it has to be proven that the development project in question and its outcomes will advance the rights and freedom of those that will benefit from the project. States can rely on the contemporary understanding of development discussed in Chap. 8 to make the necessary correlation between development and human rights. Overall, DID and the interferences to human rights it involves can only be justified if they aim to advance the general welfare or the rights of others.

---

[17] ICESCR (n 11) Article 4; see also Muller 2009, p. 570.

[18] Limburg Principles (n 12) para 52; see the discussion in Chap. 3 on the limitation to ESC rights (Sect. 3.5).

[19] UN General Assembly, International Covenant on Civil and Political Rights, 16 December 1966, 999 United Nations Treaty Series 171 (see the specific limitation clauses of the limitable rights).

[20] Muller 2009, pp. 573 and 574.

[21] It is important to note that the rights and freedoms that the limitation aims to protect do not have to be provided in the same instrument in which the right the limitation is imposed on is provided (see Siracusa Principles (n 12) para 35; see also Limburg Principles (n 12) para 69; see also Muller 2009, p. 560).

[22] ICCPR (n 19) Article 12(1).

[23] Ibid., Article 12(3); see also UN CCPR 1999, para 11.

10.2.1.3 Necessity and Proportionality

The limitation clauses of the relevant human rights treaties require that the interference needs to be necessary to achieve the legitimate aim pursued.[24] This condition of necessity embodies two requirements: the interference has to be, first, necessary to "[respond] to a pressing public or social need"[25] and, second, "proportionate to the aim pursued".[26] States have to demonstrate that there is an overarching need to protect or advance the public interest pursued at that particular moment. Moreover, there has to be a causal relationship between the measures proposed and the legitimate aim it seeks to achieve.[27] In other words, the measures need to be relevant and reasonably effective to achieve the objective.[28] In the context of DID, the state has to show how the proposed development project can reasonably achieve the public interest or advance the realization of rights.

Proportionality pertains to the scope and severity of the interference with human rights compared to the individual or public interest that the legitimate aim seeks to advance. Accordingly, the condition of proportionality demands that, first, the state needs to use the least intrusive or restrictive means to achieve the legitimate aim.[29] Second, the individual or public interest the legitimate aim seeks to protect or advance should outweigh the rights affected by the interference. This requires balancing competing interests—the protection of individual rights, on the one hand, and advancing the individual or public interest concerned, on the other hand.[30] This balancing exercise involves both objective and subjective considerations. The impact of the interference on the enjoyment of rights and the circumstances of the case or the people involved need to be duly considered to determine the proportionality of the measures.[31]

In the context of DID, a state needs to undertake a balancing exercise taking into account the benefits of the development project for public interest or realization of rights and the adverse consequences of the project. To this end, various factors, such as the number of people affected by the displacement, the severity of the potential impacts of the displacement, and whether or not these impacts can be fully redressed, should be weighed against the public interest sought to be advanced. This requires the state to undertake comprehensive social, environmental, and human rights impact

[24] For instance, see ICCPR (n 19) Article 12(3); see also ICESCR (n 11) Article 4.

[25] Siracusa Principles (n 12) para 10(b); see also see also Sommario 2018, p. 101; see also Muller 2009, p. 583.

[26] Siracusa Principles (n 12) para 10; see also Muller 2009, p. 583; see also Sommario 2018, p. 101.

[27] Conte 2016, p. 48.

[28] Muller 2009, p. 584.

[29] Ibid; see also UN CCPR 1999, para 14.

[30] Muller 2009, 559; see also Conte 2016, pp. 49 and 50.

[31] Conte 2016, pp. 49 and 50.

assessments to fully appreciate the impacts of the proposed project. These assessments particularly need to take into account the differential impacts of the project on vulnerable and marginalized groups.[32]

In some cases, however, DID and its consequences can be evidently disproportionate despite the level or importance of the public interest it aims to achieve. For instance, if the eviction that DID involves puts those affected at risk of homelessness, it cannot be justified, as elucidated in Chap. 3.[33] This is also the case for other core contents of ESC rights as can be deduced from the requirement of "compatibility with the nature of the rights" under the general limitation clause of the ICESCR.[34] Consequently, the limitation should not be incompatible with the very objective and essence of the right,[35] and hence, it should not affect the minimum core contents these rights.[36] Not only for socio-economic rights but also generally limitations are strict exceptions that "…shall not be interpreted so as to jeopardize the essence of the right concerned."[37] Hence, there are certain elements or aspects of rights the protection of which inherently outweigh the public interest pursued.

In relation to ESC rights, there is another caveat that needs to be taken into account in the assessment of limitations, i.e. whether or not the interference in question constitutes a retrogressive measure—a measure that reduces the (level of) enjoyment of rights.[38] While the concepts of retrogressive measures and limitations are distinct theoretically, retrogressive measures essentially constitute limitations,[39] but not always vice versa. Limitations that do not have the effect of reducing the level of enjoyment of rights already achieved will not amount to retrogressive measures. For instance, in the context of eviction, if a state provides a replacement housing of equal or better quality than the housing the people concerned are evicted from, the eviction may not amount to a retrogressive measure. In principle, retrogressive measures are prohibited under the Covenant since states are instead obliged to move progressively towards the realization of these rights.[40] There are, however, exceptional circumstances, which need to be construed even more strictly, that can justify these measures, such as economic recession, natural disaster, or other comparable

---

32 The Special Rapporteur on Adequate Housing 2007, para 33.

33 As the Committee on Economic, Social and Cultural Rights (CESCR) repeatedly stressed "eviction should not render individuals homeless." (see *Mohamed Ben Djazia and Naouel Bellili v. Spain*, Communication No. 5/2015, adoption of views, UN Doc. E/C.12/61/D/5/2015, CESCR, 20 June 2017, para 15.2; see also UN CESCR 1997, para 16.

34 ICESCR (n 11) Article 4 (this provision requires that "…the State may subject such rights only to such limitations as are determined by law only in so far as this may be compatible with the nature of these rights…"); see also Muller 2009, pp. 579–583.

35 Limburg Principles (n 12) para 56; see also Saul et al. 2014, p. 257.

36 Saul et al. 2014, pp. 257 and 258.

37 Siracusa Principles (n 12) para 2; see also Limburg (n 12) para 56; see also Muller 2009, p. 581; see also UN CCPR 1999, para 13.

38 International Commission of Jurists (ICJ), Maastricht Guidelines on Violations of Economic, Social and Cultural Rights, 26 January 1997, para 14(e).

39 Muller 2009, pp. 584 and 585.

40 UN CESCR 1990, para 9.

circumstances that put a severe strain on the available resources.[41] In addition, these measures can only be justified if they are taken to advance other Covenant rights.[42] Accordingly, in cases where DID and the interference to human rights it involves amount to retrogressive measures, the state has to go beyond the conditions of limitation and prove the existence of an extenuating circumstance that warrants such measure as well as justify that such measure is necessary to protect other rights. Since DID is often actively initiated by the state in pursuit of economic development or the provision of public services rather than as a response to an external crisis, it can seldom be justified if it involves a retrogressive measure. Moreover, as this book established, retrogressive outcomes can be avoided by the provision of adequate safeguards that can effectively restore or improve the enjoyment of ESC rights after displacement.

Overall, the first step in applying a HRBA to DID is framing displacement as an interference with human rights and justifying it using the three-part test of limitations. DID constitutes a violation of human rights when the development project and the resulting displacement are not justified based on the relevant conditions of limitations. This alone, however, does not exhaust the obligations of the state under international human rights law. In addition, the state has to put in place various procedural and substantive safeguards at all phases of DID, which will be elucidated in the following sections, to prevent or at least mitigate the adverse consequences of DID and preclude human rights violations.

10.2.2 Human Rights Safeguards in the Course of Development-Induced Displacement

As this book has established, most of the adverse consequences of DID and its human rights impacts are attributable to the lack or inadequacy of procedural and substantive safeguards put in place by states. Displaced persons are often left out of the decision-making process. In some cases, even if they are consulted, their participation is not meaningful in the sense that they did not have a genuine opportunity to influence decision-making. In other cases, the methods and means of participation fail to take into account the language, culture, and way of life of those affected. Moreover, in several cases, the substantive remedies or safeguards provided by states are not adequate or effective to restore the livelihoods of the people concerned. In some cases, displaced persons are not offered a replacement of real assets—land and housing. In other cases, the replacement land provided is not adequate in terms of size, location, and cultivability. The same is true for housing; displaced persons are not often provided with replacement housing of adequate quality that complies with the pertinent human rights standards. In addition, those who lost their jobs or incomes as a result of forcible displacement are not often provided with sustainable

[41] Muller 2009, pp. 586 and 587.

[42] UN CESCR 1990, para 9.

jobs or resettled in income-generating activities. States also often fail to put in place benefit-sharing schemes where the people paying the price of development equitably share the benefits of development. States usually rely on one-off monetary compensation, which is not sufficient and effective to restore the real assets and livelihoods of displaced persons. Moreover, the resettlement sites often lack adequate public service facilities, such as health and educational institutions.

Thus, most of the adverse consequences of DID are attributable to procedural irregularities and/or lack or inadequacy of substantive safeguards mentioned above. This entails that most of these consequences and the resulting human rights interference can be prevented or at least mitigated with a provision of adequate safeguards at all phases of displacement and resettlement. Some of the positive resettlement experiences cited in this book also attest that it is, in fact, possible to prevent the adverse consequences of DID and restore or even improve the livelihoods of the people affected thereby. What these positive cases have in common are extensive participation of those affected in the process of displacement and resettlement; an inclusive process that respects the agency and livelihood choices of those affected; and the provision of adequate safeguards and remedial schemes that take into account the specific needs of the people concerned.

This brings into the picture the other specific question this book asked: *what rights-based procedural and substantive safeguards states need to provide at all phases of displacement in order to protect the rights of people affected by DID?* The following sections offer the general overview of the procedural and substantive safeguards states need to put in place at all phases of DID based on the human rights norms discussed in the preceding chapters.

10.2.2.1 Procedural Safeguards

As discussed before, the HRBA seeks to make both the process and outcome of development—DID in this context—equitable and compliant with human rights norms. Accordingly, the application of the HRBA to DID demands that states put in place various procedural safeguards at all phases of displacement and resettlement. Apart from offering legitimacy to the process of DID, the provision of adequate procedural safeguards arguably leads to a better outcome in terms of preventing or mitigating the adverse consequences of involuntary displacement and protecting the rights of those affected thereby. Particularly when severe or grave interferences to human rights are concerned, as is the case for involuntary displacement that comes with a range of human rights impacts, procedural safeguards are not only desirable but also indispensable for the protection of human rights. As the Committee on Economic, Social, and Cultural Rights (CESCR) stressed in relation to forced eviction, "[a]ppropriate procedural protection and due process are essential aspects of all human rights but are especially pertinent in relation to a matter such as forced evictions which directly invokes a large number of the rights recognized in both the International Covenants on Human Rights."[43] In light of this, the following sections will explore the main procedural safeguards that need to be provided in the course of DID by drawing on the relevant human rights norms and principles.

A. **Access to Information**

As established in the preceding chapters, access to relevant information is one of the procedural safeguards states need to put in place in the course of DID. The right to access to information, which some call "the right to know",[44] is both a self-standing right and an underlying human rights principle that is instrumental for the protection of most, if not all, human rights.[45] Access to information is recognized as an integral part of the right to freedom of expression as confirmed by the Human Rights Committee and the regional human rights monitoring bodies.[46] The terms "seek and receive information" under Article 19(2) of the ICCPR indicate that the right to access to information falls within the scope of freedom of expression.[47] This obliges states not only to provide information when right-holders are actively seeking information but also to "proactively put in the public domain Government information of public interest."[48] In addition, access to information is also instrumental for the protection and realization of a range of other rights, such as the right to vote, the right to fair trial, the right to housing, and the right to health, among others.[49] As discussed in the previous chapters, the right to access to relevant information as to the process of displacement and the remedies provided along the way is one of the procedural safeguards envisaged under the frameworks on IDPs, the rights of indigenous peoples, and the right to development. It is also an integral part of the right to effective remedies,[50] which will be discussed subsequently.

In cases where the state engages in activities that severely disrupt the enjoyment of rights, as is the case for DID, it has a heightened positive obligation to actively provide all pertinent information.[51] This includes information on the (purpose and process

---

[43] UN CESCR 1997, para 15; see also *I.D.G. v Spain*, Communication No. 002/2014, adoption of views, E/C.12/55/D/2/2014, CESCR, 13 October 2015, para 12.1.

[44] Riccardi 2018, p. 228.

[45] McDonagh 2013, p. 26; see also Riccardi 2018, p. 228.

[46] UN CCPR 2011, para 18 (the Committee has noted that "Art 19, paragraph 2 embraces a right of access to information held by public bodies."); see also *Nurbek Toktakunov v Kyrgyzstan*, Communication No. 1470/2006, adoption of views, CCPR/C/101/D/1470/2006, Human Rights Committee, 28 March 2011, para 7.4; see also McDonagh 2013, pp. 29, 33–34 and 36–37.

[47] ICCPR (n 19) Article 19(2); see also UN CCPR 2011, para 18; see also McDonagh 2013, p. 32.

[48] UN CCPR 2011, para 19; see also McDonagh 2013, p. 31.

[49] McDonagh 2013, pp. 38–44.

[50] UN General Assembly, Basic Principles and Guidelines on the Right to a Remedy and Reparation for Victims of Gross Violations of International Human Rights Law and Serious Violations of International Humanitarian Law: resolution/adopted by the General Assembly, 21 March 2006, A/RES/60/147, paras 11 & 12 (while this Resolution deals with gross violations of human rights, it is grounded on the provisions of the right to effective remedies provided under general human rights treaties (see the preamble). Hence, it is relevant for the interpretation of the right to effective remedies in general).

[51] UN CESCR 1997, para 15.

of the) development project that is potentially causing the displacement, the process of relocation, the resettlement options, and the safeguards put in place by the state.[52] In general, states need to provide "timely and appropriate information" to those potentially affected by the displacement, particularly to those who are vulnerable and marginalised, "through culturally appropriate channels and methods."[53] Accordingly, the information should be provided in a language and format most suitable to the people concerned.[54] Moreover, information should be provided at the earliest possible time to allow those affected by the displacement participate in the process, challenge the decision using available administrative and judicial mechanisms, and prepare for relocation, if need be.[55] The effectiveness of the following two procedural safeguards, i.e. public participation and access to remedies, also hinges upon the provision of adequate and timely information.

B. **Public Participation**

Another procedural safeguard that needs to be provided in the course of DID is public participation. Similar to the right to access to information, public participation is also both a standalone right and a fundamental human rights principle that is essential for the realization of other rights. Article 25 of the ICCPR recognizes a right to participate "…in the conduct of public affairs, directly or through freely chosen representatives".[56] Public participation—specifically, participation in the process of development—is also one of the normative elements of the right to development as established in the preceding chapters. In addition, public participation is instrumental to the realization of several other rights, such as the right to an adequate standard of living and the right to health, as the interpretations by the relevant human rights monitoring bodies affirm.[57] Particularly those affected by a state decision, policy, and development activity should be given an opportunity to participate in the decision-making process.

Public participation can take different forms. In the context of DID, meaningful consultation with the people affected by the displacement is particularly necessary.[58] Consultation should not be a mere formality. As the relevant human rights documents also postulate, it should be "meaningful" in a sense that the individuals or the people

---

52 Ibid; see also Koenig 2006, p. 127.

53 The Special Rapporteur on Adequate Housing 2007, paras 35 & 37; see also van der Ploeg and Vanclay 2017, p. 39.

54 van der Ploeg and Vanclay 2017, p. 39.

55 The Special Rapporteur on Adequate Housing 2007, paras 37 & 38.

56 ICCPR (n 19) Article 25(a). The regional human rights frameworks also contain a comparable provisions (see Organization of African Unity (OAU), African Charter on Human and Peoples' Rights, 27 June 1981, CAB/LEG/67/3 rev. 5, 21 I.L.M. 58 (1982), Article 13(1); see also Organization of American States (OAS), American Convention on Human Rights, 22 November 1969, 36 OAS Treaty Series, Article 23(1)(a).

57 See, for instance, UN CESCR 1991, para 12; see also UN CESCR 1999, para 23; see also UN CESCR 2000, paras 11, 17, & 54.

58 UN CESCR 1997, para 15; see also van der Ploeg and Vanclay 2017, p. 36; see also Adeola 2017, p. 99.

concerned should have a genuine opportunity to influence decision-making.[59] Thus, consultation should offer those affected a chance to challenge the proposed plan, propose new alternatives, and present their demands.[60] The extent of this influence or the decision-making power left to the people, however, depends on the circumstances of the case and the identity of the people concerned. For instance, indigenous peoples can only be subjected to land acquisition and relocation based on their "free, prior, and informed consent".[61] Moreover, consultation and participation should not only pertain to the development project concerned and the displacement it results in but also to the resettlement options and the remedies available to those affected by the displacement.[62] Hence, displaced people(s) should have a say in the resettlement process as well.

In addition, participation needs to be inclusive to be considered "meaningful". Particularly those economically and socially vulnerable and marginalized should be given a chance to participate in a manner, i.e. language, format, location, and venue, conducive to their specific conditions and needs.[63] Accordingly, it is imperative that states put in place special procedures and measures, if necessary, to accommodate these groups.[64] In other words, the participation and consultation process should be guided by the principles of non-discrimination and formal and substantive equality.[65] Overall, a state wishing to displace individuals from their homes and/or residences for development purposes needs to conduct extensive, inclusive, and genuine consultations with those affected.

Several case studies on positive resettlement experiences show that extensive and meaningful participation is essential not only to legitimatize the process of displacement but also to avoid the risk of impoverishment and restore the livelihoods of those affected in the long run.[66] The case of the Yacyreta Hydroelectric Project in Argentina, which displaced an estimated number of 80,000 individuals,[67] is a good example of this. Some of these displaced persons are "artisanal brick makers", a group locally known as "*olero*", who were considered "highly vulnerable" due to their dependence on common resources affected by the project, such as the clay deposits they use to make bricks, firewood, and water from the river.[68] In order to

---

[59] van der Ploeg and Vanclay 2017, p. 40; see also Adeola 2017, p. 100; see also Koenig 2006, p. 125.

[60] The Special Rapporteur on Adequate Housing 2007, paras 37 & 38.

[61] UN General Assembly, United Nations Declaration on the Rights of Indigenous Peoples: resolution/adopted by the General Assembly, 2 October 2007, A/RES/61/295 (UNDRIP), Article 10; see also International Labour Organization (ILO), Indigenous and Tribal Peoples Convention, C169, 27 June 1989, Article 16; see the details in Chap. 7, Sect. 7.4.

[62] van der Ploeg and Vanclay 2017, p. 40.

[63] Ibid., pp. 39 and 40.

[64] The Special Rapporteur on Adequate Housing 2007, para 39.

[65] van der Ploeg and Vanclay 2017, p. 40.

[66] Randell 2016, p. 386.

[67] Mejia 2000, p. 145.

[68] Ibid., p. 146.

avoid, or at least reduce, their risk of impoverishment, a resettlement and rehabilitation plan was prepared with extensive participation of the people affected.[69] The *oleros* were provided with several alternatives including an option to be resettled nearby and continue their economic activity (brick making) "…with technical assistance to improve their production system";[70] an option to be resettled in rural areas to engage in farming; and cash compensation to start new businesses.[71] Each household was given a choice to freely select the alternative that best suited their interests.[72] This meaningful participation coupled with the substantive safeguards put in place by the state was the main reason the incomes and overall livelihoods of the majority of the *oleros* displaced by the project improved after relocation.[73] Similarly, case studies conducted on the Shuikou and Yantan Dams in China and the Arenal Hydroelectric Project in Costa Rica have identified extensive and meaningful consultation with those affected as one of the main factors behind the relative success of the resettlement plans.[74] Overall, these cases demonstrate that meaningful participation is significant to rebuild the lives of those uprooted from their homes and residences to make room for development projects. Besides, it creates a sense of ownership and offers legitimacy to the process.

C. **Access to (Judicial) Remedies**

Access to effective remedies is another procedural safeguard that needs to be provided for those affected by DID. The right to effective remedies is a cross-cutting human rights norm on which the full protection of all human rights is contingent. It is explicitly recognized under Article 2(3) of the ICCPR, which obliges states "[t]o ensure that any person whose rights or freedoms as herein recognized are violated shall have an effective remedy, notwithstanding that the violation has been committed by persons acting in an official capacity".[75] The provision also requires states to ensure that individuals and groups whose rights are allegedly violated have access to competent remedial institutions—preferably judicial—and that the remedies granted by these institutions are properly enforced.[76] While the ICESCR does not contain a similar provision, the right to effective remedies is read into the Covenant by the Committee. According to the Committee, "…there cannot be a right without an effective remedy"[77] and "the obligation to take appropriate steps" envisaged under Article 2(1) of the Covenant involves, *inter alia*, the duty to provide judicial and

---

[69] Ibid., pp. 151–159; see also Randell 2016, p. 386 (the plan was prepared based on the resettlement policy of the World Bank).

[70] Mejia 2000, p. 150.

[71] Ibid., pp. 150 and 51.

[72] Ibid., p. 151; see also Randell 2016, p. 386.

[73] Mejia 2000, pp. 154–159 and 163; see also Randell 2016, p. 386.

[74] Randell 2016, p. 386; see also World Bank Report, Recent Experience With Involuntary Resettlement China Shuikou (and Yantan), Report No. 17539, 2 June 1998, 16.

[75] ICCPR (n 19) Article 2(3)(a).

[76] Ibid., Article 2(3)(b) & (c).

[77] *Mohamed Ben Djazia and Naouel Bellili Spain* (n 33) para 13.4.

other remedies.[78] In addition, the right to effective remedies is also recognized in the UDHR,[79] several special human rights frameworks,[80] and the main regional human rights instruments.[81] There is also a compelling argument that this right has obtained the status of customary international law.[82]

The right to effective remedies involves two aspects, namely procedural and substantive remedies.[83] The procedural aspect denotes "the processes by which arguable claims of human rights violations are heard and decided, whether by courts, administrative agencies, or other competent bodies."[84] The substantive aspect, on the other hand, pertains to the outcome of those processes or the redress accorded to those whose rights are affected.[85] The current section will only deal with the procedural aspect, which it refers to as "access to remedies"; substantive remedies will be covered in the subsequent section.

Access to remedies constitutes several elements. One of these elements is the existence of independent institutions competent to afford redress to which right holders can resort.[86] While this does not necessarily imply that these institutions have to be judicial bodies, international human rights frameworks and monitoring bodies highly encourage the provision of judicial remedies.[87] In some cases, for instance, in cases involving gross violations of human rights and the duty of non-discrimination,

---

[78] UN CESCR 1990, para 5; UN CESCR 1998, para 3; see also ICESCR (n 11) Article 2(1); see also *I.D.G. v Spain* (n 43) para 11.3; see also UN CESCR 1997, para 13; see also Maastricht Guidelines (n 38) para 22.

[79] UDHR (n 11) Article 8.

[80] UN General Assembly, International Convention on the Elimination of All Forms of Racial Discrimination, 21 December 1965, 660 United Nations Treaty Series at 195, Article 6; see also UN General Assembly, Convention on the Rights of Persons with Disabilities, 3 December 2006, 2515 United Nations Treaty Series 3, Article 13; see also UN General Assembly, Convention Against Torture and Other Cruel, Inhuman or Degrading Treatment or Punishment, 10 December 1984, 1465 United Nations Treaty Series 85, Article 14.

[81] Council of Europe, European Convention for the Protection of Human Rights and Fundamental Freedoms, as amended by Protocols Nos. 11 and 14, 4 November 1950, 5 ETS, Article 13; see also African Charter (n 56) Article 26; see also Inter-American Convention (n 56) Article 25.

[82] Wewerinke-Singh 2019, p. 226. It is also an integral part of the principle of accountability, which is one of the core principles of the HRBA (see van der Ploeg and Vanclay 2017, p. 42).

[83] Shelton 2015, p. 17; see General Assembly Basic Principles and Guidelines on the Right to a Remedy (n 50) para 11.

[84] Shelton 2015, p. 17; see also General Assembly Basic Principles and Guidelines on the Right to a Remedy (n 50) para 12.

[85] General Assembly Basic Principles and Guidelines on the Right to a Remedy (n 50) para 12; see also Shelton 2015, p. 17.

[86] Shelton 2015, p. 18; see also UN CCPR 2004, para 15.

[87] ICCPR (n 19) Article 2(3)(b); see also UN CESCR 1990, para 5; see also I.*D.G. v Spain* (n 43) paras 11.3 & 11.4; see also UN CESCR 1998, para 9; see also General Assembly Basic Principles and Guidelines on the Right to a Remedy (n 50) para 12.

judicial remedies can even be indispensable.[88] In any case, the available mechanisms have to be "accessible, affordable, timely and effective."[89] Another element of access to remedies is the provision of adequate due process guarantees that ensure procedural fairness.[90] A further important element of access to remedies is the justiciability—the ability to be invoked and enforced judicially—of the claims or rights concerned. This is particularly an issue with regard to economic, social, and cultural rights since they are traditionally considered policy issues, which might fall outside of the competence of courts or are best addressed by political decisions.[91] Currently, however, this conception is largely debunked and it is widely accepted that, as the CESCR also affirmed, "there is no Covenant right which could not, in the great majority of systems, be considered to possess at least some significant justiciable dimensions."[92] Hence, states need to ensure that all human rights or at least their aspects are justiciable. Overall, access to remedies can only be "effective" if all the above elements are fulfilled.

Accordingly, people affected by DID should have access to appropriate judicial and administrative mechanisms to challenge the decision and invoke their rights. Besides, they should have due process guarantees including adequate notice, for instance, about eviction proceedings, and provision of legal aid, among others.[93] Given the gravity of human rights interferences that DID often involves, the provision of free legal aid, if needed, is particularly pertinent.[94] Moreover, access to remedies needs to be provided both before and after the displacement takes place. The people concerned should be given an opportunity to contest the decision of eviction, expropriation, or relocation as the case may be. Moreover, displaced persons whose rights are affected by the displacement and/or lack or inadequacy of safeguards provided by the state should have recourse to remedial procedures after displacement.

10.2.2.2 Substantive Safeguards

A breach of an international obligation necessarily entails a duty to make good the damage through the provision of adequate pecuniary and non-pecuniary remedies.[95] As the predecessor of the International Court of Justice, the Permanent Court of International Justice, asserted in its seminal judgment, the *Chorzow Factory case*, "[i]t is

---

[88] General Assembly Basic Principles and Guidelines on the Right to a Remedy (n 50) para 12; see also UN CESCR 1998, para 9.

[89] UN CESCR 1998, para 9.

[90] General Assembly Basic Principles and Guidelines on the Right to a Remedy (n 50) para 12.

[91] UN CESCR 1998, para 10.

[92] Ibid.

[93] UN CESCR 1997, para 15; see also Special Rapporteur Principles and Guidelines (n 32) paras 37 & 41.

[94] UN CESCR 1997, para 15.

[95] International Law Commission, Draft Articles on Responsibility of States for Internationally Wrongful Acts, November 2001, Supplement No. 10 (A/56/10), chp.IV.E.1 ('ARSIWA'), Article 31.

a principle of international law…that the breach of an engagement involves an obligation to make reparation in an adequate form."[96] The type and scope of substantive remedies should be proportionate to the harm suffered by the victim.[97] Generally, remedies have dual objectives, i.e. they aim to correct the past by providing monetary and non-monetary reparations that rectify the damage sustained in the particular case and to shape the future by prescribing reform measures to guarantee the non-repetition of the violation.[98] It is worth noting here that, technically, the substantive remedies under the right to effective remedies are provided to redress "violations" of human rights. In the context of DID, nevertheless, substantive remedies should not only be provided once violations occur but also be put in place as "safeguards" to prevent violations. Based on this understanding, the norms on the right to effective remedies can be analogously applied in conjunction with the norms on the specific rights affected by DID.

It is important to recall that one of the peculiar aspects of DID is that the state is actively engaging in activities, i.e. the implementation of development projects, which interfere with the enjoyment of rights. Thus, the displacement and interferences it results in are pre-planned, foreseeable, and, hence, avoidable. The state in this case is relinquishing its minimum obligation to respect human rights—to refrain from engaging in activities that interfere with the enjoyment of rights. Thus, the state has or should have heightened positive obligations to put in place adequate substantive remedies or safeguards to prevent or mitigate the adverse impacts of its development endeavours. The principal objectives of these substantive safeguards should be to restore and, preferably, improve the livelihoods of those affected and protect their rights. In fact, priority should be given to improving the conditions of displaced persons and addressing the socio-economic difficulties they were facing before relocation and, hence, in effect turning DID into a development opportunity.[99] These objectives also align with the obligation of progressive realization and the prohibition of retrogressive measures under the ICESCR.[100] DID that deteriorates the lives of those affected and, consequently, reduces the enjoyment of rights can constitute a retrogressive measure. This retrogressive measure can seldom be justified as DID is not prompted by a force majeure situation or an extraordinary circumstance that puts a severe strain on the resources of the state. Thus, the state needs to improve or at least restore the livelihoods of displaced persons to avoid retrogression. Moreover,

[96] *Factory at Chorzów, Germany v. Poland*, Judgment, Claim for Indemnity, Merits, Judgment No. 13, (1928) PCIJ Series A No. 17, ICGJ 255 (PCIJ 1928), 13 September 1928, para 29; see also Bassiouni 2006, p. 207; see also ARSIWA (n 95) Article 31.

[97] General Assembly Basic Principles and Guidelines on the Right to a Remedy (n 50) para 15.

[98] Roach 2021, p. 12.

[99] Vanclay 2017, pp. 6 and 4 (as Vanclay rightly contended, "…rather than 'restoring' people to situations similar to their previous contexts and potentially condemning them to ongoing poverty, contemporary thinking has become more focused on improving their livelihoods and enabling them to transition to new circumstances, either by enhancing existing livelihood activities or identifying alternative activities that are compatible with their new situation."); see also van der Ploeg and Vanclay 2017, p. 44; see also Price 2009, p. 276.

[100] ICESCR (n 11) Article 2(1); see also UN CESCR 1990, para 9.

"the constant improvement of the well-being of the entire population" is also the definitional element of the right to development.[101] Overall, this is to say that the underlying objectives of substantive safeguards in the case of DID, i.e. improving or restoring livelihoods, have a legal basis. As the examples of case studies of positive resettlement experiences mentioned in this book also demonstrate, comprehensive and adequate safeguards not only prevent the risk of impoverishment that often taints DID but can also effectively restore or improve the livelihoods of those affected.

As the wording of the relevant human rights provisions indicates, substantive remedies need to be "effective",[102] i.e. capable of redressing the pecuniary and non-pecuniary damage sustained by the victim. Human rights frameworks do not, however, enumerate the types and scope of effective substantive remedies and the manner they are evaluated. Nor do they set out standards for the assessment of substantive remedies. This is one of the prevalent gaps in international human rights law in relation to DID, as will be elucidated below. However, certain substantive remedies can be deduced from the interpretations and case law of human rights monitoring bodies as well as other relevant general public international law frameworks. These substantive remedies include restitution, compensation, and rehabilitation.[103] It is important to reiterate here that the people(s) affected should also be meaningfully consulted about the substantive remedies put in place and, when possible, given an opportunity choose the option most suitable for them. The subsequent section will explore the substantive remedies relevant to DID or the substantive safeguards that need to be provided in the course of DID to restore and improve the livelihoods of those affected.

A. **Replacement Housing and/or Land**

The primary remedy states need to provide for people who are ousted from their homes or land for development purposes is replacement housing and/or land of adequate quality. These remedies resemble restitution, which is the primary remedy in international law for breach of international obligations.[104] Restitution entails an in-kind remedy that restores what is taken from the victim of human rights violation or "restore[s] the victim to the original situation before [the violation occurred]."[105] In human rights proceedings, it is mostly used in cases that involve deprivation of liberty, acquisition of property, termination of employment, and other similar cases where restoring what the victim has lost is feasible.[106] Restitution is considered the most effective and preferred remedy since the principal aim of remedies is "to

---

[101] See also van der Ploeg and Vanclay 2017, p. 37; see also UN General Assembly, Declaration on the Right to Development: resolution/adopted by the General Assembly, 4 December 1986, A/RES/41/128, Preamble.

[102] Bassiouni 2006, p. 214.

[103] UN CCPR 2004, para 16; see also Maastricht Guidelines (n 38) para 23.

[104] ARSIWA (n 95) Article 35.

[105] *Chorzow factory case* (n 96) 47; see also Shelton 2015, p. 298; see also General Assembly Basic Principles and Guidelines on the Right to a Remedy (n 50) para 19.

[106] Shelton 2015, p. 298; see also General Assembly Basic Principles and Guidelines on the Right to a Remedy (n 50) para 19.

place an aggrieved party in the same position as he or she would have been had no injury occurred."[107] Restitution, when feasible, is best able to directly and effectively achieve this purpose.

In the context of DID, restitution is evidently infeasible since the acquisition of properties—land and housing—and relocation that DID involves is often permanent.[108] However, the rationales that make restitution the primary remedy can be used to support the argument that in-kind remedies, i.e. replacement housing and/or land and access to common resources, should be the preferred remedies for DID. In other words, replacing the housing, land, and other properties taken away from those affected by DID can serve the purpose of restitution provided that the replaced properties are of comparable or higher quality than the ones taken away. As mentioned before, the main aim of substantive remedies in the case of DID is restoring and, preferably, improving the livelihoods of those affected. There is no better way to achieve this than in-kind remedies that physically replace the properties and resources taken away from the people concerned. This is also affirmed by the CESCR and the Special Rapporteur on the right to housing as discussed in Chap. 3—in relation to forced evictions, in-kind remedies should be given priority.[109]

Accordingly, people who have been involuntarily removed from their homes and lands should be given replacement housing and/or land that meet human rights standards.[110] The replacement housing provided for displaced persons needs to comply with the conditions of "adequacy" enumerated under General Comment No. 4 and discussed under Chap. 3.[111] In exceptional cases where this is not possible, displaced persons should at least be provided with basic shelter as this is the minimum core content of the right to housing.[112] However, this does not sufficiently exhaust states' human rights obligations and it should only be used as a temporary measure. States, eventually, need to provide displaced persons with adequate housing or, in lieu of that, a commensurate amount of compensation and other assistance to enable them to obtain adequate housing. It is worth reiterating here that DID is not a response to a force majeure situation; rather, it is a pre-planned interference instigated by the state. Hence, reaching the bare minimum standards alone cannot and should not relieve a state of its human rights obligations.

In addition to replacement housing, displaced persons should also be provided with replacement "land of better or equal quality"[113] in terms of size, location, and cultivability.[114] Particularly in cases where displaced persons depend on land for their

[107] Shelton (2015) (n 83) 19 & 298; see also General Assembly Basic Principles and Guidelines on the Right to a Remedy (n 50) para 19.

[108] Vanclay 2017, p. 6.

[109] The Special Rapporteur on Adequate Housing 2007, para 60.

[110] Ibid., para 16.

[111] Ibid; see also UN CESCR 1991, para 8.

[112] The Special Rapporteur on Adequate Housing 2007, para 52.

[113] Ibid., paras 16 & 60; see also Vanclay 2017, p. 11; see also van der Ploeg and Vanclay 2017, p. 36.

[114] The Special Rapporteur on Adequate Housing 2007, para 60; see also Vanclay 2017, p. 11.

livelihoods, providing replacement land is essential. It is pertinent to note that land is much more than an economic asset for most communities and, hence, the location and nature of the replacement land should take into account and maintain as much as possible the social and cultural significance of land. Overall, the replacement land provided for displaced persons should be of equal or better quality than the land taken.

The other important factor that needs to be taken into account in the replacement of real properties is access to common resources that displaced persons depend upon for their livelihoods and cultural and social life.[115] Loss of access to common resources is one of the factors that contributes to the economic impoverishment, which DID often causes.[116] Thus, it is essential to take them into consideration in the determination of the location of the replacement assets. When that is not possible, they should be factored into the pecuniary compensation. Overall, the replacement of real assets taken away from the displaced persons is the first and preferred remedy that needs to be provided in the case of DID.

B. **Compensation**

In addition to or in lieu of in-kind remedies, i.e. replacement housing and land and access to common resources, displaced persons should also be provided with monetary compensation. The monetary compensation needs to be commensurate to redress the pecuniary and non-pecuniary damage they sustained and to restore their livelihoods.[117] Accordingly, states need to provide "fair and just compensation" to displaced persons for any damage they incurred due to the displacement including, *inter alia*, loss of property and assets, loss of income and other opportunities.[118]

In general, compensation is a substitute remedy that needs to be provided in lieu or in addition to restitution or in-kind remedies.[119] In the context of DID, in particular, states should always give priority to in-kind remedies that are capable of replacing the assets taken from those affected.[120] Studies show that monetary compensation alone can hardly restore the livelihoods and real assets of displaced persons. In fact, using monetary compensation as a sole remedy, in some cases, contributes to the impoverishment of people that often follows DID, particularly when it is a one-off payment.[121]

---

[115] The Special Rapporteur on Adequate Housing 2007, para 52.

[116] Cernea 2000, p. 29.

[117] General Assembly Basic Principles and Guidelines on the Right to a Remedy (n 50) para 120; see also van der Ploeg and Vanclay 2017, p. 42 ("Compensation programmes that are not adequate in protecting families from impoverishment can adversely impact on the right to an adequate standard of living"); see also ARSIWA (n 95) Article 36.

[118] Special Rapporteur Principles and Guidelines (n 32) para 60; see also General Assembly Basic Principles and Guidelines on the Right to a Remedy (n 54) para 20; see also Shelton 2015, p. 319.

[119] Shelton 2015, p. 315.

[120] The Special Rapporteur on Adequate Housing 2007, para 60; see also van der Ploeg and Vanclay 2017, p. 43.

[121] van der Ploeg and Vanclay 2017, p. 45.

International human rights frameworks do not offer adequate standards on the type of pecuniary and non-pecuniary damages that warrant compensation and on how the commensurate amount of compensation should be determined.[122] Human rights monitoring bodies often use some version of the market value standard of assessment, i.e. the (selling) price of the property at the time of the violation, for claims involving property rights.[123] The European Court of Human Rights, for instance, assesses whether the amount of paid by the state is "reasonably related to [the market] value" of the property to determine the adequacy of compensation for deprivation of property.[124] However, this standard does not fully redress the damage caused by the acquisition of properties or meet the objective of re-establishing the livelihoods of displaced persons in the context of DID as will be discussed below.

C. **Rehabilitation**

Rehabilitation measures are various types of fairly long-term assistances provided for displaced persons to ensure that their livelihoods are sustainably restored or improved. Rehabilitation measures include, for instance, creating employment opportunities. The focus here should be on providing long-term jobs or income sources or facilitating ways in which displaced persons can create and participate in income-generating activities.[125] In the cases of the Shuikou and Yantan Dams in China, for instance, in addition to providing a commensurate amount of compensation, the state has taken proactive measures to create jobs and restore the livelihoods of those affected.[126] As a result, most of the people displaced by these projects were

---

[122] Shelton 2015, p. 321.

[123] Ibid., p. 337; see also *Case of Salvador Chiriboga v. Ecuador*, Inter-American Court of Human Rights, Judgment of 6 May 2008 (Preliminary Objection and Merits), para 98; see also European Court of Human Rights, Guide on Article 1 of Protocol No. 1 to the European Convention on Human Rights: the Protection of Property, Updated on 31 December 2021, paras 173–190; see also African Commission on Human and Peoples' Rights, Principles and Guidelines on the Implementation of Economic, Social, and Cultural Rights, 2010, para 55(E).

[124] *The case of The Holy Monasteries v. Greece*, Application no. 13092/87; 13984/88, Judgment, European Court of Human Rights, 09 December 1994, para 71; see also *the case of Platakou v. Greece*, Application no. 38460/97, judgment, European Court of Human Rights, 11 January 2001, para 55; see also European Court of Human Rights, Guide on Article 1 of Protocol No. 1 (n 123) paras 173–190. This does not always equate to the full market value (see *the case of Pincová and Pinc v. the Czech Republic*, Application no. 36548/97, judgment, European Court of Human Rights, 5 November 2002, para 53). The court also leaves a "wide margin of appreciation" for states in determination of compensation (see *the case of James and Others v. United Kingdom*, Application no. 8793/79, judgment, European Court of Human Rights, 21 February 1986, para 54).

[125] This is grounded on the norms on the right to work discussed in Chap. 5. As the joblessness or loss of income that DID involves might constitute deprivation of work, as discussed in Chap. 5, a state needs to take necessary measures to sustainable restore the sources pf income of the people concerned.

[126] Randell 2016, p. 386; World Bank Report (n 74) 10.

able to regain their income and earn even more after displacement.[127] As a joblessness and a decrease in income sources after displacement are among the main causes of impoverishment,[128] it is imperative to address these calamities.

Rehabilitation measures also include benefit-sharing schemes where those displaced by DID can sustainably share the benefits of the development project for which they are displaced. Equitable benefit-sharing is one of the normative elements of the right to development as discussed in Chap. 4.[129] Thus, benefit-sharing is not only a demand of social justice but also constitutes a human rights norm. Benefit-sharing schemes can include various financial and non-financial benefits including project-related jobs, training and other capacity-building opportunities, a percentage share in the project revenue, provision of public services, and discounted rates in services generated by the project, such as electricity.[130] These schemes have proven to be effective in averting the risk of impoverishment and restoring the livelihoods of those displaced. For instance, a study conducted on a series of eviction cases in Jakarta found that benefit-sharing schemes implemented by the government improved the living conditions of evicted households.[131] Moreover, these benefit-sharing schemes would help to address one of the pervasive practices in DID where those who bear the costs of development do not benefit from the fruits of development, which raises numerous human rights and social justice concerns. Thus, these schemes are essential to transform DID into a development opportunity.

The other important rehabilitation measure is integrating resettled individuals or groups into the social and political fabric of the host communities when applicable. In any case, rehabilitation measures need to be responsive to the specific economic, social, and political risks displaced persons face. The human rights, social, and environmental impact assessments that states are expected to undertake, which will be explored in the subsequent section, should be used as input to design these measures.

Overall, states need to provide a range of in-kind and/or monetary remedies to sustainably restore the livelihoods of those affected and avert the risk of impoverishment. Relocation should only take place after these substantive remedies have been arranged.[132] It is imperative to emphasize that the remedies discussed above are not an exhaustive list of the substantive remedies states need to provide to prevent or at least mitigate the adverse consequences of DID. Depending on the context and taking into account the special circumstances of the people affected, states need to provide a range of substantive safeguards. The litmus test should be that the safeguards provided by the state need to be adequate and effective enough to restore and,

---

[127] Randell 2016, p. 386; see also World Bank Report (n 74) 10 & 11.

[128] See the discussion and the examples of case studies in Chap. 5, Sect. 5.6.

[129] The Declaration on the Right to Development (n 101) Articles 1(1), 2(1), and 8(1).

[130] Vanclay 2017, pp. 16 and 17; see also Sholihah and Shaojun 2020, pp. 1 and 2 (for instance, Colombia has a law that demands a specific percentage of the revenue generated from the development project to be used or invested in resettlement areas); see also Koenig 2021, pp. 418 and 419.

[131] Sholihah and Shaojun 2020, p. 10.

[132] Special Rapporteur Principles and Guidelines (n 32) para 56; see also Vanclay 2017, p. 6.

preferably, improve the livelihoods of the people affected and protect their human rights.

10.2.3 Non-discrimination

As established in this book, one of the ways DID can potentially violate human rights is when the process and/or outcome of displacement involves direct or indirect discrimination. The adverse consequences of DID particularly hit vulnerable and marginalized groups the hardest. Not only are these groups disproportionately represented in the number of people displaced by DID but they also face special challenges and adversities due to their specific socio-economic standing and their historical and ongoing marginalization. This book has demonstrated how indigenous peoples, women, and children, in particular, endure special challenges in the course of DID. In addition, those who depend on land for their livelihoods, such as farmers and pastoralists, are severely affected by the consequences of forced displacement. This is compounded by the fact that socially and economically marginalized groups are often not the participants or beneficiaries of the envisaged development, while they bear the costs, including DID, at a higher proportion. The process of development often fails to be inclusive and accommodate the needs and interests of these groups. In addition, the process and outcome of displacement often involve direct or indirect discrimination, which further exacerbates the vulnerability of marginalized groups. Hence, involuntary displacement has the potential to perpetuate existing vulnerabilities or disadvantages and even create new ones particularly when it is not accompanied by appropriate safeguards.

Hence, the process and outcome of DID need to be guided by the principle of non-discrimination, which is a cross-cutting norm of international human rights law.[133] Rights stipulated under human rights treaties should be protected and realized without any discrimination based on any of the protected grounds, *inter alia*, race, gender, ethnicity, political opinion, and social origin.[134] This entails an immediate obligation,[135] or in other words, the duty of non-discrimination is not qualified by the principle of progressive realization. As discussed in Chap. 3, discrimination can be formal or substantive and direct or indirect.[136] States need to take necessary measures to prevent and address all forms of discrimination.[137] States particularly

---

[133] UN CESCR 2009, para 7.

[134] ICCPR (n 19) Article 2(1); see also ICESCR (n 11) Article 2(2).

[135] UN CESCR 2009, para 7.

[136] UN CESCR 2009, paras 8–10 (formal discrimination pertains to discriminatory laws or policies while substantive discriminations denotes differential treatment or prejudice manifested in practice. Direct discrimination occurs when the differential treatment is embedded in the laws or policies and practices of the state. Whereas, indirect discrimination happens when neutral laws or practices have disproportionate impact on certain protected groups).

[137] UN CESCR 2009, paras 8–10.

need to take steps to correct structural problems and rectify cultural and social norms that marginalize certain groups and perpetuate inequalities.[138]

The disproportionate impact of DID on marginalized groups is usually a result of systemic problems in the state and a deliberate attempt of targeting those who have minimal political leverage and lack adequate resources to defend their rights. On the contrary, human rights frameworks require states to take extra steps and implement special measures to protect and empower vulnerable and marginalized groups,[139] rather than take advantage of their vulnerability. In some cases, states are required to adopt differential measures—"temporary special measures"—in order to address historical and systemic inequalities.[140] Marginalised groups that have been historically excluded from participating in development and disproportionately targeted by DID, such as indigenous peoples, should be offered a special protection. Hence, it is important to adopt a vulnerability lens in order to understand and address the differential degrees of risk that DID poses to different groups of people.

10.2.4 Due Diligence: The Principle of "Do No Harm"

The duty of due diligence is a general principle that requires states to take "reasonable measures" in order to identify, prevent, and address human rights risks.[141] It is initially developed and often employed to determine state responsibility particularly for the conduct of private actors.[142] However, the principle of due diligence is increasingly accepted as a standard of conduct against which the compliance of states with their human rights obligations is assessed. States particularly have to exercise a heightened duty of care when they themselves are engaging in activities that create human rights risks,[143] as is the case for DID. The duty of due diligence also coincides with the principle of "do no harm", which is one of the core principles of the HRBA.

The seminal human rights case that explicitly employed due diligence as a standard of assessment of states' human rights obligations is the *Velásquez case* decided by the Inter-American Human Rights Court.[144] In this case, which concerns enforced disappearance, the Court remarked that "an illegal act which violates human rights and which is initially not directly imputable to a State…can lead to international responsibility of the State, not because of the act itself, but because of the lack of due diligence to prevent the violation or to respond to it."[145] This principle was

138 Ibid., paras 8 & 9.

139 Ibid., paras 8 & 9.

140 Ibid., para 9.

141 Monnheimer 2021, p. 69; see also Shelton and Gould 2013, pp. 578 and 579.

142 Monnheimer 2021, p. 78.

143 Ibid 213.

144 *Velásquez Rodríguez v. Honduras*, Judgment, Inter-American Court of Human Rights, 29 July 1988 see also Monnheimer (n 141) 69; see also Shelton and Gould 2013, p. 579.

145 *Velásquez Rodríguez v. Honduras* (n 144) para 172.

later confirmed by the Human Rights Committee in General Comment No. 3, which required states "to exercise due diligence to prevent, punish, investigate or redress the harm caused by…private persons or entities."[146] The African Commission on Human and Peoples Rights also accepted the principle of due diligence as a standard of assessment of states' compliance with their human rights obligations in a case against Zimbabwe.[147] While these jurisprudences mainly relate to the obligations of states for third-party conduct, the principles developed in these cases and interpretative documents can inform the standard of conduct generally expected from states.[148] Overall, it is widely accepted that states should exercise due diligence in complying with their human rights obligations.

The principle of due diligence should guide the process of DID in general and the application of the HRBA to DID in particular. Generally, the duty of due diligence consists of two elements: the duty to prevent harm—human rights violations in this context—and the duty to respond or effectively remedy the harm if it has occurred.[149] The first element requires states to take appropriate legislative, administrate, and other pertinent steps to prevent human rights violations.[150] Accordingly, states need to take reasonable measures to identify and address the human rights impacts of their activities. In the context of DID, states should provide legal protection against arbitrary displacement, eviction, and expropriation as elucidated in the preceding chapters. The relevant laws should also specify the circumstances under which these actions can be justified and the remedies available for those affected.

The other important preventive measure states need to take is to conduct a human rights impact assessment in order to identify and duly address the human rights impact of their activities.[151] Human rights impact assessment is a process that identifies, measures, and responds to the adverse impacts of policies and projects on the enjoyment or realization of human rights.[152] In the context of DID, a human rights impact assessment should identify and assess the human rights impact of the development project in general and the involuntary displacement it (potentially) induces in particular. Human rights impact assessment needs to be undertaken both before the project is implemented to identify its potential impact—"*ex ante* assessment"—and during or after the project and displacement take place to identify the actual impact of the

---

[146] UN CCPR 2004, para 8; see also Monnheimer 2021, p. 70.

[147] *Zimbabwe Human Rights NGO Forum v. Zimbabwe*, Communication No. 245/2002, EX.CL/322 (X), African Commission on Human and Peoples' Rights, 15 May 2006, para 146 (in this case, the African Commission, in fact, explicitly drew lessons from the Inter-American Court case mentioned above); see also Monnheimer 2021, p. 70.

[148] Bourke-Martignoni 2008, p. 51.

[149] Monnheimer 2021, p. 116.

[150] Ibid., p. 71.

[151] The Special Rapporteur on Adequate Housing 2007, para 32. While the present work only deals with human rights impact assessment for apparent reasons—as the scope of this book is limited to international human rights law—states have to undertake other impact assessments that cover the environmental and social impacts, among others, of the proposed project.

[152] Walker 2014, p. 394; see also Harrison 2011, p. 166.

project and respond accordingly—"*ex post* assessment".[153] In addition, the content and process of these impact assessments need to be informed by relevant human rights norms and principles. The human rights impact assessment "...should use human rights norms and standards as measures, and further, should also ensure that the...methodology respects human rights in the process of undertaking the assessment."[154] The assessment needs to identify the rights potentially affected by the project by referring to the pertinent human rights treaties, soft-law frameworks, and interpretative documents.[155] The impact assessment should particularly take into account the specific and divergent impacts of the project on vulnerable and marginalized groups or the groups protected under the non-discrimination clauses.[156] Further, the process and methodology in which the assessment is conducted need to be inclusive, participatory, and non-discriminatory.[157] In other words, the content and the process of the human rights impact assessment itself should follow the human rights-based approach.[158] Overall, the aim of the human rights impact assessment, or the due diligence process for that matter, is to ensure that development projects are implemented in such a way that complies with human rights norms. Thus, conducting a human rights impact assessment is an essential step in the application of the HRBA to DID.

The findings of the human rights impact assessment should be used as input in designing the resettlement plan and inform the determination of the type and scope of safeguards necessary under specific circumstances. In other words, the safeguards put in place by the state need to address the specific human rights impacts identified in the impact assessment with a view to preventing human rights violations. Thus, appropriate responses or measures, which are determined on a case-by-case basis, should be adopted based on the impact assessment. In some extreme cases, the appropriate response could be cancelling the project entirely—if the human rights impact of the project outweighs its public benefit—or changing the site of the project. This ties back to the proportionality assessment discussed previously. In addition, the right to access to information also extends to the human rights impact assessment and the other impact assessments of the proposed project. This information needs to be made public.[159] Particularly those affected by the project and the displacement it causes, their representatives, and other stakeholders including human rights NGOs and the media should have unfettered access. This would allow them to use the findings of these assessments in their advocacy and to challenge the decision through judicial and other mechanisms.[160] Overall, the principle of due diligence urges states

153 Walker 2014, pp. 395 and 396; see also Harrison 2011, p. 166.

154 Walker 2014, p. 398.

155 Ibid., p. 399; see also Harrison 2011, p. 176.

156 The Special Rapporteur on Adequate Housing 2007, para 33; see also Walker 2014, pp. 392 and 393.

157 Walker 2014, p. 399; see also Harrison 2011, pp. 175 and 176; see also Adeola 2017, p. 99.

158 Walker 2014, p. 399.

159 Harrison 2011, p. 179.

160 Ibid., pp. 167 and 179.

not only to use displacement as a last resort but also to take precautionary measures in order to prevent the adverse impact of displacement when it is inevitable.

The second element of due diligence entails investigating and providing redress for human rights violations.[161] This pertains to the right to effective remedies elaborated in the preceding sections and, thus, a further discussion is not desirable here.

10.3 Normative Gaps in International Human Rights Law

The final question this book asked was: *to what extent do the existing human rights frameworks adequately address the adverse consequences of DID and its salient features?*

While the procedural and substantive safeguards that need to be provided in the course of displacement and resettlement can be drawn from existing human rights norms and principles, there are substantial gaps and inconsistencies in international human rights law vis-à-vis DID. It is to be recalled that some of the specific gaps have been discussed in the previous chapters in relation to the rights and frameworks to which they correspond. These normative gaps and limitations can be summarised under three main categories: gaps in the recognition of land rights, the inadequacy of normative guidance on the substantive safeguards or remedies, and a lack of contextualization of the existing norms to sufficiently respond to DID, which will be elaborated in the subsequent sections.

10.3.1 The Gap in the Recognition of Land Rights

The principal normative gap in international human rights law in relation to DID pertains to the lack of recognition of a general right to land. As discussed in Chap. 4, the existing universal and regional human rights frameworks do not explicitly recognize land rights.[162] While land rights partly fall within the scope of certain rights, such as the rights to property, housing, and food, this is far from being comprehensive. For instance, relying on property rights to protect land rights comes with two main challenges. First, property rights are not adequately recognized in international human rights law, particularly at the universal level.[163] While Article 17 of the UDHR explicitly enunciates "the right to own property" and offers protection against

[161] Monnheimer 2021, pp. 71 and 72.

[162] Gilbert 2013, p. 115.

[163] On the other hand, all the major regional human rights instruments contain a provision that guarantees the right to property (see Council of Europe, Protocol 1 to the European Convention for the Protection of Human Rights and Fundamental Freedoms, 20 March 1952, 9 ETS, Article 1; see also Inter-American Convention on Human Rights (n 56) Article 21; see also African Charter (n 56) Article 14).

arbitrary deprivation of property,[164] this right is left out of the two Covenants.[165] Moreover, although a compelling argument can be made that the right to property has obtained the status of customary international law as discussed previously,[166] it is one of the most underdeveloped rights and there is hardly any guidance from the universal human rights monitoring bodies as to its normative contents. Second, property rights cannot fully protect the broad scope of land rights. Land is more than property or an economic asset, and it has cultural, social, and spiritual significance,[167] which the right to property cannot fully protect.[168] Moreover, the scope of land rights should not be confined to formal ownership or possessions. Rather, it should also extend to informal settlements, traditional land tenures, and communal properties, which are particularly relevant in the context of DID. Thus, property rights do not comprehensively protect land rights. This is also true for the recognition of land rights through the rights to housing and food. These rights protect land to the extent that it is essential to the procurement of the objects of those rights—shelter and food, respectively.[169] In other words, the norms on the rights to housing and food only protect land based on its instrumental value in the protection of these rights. Hence, these norms do not fully capture the economic, social, and cultural significance of land and the broad scope of land rights.[170]

International human rights law, on the other hand, offers special protection to indigenous peoples' rights to their ancestral land, as elucidated in Chap. 7.[171] The frameworks on indigenous peoples particularly protect these peoples against the acquisition of and involuntary removal from their lands.[172] Indigenous peoples cannot be removed from the lands they traditionally occupy for development or other purposes without their "free, prior, and informed consent".[173] The protections accorded to indigenous peoples, however, are not applicable and cannot even be analogously applied to individuals or groups that do not have "indigenous status". This is due to the fact that the norms on indigenous peoples' land rights are developed based

164 UDHR (n 11) Article 17.

165 Gilbert 2013, p. 118 (this "[makes] property rights one of the only human rights affirmed in the UDHR which was not integrated into one of the legally binding Covenants").

166 See Chap. 4, Sect. 4.2. Evidence of state practice and opinio juris in particular show that the first paragraph of Article 17 of the UDHR, which guarantees "the right to own property alone as well as in association with others", has obtained the status of customary international law (see Golay and Cismas 2010, p. 10).

167 Gilbert 2013, p. 129.

168 The right to property has been largely associated with the liberal conception of individualism and conceived as a right that protects already acquired properties from interference by others (see Heri 2020, p. 434).

169 Diergarten 2019, pp. 40 and 41; see also Gilbert 2013, pp. 124–128.

170 Gilbert 2013, p. 126.

171 See Chap. 7, Sect. 7.4.

172 UNDRIP (n 61) Article 10; see also ILO Convention No. 169 (n 61) Articles 13–19.

173 UNDRIP (n 61) Article 10; see also ILO Convention No. 169 (n 61) Article 16.

on the distinct cultural or spiritual connection these groups have with their ancestral land.[174] In other words, the rationale that indigenous peoples are bestowed with heightened protection against interference with their lands is this special connection, which is also the very fact on which their existence or identification as indigenous communities depends.[175] The jurisprudence of the human rights monitoring bodies is also developed along the same lines; these bodies heavily rely on this special connection in their reasonings in cases where the land rights of these communities are invoked.[176] Hence, the protection of land rights accorded to indigenous peoples cannot be readily transferred to other groups as their rationale is closely linked to the very fact of being indigenous.

Land is an important, if not the most important, variable in DID discourse. The acquisition of land that DID often involves "…removes the main foundation upon which people's productive systems, commercial activities, and livelihoods are constructed."[177] In most cases, the people affected by DID depend on land for their livelihoods and social and cultural subsistence. While indigenous peoples are often disproportionately affected by DID, not all individuals and groups displaced to make room for development projects have such status. Hence, they cannot enjoy the same level of protection accorded to indigenous peoples despite their reliance on land. Those that have been economically and politically marginalized, in some cases to a comparable degree to indigenous peoples, such as peasants and pastoralists, remain vulnerable to arbitrary land acquisitions and other interferences with their lands. This is one of the reasons peasant rights advocates have been pushing for the adoption of a human rights framework that protects the rights of peasants.[178] As a result, the Working Group on the Rights of Peasants, established under the auspices of the Human Rights Council, drafted a "Declaration on the Rights of Peasants and Other People Working in Rural Areas", which was adopted in 2018.[179]

The Declaration, which heavily draws on the frameworks on indigenous peoples rights, among others,[180] envisages, *inter alia*, individual and collective rights to land, legal security of tenure including for informal or traditional tenures, and protection

---

[174] Diergarten 2019, p. 46; see also ILO Convention No. 169 (n 61) Article 13; see also UNDRIP (n 61) Article 25; see also Gilbert 2013, p. 119.

[175] UNDRIP (n 11) Article 25; see also *Centre for Minority Rights Development (Kenya) and Minority Rights Group International on behalf of Endorois Welfare Council v. Kenya*, 276/2003, African Commission on Human and Peoples' Rights, 4 February 2010, para 154.

[176] Diergarten 2019, pp. 46–48; see for instance, *Case of the Saramaka People v Suriname*, Preliminary objections, merits, reparations and costs, 28th November 2007, para 122; see also *Endorois case* (n 175) para 151; see also *Daniel Billy et al. v Australia*, communication No. 3624/2019, adoption of views, UN Human Rights Committee, 22 September 2022, CCPR/C/135/D/3624/2019, paras 8.13 & 8.13; see also Gilbert 2013, pp. 119 and 120.

[177] Cernea 2000, p. 23.

[178] Diergarten 2019, p. 50.

[179] UN Human Rights Council, Resolution 39/12, Declaration on the Rights of Peasants and Other People Working in Rural Areas, A/HRC/RES/39/12, 8 October 2018.

[180] Diergarten 2019, pp. 50 and 51; see also the Declaration on the rights of peasants (n 179) Preamble.

against arbitrary displacement or forced eviction.[181] Yet, the Declaration does not enunciate standards for a justified displacement or eviction of peasants from their land and the safeguards that need to be provided along the way. It only requires states to undertake meaningful consultation prior to engaging in any activity that affects the rights of peasants and those working in rural areas.[182] The Declaration, however, does not extend the requirement of "free, prior, and informed consent" to these groups. These land-related rights are predicated on the recognition of peasants' special relationship with their lands and the corresponding environment as well as their reliance on those resources for their livelihoods.[183] The adoption of the Declaration is a momentous step not only for the protection of the rights of peasants but also for the development of land rights in general. The norms incorporated therein will substantially contribute to filling the existing normative gap in international human rights law with regard to the recognition of land rights,[184] although they are not impervious to limitations. Moreover, the rights enshrined under the Declaration frame land as a natural resource that the people concerned utilize to make a living rather than as a mere commodity,[185] which challenges the liberal and individualistic conception of land under the property rights regime. Nevertheless, the recognition of land rights under the Declaration is status-based similar to the frameworks on indigenous peoples rights. In other words, it only applies to those who are considered peasants,[186] albeit this group is broader than the indigenous status, and it does not offer a general right to land. Thus, those who do not fit in the definitions of indigenous peoples or peasants fall outside the normative scope of (meaningful) land rights protection in international law. While these groups evidently need a specific protection due to their special dependence on land, other groups, such as urban residents, also use land for various socio-economic and cultural purposes.[187] Hence, a general and comprehensive right to land, which embraces the economic, social, and cultural significance of land and protects right-holders from arbitrary interference, is overdue.

As established in the preceding chapters, disruption of access to land—landlessness or decrease of landholdings—that DID often results in is the principal reason for the impoverishment of those displaced by DID. The lack of a general and comprehensive right to land and normative guidance on the legitimate acquisition of land

[181] Declaration on the rights of peasants (n 179) Article 17.

[182] Ibid., Articles 2(3) & 5.

[183] Ibid., Preamble.

[184] Diergarten 2019, p. 51.

[185] Heri 2020, p. 445.

[186] The Declaration defines a peasant as "any person who engages or who seeks to engage, alone, or in association with others or as a community, in small-scale agricultural production for subsistence and/or for the market, and who relies significantly, though not necessarily exclusively, on family or household labour and other non-monetized ways of organizing labour, and who has a special dependency on and attachment to the land" (see Declaration on the rights of peasants (n 183) Article 1(1)). In addition, the Declaration also applies to those working in agriculture in different capacities and related activities in rural areas (see Declaration on the rights of peasants (n 179) Article 1(2–4)).

[187] For instance, for business operations and rental properties. Not to mention the spiritual and cultural significance of land.

exacerbates this problem. This is the main normative gap in international human rights law when it comes to DID.

This normative gap can be addressed through the development of a separate and general instrument on land rights either in the form of a treaty, although the adoption of a treaty can be unlikely, or a soft law instrument that emulates, for instance, the Declarations on the rights of indigenous peoples or peasants. This instrument needs to recognize the right to access, utilize, and control land as well as offer protection against arbitrary acquisition of land or deprivation of land rights. The instrument should also stipulate circumstances under which land acquisition can be justified, the conditions that need to be fulfilled, and the safeguards that need to be provided for the acquisition of land. These norms can be informed by the pertinent human rights norms identified in this book, other norms and principles of international law and domestic law. In lieu of a separate instrument or until such an instrument is adopted, human rights monitoring bodies can and should clarify the normative contents of land rights by drawing on existing human rights norms that directly or indirectly recognize land rights.

The CESCR has recently taken steps towards this by developing a general comment "on land and economic, social and cultural rights".[188] The general comment affirms that land rights are instrumental to the realization of several rights enunciated under the ICESCR, such as the rights to housing, food, and water, and outlines the specific obligations of states.[189] The general comment potentially contributes towards filling the normative underdevelopment discussed above and catalysing the international law discourse on land rights.

10.3.2 *Inadequacy of Normative Guidance on Substantive Safeguards*

The other protection gap evident in international human rights law is the inadequacy of normative guidance on the type, scope, and assessment of substantive remedies or safeguards that need to be provided for people(s) affected by DID. The law of remedies is one of the most underdeveloped areas in international human rights law.[190] While the right to effective remedies is enshrined in numerous human rights frameworks, these frameworks "provide limited guidance in shaping remedies."[191] As mentioned before, international human rights instruments do not specify when substantive remedies are due; nor do they provide guidelines or standards for the evaluation of these remedies.[192] This is particularly true for determination of "adequate compensation". One could argue that the assessment of compensation, which

188 UN CESCR 2022.

189 Ibid.

190 Roach 2021, p. 4.

191 Ibid., p. 4.

192 Shelton 2015, p. 321.

involves taking into account various financial, market, and social factors, is outside of the reach of legal norms—particularly international human rights law. Moreover, what adequate compensation means is contextual and subjective, which should best be assessed on a case-by-case basis. Nevertheless, although these arguments are to some extent valid, human rights law should provide normative standards against which the "effectiveness" of remedies is measured. As substantive remedies are one of the important prerequisites for the effectiveness of remedies, international human rights law should not leave the determination of these remedies to the discretion of states or domestic laws.

Although the practice of human rights bodies can inform the determination of remedies, they still fall short of covering the full range of remedies that need to be provided in the context of DID. For instance, the market value standard of assessment commonly employed by these bodies fails to take into account fluctuations in the market value of the property concerned—between the time of acquisition of the property and the time of resettlement, the cost of obtaining a similar property in the resettlement site, and other related costs, such as transaction costs.[193] Moreover, this standard of assessment does not duly consider other relevant factors that affect the value of the property and, in turn, affect the livelihoods of the people affected, such as the location of the property and its proximity to essential public services, access to common resources, and the cultural and sentimental significance of the property to the people affected. Thus, the market value standard of assessment for the acquisition of properties might not be adequate to allow those affected to obtain properties of similar value in the resettlement location.

In addition, the norms on the right to effective remedies are theoretically applicable when violations of human rights occur. In other words, states are obliged to provide adequate and effective remedies to rectify the pecuniary and non-pecuniary damage incurred due to violations of human rights. Consequently, the main objective of remedies is to correct the wrong following a breach of obligation.[194] In the context of DID, however, substantive remedies or safeguards, such as the replacement of real assets and compensation, need to be provided not only to redress the violations but also to prevent violations of human rights. Ideally, states would put in place adequate procedural and substantive safeguards to justify the human rights interferences that DID results in and, hence, avoid the violation of human rights. Thus, the main objective of remedies in the case of DID is to restore or preferably improve the livelihoods of those affected. This distinction between the general law of remedies and the remedies needed in the context of DID makes the existing substantive remedies in international human rights law inadequate, albeit not irrelevant, to accommodate the peculiar issues and adverse impacts to human rights that DID involves.

---

[193] On the contrary, as mentioned in Chap. 9, the resettlement policies of international financial institutions use a "replacement cost" standard of assessment, which is calculated based on the market value of replacing the property of a similar value plus the transaction costs (see Vanclay 2017, p. 13; see also van der Ploeg and Vanclay 2017, p. 43).

[194] Shelton 2015, pp. 19 and 13.

In addition, international human rights law does not offer adequate normative guidance on the rehabilitation measures that need to be provided for people affected by DID. As the preceding chapters have established, DID often results in long-term adverse consequences and, in some cases, the consequences of DID only materialize after a significant time lapse. These long-term consequences make displaced persons susceptible to chronic impoverishment. Studies conducted on DID indicate that long-term rehabilitation measures are essential to fully restore the livelihoods of those affected and to prevent the risk of impoverishment that often taints this form of displacement. Hence, it is important that there is normative guidance on the follow-up and rehabilitation measures states need to undertake to ensure that the livelihoods of those affected are sustainably restored. This will not only offer guidance for states but also allow the people affected by DID to formulate and claim their rights.

Overall, international human rights law falls short of providing comprehensive guidelines that can be used to determine the type, scope, and amount of substantive remedies that need to be provided in the course of DID as well as accommodating the peculiar features of DID. This normative underdevelopment along with the next one, i.e. the lack of contextualization, can be addressed through the adoption of a guiding framework that contextually elucidates how the existing norms can be used to determine and provide the necessary safeguards in the course of DID. It can also be rectified by the interpretations of human rights monitoring bodies.

10.3.3 Lack of Contextualization of Existing Norms

Displacement prompted by development projects is the most neglected and under-explored form of internal displacement in international human rights law in general and in the frameworks on the rights of IDPs in particular. The discourse on internal displacement seldom takes into account the involuntary displacement caused to make room for development projects and its adverse consequences. Rather, it principally focuses on displacement induced by extraordinary or unforeseen circumstances, i.e. conflict and natural disasters. As elucidated in Chap. 6, most of the norms on the rights of IDPs appear to be drafted having these unforeseen displacements, particularly conflict-induced displacement, in mind. The UN special procedures established to monitor internal displacement have rarely paid attention to displacement instigated by development projects.[195] In addition, "[w]hile the UNHCR has expanded its mandate to include the responsibility to protect not only refugees but also those who have not crossed a border and yet are in a refugee like situation, the agency has repeatedly rejected an expansion of the definition of displacement to include those people who lose their homes and their assets in the development process."[196] Similarly, international institutions that track and keep a database on internal displacement

[195] Sánchez 2017, p. 89.

[196] McDowell 2014, pp. 340 and 341.

fail to duly document the statistics on DID.[197] This neglect of DID is also reflected in academic works in international law where issues related to DID are ostensibly understudied despite a myriad of legal questions they raise. Similar to the development of norms, the existing literature disproportionately focuses on conflict-induced displacement and, to some extent, disaster-induced displacement.

However, as established throughout this book, displacement caused by development can be equally disruptive and result in a plethora of adversities if adequate safeguards are not provided. In addition, contrary to the other forms of internal displacement, DID is prompted by the state and is pre-planned, foreseeable, and hence, it can be readily avoided. Thus, the degree of safeguards and humanitarian assistance states are obliged to provide in the case of unforeseen displacements caused by external factors would not be adequate in the context of DID. The frameworks on IDPs, i.e. the UN Guiding Principles on the Rights of IDPs and the AU Convention for the Protection and Assistance of IDPs, for the most part, reflect the bare minimum standards of protection.[198] These standards might be adequate when a state is faced with an emergency or unforeseen displacements caused by external factors but not when the state itself is prompting the displacement. Thus, states should have heightened obligations to put in place adequate safeguards before, during, and after displacement when they themselves are planning and causing the involuntary displacement. The existing human rights norms on internal displacement do not duly take into account these distinguishing features of DID.

Consequently, the relevant human rights norms are not sufficiently developed and contextualized through interpretation to accommodate the peculiar features of DID and the risks people(s) affected thereby face. For instance, the human rights norms mentioned in this chapter, such as access to information, access to justice, and substantive remedies, can be found scattered in various human rights frameworks or can be drawn from the interpretive documents and case law of human rights bodies. Nevertheless, they have not been adequately contextualized to respond to the specific issues that arise when people(s) are uprooted from their homes or residences to make room for development projects. In a similar vein, although the duty of due diligence, particularly the desirability of the human rights impact assessment, is fairly accepted, its application in the context of DID has not been explored to a sufficient degree. Thus, the existing norms do not lend themselves to proper utilization by duty-bearers in designing development projects as well as by right-holders in invoking their rights.

---

197 Sánchez 2017, p. 89. For instance, the Internal Displacement Monitoring Centre (IDMC), the organization that keeps up-to-date data on internal displacement, does not track and publish data on DID while it does for conflict and disaster-induced displacement (see IDMC, Global Internal Displacement Database, available at https://www.internal-displacement.org/database/displacement-data, accessed 2 July 2025); see also Stanley 2004, p. 3.

198 See Chap. 6, Sect. 6.3; see also Kälin 2005, p. 30. For instance, the Guiding Principles on IDPs requires states "…ensure, to the greatest practicable extent, that proper accommodation is provided to the displaced persons, that such displacements are effected in satisfactory conditions of safety, nutrition, health and hygiene, and that members of the same family are not separated" (see UN Commission on Human Rights, Guiding Principles on Internal Displacement, 11 February 1998, E/CN.4/1998/53/Add.2, Principle 7(2)). This does not reflect the comprehensive substantive safeguards states need to provide in the context of DID as discussed in the preceding sections.

As mentioned before, there is no specific and comprehensive framework in international human rights law that sets norms on DID. Besides, there are hardly any guidelines, interpretative documents, or soft-law instruments that elaborates on the application of the relevant human rights norms in the context of DID. The only notable effort in this regard is the guiding principles adopted by the UN Special Rapporteur on the right to housing, which details the application of the norms on the right to housing on forced evictions induced by development projects.[199] While this is a commendable effort, it is limited in scope as it mostly deals with only the right to housing and does not address DID in a broader sense. The only comprehensive frameworks in this regard are the involuntary resettlement policies of international financial institutions (IFIs). Nonetheless, norm-setting should not be left to these institutions since human rights are not systematically mainstreamed in the activities and policies of these institutions, as established in the preceding chapter. Moreover, not all development projects that involve displacement are funded by these institutions and, hence, cannot benefit from the policy guidance they offer.

Overall, international human rights law does not offer sufficient normative guidance to states as to the application of the relevant human rights norms in the context of DID. This normative underdevelopment also hinders right-holders or people affected by DID from invoking their rights through available human rights complaint mechanisms.

Addressing this normative underdevelopment does not necessarily require the adoption of a new right or a new international treaty. However, there should be a guiding framework that sets out the safeguards that should be put in place by states at all stages of DID to protect the rights of the people affected thereby. This requires contextualizing the existing human rights norms and principles to address the salient features of DID and the socio-economic consequences it results in. This can be achieved through a soft-law instrument that emulates the guiding principles on IDPs or the guiding principles on business and human rights. This instrument can be informed by the resettlement policies of IFIs and draw lessons from the case studies of development projects that involve involuntary displacement and resettlement. Until such framework is achieved, human rights monitoring bodies can and should provide interpretative guidance on how the respective frameworks or norms they monitor are applicable in the context of DID.

10.4 Conclusion

As the current book has established, most of the adverse consequences of DID are attributable to the lack or inadequacy of the procedural and substantive safeguards put in place by states rather than the mere fact of displacement. As invasive as DID can be, its adverse impacts can be avoided, or at least mitigated, with the provision of adequate safeguards at all phases of displacement and resettlement. As the case

[199] The Special Rapporteur on Adequate Housing 2007.

studies of positive resettlement experiences also attest, it is, in fact, possible to avoid the looming risk of impoverishment in DID as well as to restore and even improve the livelihoods of those affected. Against this background, the current chapter quested how international human rights law can be utilized to this effect or how DID and the involuntary resettlements it involves can be justified and designed based on human rights norms and principles. Thus, it has proposed the HRBA to DID as a guiding framework. The HRBA—the integration of human rights norms and principles in the process of DID—can aid the provision of adequate safeguards. The HRBA not only offers legitimacy to the process of DID but also potentially leads to a better outcome in terms of averting the adverse consequences of DID and protecting the rights of the people affected thereby.

The first step in the application of the HRBA to DID is (re)framing DID as human rights interferences and justifying those interferences based on the norms on limitations to human rights. As most human rights are not absolute and can be limited to protect a higher individual or public interest, the interferences that DID results in can also be justified provided that the conditions of limitation under the relevant human rights treaties are fulfilled. Generally, a justified limitation has to comply with three cumulative conditions: it has to be provided by law, pursue a legitimate aim, and be necessary and proportionate. Hence, the proposed development project that causes displacement as well as the specific interferences that DID involves have to be justified based on these three conditions.

If displacement is inevitable and justified based on the three-part test, states have to put in place comprehensive procedural and substantive safeguards at all phases of displacement—from the planning of the development project concerned to resettlement and beyond. These safeguards should be aimed at avoiding, or at least mitigating, the adverse consequences of DID and protecting the rights of those affected. The relevant human rights frameworks and norms indicate that procedural safeguards include access to relevant and timely information, meaningful participation, and access to remedies, preferably judicial remedies. Overall, the process of DID needs to be inclusive, participatory, and human-centred. In addition, adequate substantive safeguards that are aimed at restoring and preferably improving the livelihoods of displaced persons need to be provided. These safeguards include the replacement of real assets—housing and/or land—of comparable or better quality than the ones taken, access to common resources, a commensurate amount of compensation, and follow-up and rehabilitation measures to ensure that the livelihoods of those concerned are sustainably restored.

Moreover, the process of DID and the provision of remedies or safeguards need to be guided by the principle of non-discrimination, which is a cross-cutting norm in human rights law. Rights recognized under human rights treaties should be guaranteed without any discrimination based on any of the protected grounds. In this regard, states not only need to refrain from applying unjustified differential treatment but also take positive measures to address the structural inequalities that marginalized groups face. In all of these processes, states should exercise due diligence to identify, prevent, and redress the human rights risks of their activities, which particularly involves conducting human rights impact assessment.

International human rights law, however, does not have all the answers. In fact, the existing human rights frameworks and norms grapple with substantial normative gaps and limitations that potentially impede the effective protection of the rights of people(s) affected by DID. The first normative gap pertains to the lack of recognition of a general right to land. While land rights are partly covered by the scope of certain rights, such as the rights to property, housing, and food, and are protected for specific groups, i.e. indigenous peoples and peasants, international human rights law does not recognize a general right to land. As land acquisition is the main factor behind the impoverishment of the people affected by DID and the human rights risks they face, this poses a significant protection gap. Another normative gap in international human rights law vis-à-vis DID is the lack of sufficient normative guidance on the type, scope, and assessment of substantive safeguards or remedies that need to be provided for the people affected by DID. Not only is the law of remedies one of the most underdeveloped areas in international human rights law but it also does not provide normative guidance as to the specific remedies required in the context of DID. The other normative gap pertains to the lack of contextualization and development of the existing human rights norms to accommodate the peculiar features of DID and the risks the people affected thereby face. The development of norms on internal displacement, the interpretation by human rights bodies, and the academic discourse mainly focus on displacements caused by unforeseen and external circumstances, i.e. conflict and natural disasters. As DID is pre-planned, foreseeable, and prompted by the state, the norms developed having those unforeseen forms of displacements in mind would not be adequate. Thus, the existing norms are underdeveloped and not sufficiently contextualized to respond to DID. Hence, international human rights law does not offer adequate and sufficient guidance when it comes to displacement caused to make room for development projects. Overall, these normative gaps need to be addressed to make human rights law more responsive to DID and allow rights-holders to effectively enjoy and invoke their rights.

References

Adeola R (2017) The Legal Protection of Development-Induced Displaced Persons in Africa. 10 African Journal of Legal Studies 91–104.

Bassiouni M C (2006) International Recognition of Victims' Rights. (2006) 6(2) Human Rights Law Review 203–279.

Boesen J K, Sano H-O (2010) The Implications and Value-Added of a Human Rights-Based Approach. In: Andreassen B V, Marks S P (eds) Development as a Human Right: Legal, Political and Economic Dimensions, 2nd edn. Intersentia, Antwerp.

Bourke-Martignoni J (2008) The History and Development of the Due Diligence Standard in International Law and Its Role in the Protection of Women against Violence. In: Benninger-Budel C (ed) Due Diligence and its Application to Protect Women from Violence. Martinus Nijhoff Publishers, Leiden/Boston.

Braniff M, Hainsworth P (2015) A Human Rights Based Approach to Development. In: McCann G, McCloskey S (eds) From the Local to the Global: Key Issues in Development Studies, 3rd edn. Pluto Press, London.

Cernea M M (2000) Risks, safeguards, and reconstruction: a model for population displacement and resettlement. In: Cernea M M, McDowell C (eds) Risks and Reconstruction: Experiences of Resettlers and Refugees. The World Bank, Washington DC.

Conte A (2016) Defining Civil and Political Rights: The Jurisprudence of the United Nations Human Rights Committee, 2nd edn. Routledge, London.

Diergarten Y (2019) Indigenous or Out of Scope? Large-scale Land Acquisitions in Developing Countries, International Human Rights Law and the Current Deficiencies in Land Rights Protection. (2019) 19(1) Human Rights Law Review 37–52.

Gilbert J (2013) Land Rights as Human Rights: the Case for a Specific Right to Land. (2013) 10(18) International Journal on Human Rights 115–135.

Golay C, Cismas I (2010) Legal Opinion: The Right to Property from a Human Rights Perspective. International Centre for Human Rights and Democratic Development.

Gready P (2008) Rights-based approaches to development: what is the value added? (2008) 18(6) Development in Practice 735–747.

Hamm B I (2001) A Human Rights Approach to Development. (2001) 23(4) Human Rights Quarterly 1005–1031.

Harrison J (2011) Human Rights Measurement: Reflections on the Current Practice and Future Potential of Human Rights Impact Assessment. (2011) 3(2) Journal of Human Rights Practice 162–187.

Heri C (2020) The Human Right to Land, for Peasants and for All: Tracing the Social Function of Property to 1948. (2020) 20(3) Human Rights Law Review 433–452.

Kälin W (2005) The Guiding Principles on Internal Displacement as International Minimum Standard and Protection Tool. (2005) 24(3) Refugee Survey Quarterly 27–36.

Koenig D (2006) Enhancing Local Development in Development-Induced Displacement and Resettlement Projects. In: de Wet C (ed) Development-induced Displacement: Problems, Policies, and People. Berghahn Books, New York.

Koenig D (2021) Advantages and Obstacles to Retrofitting Benefit-Sharing after Development-Induced Displacement and Resettlement. 35(5) Impact Assessment and Project Appraisal 417–428.

McDonagh M (2013) The Right to Information in International Human Rights Law. (2013) 13(1) Human Rights Law Review 25–55.

McDowell C (2014) Development Created Population Displacement. In: Fiddian-Qasmiyeh E, Loescher G, Long K, Sigona N (eds) The Oxford Handbook of Refugee and Forced Migration Studies. Oxford University Press, Oxford.

Mejia M C (2000) Economic Recovery After Involuntary Resettlement: the Case of Brickmakers Displaced by the Yacyereta Hydroelectric Project. In: Cernea M M, McDowell C (eds) Risks and Reconstruction: Experiences of Resettles and Refugees. The World Bank, Washington DC.

Monnheimer M (2021) Due Diligence Obligations in International Human Rights Law. Cambridge University Press, Cambridge.

Muller A (2009) Limitations to and Derogations from Economic, Social and Cultural Rights. (2009) 9(4) Human Rights Law Review 557–601.

Office of the United Nations High Commissioner for Human Rights (OHCHR) (2006) Frequently asked questions on human rights based approach to development cooperation, 2006, HR/PUB/06/8.

Osmani S R (2005) An Essay on the Human Rights Approach to Development. In: Sengupta A, Negi A, Basu M (eds) Reflections on the Right to Development. SAGE Publications, India.

Price S (2009) Prologue: Victims or Partners? The Social Perspective in Development-Induced Displacement and Resettlement. (2009) 10(4) The Asia Pacific Journal of Anthropology 266–282.

Randell H (2016) The short-term impacts of development-induced displacement on wealth and subjective well-being in the Brazilian Amazon. (2016) 87 World Development 385–400.

Riccardi A (2018) The Right to Know: the Role of Transparency, Access to Information, Freedom of Expression in Overcoming Disasters. In: Giustiniani F Z, Sommario E, Casolari F, Bartolini G (eds) Routledge Handbook of Human Rights and Disasters. Routledge, London/New York.
Roach K (2021) Remedies for Human Rights Violations: a Two-Two Approach to Supra-National and National Law. Cambridge University Press, Cambridge.
Sánchez B E (2017) Colombian Development-Induced Displacement – Considering the Impact of International Law on Domestic Policy. (2017) 5(1) Groningen Journal of International Law 73–95.
Saul B, Kinley D, Mowbray J (2014) The International Covenant on Economic, Social and Cultural Rights: Commentary, Cases, and Materials. Oxford University Press, Oxford.
Shelton D (2015) Remedies in International Human Rights Law, 3rd edn. Oxford University Press, Oxford.
Shelton D, Gould A (2013) Positive and Negative Obligations. In: Shelton D (ed) Oxford Handbook of International Human Rights Law. Oxford University Press.
Sholihah P I, Shaojun C (2020) Improving living conditions of displacees: A review of the evidence benefit sharing scheme for development induced displacement and resettlement (DIDR) in urban Jakarta Indonesia. (2020) 20 World Development Perspectives 1–12.
Sommario E (2018) Limitations and derogation provisions in international human rights law treaties and their use in disaster settings. In: Giustiniani F Z, Sommario E, Casolari F, Bartolini G (eds) Routledge Handbook of Human Rights and Disasters. Routledge, London/New York.
Special Rapporteur on Adequate Housing (2007) Basic Principles and Guidelines on Development-based Evictions and Displacement, 5 February 2007, A/HRC/4/18.
Stanley J (2004) Development-induced Displacement and Resettlement. (2004) Forced Migration Online.
UN Committee on Economic, Social and Cultural Rights (UN CESCR) (1990) General Comment No. 3: The Nature of States Parties' Obligations (Article 2, Para 1, of the Covenant), 14 December 1990, E/1991/23.
UN Committee on Economic, Social and Cultural Rights (UN CESCR) (1991) General Comment No. 4: The Right to Adequate Housing (Article 11 (1) of the Covenant), 13 December 1991, E/1992/23.
UN Committee on Economic, Social and Cultural Rights (UN CESCR) (1997) General Comment No. 7: The right to adequate housing (Article 11.1): forced evictions, 20 May 1997, E/1998/22.
UN Committee on Economic, Social and Cultural Rights (UN CESCR) (1998) General Comment No. 9: The domestic application of the Covenant, 3 December 1998, E/C.12/1998/24.
UN Committee on Economic, Social and Cultural Rights (UN CESCR) (1999) General Comment No. 12: The Right to Adequate Food (Article 11 of the Covenant), 12 May 1999, E/C.12/1999/5.
UN Committee on Economic, Social and Cultural Rights (UN CESCR) (2000) General Comment No. 14: The Right to the Highest Attainable Standard of Health (Article 12), 11 August 2000, E/C.12/2000/4.
UN Committee on Economic, Social and Cultural Rights (UN CESCR) (2009) General Comment No. 20: Non-discrimination in economic, social and cultural rights (Article 2, para 2, of the International Covenant on Economic, Social and Cultural Rights), 2 July 2009, E/C.12/GC/20.
UN Committee on Economic, Social and Cultural Rights (UN CESCR) (2022) General Comment No. 26 (2022) on Land and Economic, Social and Cultural Rights, E/C.12/GC/26, 22 December 2022.
UN Human Rights Committee (UN CCPR) (1999) General Comment No. 27: Article 12 (Freedom of Movement), 2 November 1999, CCPR/C/21/Rev.1/Add.9.
UN Human Rights Committee (UN CCPR) (2004) General comment No. 31 [80], The nature of the general legal obligation imposed on States Parties to the Covenant, 26 May 2004, CCPR/C/21/Rev.1/Add.13.
UN Human Rights Committee (UN CCPR) (2011) General Comment No. 34, Article 19, Freedoms of opinion and expression, 12 September 2011, CCPR/C/GC/34.

Uvin P (2007) From the right to development to the rights-based approach: how 'human rights' entered development. (2007) 17(4/5) Development in Practice 597–606.
Vanclay F (2017) Project-induced displacement and resettlement: from impoverishment risks to an opportunity for development? (2017) 35(1) Impact Assessment and Project Appraisal 3–21.
van der Ploeg L, Vanclay F (2017) A human Rights-based Approach to Project Induced Displacement and Resettlement. (2017) 35(1) Impact Assessment and Project Appraisal 34–52.
Walker S (2014) Human Rights Impact Assessments: Emerging Practice and Challenges. In: Riedel E, Giacca G, Golay C (eds) Economic, Social, and Cultural Rights in International Law: Contemporary Issues and Challenges. Oxford University Press, Oxford.
Wewerinke-Singh M (2019) Remedies for Human Rights Violations Caused by Climate Change. (2019) 9 Climate Law 224–243.
World Bank (1998) Recent Experience With Involuntary Resettlement China Shuikou (and Yantan), Report No. 17539, 2 June 1998.

Bibliography

Books

Alston, Philip and Robinson, Mary, *Human Rights and Development: Towards Mutual Reinforcement* (Oxford: Oxford University Press, 2005).

Anaya, S. James, *International Human Rights and Indigenous Peoples* (Aspen Publishers, 2009).

Anaya, S. James, *International Human Rights and Indigenous Peoples* (Wolters Kluwer Law & Business, 2010).

Bennett, Olivia and McDowell, Christopher, *Displaced: The Human Cost of Development and Resettlement* (Palgrave Macmillan, 2012).

Cernea, Michael M. and McDowell, Christopher (eds), *Risks and Reconstruction: Experiences of Refugees and Resettlers* (The World Bank, Washington DC., 2000).

Chambers, Robert, *Settlement schemes in Tropical Africa: A Study of Organizations and Development* (Routledge & Kegan Paul, 1969).

Clapham, Andrew, *Human Rights Obligations of Non-State Actors* (Oxford: Oxford University Press, 2006).

Cohen, Roberta and Deng, Francis M., *Masses in Flight: The Global Crisis of Internal Displacement* (Washington, D.C: Brookings Institution Press, 1998).

Colson, Elizabeth, *The Social Consequences of Resettlement: The Impact of the Kariba Resettlement upon the Gwembe Tonga* (Manchester University Press, 1971).

Conte, Alex, *Defining Civil and Political Rights: The Jurisprudence of the United Nations Human Rights Committee*, 2nd edition (London: Routledge, 2016).

Darrow, Mac, *Between Light and Shadow: The World Bank, The International Monetary Fund and International Human Rights Law* (Hart Publishing 2003).

Deng, Francis M., *Internally Displaced Persons* (Office of the United Nations High Commissioner for Human Rights, Geneva, 1998).

Deng, Francis M., *Internally displaced persons: compilation and analysis of legal norms* (New York: United Nations, 1998).

Fujita, Sanae, *The World Bank, Asian Development Bank and Human Rights: Developing Standards of Transparency, Participation and Accountability* (Edward Elgar Publishing, 2013).

Ghai, Yash P, *Whose Human Right to Development?* (Human Rights Unit Occasional Paper, 1989).

Giacca, Gilles, Economic, Social, and Cultural Rights in Armed Conflicts (Oxford: Oxford University Press, 2014).

Henckaerts, Jean-Marie and Doswald-Beck, Louise, *Customary International Humanitarian Law, Volume I: Rules* (Cambridge University Press, 2005).

Hohmann, Jessie and Weller, Marc 'Introduction' in Jessie Hohmann and Marc Weller (eds), *The UN Declaration on the Rights of Indigenous Peoples: A Commentary* (Oxford: Oxford University Press, 2018).

© T.M.C. ASSER PRESS and the authors 2026

R. G. Teshome, *The Human Cost of Development*, Human Rights Research Series 104,
https://doi.org/10.1007/978-94-6265-751-9

International Labour Organization, *Understanding the Indigenous and Tribal Peoples Convention, 1989 (No. 169): Handbook for ILO Tripartite Constituents* (Geneva: International Labour Office, 2013).

Jayawickrama, Nihal, *The Judicial Application of Human Rights Law: National, Regional and International Jurisprudence*, 2nd edition (Cambridge University Press, 2017).

Kälin, Walter, *Guiding Principles on Internal Displacement: Annotations*, 2nd edition (Studies in Transnational Legal Policy No. 38, Washington DC.: The American Society of International Law, 2008).

Lindroos, Anja, *The Right to Development* (Faculty of Law, University of Helsinki, Helsinki, 1999).

Mahapatra, Lakshman Kumar, *Resettlement, Impoverishment, and Reconstruction in India: Development for the Deprived* (Vikas Publishing House, 1999).

Maru, Mehari Taddele, *The Kampala Convention and Its Contributions to International Law: Legal Analyses and Interpretations of the African Union Convention for the Protection and Assistance of Internally Displaced Persons* (The Hague, Netherlands: Eleven International Publishing, 2014).

Mathur, Hari Mohan and Marsden, David (eds), *Development Projects and Impoverishment Risks: Resettling Project-Affected People in India* (Oxford: Oxford University Press, 1998).

McDowell, Christopher (ed), *Understanding Impoverishment: the Consequences of Development-Induced Displacement,* 1st edition (New York: Berghahn Books, 1996).

McDowell, Christopher, and Morrell, Gareth, *Displacement Beyond Conflict: Challenges for the 21st Century* (Berghahn Books, 2010).

Mclnerney-Lankford, Siobhan and Sano, Hans-Otto, *Human Rights Indicators in Development: An Introduction* (Washington DC: the World Bank, 2010).

Monnheimer, Maria, *Due Diligence Obligations in International Human Rights Law* (Cambridge: Cambridge University Press, 2021).

Office of the UN High Commissioner for Human Rights, *Human Rights and Poverty Reduction: A Conceptual Framework* (New York and Geneva: United Nations, 2004).

Oliver-Smith, Anthony, *Development & Dispossession: The Crisis of Forced Displacement and Resettlement* (School for Advanced Research Press, 2009).

Pahuja, Sundhya, *Decolonizing International Law: Development, Economic Growth and the Politics of Universality* (Cambridge: Cambridge University Press, 2011).

Phuong, Catherine, *The International Protection of Internally Displaced Persons* (Cambridge: Cambridge University Press, 2005).

Picciotto, Robert; Van Wicklin, Warren, and Rice, Edward (eds), *Involuntary Resettlement Comparative Perspectives*, World Bank Series on Evaluation and Development Volume 2, 2nd edition, (New York: Routledge, 2017).

Rawls, John, *A Theory of Social Justice* (Harvard University Press, 1971).

Rawls, John, *A Theory of Social Justice*, revised edition (Harvard University Press, 1999).

Rew, Alan; Fisher, Eleanor and Pande, Balaji, *Addressing Policy Constraints and Improving Outcomes in Development-Induced Resettlement Projects* (Oxford: Refugee Studies Center, 2000).

Roach, Kent, *Remedies for Human Rights Violations: a Two-Two Approach to Supra-National and National Law* (Cambridge: Cambridge University Press, 2021).

Robinson, Courtland W., *Risks and Rights: The Causes, Consequences, and Challenges of Development-Induced Displacement*, (The Brookings Institution-SAIS Project on Internal Displacement, An Occasional Paper May 2003).

Sarfaty, Galit A., *Values in Translation: Human Rights and the Culture of the World Bank* (Stanford: California: Stanford University Press, 2012).

Saul, Ben, *The International Covenant on Economic, Social and Cultural Rights: Travaux Preparatoires 1946–1966*, Volume I (Oxford: Oxford University Press, 2016).

Saul, Ben; Kinley, David; and Mowbray, Jaqueline, *The International Covenant on Economic, Social and Cultural Rights: Commentary, Cases, and Materials* (Oxford: Oxford University Press, 2014).

Schabas, William (ed), *The Universal Declaration of Human Rights: the Travaux Préparatoires* (Cambridge University Press, 2013).
Shelton, Dinah, *Remedies in International Human Rights Law*, 3rd edition (Oxford: Oxford University Press, 2015).
Skogly, Sigrun, *The Human Rights Obligations of the World Bank and the International Monetary Fund* (Cavendish Publishing, 2001).
Terminski, Bogumil, *Development-Induced Displacement and Resettlement: Causes, Consequences, and Socio-Legal Context* (Stuttgart: Ibidem-Verlag, 2015).
The African Development Bank (AfDB), *AfDB in Brief* (published by the African Development Bank, May 2013).
The Independent Evaluation Group (IEG), *Safeguards and Sustainability Policies in changing World: An Independent Evaluation of World Bank Group Experience* (Washington DC: The World Bank, 2010).
The World Bank, *Governance: the World Bank Experience* (the World Bank, 1994).
The World Bank, *Resettlement and Development: The Bankwide Review of Projects Involving Involuntary Resettlement 1986–1993* (World Bank, 1994).
The World Bank, *Involuntary Resettlement Sourcebook: Planning and Implementation in Development Projects* (The World Bank, 2004).
The World Bank, *A Guide to the World Bank*, 3rd edition (Washington DC: the World Bank, 2011).
The World Bank Inspection Panel, *Involuntary Resettlement, Emerging Lessons Series No. 1* (The World Bank, 2016).
Tomuschat, Christian, *Human Rights: Between Idealism and Realism*, 3rd edition (Oxford: Oxford University Press, 2014).
UNHCR, *Sexual and Gender-Based Violence against Refugees, Returnees and Internally Displaced Persons: Guidelines for Prevention and Response* (UNHCR, May 2003).
Van Banning, Theo R.G,, *The Human Right to Property* (Intersentia, 2002).
Verdirame, Guglielmo, *The UN and Human Rights: Who Guards the Guardians?* (Cambridge: Cambridge University Press, 2011).

Book Chapters

Ahmed, Iman A.I. 'The Merowe Dam in Northern Sudan: A Case of Population Displacement and Impoverishment' in Johannes Dragsbaek Schmidt, Leah Kimathi, and Michael Omondi Owiso (eds), *Refugees and Forced Migration in the Horn and Eastern Africa: Trends, Challenges and Opportunities* (Springer, 2019).
Anaya, James S, 'The Right of Indigenous Peoples to Self-Determination in the Post- Declaration Era' in Charters and Rodolfo Stavenhagen (eds), *Making the Declaration Work: The United Nations Declaration on the Rights of Indigenous Peoples* (Copenhagen 2009 – Document No. 127).
Anaya, James S. and Rodríguez-Piñero, Luis, 'Part I The UNDRIP's Relationship to Existing International Law: the Making of the UNDRIP' in Jessie Hohmann and Marc Weller (eds), *The UN Declaration on the Rights of Indigenous Peoples: A Commentary* (Oxford: Oxford University Press, 2018).
Bakewell, Oliver, 'Conceptualising Displacement and Migration: Processes, Conditions, and Categories' in Khalid Koser and Susan Martin, *The Migration-Displacement Nexus: Patterns, Processes, and Policies* (New York: Berghahn Books, 2011).
Barutciski, Michael, 'International Law and Development-induced Displacement' in Chris de Wet (ed), *Development-induced displacement: Problems, Policies and People*, (New York: NY Berghahn, 2006).

Beetham, David, 'The Right to Development and its Corresponding Obligations' in Bård-Anders Andreassen and Stephen Powys Marks (eds), *Development as a Human Right*, 2nd edition (Antwerp: Intersentia, 2010).

Boesen, Jacob Kirkemann and Sano, Hans-Otto, 'The Implications and Value-Added of a Human Rights-Based Approach' in Bard V. Andreassen and Stephen P. Marks (eds), *Development as a Human Right: Legal, Political and Economic Dimensions*, 2nd edition (Intersentia, 2010).

Bourke-Martignoni, Joanna, 'The History and Development of the Due Diligence Standard in International Law and Its Role in the Protection of Women against Violence' in Carin Benninger-Budel (ed), *Due Diligence and its Application to Protect Women from Violence* (Leiden; Boston: Martinus Nijhoff Publishers, 2008).

Bradlow, Daniel D., 'International Law and the Operations of the International Financial Institutions' in Daniel D. Bradlow and David B. Hunter (eds), *International Financial Institutions and International Law* (Kluwer Law International, 2010).

Braniff, Máire, and Hainsworth, Paul, 'A Human Rights Based Approach to Development' in Gerard McCann and Stephen McCloskey (eds), *From the Local to the Global: Key Issues in Development Studies*, 3rd edition (London, England: Pluto Press, 2015).

Castellino, Joshua and Doyle, Cathal, 'Part I The UNDRIP's Relationship to Existing International Law, Ch. 1 Who Are 'Indigenous Peoples'?: An Examination of Concepts Concerning Group Membership in the UNDRIP' in Jessie Hohmann and Marc Weller, *The UN Declaration on the Rights of Indigenous Peoples: A Commentary* (Oxford: Oxford University Press, 2018).

Cernea, Michael M., 'Preface' in Hari Mohan Mathur and Michael Cernea (eds), *Development, Displacement and Resettlement: Focus on Asian Experience* (New Delhi: Vikas Publishing House, 1995).

Cernea, Michael M., 'Bridging the Research Divide: Studying Development Oustees' in Tim Allen (ed), *In Search of Cool Ground: War, Flight and Homecoming in Northeast Africa* (London: United Nations Research Institute for Social Development, Africa World Press and James Currey, 1996).

Cernea, Michael M., 'Understanding and Preventing Impoverishment from Displacement' in Christopher McDowell (ed), *Understanding Impoverishment: the Consequences of Development-induced Displacement* (Berghahn Books, 1996).

Cernea, Michael, 'Why Economic Analysis is Essential to Resettlement: A Sociologist's View' in Michael Cernea (ed), *The Economics of Involuntary Resettlement: Questions and Challenges* (Washington DC: World Bank, 1999).

Cernea, Michael M., 'Risks, safeguards, and reconstruction: a model for population displacement and resettlement' in Michael M. Cernea and Christopher McDowell (eds), *Risks and Reconstruction: Experiences of Resettlers and Refugees* (The World Bank, Washington DC., 2000).

Cernea, Michael, 'Compensation and Investment in Resettlement: Theory, Practice, Pitfalls, and Needed Policy Reform' in Michael Cernea and Hari Mohan Mathur (eds), *Can Compensation Prevent Impoverishment? Reforming Resettlement through Investments* (Oxford: Oxford University Press, 2008).

Cernea, Michael, 'Preface: An original contribution to country-wide displacement analysis' in Alula Pankhurst & Francois Piguet (eds), *Moving People in Ethiopia: Development, Displacement and The State*, (Woodbridge, Suffolk; Rochester, NY: James Currey, 2009)

Cernea, Michael M. and McDowell, Christopher, 'Introduction: Reconstructing resettlers' and refugees' livelihoods' in Michael M. Cernea and Christopher McDowell (eds), *Risks and Reconstruction: Experiences of Refugees and Resettlers* (Washington DC: The World Bank, 2000).

Charters, Claire, 'Part IV Rights to Land and Territory, Natural Resources, and Environment, Ch. 14 Indigenous Peoples' Rights to Lands, Territories, and Resources in the UNDRIP: Articles 10, 25, 26, and 27' in Jessie Hohmann and Marc Weller, *The UN Declaration on the Rights of Indigenous Peoples: A Commentary* (Oxford: Oxford University Press, 2018).

Cohen, Roberta, 'Protection of Internally Displaced Persons: National and International Responsibilities' in Vincent Chetail and Céline Bauloz (eds), *Research handbook on international law and migration* (Cheltenham, UK: Edward Elgar, 2014).

Colson, Elizabeth, 'Gendering Those Uprooted by 'Development'' in Doreen Indra (ed), *Engendering Forced Migration: Theory and Practice* (New York: Berghahn Books, 2008).

Daes, Erica-Irene A, 'The Contribution of the Working Group on Indigenous Populations to the Genesis and Evolution of the UN Declaration on the Rights of Indigenous Peoples' in Charters and Rodolfo Stavenhagen (eds), *Making the Declaration Work: The United Nations Declaration on the Rights of Indigenous Peoples* (Copenhagen 2009 – Document No. 127).

d'Aspremont, Jean, 'The Multifaceted Concept of the Autonomy of International Organizations and International Legal Discourse' in Richard Collins and Nigel D. White (eds), *International Organizations and the Idea of Autonomy* (Routledge publishing, 2011).

Duchatellier, Moetsi and Phuong, Catherine, 'The African Contribution to the protection of internally displaced persons: A commentary on the 2009 Kampala Convention' in Vincent Chetail and Céline Bauloz (eds), *Research handbook on international law and migration* (Cheltenham, UK: Edward Elgar publishing, 2014).

Dunning, Millard H., 'Government managed land settlement and resettlement in Thailand' in L.A. Peter Gosling (ed), *Population resettlement in the Mekong River Basin: Papers of the Third Carolina Geographical Symposium* (Chapel Hill: University of North Carolina Press, 1979).

Fitzmaurice, Malgosia, 'Interpretation of Human Rights Treaties' in Dina Shelton (ed), *The Oxford Handbook of International Human Rights Law* (Oxford University Press: Oxford, 2013).

Goodwin-Gill, Guy S., 'The International Law of Refugee Protection' in Elena Fiddian-Qasmiyeh, Gil Loescher, Katy Long, and Nando Sigona (eds), *The Oxford Handbook of Refugee and Forced Migration Studies* (Oxford: Oxford University Press, 2014).

Henriksen, John B, 'The UN Declaration on the Rights of Indigenous Peoples: Some Key Issues and Events in the Process' in Charters and Rodolfo Stavenhagen (eds), *Making the Declaration Work: The United Nations Declaration on the Rights of Indigenous Peoples* (Copenhagen 2009 – Document No. 127).

Kälin, Walter, 'Internal Displacement' in Elena Fiddian-Qasmiyeh, Gil Loescher, Katy Long, and Nando Sigona (eds), *The Oxford Handbook of Refugee and Forced Migration Studies* (Oxford: Oxford University Press, 2014).

Kälin, Walter, 'The Guiding Principles on Internal Displacement and the search for a universal framework of protection for internally displaced persons' in Vincent Chetail and Céline Bauloz (eds), *Research handbook on international law and migration* (Cheltenham, UK: Edward Elgar publishing, 2014).

Keller, Helen and Grover, Leena, 'General Comments of the Human Rights Committee and their Legitimacy' in Helen Keller and Geir Ulfstein (eds), *UN Human Rights Treaty Bodies: Law and Legitimacy* (Cambridge University Press, 2012).

Kibreab, Gaim, 'Common property resources and resettlement' in Michael M. Cernea and Christopher McDowell (eds), *Risks and Reconstruction Experiences of Resettlers and Refugees* (Washington DC: The World Bank, 2000).

Koenig, Dolores, 'Enhancing Local Development in Development-Induced Displacement and Resettlement Projects' in Chris de Wet (ed), *Development-induced Displacement: Problems, Policies, and People* (New York: NY Berghahn Books, 2006).

Leckie, Scott, 'The Right to Housing' in Asbjorn Eide, Catarina Krause and Allan Rosas (eds), *Economic, Social and Cultural Rights: A Textbook,* 1st edition (Martinus Nijhoff Publishers, 1995).

Liebenberg, Sandra, 'Masking a Difference: Human Rights and Development- Reflecting on the South African Experience' in Bård-Anders Andreassen and Stephen Powys Marks (eds), *Development as a Human Right*, 2nd edition (Antwerp: Intersentia, 2010).

Loescher, Gil, 'Refugees and Internally Displaced Persons' in Jacob Katz Cogan, Ian Hurd, and Ian Johnstone (eds), *The Oxford Handbook of International Organizations* (Oxford: Oxford University Press, 2016).

Mathur, Mohan Hari, 'The Resettlement of People Displaced by Development Projects: Issues and Approaches' in in Hari Mohan Mathur and Michael Cernea (eds), *Development, Displacement and Resettlement: Focus on Asian Experience*, 1st edition (New Delhi: Vikas Publishing House, 1995).

Mburugu, Edward K., 'Dislocation of Settled Communities in the Development Process: The Case of Kiambere Hydroelectric Project' in Cynthia C Cook (ed), *Involuntary Resettlement in Africa*, World Bank Technical Paper No. 227 (Washington DC: World Bank, 1994).

McDowell, Christopher, 'Development Created Population Displacement' in Elena Fiddian-Qasmiyeh, Gil Loescher, Katy Long, and Nando Sigona (eds), *The Oxford Handbook of Refugee and Forced Migration Studies* (Oxford: Oxford University Press, 2014).

Mejia, Maria Clara, 'Economic Recovery After Involuntary Resettlement: the Case of Brickmakers Displaced by the Yacyereta Hydroelectric Project' in Michael M. Cernea and Christopher McDowell (Eds.), *Risks and Reconstruction: Experiences of Resettles and Refugees* (Washington DC: The World Bank, 2000).

Montes, A Regino and Cisneros, G Torres, 'The United Nations Declaration on the Rights of Indigenous Peoples: The Foundation of a New Relationship between Indigenous Peoples, States and Societies' in Claire Charters and Rodolfo Stavenhagen (eds), *Making the Declaration Work: The United Nations Declaration on the Rights of Indigenous Peoples* (Copenhagen 2009 – Document No. 127).

O'cinneide, Colm, 'The Right to Work in International Human Rights Law' in Virginia Mantouvalou (ed), *The Right to Work: Legal and Philosophical Perspectives*, (Hart Publishing, 2014).

Osmani, Siddiqur Rahman, 'An Essay on the Human Rights Approach to Development' in Arjun Sengupta, Archna Negi & Moushumi Basu (eds), *Reflections on the Right to Development* (India: SAGE Publications, 2005).

Partridge, William L., 'Successful Involuntary Resettlement: Lessons from the Costa Rican Arenal Hydroelectric Plant' in Michael M. Cernea and Scott E. Guggenheim (eds), *Anthropological Approaches to Resettlement: Policy, Practice and Theory* (Routledge, 1993).

Piovesan, Flávia, 'Active, free and meaningful participation in development' in The United Nations, *Realizing the Right to Development* (Essays in Commemoration of 25 Years of the United Nations Declaration on the Right to Development), (New York and Geneva: United Nations Publications, HR/PUB/12/4, December 2013), available at https://www.un-ilibrary.org/economic-and-social-development/realizing-the-right-to-development_49006c2a-en, accessed 26 July 2025.

Reidel, Eibel; Giacca, Gilles and Golay, Christophe 'The Development of Economic, Social and Cultural Rights in International Law' in Eibel Reidel, Gilles Giacca, and Christophe Golay (eds), *Economic, Social and Cultural Rights in International Law: Contemporary Issues and Challenges* (Oxford: Oxford University Press, 2014).

Riccardi, Alice, 'The Right to Know: the Role of Transparency, Access to Information, Freedom of Expression in Overcoming Disasters' in Flavia Zorzi Giustiniani, Emanuele Sommario, Federico Casolari, and Giulio Bartolini (eds), *Routledge Handbook of Human Rights and Disasters* (London; New York: Routledge, 2018).

Salomon, Margot E., 'International Human Rights Obligations in Context: Structural Obstacles and the Demands of Global Justice' in Bård-Anders Andreassen and Stephen Powys Marks (eds.), Development as a Human Right, 2nd edition (Antwerp: Intersentia, 2010).

Schrijver, Nicolaas, 'Self-determination of Peoples and Sovereignty over Natural Wealth and Resources' in The United Nations, *Realizing the Right to Development* (Essays in Commemoration of 25 Years of the United Nations Declaration on the Right to Development), (New York and Geneva: United Nations Publications, HR/PUB/12/4, December 2013), available at https://www.un-ilibrary.org/economic-and-social-development/realizing-the-right-to-development_49006c2a-en, accessed 26 July 2025.

Shelton, Dinah and Gould, Ariel, 'Positive and Negative Obligations' in Dinah Shelton (ed.), *Oxford Handbook of International Human Rights Law* (Oxford University Press, 2013).

Skogly, Sigrun I., 'The Human Rights Obligations of the World Bank and the International Monetary Fund' in Willem Van Genugten, Paul Hunt, and Susan Mathews (eds), *World Bank, IMF, and Human Rights* (Nijmegen: Wolf Legal Publishers, 2003).

Sen, Amartya, 'Human Rights and Development' in Bård-Anders Andreassen and Stephen Powys Marks (eds), *Development as a Human Right*, 2nd edition (Antwerp: Intersentia, 2010).

Sengupta, Arjun, 'The Human Right to Development' in Bård-Anders Andreassen and Stephen Powys Marks (eds), *Development as a Human Right*, 2nd edition (Antwerp: Intersentia, 2010) at 13; see also Sengupta (2000).

Sommario, Emanuele, 'Limitations and derogation provisions in international human rights law treaties and their use in disaster settings' in Flavia Zorzi Giustiniani, Emanuele Sommario, Federico Casolari and Giulio Bartolini (eds), *Routledge Handbook of Human Rights and Disasters* (London; New York: Routledge, 2018).

Turton, David, 'Who is a Forced Migrant?' in Chris de Wet (ed), *Development-induced Displacement: Problems, Policies and People* (Berghahn Books, 2006).

Van Hoof, G.J.H. 'The Legal Nature of Economic, Social and Cultural Rights: a Rebuttal of Some Traditional Views' in Katarina Tomaševski and Philip Alston (eds), *The Right to Food* (International Studies in Human Rights Series, Volume 4, 1984).

Waincymer, Jeff, 'Balancing Property Rights and Human Rights in Expropriation' in Pierre-Marie Dupuy, Ernst-Ulrich Petersmann, and Francesco Francioni (eds), *Human Rights in International Investment Law and Arbitration* (Oxford: Oxford University Press, 2009).

Walker, Simon, 'Human Rights Impact Assessments: Emerging Practice and Challenges' in Eibe Riedel, Gilles Giacca, and Christophe Golay (eds), *Economic, Social, and Cultural Rights in International Law: Contemporary Issues and Challenges* (Oxford: Oxford University Press, 2014).

Journal Articles

Aboda, Caroline; Mugagga, Frank; Byakagaba, Patrick; and Nabanoga, Goretti, 'Development Induced Displacement: A Review of Risks Faced by Communities in Developing Countries' (2019) 7(2) Sociology and Anthropology 100–110.

Adeola, Romola, 'The right not to be arbitrarily displaced under the United Nations Guiding Principles on Internal Displacement' (2016) 16(1) African Human Rights Law Journal 83–98.

Adeola, Romola, 'The Legal Protection of Development-Induced Displaced Persons in Africa' (2017) 10(1) African Journal of Legal Studies 91–104.

Adeola, Romola, (2017), 'The Responsibility of Businesses to Prevent Development-induced Displacement in Africa' (2017) 17(1) African Human Rights Journal 245–265.

Adeola, Romola, 'The Kampala Convention and the right not to be arbitrarily displaced' (2018) 59 Forced Migration Review 15–17.

Anaya, S James and Williams, Robert A Jr, 'The Protection of Indigenous Peoples' Rights over Lands and Natural Resources under the Inter-American Human Rights System' (2001) 14 Harvard Human Rights Journal 33–86.

Assefa, Mesenbet, 'Defining the Minimum Core Obligations-Conundrums in International Human Rights Law and Lessons from the Constitutional Court of South Africa' (2010) 1(1) Mekelle University Law Journal 1.

Alston, Philip and Quinn, Gerard, 'The Nature and Scope of States Parties' Obligations under the International Covenant on Economic, Social and Cultural Rights' (1987) 9(2) Human Rights Quarterly 156–229.

Arts, Karin, and Tamo, Atabongawung, 'The Right to Development in International Law: New Momentum Thirty Years Down the Line?' (2016) 63(3) Netherlands International Law Review at 221–249.

Bagshaw, Simon, 'Internally Displaced Persons at the Fifty-Fourth Session of the United Nations Commission on Human Rights' (1998) 10(3) International Journal of Refugee Law 548–556.

Baird, Ian G.; Shoemaker, Bruce P. and Manorom, Kanokwan, 'The People and their River, the World Bank and its Dam: Revisiting the Xe Bang Fai River in Laos' (2015) 46(5) Development and Change 1080–1105.

Barelli, Mauro, 'Free, prior and informed consent in the aftermath of the UN Declaration on the Rights of Indigenous Peoples: developments and challenges ahead' (2012) 16(1) The International Journal of Human Rights 1–24.

Barnabas, Sylvanus Gbendazhi, 'The Legal Status of the United Nations Declaration on the Rights of Indigenous Peoples in Contemporary International Human Rights Law' (2017) 6 International Human Rights Law Review 242–261.

Barutciski, Michael, 'Addressing legal constraints and improving outcomes in DIDR projects' in a compilation by Chris de Wet, 'Improving outcomes in development-induced displacement and resettlement projects' (2002) 12 Forced Migration Review 7.

Bassiouni, M. Cherif, 'International Recognition of Victims' Rights' (2006) 6(2) Human Rights Law Review 203–279.

Beirne, Jonny, 'Gilgel Gibe III: Dam-Induced Displacement in Ethiopia and Kenya', SEM 2014.

Bisht, Tulsi Charan, 'Development-Induced Displacement and Women: The Case of the Tehri Dam, India' (2009) 10(4) The Asia Pacific Journal of Anthropology 301–317.

Bøås, Morten, 'Governance as multilateral development bank policy: The cases of the African development bank and the Asian development bank' (1998) 10(2) The European Journal of Development Research 117–134.

Bradley, Megan, 'Durable Solutions and the Right of Return for IDPs: Evolving Interpretations' (2018) 30(2) International Journal of Refugee Law 218–242.

Bugalski, Natalie, 'The Demise of Accountability at the World Bank' (2016) 31(1) American University International Law Review 1–56.

Bunn, Isabella D, 'The Right to Development: Implications for International Economic Law' (2000) 15(6) American University International Law Review 1425–1467.

Byrnes, Andrew, 'The Asian Development Bank and the Role of Human Rights in the Pursuit of just and Sustainable Development in the Asia-Pacific Region: An Advocacy Role for Australia?' (2011) 18 Australian International Law Journal 1–21.

Cernea, Michael M., 'Understanding and Preventing Impoverishment from Displacement: Reflections on the state of Knowledge' (1995) 8(3) Journal of Refugee Studies 245–264.

Cernea, Michael M., 'The Risks and Reconstruction Model for Resettling Displaced Populations' (1997) 25(10) World Development 1569–1587.

Cernea, Michael M., 'Risks, Safeguards and Reconstruction: A Model for Population Displacement and Resettlement' (2000) 35(41) Economic and Political Weekly 3659–3678.

Chapman, Audrey R., 'A "Violations Approach" for Monitoring the International Covenant on Economic, Social and Cultural Rights' (1996) 18(1) Human Rights Quarterly 23–66.

Chen, Muyang, 'Beyond Donation: China's Policy Banks and the Reshaping of Development Finance' (2020) 55 Studies in Comparative International Development 436–459.

Ciorciari, John D., 'The Lawful Scope of Human Rights Criteria in World Bank Credit Decisions: An Interpretive Analysis of the IBRD and IDA Articles of Agreement' (2000) 33(2) Cornell International Law Journal 331–371.

Cisse, Hassane, 'Should the Political Prohibition in Charters of International Financial Institutions Be Revisited: The Case of the World Bank' (2012) 3 World Bank Legal Review 59–92.

Clark, Dana, 'The World Bank and Development-Induced Displacement in South Asia' (1997) 4(2) The Brown Journal of World Affairs 215–231.

Clark, Dana L, 'The World Bank and Human Rights: The Need for Greater Accountability' (2002) 15 Harvard Human Rights Journal 205–226.

Cohen, Roberta, 'The Guiding Principles on Internal Displacement: An Innovation in International Standard Setting' (2004) 10(4) Global Governance 459–480.

Cohen, Roberta, 'Developing an International System for Internally Displaced Persons' (2006) 7(2) International Studies Perspectives 87–101.
Cohen, Roberta, 'Response to Hathaway' (2007) 20(3) Journal of Refugee Studies 370–376.
Crippa, Leonardo A., 'Multilateral Development Banks and Human Rights Responsibility' (2010) 25(3) American University International Law Review 531–577.
Debasree, De, 'Development-induced displacement: impact on Adivasi women of Odisha' (2015) 50(3) Community Development Journal 448–462.
Deng, Francis M and Adeola, Romola 'The Normative Influence of the UN Guiding Principles on the Kampala Convention in the Protection of Internally Displaced Persons in Africa' (2021) 65(S1) Journal of African Law 59–72.
DeWind, Josh, 'Response to Hathaway' (2007) 20(3) Journal of Refugee Studies 381–385.
Diergarten, Yorck, 'Indigenous or Out of Scope? Large-scale Land Acquisitions in Developing Countries, International Human Rights Law and the Current Deficiencies in Land Rights Protection' (2019) 19(1) Human Rights Law Review 37–52.
Downing, Theodore E., 'Avoiding New Poverty: Mining-Induced Displacement and Resettlement' (2002) 58 Mining, Minerals and Sustainable Development.
Downing, Theodore E., 'Creating poverty: the flawed economic logic of the World Bank's revised involuntary resettlement policy' (2012) 12 Forced Migration Review 13–14.
Evans, Jessica, 'Abuse-Free Development: How the World Bank Should Safeguard Against Human Rights Violations' (2013) 107 Proceedings of the Annual Meeting- American Society of International Law (International Law in a Multipolar World) 298–302.
Feyter, Koen De, 'The Declaration on the Right to Development Revisited' (2013) 1(1) Journal of National Law University 15–32.
Foster, Sheila R., 'The Social Function of Property: A Comparative Law Perspective' (2011) 80(3) Fordham Law Review 101–113.
Freccero, Julie, 'Sheltering Displaced Persons from Sexual and Gender-based Violence' (2015) 50 Forced Migration Review 55–58.
Fuentes-Julio, Claudia and Ibrahim, Raslan, 'A Human Rights Approach to Conflict Resolution' (2019) 33(3) Ethics & International Affairs 261–276.
Fujita, Sanae, 'The challenges of mainstreaming human rights in the World Bank' (2011) 15(3) The International Journal of Human Rights 374–396.
Gebreyesus, Ataklti and Tadesse, Shishay, 'Livelihood Impacts of Development-Induced Displacements: an Investigation into Post-Project Livelihoods of PAPs' (2019) 35(1/2) Eastern Africa Social Science Research Review 123–151.
George, Ann and Rajan, Irudaya, 'Changing Cities and Changing Lives: Development Induced Displacement in Kochi, Kerala' (2015) 1(1) International journal on urban environments 1–18.
Gilbert, Jérémie, 'Indigenous peoples' human rights in Africa: the pragmatic revolution of the African Commission on Human and Peoples' Rights' (2011) 60(1) The International and Comparative Law Quarterly 245–270.
Gilbert, Jérémie, 'Land Rights as Human Rights: the Case for a Specific Right to Land' (2013) 10(18) International Journal on Human Rights 115–135.
Gismondi, Giovanna, 'Denial of Justice: The Latest Indigenous Land Disputes Before the European Court of Human Rights and the Need for an Expansive Interpretation of Protocol 1' (2016) 18 Yale Human Rights & Development Law Journal 1–58.
Giustiniani, Flavia Zorzi, 'New hopes and challenges for the protection of IDPs in Africa: the Kampala Convention for the Protection and Assistance of Internally Displaced Persons in Africa' (2011) 39(2) Denver Journal of International Law and Policy 347–370.
Gizachew, Andnet, 'Causes of Big Development Projects: Development-induced Displacement and its Socio-economic Impacts on Displaced People in Tekeze Dam' (2017) 9(9) International Journal of Sociology and Anthropology 114–130.
Glendon, Mary A., 'Knowing the Universal Declaration of Human Rights' (1998) 73(5) Notre Dame Law Review 1153–1190.

Gready, Paul, 'Rights-based approaches to development: what is the value-added?' (2008) 18(6) Development in Practice 735–747.

Hamm, Brigitte I., 'A Human Rights Approach to Development' (2001) 23(4) Human Rights Quarterly 1005–1031.

Hannum, Hurst, 'The UDHR in National and International Law' (1998) 3(2) Health and Human Rights 144–158.

Harrison, James, 'Human Rights Measurement: Reflections on the Current Practice and Future Potential of Human Rights Impact Assessment' (2011) 3(2) Journal of Human Rights Practice 162–187.

Hathaway, James C., 'Forced Migration Studies: Could We Agree Just to 'Date'?' (2007) 20(3) Journal of Refugee Studies 349–365.

Heri, Corina, 'The Human Right to Land, for Peasants and for All: Tracing the Social Function of Property to 1948' (2020) 20(3) Human Rights Law Review 433–452.

Hong, Philip Young P.; Singh, Shweta & Ramic, Juliane, 'Development-induced impoverishment among involuntarily displaced populations' (2009) 25(3) Journal of Comparative Social Welfare 221–238.

Huang, Youliang; Lin, Wensheng; Li, Shan and Ning, Yan 'Social Impacts of Dam-Induced Displacement and Resettlement: A Comparative Case Study in China' (2018) 10(11) Sustainability.

Hugo, Graeme and Bun, Chan Kwok 'Conceptualizing and Defining Refugee and Forced Migrations in Asia' (1990) 18(1) Asian Journal of Social Science 19–42.

Hwang, Sean-Shong; Cao, Yue and Xi, Juan, 'The Short-Term Impact of Involuntary Migration in China's Three Gorges: A Prospective Study' (2011) 101(1) Social Indicators Research at 73–92.

Juma, Laurence, 'An Overview of Normative Frameworks for the Protection of Development-Induced IDPs in Kenya' (2013) 6(1) African Journal of Legal Studies 17–47.

Juma, Laurence, 'Protection of development-induced internally displaced persons under the African Charter: the case of the Endorois community of Northern Kenya' (2013), 46(2) The Comparative and International Law Journal of Southern Africa 211–233.

Kahsay, Bereket Godifay, 'Socio-cultural and economic impacts of development induced displacement on resettled people: The case of Welkayt Sugar Factory in Tigray Region, Ethiopia' (2020) 12(4) International Journal of Sociology and Anthropology 94–103.

Kälin, Walter, 'The Guiding Principles on Internal Displacement—Introduction' (1998) 10(3) International Journal of Refugee Law 557–562.

Kälin, Walter, 'The Guiding Principles on Internal Displacement as International Minimum Standard and Protection Tool' (2005) 24(3) Refugee Survey Quarterly 27–36.

Kamski, Benedikt, 'The Kuraz Sugar Development Project (KSDP) in Ethiopia: between 'sweet visions' and mounting challenges', (2016) 10(3) Journal of Eastern African Studies 568–580.

Kangave, Jalia, 'Investigating the failure of resettlement and rehabilitation in development projects: a critical analysis of the World Bank's policy on involuntary resettlement using lessons from Uganda's Bujagali hydroelectric project' (2012) 45(2) University of British Columbia Law Review 329–392.

Kanosue, Yu, 'When Land is Taken Away: States Obligations under International Human Rights Law Concerning Large-Scale Projects Impacting Local Communities' (2015) 15(4) Human Rights Law Review 643–667.

Kates, Robert W.; Parris, Thomas M. and Leiserowitz, Anthony A., 'What IS Sustainable Development? Goals, Indicators, Values, and Practice' (2005) 47(3) Environment: Science and Policy for Sustainable Development 8–21.

Koenig, Dolores, Advantages and obstacles to retrofitting benefit-sharing after development-induced displacement and resettlement, (2020) 39(5) Impact Assessment and Project Appraisal 417–428.

Koivurova, Timo, 'Jurisprudence of the European Court of Human Rights Regarding Indigenous Peoples: Retrospect and Prospects' (2011) 18 International Journal on Minority and Group Rights 1–37.

Kovacs, Peter, 'Indigenous Issues under the European Convention of Human Rights, Reflected in an Inter-American Mirror' (2016) 48(4) The George Washington International Law Review 781–806.

Kucs, Arturs; Sedlova, Zane and Pierhorovica, Liene, 'The Right to Housing: International, European and National Perspectives' (2008) 64/65 Cuadernos Constitucionales de la Cátedra Fadrique Furió Ceriol 101–123.

Lane, Lottie, 'The Horizontal Effect of International Human Rights Law in Practice' (2018) 5(1) European Journal of Comparative Law and Governance 5–88.

Langford, Malcolm and Du Plessis, Jean. 'Dignity in Rubble? Forced Evictions and Human Rights Law' (2006) Centre on Housing Rights and Evictions, available at https://www.jus.uio.no/ior/english/people/aca/malcolml/dignity-in-the-rubble---human-rights-law-and-forced-evictions.pdf, accessed 26 July 2025.

Lischer, Sarah Kenyon, 'Causes and Consequences of Conflict-Induced Displacement' (2007) 9(2) Civil Wars 142–155.

MacInnes, Angus; Colchester, Marcus; and Whitmore, Andrew, 'Free, prior and informed consent: how to rectify the devastating consequences of harmful mining for indigenous peoples" (2017) 15 Perspectives in Ecology and Conservation 152–160.

Maitra, Sreya, 'Compensation and Resettlement – Experiences from the Narmada Valley and Sardar Sarovar Project' (2009) 10(2) Japanese Journal of Political Science 191–211.

Manjula, K.; Kumar, T.A. and Aneesh, K.A., 'Impact of Development-induced Displacement in Kerala, India' (2013) 3(1) Journal of Internal Displacement 2–18.

Mazel, Odette, 'The Evolution of Rights: Indigenous Peoples and International Law' (2009) 13(1) Australian Indigenous Law Review 140–158.

Mcbeth, Adam, 'Breaching the Vacuum: A Consideration of the Role of International Human Rights Law in the Operations of the International Financial Institutions' (2006) 10(4) The International Journal of Human Rights 385–404.

McDonagh, Maeve, 'The Right to Information in International Human Rights Law' (2013) 13(1) Human Rights Law Review 25–55.

McDowell, Christopher, 'Involuntary resettlement, impoverishment risks, and sustainable livelihoods' (2002), 2 Australasian Journal of Disaster and Trauma Studies 1–10.

McInerney-Lankford, Siobhan, 'Human Rights and Development: A Comment on Challenges and Opportunities from a Legal Perspective' (2009) 1(1) Journal of Human Rights Practice 51–82.

Meidinger, Errol E., 'The "Public Uses" of Eminent Domain: History and Policy' (2008) 11(1) Journal of Environmental Law 1–66.

Mooney, Erin, 'The Concept of Internal Displacement and the Case for Internally Displaced Persons as a Category of Concern' (2005) 24(3) Refugee Survey Quarterly 9–26.

Muggah, Robert, 'A Tale of Two Solitudes: Comparing Conflict and Development induced Internal Displacement and Involuntary Resettlement' (2003) 41(5) International Migration 5–31.

Muller, Amrei, 'Limitations to and Derogations from Economic, Social and Cultural Rights' (2009) 9(4) Human Rights Law Review 557–601.

Nayak, Arun Kumar, 'Development, Displacement and Justice in India: Study of Hirakud Dam' (2013) 43(3) Social Change 397–419.

Nykolaishen, Sarah, 'Customary International Law and the Declaration on the Rights of Indigenous Peoples' (2012) 17(1) Appeal 111–128.

Okello, JO Moses, 'In Lieu of a Travaux Préparatoires: A Commentary on the Kampala Convention for IDPs' (2019) 31(2/3) International Journal of Refugee Law 349–378.

Orchard, Phil, 'Protection of internally displaced persons: soft law as a norm-generating mechanism' (2010) 36(2) Review of International Studies 281–303.

Parasuraman, S., 'Development Projects, Displacement and Outcomes for Displaced: Two Case Studies' (1996) 31(24) Economic and Political Weekly 1529–1532.

Partridge, William L., 'Involuntary Resettlement in Development Projects' (1989) 2(3) Journal of Refugee Studies 373–384.

Pasqualucci, Jo M, 'International Indigenous Land Rights: A Critique of the Jurisprudence of the Inter-American Court of Human Rights in Light of the United Nations Declaration on the Rights of Indigenous Peoples' (2009) 27(1) Wisconsin International Law Journal 51–98.

Patel, Sejal; Sliuzas, Richard and Mathur, Navdeep, 'The risk of impoverishment in urban development-induced displacement and resettlement in Ahmedabad' (2015) 27(1) Environment & Urbanization 231–256.

Price, Susanna, 'Prologue: Victims or Partners? The Social Perspective in Development-Induced Displacement and Resettlement', (2009) 10(4) The Asia Pacific Journal of Anthropology 266–282.

Rahmato, Dessalegn, Resettlement in Ethiopia: The Tragedy of Population Relocation in the 1980s, (Forum for Social Studies, Addis Ababa, June 2003).

Ramanathan, Usha, 'Displacement and the Law' (1996) 31(24) Economic and Political Weekly 1486–1491.

Randell, Heather, 'The short-term impacts of development-induced displacement on wealth and subjective well-being in the Brazilian Amazon' (2016) 87 World Development 385–400.

Sánchez, Beatriz Eugenia, 'Colombian Development-Induced Displacement – Considering the Impact of International Law on Domestic Policy' (2017) 5(1) Groningen Journal of International Law 73–95.

Sarfaty, Galit A, 'Why Culture Matters in International Institutions: The Marginality of Human Rights at the World Bank' (2009) 103(4) American Journal of International Law 647–683.

Schapper, Andrea and Urban, Frauke, 'Large dams, norms and Indigenous Peoples' (2021), 39(S1) Development Policy Review O61–O80.

Scholten, Andrew, 'International Human Rights Law Aspects of Forced Migrations, Evictions and Displacement: Current Issues and Challenges', available at https://www.ssoar.info/ssoar/handle/document/47750, accessed 26 July 2025.

Schulz, Christopher and Adams, William A., Debating dams: The World Commission on Dams 20 years on (2019) 6(5) WIREs Water 1–19.

Sen, Amartya, 'Development as Capability Expansion' (1989) 19 Journal of Development Planning 3–16.

Sengupta, Arjun, 'Realizing the Right to Development' (2000) 31(3) Development and Change 553–578.

Sholihah, Puput Ichwatus and Shaojun, Chen, 'Improving living conditions of displacees: A review of the evidence benefit sharing scheme for development induced displacement and resettlement (DIDR) in urban Jakarta Indonesia' (2020) 20 World Development Perspectives 1–12.

Sprankling, John G., 'The Global Right to Property' (2014) 52(2) Columbia Journal of Transnational Law 464–505.

Ssenyonjo, Manisuli, 'Reflections on State Obligations with Respect to Economic, Social and Cultural Rights in International Human Rights Law' (2011) 15(6) The International Journal of Human Rights 969–1012.

Stanley, Jason, 'Development-induced Displacement and Resettlement' (2004) Forced Migration Online.

Stein, Martin, 'The Three Gorges Dam: the Unexamined Toll of Development-induced Displacement' (1998) 1 Forced Migration Review 7–10.

Stevenson, Edward G. J. and Buffavand, Lucie, '"Do Our Bodies Know Their Ways?" Villagization, Food Insecurity, and Ill-Being in Ethiopia's Lower Omo Valley' (2018) 61(1) African Studies Review 109–133.

Terminski, Bogumil, 'Mining-Induced Displacement and Resettlement: Social Problem and Human Rights Issue' (2012) Universite de Geneve, Faculte de Droit, 2012.

Terminski, Bogumil, 'Oil-Induced Displacement: Social Problem and Human Rights Issue' (2012) Research Paper, Simon Fraser University, School For International Studies.

Teshome, Roman Girma, 'The Draft Convention on the Right to Development: A New Dawn to the Recognition of the Right to Development as a Human Right?' (2022) 22(2) Human Rights Law Review.

Thiele, Bret, 'Litigating against Forced Evictions under the American Convention on Human Rights' (2003) 21(3) Netherlands Quarterly of Human Rights 463–478.

Thukral, Enaski Ganguly, 'Development, Displacement and Rehabilitation: Locating Gender' (1996) 31(24) Economic and Political Weekly 1500–1503.

Uvin, Peter, 'From the right to development to the rights-based approach: how 'human rights' entered development' (2007) 17(4/5) Development in Practice 597–606.

Van Den Meerssche, Dimitri, 'A Legal Black Hole in the Cosmos of Virtue—The Politics of Human Rights Critique Against the World Bank' (2021) 21(1) Human Rights Law Review 80–107.

Van der Ploeg, Lideweji & Vanclay, Frank, 'A human Rights-based Approach to Project Induced Displacement and Resettlement' (2017) 35(1) Impact Assessment and Project Appraisal 34–52.

Vanclay, Frank, 'Project-induced displacement and resettlement: from impoverishment risks to an opportunity for development?' (2017) 35(1) Impact Assessment and Project Appraisal 3–21.

Victoria, Maria; Ormaza, Cabrera and Ebert, Franz Christian, 'The World Bank, human rights, and organizational legitimacy strategies: The case of the 2016 Environmental and Social Framework' (2019) 32(3) Leiden Journal of International Law 483–500.

Wewerinke-Singh, Margaretha, 'Remedies for Human Rights Violations Caused by Climate Change' (2019) 9 Climate Law 224–243.

Wilmsen, Brooke; Webber, Michael and Duan, Yuefang, 'Involuntary Rural Resettlement: Resources, Strategies, and Outcomes at the Three Gorges Dam, China' (2011) 20(4) Journal of Environment & Development 355–380.

Zhou, Suzanne, 'Reassessing the Prospects of Human Rights Safeguard Policy at the World Bank' (2012) 15(3) Journal of International Economic Law 823–841.

Zikargie, Yidneckachew Ayele and Cochrane, Logan, 'Modernist Land Development-Induced Villagisation: Deconstructing Socio-Economic Rights of Pastoralists in South Omo, Ethiopia' (2022) Forum for Development Studies 1–24.

Zvobgo, Kelebogile and Graham, Benjamin A. T., 'The World Bank as an enforcer of human rights' (2020) 19(4) Journal of Human Rights 425–448.

Reports

Human Rights Council, Report of the Special Rapporteur on the right to food, Olivier De Schutter, Large-Scale Land Acquisitions and Leases: A Set of Minimum Principles and Measures to Address the Human Rights Challenge, 28 December 2009, A/HRC/13/33/Add.2.

Human Rights Council, Report of the Independent Expert on the effects of foreign debt and other related international financial obligations of States on the full enjoyment of all human rights, particularly economic, social and cultural rights, Juan Pablo Bohoslavsky, 22 December 2014, A/HRC/28/59.

Human Rights Council, Report of the Special Rapporteur on the human rights of internally displaced persons, 18 April 2017, A/HRC/35/27.

Human Rights Watch, *"What Will Happen if Hunger Comes?": Abuses against the Indigenous Peoples of Ethiopia's Lower Omo Valley* (Human Rights Watch, June 2012).

Internal Displacement Monitoring Centre (IDMC), Pushed Aside: Displaced for 'Development' in India, IDMC report, July 2016, available at http://www.internal-displacement.org/publications/pushed-aside-displaced-for-development-in-india, last accessed 26 July 2025..

IDMC, Africa Report on Internal Displacement, 2019, available at https://www.internal-displacement.org/publications/africa-report-on-internal-displacement, accessed 26 July 2025.

Internal Displacement Monitoring Centre (IDMC), Global Report on Internal Displacement 2018, available at http://www.internal-displacement.org/global-report/grid2018/, accessed 26 July 2025.

Internal Displacement Monitoring Centre (IDMC), Internal displacement in a changing climate, 2021 ('IDMC report 2020') available at https://www.internal-displacement.org/global-report/grid2021/#part1, accessed 26 July 2025.

Report of the Secretary-General, In larger freedom: towards development, security and human rights for all, 21 March 2005, A/59/2005.

Report of the UN Secretary-General, 'The emergence of the right to development' in the United Nations, *Realizing the Right to Development* (Essays in Commemoration of 25 Years of the United Nations Declaration on the Right to Development), (New York and Geneva: United Nations Publications, HR/PUB/12/4, December 2013), available at https://www.un-ilibrary.org/economic-and-social-development/realizing-the-right-to-development_49006c2a-en, accessed 26 July 2025.

The Oakland Institute, *"How They Tricked Us": Living with the Gibe III Dam and Sugarcane Plantations in Southwest Ethiopia* (the Oakland Institute, 2019).

UN Commission on Human Rights, Analytical report of the Secretary-General on Internally Displaced Persons, 14 February 1992, UN Doc. E/CN.4/1992/23.

The UN Commission on Human Rights, Study on the current state of progress in the implementation of the right to development submitted by Mr. Arjun K. Sengupta, independent expert, pursuant to Commission resolution 1998/72 and General Assembly resolution 53/155, 27 July 1999, E/CN.4/1999/WG.18/2.

UN Commission on Human Rights, The right to food Report of the Special Rapporteur on the right to food, Jean Ziegler, 20 March 2006, E/CN.4/2006/44.

UN Economic and Social Council, Commission on Human Rights, Drafting Committee, Report of the Drafting Committee to the Commission on Human Rights, 21 May 1948, UN Doc E/CN.4/95.

UN General Assembly, Report of the Independent Expert on the Right to Development, 17 August 2000, A/55/306.

UN General Assembly, Report of the Independent Expert on the Right to Development, 17 August 2002, A/55/306.

UN General Assembly, Philip Alston, Report of the Special Rapporteur on extreme poverty and human rights, 4 August 2015, A/70/274.

UN Human Rights Council, Report of the Special Rapporteur on adequate housing as a component of the right to an adequate standard of living, Miloon Kothari, mission to Spain, 7 February 2008, A/HRC/7/16/Add.2.

UNHCR, Global Trends: Forced Displacement in 2021, available at https://www.unhcr.org/global trends.html, accessed 26 July 2025.

UN Population Fund (UNFPA), *Report of the International Conference on Population and Development: Cairo, 5–13 September 1994*, A/CONF.171/13/Rev.1 (New York: United Nations, 1995).

World Bank Report, Recent Experience With Involuntary Resettlement China Shuikou (and Yantan), Report No. 17539, 2 June 1998.

World Bank, Knowledge and Learning for Human Rights and Development: Nordic Trust Fund Progress Report November 2010 – October 2011, available at https://documents.worldbank.org/en/publication/documents-reports/documentdetail/857101468188367170/knowledge-and-learning-for-human-rights-and-development-nordic-trust-fund-progress-report-september-2009-october-2010, accessed 26 July 2025.

World Bank, International Debt Statistics 2022, (World Bank, 2022), available at https://openknowledge.worldbank.org/entities/publication/47f55cbf-ee14-531a-8acb-8e2406f4354d, accessed 26 July 2025.

World Commission on Environment and Development, *Our Common Future* (Oxford; New York: Oxford University Press, 1987).

World Commission on Dams, *Dams and Development: a New Framework for Decision-Making*, the Report of the World Commission on Dams, (Earthscan Publications, 2000).

Blog Posts and Other Online Sources

Avery, Sean, 'Fears over Ethiopian dam's costly impact on environment, people' (The Conversation, 12 September 2017), available at https://theconversation.com/fears-over-ethiopian-dams-costly-impact-on-environment-people-80757, accessed 8 October 2022.

Brookings-Bern Project on Internal Displacement, Addressing Internal Displacement: A Framework for National Responsibility, April 2005, available at https://www.brookings.edu/research/addressing-internal-displacement-a-framework-for-national-responsibility/, accessed 26 July 2025.

Claridge, Lucy, 'Landmark ruling provides major victory to Kenya's indigenous Endorois', Minority Rights Groups International briefing, 26 August 2010, available at https://minorityrights.org/publications/landmark-ruling-provides-major-victory-to-kenyas-indigenous-endorois-august-2010/, accessed 26 July 2025.

European Committee of Social Rights, available at https://www.coe.int/en/web/european-social-charter/european-committee-of-social-rights, accessed 26 July 2025.

Food Agricultural Organization of the United Nations (FAO), The gender gap in land rights, available at http://www.fao.org/3/I8796EN/i8796en.pdf, accessed 26 July 2025.

Himanshu, Thakkar, 'Displacement and Development: Construction of the Sardar Dam' (Cultural Survival, September 1999) available https://www.culturalsurvival.org/publications/cultural-survival-quarterly/displacement-and-development-construction-sardar-dam, accessed 26 July 2025.

IDMC, Global Internal Displacement Database, available at https://www.internal-displacement.org/database/displacement-data, accessed 26 July 2025.

Internal Displacement monitoring Centre (IDMC), 'Dams and Internal Displacement: an Introduction' (IDMC, 11 April 2017) available at https://www.internal-displacement.org/publications/case-study-series-dam-displacement, 26 July 2025.

Internal Displacement Monitoring Centre, 'Who are Internally Displaced People?', available at http://www.internal-displacement.org/internal-displacement, accessed 26 July 2025.

International Committee of the Red Cross (ICRC), 'How is the Term "Armed Conflict" Defined in International Humanitarian Law?' (ICRC Opinion Paper, March 2008), available at https://www.icrc.org/en/doc/assets/files/other/opinion-paper-armed-conflict.pdf, accessed 26 July 2025.

International Rivers Network (IRN), Tehri Dam, IRN fact sheet, October 2002, available at https://www.internationalrivers.org/resources/tehri-dam-2666, accessed 26 July 2025.

International Rivers: people, water, life, Questions and Answers About Large Dams, available at https://www.internationalrivers.org/questions-and-answers-about-large-dams, accessed 26 July 2025.

OHCHR, Free, Prior and Informed Consent of Indigenous Peoples, September 2013, available at https://www.ohchr.org/sites/default/files/Documents/Issues/IPeoples/FreePriorandInformedConsent.pdf, accessed 26 July 2025.

OHCHR, The principle of non-refoulement under international human rights law, available at https://www.ohchr.org/Documents/Issues/Migration/GlobalCompactMigration/ThePrincipleNon-RefoulementUnderInternationalHumanRightsLaw.pdf, accessed 26 July 2025.

OHCHR, Human Rights and Development Trust Fund Launch: Statement by UN High Commissioner for Human Rights, Michelle Bachelet, 12 April 2019, available at https://www.ohchr.org/en/newsevents/pages/DisplayNews.aspx?NewsID=24487&LangID=E, accessed 26 July 2025.

Solomon, Salem, 'Forced Displacement Causes Controversy in Ethiopia's Omo Valley' (VOA News, 19 July 2019), available at https://www.voanews.com/a/africa_forced-displacement-causes-controversy-ethiopias-omo-valley/6172224.html, accessed 26 July 2025.

The Economist, 21 December 2016), available at https://www.economist.com/middle-east-and-africa/2016/12/21/ethiopia-opens-africas-tallest-and-most-controversial-dam, accessed 26 July 2025.

The World Bank, Development and human rights: the role of the World Bank, 1998, available at https://documents.worldbank.org/en/publication/documents-reports/documentdetail/820031468767358922/development-and-human-rights-the-role-of-the-world-bank, accessed 26 July 2025.

The World Bank, Urban Development, last updated 20 April 2020, available at https://www.worldbank.org/en/topic/urbandevelopment/overview#1, accessed 26 July 2025.

UNHCR, Who is a Refugee?, UNHCR Protection Training Manual for European Border and Entry Officials, available at https://www.unhcr.org/publications/manuals/4d944dfc9/unhcr-protection-training-manual-european-border-entry-officials-3-refugee.html, accessed 26 July 2025.

United Nations Department of Economic and Social Affairs, 68% of the world population projected to live in urban areas by 2050, says UN, News, available at https://www.un.org/development/desa/en/news/population/2018-revision-of-world-urbanization-prospects.html, 26 July 2025.

Wang, Kai, 'China: Is it burdening poor countries with unsustainable debt?', BBC, 6 January 2022, available at https://www.bbc.com/news/59585507, accessed 26 July 2025.

Miscellaneous

African Development Bank Group's Integrated Safeguards System: Policy statement and operational safeguard, Safeguards and Sustainability Series, Volume 1 - Issue 1, December 2013, Preamble.

Clark, Lance, 'Internal Refugees- The Hidden Half', World Refugee Survey (Washington DC: US Committee for Refugees, 1989).

Cobo, J Martínez, Special Rapporteur of the UN Sub-Commission on Prevention of Discrimination and Protection of Minorities, Study on the Problem of Discrimination against Indigenous Populations, March 1987, UN Doc E/CN.4/Sub.2/1986/Add.4.

Danino, Robert, 'Legal Opinion on Human Rights and the Work of the World Bank', 27 January 2006.

Harris, Jonathan M., 'Basic Principles of Sustainable Development' (2000) Global Development and Environment Institute Working Paper No. 00-04.

Human Rights Council, Working Group on the Right to Development, *Draft Convention on the Right to Development*, 17 January 2020, A/HRC/WG.2/21/2.

Feiring, Birgitte, Indigenous peoples' rights to lands, territories, and resources, ILC, Rome, 2013.

FIAN International, The Human Right to Land: Position Paper (Published by FIAN International Secretariat, November 2017).

Geneva Academy of International Humanitarian Law and Human Rights, Use of Force in Law Enforcement and the Right to Life: The Role of the Human Rights Council, Academy in Brief No.6 (Geneva, November 2016).

Golay, Christophe and Cismas, Ioana, 'Legal Opinion: The Right to Property from a Human Rights Perspective' (International Centre for Human Rights and Democratic Development, 2010).

Kerchmeier, Felix, 'The right to development where do we stand: the state of the debate on the right to development' (2006) Dialogue on Globalization, occasional paper No. 23.

Inclusive Development International (IDI), International Accountability Project (IAP), Bank Information Center (BIC), Habitat International Coalition- Housing and Land Rights Network (HIC-HLRN), Reforming the World Bank Policy on Involuntary Resettlement, Submission to the World Bank Safeguards Review (April 2013).

Memorandum of the Legal Department of the IBRD', A/6825 (5 May 1967) Annex II in United Nations, *Juridical Yearbook 1997: Part Two: Legal activities of the United Nations and related inter-governmental organizations* (United Nations, 1997), at 121.

Office of the High Commissioner for Human Rights (OHCHR), Forced Evictions, Fact Sheet No. 25/Rev.1 (United Nations: New York and Geneva, 1 May 2014).
Office of the United Nations High Commissioner for Human Rights (OHCHR), Frequently asked questions on a human rights-based approach to development cooperation, 1 January 2006, HR/PUB/06/8, 2006.
Office of the United Nations High Commissioner for Human Rights (OHCHR), Principles and Guidelines for a Human Rights Based Approach to Poverty Reduction Strategies, 2012, HR/PUB/06/12.
OHCHR, Indigenous Peoples and the United Nations Human Rights System, Fact Sheet No. 9/Rev.2 (United Nations, 2013).
OHCHR, Land and Human Rights: Standards and Applications, HR/PUB/15/5/Add.1, 2015.
OHCHR, Frequently Asked Questions on the Right to Development, Fact Sheet No. 37 (United Nations: New York and Geneva, 2016).
Pandey, Balaji, Impoverishment Risks: A Case Study of Five Villages in Coal Mining Areas of Talcher, Orissa, Paper presented at the workshop on Involuntary Resettlement and Impoverishment Risks, New Delhi.
Response Note to 'The Draft Aide Memoire of the African Group on the UN Declaration on the Rights of Indigenous Peoples', presented by an African group of experts, 21 March 2007.
Tagliarino, Nicholas K., Encroaching on Land and Livelihoods: How International Expropriation Laws Measure up to International Standards (Working Paper, World Resources Institute, 2016).
UN Commission on Human Rights, Internally displaced persons, 14 April 2005, UN Doc. E/CN.4/2005/L.60.
UN Committee on Economic, Social and Cultural Rights, Statement on the importance and relevance of the right to development, adopted on the occasion of the twenty-fifth anniversary of the Declaration on the Right to Development, 12 July 2011, E/C.12/2011/2.
UN General Assembly, The Third Committee, Summary Record of the Ninety-Third Meeting, 4 October 1948, UN Doc A/C.3/SR.93.
UN Human Rights Council, the Third Revised Draft of the Binding Treaty on Business and Human Rights, January 2022, A/HRC/49/65/Add.1.
UNHCR, *Internal Displacement: Responsibility and Action* (UNHCR Handbook for Parliamentarians, No. 20, 2013).
United Nations Conference on Trade and Development, Expropriation, UNCTAD Series on Issues in International Investment Agreements II, 2013.
United Nations Economic and Social Council, Statement of Essential Human Rights Presented by the Delegation of Panama, E/HR/3, 26 April 1946.
World Bank Inspection Panel, Investigation Report, Ghana: West African Gas Pipeline Project, IDA Guarantee No. B-006-0-GH, 2008, available at https://documents.worldbank.org/en/publication/documents-reports/documentdetail/664021468003035202/ghana-west-african-gas-pipeline-project-inspection-panel-request-for-inspection, accessed 26 July 2025.
World Bank Social Development Department, Involuntary Resettlement Portfolio Review: Phase I, Inventory of Bank-financed Projects Triggering the Involuntary Resettlement Policy (1990–2010), May 2012.
World Health Organization (WHO), Health principles of housing (Geneva: World Health Organization, 1989) available at https://apps.who.int/iris/handle/10665/39847, accessed 26 July 2025.

Legal Sources: Treaties, Cases, and Others

Treaties

African Union, Protocol to the African Charter on Human and People's Rights on the Rights of Women in Africa, 11 July 2003.

African Union, African Union Convention for the Protection and Assistance of Internally Displaced Persons in Africa, 23 October 2009.

Council of Europe, European Convention for the Protection of Human Rights and Fundamental Freedoms, as amended by Protocols Nos. 11 and 14, 4 November 1950, 5 ETS.

Council of Europe, Protocol 1 to the European Convention for the Protection of Human Rights and Fundamental Freedoms, 20 March 1952, 9 ETS.

Council of Europe, European Social Charter, 18 October 1961, 35 ETS.

Council of Europe, Additional Protocol to the European Social Charter, 5 May 1988, 128 ETS.

Council of Europe, European Charter for Regional or Minority Languages, 5 November 1992, 148 ETS.

Council of Europe, European Social Charter (Revised), 3 May 1996, 163 ETS.

Council of Europe, Framework Convention for the Protection of National Minorities, 1 February 1998, 157 ETS.

Council of Europe, Convention on Access to Official Documents, 205 Council of Europe Treaty Series, entered into force on 1 December 2020.

International Bank for Reconstruction and Development and United Nations, Protocol concerning the entry into force of the Agreement between the United Nations and the International Bank for Reconstruction and Development, 15 April 1948, 16 United Nations Treaty Series 341.

International Bank for Reconstruction and Development (IBRD), Articles of Agreement (As amended effective June 27, 2012).

International Development Association (IDA), Articles of Agreement (Effective September 24, 1960).

International Labour Organization (ILO), Forced Labour Convention, C29, 28 June 1930.

International Labour Organization (ILO), Abolition of Forced Labour Convention, C105, 25 June 1957.

International Labour Organization (ILO), Indigenous and Tribal Populations Convention, C107, 26 June 1957.

International Labour Organization (ILO), Discrimination (Employment and Occupation) Convention, C111, 25 June 1958.

International Labour Organization (ILO), Convention Concerning Employment Policy, C122, 9 July 1964.

International Labour Organization (ILO), Convention Concerning Termination of Employment at the Initiative of the Employer, C158, 22 June 1982.

International Labour Organization (ILO), Indigenous and Tribal Peoples Convention, C169, 27 June 1989.

Organization of African Unity (OAU), Convention Governing the Specific Aspects of Refugee Problems in Africa, 10 September 1969, 1001 U.N.T.S. 45.

Organization of African Unity (OAU), African Charter on Human and Peoples' Rights, 27 June 1981, CAB/LEG/67/3 rev. 5, 21 I.L.M. 58 (1982).

Organization of American States (OAS), Protocol of Amendment to the Charter of the Organization of American States, 27 February 1967, 1-A OAS Treaty Series.

Organization of American States (OAS), American Convention on Human Rights, 22 November 1969, 36 OAS Treaty Series.

Organization of American States (OAS), Additional Protocol to the American Convention on Human Rights in the Area of Economic, Social and Cultural Rights, 17 November 1988, 69 OAS Treaty Series ('Protocol of San Salvador').

United Nations, Charter of the United Nations, 24 October 1945, 1 UNTS XVI.
United Nations, Statute of the International Court of Justice, 18 April 1946.
United Nations, Vienna Convention on the Law of Treaties, 23 May 1969, 1155 United Nations Treaty Series 331.
UN General Assembly, Statute of the Office of the United Nations High Commissioner for Refugees, 14 December 1950, A/RES/428(V).
UN General Assembly, Convention Relating to the Status of Refugees, 28 July 1951, 189 United Nations Treaty Series 137.
UN General Assembly, International Convention on the Elimination of All Forms of Racial Discrimination, 21 December 1965, 660 United Nations Treaty Series 195.
UN General Assembly, International Covenant on Civil and Political Rights, 16 December 1966, 999 United Nations Treaty Series 171.
UN General Assembly, International Covenant on Economic, Social and Cultural Rights, 16 December 1966, 993 United Nations Treaty Series 3.
UN General Assembly, Convention on the Elimination of All Forms of Discrimination Against Women, 18 December 1979, 1249 United Nations Treaty Series 13.
UN General Assembly, Convention Against Torture and Other Cruel, Inhuman or Degrading Treatment or Punishment, 10 December 1984, 1465 United Nations Treaty Series 85.
UN General Assembly, Convention on the Rights of the Child, 20 November 1989, 1577 United Nations Treaty Series 3.
UN General Assembly, International Convention on the Protection of the Rights of All Migrant Workers and Members of their Families, 18 December 1990, A/RES/45/158.
UN General Assembly, Convention on the Rights of Persons with Disabilities: Resolution/adopted by the General Assembly, 24 January 2007, A/RES/61/106.

Soft Law

African Commission on Human and Peoples' Rights, 51 Resolution on the Rights of Indigenous Peoples' Communities in Africa, 6 November 2000, ACHPR/Res.51(XXVIII)00.
African Commission on Human and Peoples' Rights, Resolution on the Adoption of the Report of the African Commission's Working Group on Indigenous Populations/Communities, ACHPR/ Res 51 (XXVII), 34th Ordinary Session, November 2003.
Basic Principles on the Use of Force and Firearms by Law Enforcement Officials, Adopted by the Eighth United Nations Congress on the Prevention of Crime and the Treatment of Offenders, Havana, Cuba, 27 August to 7 September 1990.
Cartagena Declaration on Refugees, Colloquium on the International Protection of Refugees in Central America, Mexico and Panama, 22 November 1984, III(3).
Economic and Social Council Resolution 1982/34, Study of the problem of discrimination against indigenous populations, 7 May 1982.
Human Rights Council, Resolution 6/32, Mandate of the Representative of the Secretary-General on the human rights of internally displaced persons, 14 December 2007, UN Doc. A/HRC/RES/ 6/32.
Human Rights Council, Resolution 23/8, Mandate of the Special Rapporteur on the human rights of internally displaced persons, 20 June 2013, UN Doc. A/HRC/RES/23/8.
Human Rights Council, Resolution 39/9, The Right to Development, 25 September 2018, A/HRC/ 39/L.12.
Human Rights Council, Resolution 42/23, The Right to Development, 20 September 2019, A/HRC/ 42/L.36.
International Law Commission, Draft Articles on Responsibility of States for Internationally Wrongful Acts, November 2001, Supplement No. 10 (A/56/10), chp.IV.E.1.

International Law Commission, Draft Articles on the Responsibility of International Organizations, Yearbook of the International Law Commission, 2011, vol. II, Part Two, A/CN.4/SER.A/2011/Add.1.

International Law Commission, Draft conclusions on subsequent agreements and subsequent practice in relation to the interpretation of treaties, 2018, Yearbook of the International Law Commission, 2018, vol. II, Part Two.

Office of the UN High Commissioner for Human Rights, Principles and Guidelines for a Human Rights Approach to Development, 2006, HR/PUB/06/12.

OHCHR, Guiding Principles on Business and Human Rights: Implementing the United Nations "Protect, Respect and Remedy" Framework, HR/PUB/11/04, 2011.

Organization of American States, American Declaration on the Rights of Indigenous Peoples, 15 June 2016, AG/RES. 2888 (XLVI-O/16).

The Guiding Principles on Business and Human Rights: Implementing the United Nations "Protect, Respect and Remedy" Framework, 2011, HR/PUB/11/04.

The Johannesburg Declaration on Sustainable Development, 4 September 2002.

The UN Commission on Human Rights, Resolution 1992/73, Internally Displaced Persons, 5 March 1992, UN Doc. E/CN.4/RES/1992/73.

UN Commission on Human Rights, Forced evictions, Resolution 1993/77, 10 March 1993, E/CN.4/RES/1993/77.

UN Human Rights Commission, Resolution 1996/52, Internally Displaced Persons, 19 April 1996, UN Doc. E/CN.4/RES/1996/52.

UN Commission on Human Rights, Guiding Principles on Internal Displacement, 11 February 1998, E/CN.4/1998/53/Add.2.

The UN Commission on Human Rights, Resolution 1998/72 the Right to Development, 22 April 1998, ESCOR Supp. (No. 3) at 229 U.N. Doc. E/CN.4/1998/72).

UN Economic and Social Council, Implementation of the International Covenant on Economic, Social and Cultural Rights Resolution 1985/17, 28 May 1985, E/RES/1985/17.

UN General Assembly, Universal Declaration of Human Rights, 10 December 1948, 217 A (III).

UN General Assembly, Resolution 1720 (XVI), Permanent sovereignty over Natural Resources, 19 December 1961, A/RES/1720.

UN General Assembly, Resolution 2184 (XXI), Questions of Territories under Portuguese Administration, 12 December 1966, A/RES/2184.

UN General Assembly, Resolution 2202 (XXI), The policies of apartheid of the Government of the Republic of South Africa, 16 December 1966, A/RES/2202.

UN General Assembly, Resolution 2270 (XXII), Questions of Territories under Portuguese Administration, 3 November 1967, A/RES/2270 (XXII).

UN General Assembly, Code of Conduct for Law Enforcement Officials, Resolution 34/169, 17 December 1979.

UN General Assembly, Resolution 45/98 Respect for the right of everyone to own property alone as well as in association with others and its contribution to the economic and social development of Member States, 14 December 1990, A/RES/45/98.

UN General Assembly, Rio Declaration on Environment and Development, 12 August 1992, A/CONF.151/26 (Vol. I).

UN General Assembly, Vienna Declaration and Programme of Action, 12 July 1993, A/CONF.157/23.

UN General Assembly, Declaration on the Right to Development: resolution/adopted by the General Assembly, 4 December 1986, A/RES/41/128.

UN General Assembly, Resolution 60/1, 2005 World Summit Outcome, 24 October 2005, A/RES/60/1.

UN General Assembly, Basic Principles and Guidelines on the Right to a Remedy and Reparation for Victims of Gross Violations of International Human Rights Law and Serious Violations of International Humanitarian Law: resolution/adopted by the General Assembly, 21 March 2006, A/RES/60/147.

UN General Assembly, United Nations Declaration on the Rights of Indigenous Peoples: resolution/ adopted by the General Assembly, 2 October 2007, A/RES/61/295.

UN General Assembly, Transforming our world: the 2030 Agenda for Sustainable Development, 21 October 2015, A/RES/70/1.

UN Human Rights Council, Resolution 39/12, Declaration on the Rights of Peasants and Other People Working in Rural Areas, A/HRC/RES/39/12, 8 October 2018.

United Nations, Charter of the United Nations, 24 October 1945, 1 United Nations Treaty Series XVI.

United Nations, Final Act of the International Conference on Human Rights (The Proclamation of Teheran), 1968, UN doc. A/CONF.32/41.

United Nations World Summit for Social Development, Copenhagen Declaration on Social Development, 14 March 1995, A/CONF.166/9.

UN ECOSOC Res 1589(L) (21 May 1971) UN Doc E/5044.

Policy Frameworks

Agreement Establishing the African Development Bank, 2016 edition, Article 38(2), available at https://www.afdb.org/en/documents/agreement-establishing-african-development-fund-2016-edition, accessed 26 July 2025.

Agreement Establishing the Asian Development Bank, December 1965, Article 36(2), available at https://www.adb.org/documents/agreement-establishing-asian-development-bank-adb-charter, accessed 26 July 2025.

Agreement Establishing the Inter-American Development Bank, entered into force on 30 December 1959, last amended 31 December 1987.

African Development Bank Involuntary Resettlement Policy, November 2003.

African Development Bank Group's Policy on the Environment, February 2004.

Asian Development Bank Involuntary Resettlement Policy, August 1995.

International Bank for Reconstruction and Development and International Development Association, Resolution No. IBRD 93-10 and Resolution No. IDA 93-6 (1993).

International Bank for Reconstruction and Development and International Development Association, Resolution No. IBRD 2020-0004 and Resolution No. IDA 2020-0003, The World Bank Inspection Panel, September 8, 2020.

International Bank for Reconstruction and Development and International Development Association, Resolution No. IBRD 2020-0005 and Resolution No. IDA 2020-0004, The World Bank Accountability Mechanism September 8, 2020.

Inter-American Development Bank, Operational Policy on Involuntary Resettlement, OP-710, October 1998.

Inter-American Development Bank, Environmental and Safeguards Compliance Policy, 19 January 2006.

Inter-American Development Bank, Operational Policy on Indigenous Peoples and Strategy for Indigenous Development, July 2006.

World Bank, Operational Manual OP 4.12 - Involuntary Resettlement, December 2001.

World Bank, Operational Manual 4.10: Indigenous Peoples, adopted in July 2005.

The World Bank, Environmental and Social Framework (ESF), 2017, available at https://documents1.worldbank.org/curated/en/383011492423734099/pdf/The-World-Bank-Environmental-and-Social-Framework.pdf, accessed 26 July 2025.

The World Bank, Land Acquisition, Restrictions on Land Use and Involuntary Resettlement, in the Environmental and Social Framework, p. 53, 2017.

The World Bank, Indigenous Peoples/Sub-Saharan African Historically Underserved Traditional Local Communities, in the Environmental and Social Framework, p. 75, 2017.

The World Bank, Assessment and Management of Environmental and Social Risks and Impacts, in the Environmental and Social Framework, 2017.

Case Law

African Human Rights System

African Commission on Human and Peoples' Rights v. Republic of Kenya, Application No. 006/2012, African Court on Human and Peoples' Rights, 26 May 2017.

Article 19 v Eritrea, communication 275/03, African Commission on Human and Peoples' Rights, 30 May 2007.

Centre for Minority Rights Development (Kenya) and Minority Rights Group International on behalf of Endorois Welfare Council v. Kenya, 276/2003, African Commission on Human and Peoples' Rights, 4 February 2010.

Civil Liberties Organisation v Nigeria, communication 101/93, African Commission on Human and Peoples' Rights, 22 March 1995.

Malawi African Association and Others v. Mauritania, Communication Nos. 54/91, 61/91, 98/93, 164/97 à 196/97 and 210/98, African Commission on Human and Peoples' Rights, 11 May 2000.

Monim Elgak, Osman Hummeida and Amir Suliman (represented by FIDH and OMCT) v Sudan, Communication 379/09, African Commission on Human and Peoples' Rights, 10 March 2015.

Social and Economic Rights Action Center (SERAC) and Center for Economic and Social Rights (CESR) / Nigeria, 155/96, African Commission on Human and People's Rights, 27 May 2002.

Sudan Human Rights Organisation & Centre on Housing Rights and Evictions (COHRE) v. Sudan, 279/03-296/05, African Commission on Human and Peoples' Rights, 27 May 2009.

The Nubian Community in Kenya v. The Republic of Kenya, Communication 317/2006, African Commission on Human and Peoples' Rights, 30 May 2016.

Zimbabwe Human Rights NGO Forum v. Zimbabwe, Communication No. 245/2002, EX.CL/322 (X), African Commission on Human and Peoples' Rights, 15 May 2006.

Zimbabwe Lawyers for Human Rights & Associated Newspapers of Zimbabwe v Republic of Zimbabwe, Communication 284/03, African Commission on Human and Peoples' Rights, 3 April 2009.

European Human Rights System

Akdivar and Others v. Turkey, Application No. 99/1995/605/693, European Court of Human Rights, 16 September 1996.

Anheuser-Busch Inc. v. Portugal, Application no. 73049/01, Judgment, The European Court of Human Rights (the Grand Chamber), 11 January 2007.

CHAGOS ISLANDERS v United Kingdom, Application no. 35622/04, decision on admissibility, European Court of Human Rights, 11 December 2012.

Connors v. the United Kingdom, Application No. 66746/01, Judgment, European Court of Human Rights, 27 May 2004.

Doğan and Others v. Turkey, Applications 8803-8811/02, 8813/02 and 8815-8819/02, Judgment, European Court of Human Rights, 29 June 2004.

Dudgeon v United Kingdom, Application No. 7525/76, European Court of Human Rights, 22 October 1981.

European Federation of National Organisations Working with the Homeless (FEANTSA) v. France, Complaint No. 39/2006, decision on the merits, European Committee of Social Rights, 5 December 2007.

European Federation of National Organisations working with the Homeless (FEANTSA) v. Slovenia, Complaint No. 53/2008, decision on the merits, European Committee of Social Rights, 8 September 2009.

European Federation of National Organisations working with the Homeless (FEANTSA) v. the Netherlands, Complaint No. 86/2012, decision on the merits, European Committee of Social Rights, 2 July 2014.

G. & E. v Norway, Application No 9278/81 & 9415/81, decision on admissibility, European Commission on Human Rights, 3 October 1983.

Handyside v United Kingdom, Application No 5493/72, A/24, [1976] ECHR 5, (1976) 1 EHRR 737, (1979) 1 EHRR 737, IHRL 14 (ECHR 1976), Merits, European Court of Human Rights, 7 December 1976.

HINGITAQ 53 v Denmark, Application no. 18584/04, decision on admissibility, European Court of Human Rights, 12 January 2006.

Iatridis v. Greece, Application no. 31107/96, Judgment, European Court of Human Rights, 25 March 1999.

James and others v. The United Kingdom, Application no. 8793/79, Judgment, The European Court of Human Rights, 21 February 1986.

Lithgow v United Kingdom, Applications Nos. 9006/80, 9262/81, 9263/81, 9265/81, 9266/81, 9313/81, 9405/81, Merits, European Court of Human Rights, 8 July 1986.

Malhous v. the Czech Republic, Application no. 33071/96, Judgment, The European Court of Human Rights (the Grand Chamber), 13 December 2000.

Marzari v. Italy, Application No. 36448/97, decision on admissibility, European Court of Human Rights, 4 May 1999.

Moldovan and Others v. Romania, Application No. 41138/98; 64320/01, Judgment, European Court of Human Rights, 12 July 2005.

Pincová and Pinc v. the Czech Republic, Application no. 36548/97, judgment, European Court of Human Rights, 5 November 2002.

*Platakou v. Greec*e, Application no. 38460/97, judgment, European Court of Human Rights, 11 January 2001.

Sunday Times v United Kingdom, Application No 6538/74, A/30, [1979] ECHR 1, (1979-80) 2 EHRR 245, (1979) 76 LSG 328, IHRL 21 (ECHR 1979), Judgment, European Court of Human Rights, 26 April 1979.

The Holy Monasteries v. Greece, Application no. 13092/87; 13984/88, Judgment, European Court of Human Rights, 09 December 1994.

Inter-American Human Rights System

Case of Velásquez Rodríguez v. Honduras, Judgment, Inter-American Court of Human Rights, 29 July 1988, Series C, No. 4.

Case of the Mayagna (Sumo) Awas Tingni Community v Nicaragua, Merit, Inter-American Court of Human Rights, 31 August 2001.

Case of the "Five Pensioners" v. Peru, Merits, Inter-American Court of Human Rights, 28 February 2003.

Case of the Moiwana Community v. Suriname, Preliminary Objections, Merits, Reparations and Cost, Inter-American Court of Human Rights, 15 June 2005.

Case of the Yakye Axa Indigenous Community v Paraguay, Merits, Inter-American Court of Human Rights, 17 June 2005.

Case of the Mapiripán Massacre vs Colombia, Judgment, Inter-American Court of Human Rights, 15 September 2005.

Case of the Sawhoyamaxa Indigenous Community v. Paraguay, Merits, Reparations and Costs, Inter-American Court of Human Rights, 29 March 2006.

Case of the Saramaka People v Suriname, Preliminary objections, merits, reparations and costs, IACHR Series C no. 172, IHRL 3046 (IACHR 2007), 28th November 2007.

Case of Salvador Chiriboga v. Ecuador, Inter-American Court of Human Rights, Judgment of 6 May 2008 (Preliminary Objection and Merits).

UN Human Rights System

Chiara Sacchi et al. v Argentina, communication No. 104/2019, decision on admissibility, Committee on the Rights of the Child, 22 September 2021, CRC/C/88/D/104/2019.

Daniel Billy et al. v Australia, communication No. 3624/2019, adoption of views, UN Human Rights Committee, 22 September 2022, CCPR/C/135/D/3624/2019.

I.D.G v. Spain, Communication No. 2/2014, adoption of views, Committee on Economic, Social and Cultural Rights, 13 October 2015, E/C.12/55/D/2/2014.

Maribel Viviana López Albán v. Spain, communication No. 37/2018, adoption of views, Committee on Economic, Social and Cultural Rights, 11 October 2019, E/C.12/66/D/37/2018.

Mohamed Ben Djazia and Naouel Bellili v. Spain, Communication No. 5/2015, adoption of views, UN Committee on Economic, Social and Cultural Rights (CESCR), 21 July 2017, E/C.12/61/D/5/2015.

Nurbek Toktakunov v Kyrgyzstan, Communication No. 1470/2006, adoption of views, CCPR/C/101/D/1470/2006, Human Rights Committee, 28 March 2011.

Rosario Gómez-Limón Pardo v. Spain, communication No. 52/2018, adoption of views, Committee on Economic, Social and Cultural Rights, 5 March 2020, E/C.12/67/D/52/2018.

National Courts

Republic of South Africa v. Grootboom, Case No. CCT 11/00. 2000 (11) BCLR 1169, Constitutional Court of South Africa, 4 October 2000.

Sentencia C-175/09, Colombia: Corte Constitucional, 18 March 2009.

Social and Economic Rights Action Center (SERAC) and Center for Economic and Social Rights (CESR) / Nigeria, 155/96, African Commission on Human and People's Rights, 27 May 2002.

Soobramoney v Minister of Health (KwaZulu-Natal), CCT32/97) [1997] ZACC 17; 1998 (1) SA 765 (CC); 1997 (12) BCLR 1696, Constitutional Court of South Africa, 27 November 1997).

Others

Factory At Chorzów, Germany v Poland, Judgment, Claim for Indemnity, Merits, Judgment No 13, (1928) PCIJ Series A No 17, ICGJ 255 (PCIJ 1928), 13th September 1928.

North Sea Continental Shelf Cases (Federal Republic of Germany v. Denmark; Federal Republic of Germany v. the Netherlands), Judgment, International Court of Justice (ICJ), 20 February 1969.

Starrett Housing Corporation, Starrett Systems, Inc., Starrett Housing International, Inc., v. The Government of the Islamic Republic of Iran, Bank Omran, Bank Mellat (Case No. 24).

Advisory Opinions

African Commission on Human and Peoples' Rights, Advisory Opinion on the UN Declaration on the Rights of Indigenous Peoples', May 2007.

International Court of Justice, Reparation for Injuries Suffered in the Service of the United Nations, Advisory Opinion of 11 April 1949, ICJ report 1949.

International Court of Justice, Interpretation of the Agreement of 25 March 1951 between the WHO and Egypt, Advisory Opinion of 20 December 1980, ICJ report 1980.

Concluding Observations

UN Committee on Economic, Social and Cultural Rights, Concluding Observation of Committee on Economic, Social and Cultural Rights: Italy, 23 May 2000, E/C.12/1/Add.43.

UN Committee on Economic, Social and Cultural Rights, Concluding Observation of Committee on Economic, Social and Cultural Rights: Egypt, 23 May 2000, E/C.12/1/Add/44.

UN Committee on Economic, Social and Cultural Rights, Concluding Observation of Committee on Economic, Social and Cultural Rights: Belgium,1 December 2000, E/C.12/1/Add.54.

UN Committee on Economic, Social and Cultural Rights (CESCR), Concluding observations of the UN Committee on Economic, Social and Cultural Rights: Senegal, 24 September 2001, E/C.12/1/Add.62.

UN Committee on Economic, Social and Cultural Rights (CESCR), Concluding Observations of the Committee on Economic, Social and Cultural Rights: Greece, 7 June 2004, E/C.12/1/Add.97.

UN Committee on Economic, Social and Cultural Rights (CESCR), Document submitted by the United Nations Interim Administration Mission in Kosovo (UNMIK), Concluding Observations of the Committee on Economic, Social and Cultural Rights, 1 December 2008, E/C.12/UNK/CO/1.

UN Committee on Economic, Social and Cultural Rights (CESCR), Consideration of reports submitted by States parties under articles 16 and 17 of the Covenant, Concluding observations of the Committee on Economic, Social and Cultural Rights: Democratic Republic of the Congo, 16 December 2009, E/C.12/COD/CO/4.

UN Committee on Economic, Social and Cultural Rights (CESCR), Consideration of reports submitted by States parties under Articles 16 and 17 of the Covenant: concluding observations of the Committee on Economic, Social and Cultural Rights: Madagascar, 16 December 2009, E/C.12/MDG/CO/2.

UN Committee on Economic, Social and Cultural Rights, Concluding observations on the initial report of South Africa, 29 November 2018, E/C.12/ZAF/CO/1.

UN Human Rights Committee (HRC), Concluding Observations of the Human Rights Committee: Kenya, 29 April 2005, CCPR/CO/83/KEN.

UN Human Rights Committee (HRC), Concluding observations of the Human Rights Committee: Chad, 11 August 2009, CCPR/C/TCD/CO/1.

General Comments

UN Commission on Human Rights, The Siracusa Principles on the Limitation and Derogation Provisions in the International Covenant on Civil and Political Rights, 28 September 1984, E/CN.4/1985/4.

UN Commission on Human Rights, Note verbale dated 5 December 1986 from the Permanent Mission of the Netherlands to the United Nations Office at Geneva addressed to the Centre for Human Rights, 8 January 1987, E/CN.4/1987/17 ('Limburg Principles').

UN Committee on Economic, Social and Cultural Rights (CESCR), General Comment No. 1: Reporting by States Parties, 27 July 1981, E/1989/22.

UN Committee on Economic, Social and Cultural Rights (CESCR), General Comment No. 3: The Nature of States Parties' Obligations (Article 2, Para 1, of the Covenant), 14 December 1990, E/1991/23.

UN Committee on Economic, Social and Cultural Rights (CESCR), General Comment No. 4: The Right to Adequate Housing (Article 11 (1) of the Covenant), 13 December 1991, E/1992/23.

UN Committee on Economic, Social and Cultural Rights (CESCR), General Comment No. 7: The right to adequate housing (Article 11.1): forced evictions, 20 May 1997, E/1998/22.

UN Committee on Economic, Social and Cultural Rights (CESCR), General Comment No. 9: The domestic application of the Covenant, 3 December 1998, E/C.12/1998/24.

UN Committee on Economic, Social and Cultural Rights (CESCR), General Comment No. 12: The Right to Adequate Food (Article 11 of the Covenant), 12 May 1999, E/C.12/1999/5.
UN Committee on Economic, Social and Cultural Rights (CESCR), General Comment No. 13: The Right to Education (Article 13 of the Covenant), 8 December 1999, E/C.12/1999/10.
UN Committee on Economic, Social and Cultural Rights, General Comment No. 14: The Right to the Highest Attainable Standard of Health (Article 12), 11 August 2000, E/C.12/2000/4.
UN Committee on Economic, Social and Cultural Rights (CESCR), General Comment No. 15: The Right to Water (Articles 11 and 12 of the Covenant), 20 January 2003, E/C.12/2002/11.
UN Committee on Economic, Social and Cultural Rights (CESCR), General Comment No. 16: The Equal Right of Men and Women to the Enjoyment of All Economic, Social and Cultural Rights (Article 3 of the Covenant), 11 August 2005, E/C.12/2005/4.
UN Committee on Economic, Social and Cultural Rights (CESCR), General Comment No. 18: The Right to Work (Article 6 of the Covenant), 6 February 2006, E/C.12/GC/18.
UN Committee on Economic, Social and Cultural Rights (CESCR), General Comment No. 20: Non-discrimination in economic, social and cultural rights (Article 2, para 2, of the International Covenant on Economic, Social and Cultural Rights), 2 July 2009, E/C.12/GC/20.
UN Committee on Economic, Social and Cultural Rights (CESCR), General Comment No. 23: The right to just and favourable conditions of work (Article 7 of the International Covenant on Economic, Social and Cultural Rights), 7 April 2016, E/C.12/GC/23.
UN Committee on Economic, Social and Cultural Rights (CESCR), General Comment No. 24 (2017) on State obligations under the International Covenant on Economic, Social and Cultural Rights in the Context of Business Activities, 10 August 2017, E/C.12/GC/24.
UN Committee on Economic, Social and Cultural Rights (CESCR), General Comment No. 26 (2022) on Land and Economic, Social and Cultural Rights, E/C.12/GC/26, 22 December 2022.
UN Committee on the Elimination of Discrimination against Women, General Comment No. 34 on the rights of rural women, 4 March 2016, CEDAW/C/GC/34.
UN Economic and Social Council, Principles on Housing and Property Restitution for Refugees and Displaced Persons, 28 June 2005, E/CN.4/Sub.2/2005/17.
UN Human Rights Committee (HRC), General Comment No.16: Article 17 (Right to Privacy), The Right to Respect of Privacy, Family, Home and Correspondence, and Protection of Honour and Reputation, 27 May 1988, HRI/GEN/1/Rev.9 (Vol. I).
UN Human Rights Committee (HRC), CCPR General Comment No. 27: Article 12 (Freedom of Movement), 2 November 1999, CCPR/C/21/Rev.1/Add.9.
UN Human Rights Committee (HRC), CCPR General Comment No.29: Article 4: Derogations during a State of Emergency, 31 August 2001, CCPR/C/21/Rev.1/Add.11.
UN Human Rights Committee (HRC), General comment No. 31 [80], The nature of the general legal obligation imposed on States Parties to the Covenant, 26 May 2004, CCPR/C/21/Rev.1/Add.13.
UN Human Rights Committee (HRC), General Comment No. 34, Article 19, Freedoms of opinion and expression, 12 September 2011, CCPR/C/GC/34.

Other Interpretative Documents

African Commission on Human and Peoples' Rights, Principles and Guidelines on the Implementation of Economic, Social and Cultural Rights in the African Charter on Human and Peoples' Rights, available at https://achpr.au.int/index.php/en/node/871, accessed 26 July 2025.
Council of Europe, Committee of Ministers, Recommendation Rec(2006)6 of the Committee of Ministers to member states on internally displaced persons, 5 April 2006.
European Court of Human Rights, Guide on Article 8 of the European Convention on Human Rights: Right to respect for private and family life, home and correspondence (Council of Europe, December 2018).

European Court of Human Rights, Guide on Article 1 of Protocol No. 1 to the European Convention on Human Rights: the Protection of Property, Updated on 31 December 2021.
Human Rights Council, Free, prior and informed consent: a human rights-based Approach, Study of the Expert Mechanism on the Rights of Indigenous Peoples, 10 August 2018, A/HRC/39/62.
International Commission of Jurists (ICJ), Maastricht Guidelines on Violations of Economic, Social and Cultural Rights, 26 January 1997, available at http://hrlibrary.umn.edu/instree/Maastrichtguidelines_.html, accessed 26 July 2025.
Maastricht Principles on Extraterritorial Obligations of States in the Area of Economic, Social and Cultural Rights, September 2011.
The Special Rapporteur on Adequate Housing, Basic Principles and Guidelines on Development-based Evictions and Displacement, 5 February 2007, A/HRC/4/18.

Index

© T.M.C. ASSER PRESS and the authors 2026

R. G. Teshome, *The Human Cost of Development*, Human Rights Research Series 104,
https://doi.org/10.1007/978-94-6265-751-9